McLaren:
The Grand Prix
CanAm and
Indy cars.

McLaren:
The Grand Prix, CanAm and Indy Cars

Doug Nye

Hazleton Publishing, Richmond, Surrey

This first edition published in 1984 by Hazleton Publishing,
3 Richmond Hill, Richmond, Surrey TW10 6RE.

ISBN 0 905138 28 7

Printed in Holland by drukkerij de Lange/van Leer b.v., Deventer.
Typesetting by C. Leggett & Son Ltd., Mitcham, Surrey, England.

Cover photographs by Nigel Snowdon and Bob Tronolone.

Colour Photography by:

Diana Burnett	– pages 232
Geoffrey Goddard	– pages 28, 77, 229 (above)
LAT Photographic	– pages 129
Phipps Photographic	– pages 26/27, 80, 229 (below)
Bob Tronolone	– pages 25, 78/79, 130/131, 132
David Winter	– pages 230, 231

Black & White Photography by:
John Beale
Patrick Benjafield
Mr. & Mrs. P.C. Binks
Lionel Birnbom
Ian Catt
Michael Cooper (Photography) Ltd.
Cowderoy & Moss Ltd.
Edward Deaux
D.P.P.I.
Richard Garrett Services Ltd.
Geoffrey Goddard
Indianapolis Motor Speedway
E.J. Inwood
Charles Knight
T.C. March
Michael Marchant Ltd.
Alfred Marin
Barry McKay
Reynolds Metals Co.
Ronald C. Miller
Phipps Photographic
C. David Repp Photography
Shell Photographing Service
Nigel Snowdon
Peter Tempest
Dale von Treba
Bob Tronolone

The author wishes to thank the following for their time, trouble and
enthusiasm in helping to compile this detailed story of the McLaren
team's life and times: Teddy Mayer, Ron Dennis, John Barnard,
Gordon Coppuck, Robin Herd, Eoin Young, Jack Martin and Ron
McQueeney of the Indianapolis Motor Speedway, Don Davidson of
USAC, Sir Jack Brabham, John Cooper, Owen Maddock, Eddie
Stait, Mike Barney and all the men of McLaren who have been so
forthcoming over the years, notably the late Bruce McLaren and
Peter Revson, Denny Hulme, Phil Kerr, Tyler Alexander, Don
Beresford and more recently John Watson and Leo Wybrott.

Contents

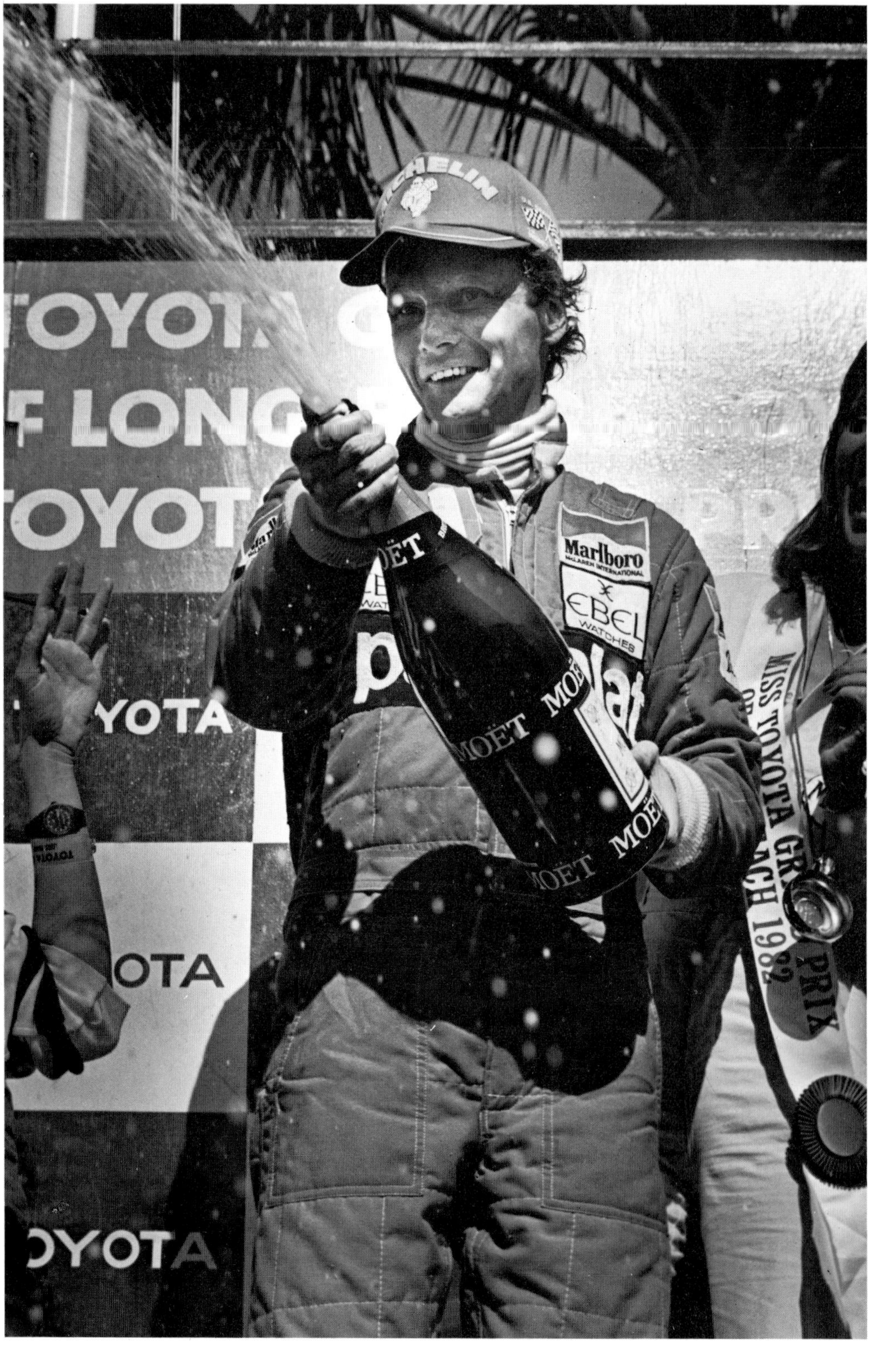
MICHELIN
Marlboro
EBEL
WATCHES
MOËT
TOYOTA

Foreword: Niki Lauda

Motor racing is a sport which demands supreme skill in the areas of technical design and development, team management and, ultimately, driving. But in order to succeed these skills must be disciplined by a dedication and unfailing attention to detail which then lead to consistent good performance and coveted championship victories. My contribution to successful Formula One teams has been chronicled annually in AUTOCOURSE, and my two seasons with the Marlboro McLaren team also qualify me to commend this first of a series of F1 marque histories as an illustration of the achievements of skilled team-work, innovative genius and forceful personalities.

With the established and respected AUTOCOURSE reputation for producing the best in motor sport publications, this new series promises to attain a similar status among the marque histories – I look forward to reading each volume.

Section I: The Men Behind McLaren

Chapter 1
Bruce McLaren – Engineer Driver

"The fact that Bruce was the same age, or younger, than many
of the people in his team helped to start the tremendous sense of
family loyalty that made the McLaren team easily the most
cheerful . . ."

Eoin Young, 1971

In motor racing there is no substitute for starting young. Bruce Leslie McLaren was just one of that long list of star drivers who had that advantage. But he had more. He was no star driver drawn merely by the lure of a charismatic competitive sport and the financial reward it might offer. He grew up with a genuine love of proper cars and proper motoring. He added the engineering background to be able to develop, design and build them. And he had the ambition to found the highly-successful marque which bore his name. What's more he was blessed with a sunny temperament and personality which made him one of the most out-going and popular drivers of his time. He was good in Grand Prix cars, an ace in sports-racers, and a gifted practical engineer whose team's products have perpetuated his name long after his tragic death . . .

Bruce was of course a New Zealander, born in Auckland on the North Island on August 30, 1937. His father Leslie ran a garage and service station there in the smart suburb of Remuera. Les McLaren and his three younger brothers competed in local motor-cycle events with considerable success through the 'thirties. He and his wife Ruth were to have three children; the eldest, Patricia, was already seven when young Bruce was born, and ten years later came another sister, Janice, born in 1947.

It was after World War Two that 'Pop' McLaren's competition ambitions transferred from two wheels to four. He sold his Singer Le Mans and replaced it with a 1935 SS1 which was run in sprints and beach races while doubling as family transport. Meanwhile young Bruce had become a useful budding sportsman in his own right. He captained his school's junior rugby football team but at the age of nine contracted Perthe's Disease.

This is a rare affection of the hip in children, caused by fragmentation of the spongy extremity of the femur (thigh-bone). It could have been caused by a heavy blow or fall, and although he had his suspicions Bruce could never be sure what started it in his case. A year earlier he had fallen from a horse onto the top of a fence post on his uncle's farm at Ngaruawahia. It might have been that. Or it might have been legacy of a trolley crash when racing his pals downhill near home in Remuera. But he would never be sure.

The result was dreadful. A month in hospital was followed by nearly three years in the Wilson Home for Crippled Children. Today it's considered that Perthe's Disease requires no active treatment, as the condition settles spontaneously within a few years. In Bruce's case he suffered the trauma of having his legs set in plaster casts and lying in traction, immobile, for weeks and months on end. Eventually he was allowed to progress to a wheelchair, though there were fears he might never walk again. But he could smile through adversity and powering his wheelchair around the hospital grounds built up muscle in his shoulders and upper arms.

He recovered completely, but the condition – or maybe its treatment – left him with his left leg 1½-inches shorter than the right. He wore a shoe with a built-up heel to compensate, but his slight limp when walking would later be as characteristic of him as it became of that other great racing driver, Graham Hill.

Bruce went back to school in 1951. He'd been kept abreast of his friends educationally by studies in the Wilson Home and by correspondence courses during his year's convalescence at home. Now rugby was one of a whole list of 'normal' sports proscribed by the doctors, anxious for him to avoid bodily contact games. He took up rowing instead, again like Graham Hill, and the powerful shoulders later as characteristic of him as the ready smile and slight limp, continued to develop. And he was a bright, adept pupil, heading his sciences and practical class by the end of his first year's engineering course at Seddon Memorial Technical College.

McLaren's garage in Remuera, Auckland, was a sizeable business and 'Pop' McLaren himself was a well-respected member of the New Zealand motor sporting fraternity.

In the early-'fifties Les McLaren decided to buy and tune a car specially for competition. He bought an ancient 1929 Ulster Austin Seven in bits and spent a year restoring it for sprint and hill-climb work. It was ancient, it was in a terrible state, but it was a proper competition car, unlike the old faithful SS1. In their heyday in England the Ulster Austin Sevens had performed brilliantly in their 750cc class. Bruce was enthralled, and helped his Pop as much as possible, watching and learning as the work progressed.

Unfortunately Pop's first test run with the completed car was an experience he preferred not to repeat, returning white and shaken. It was virtually uncontrollable, and after all that time and trouble he wanted to advertise it for sale. Bruce pleaded to keep the car if Pop didn't want it, and won the day, but he had to maintain it himself, and he had more than a year to wait until he'd be old enough to hold a driving licence.

Just days after his fifteenth birthday, in 1952, Bruce passed his driving test in a Morris Minor borrowed from a friend. Soon after, he took the redeveloped Ulster into his first competitive event; a hill-climb at Muriwai close to the beach where the family had a weekend home. Pop was in hospital at the time, having decreed that Bruce should curb his ambitions, but after wheeling the Ulster to the top of that shingle hill Bruce visited his father in the hospital to announce he'd won his class and beaten another youngster in an Austin Nippy. The other lad's name was Phil Kerr, and he and Bruce became firm friends.

Thereafter Pop McLaren allowed Bruce and Phil to work on their Austins in the Remuera garage, he and his staff taking care they did the job right, and learned!

In January 1954, in the New Zealand mid-summer, Bruce and Phil were

Bruce poses proudly with 'Pop' and the trusty little Ulster Austin Seven on which he cut his competition driving teeth in 1955. Every would-be racing driver in New Zealand had to be able to turn his hand to all kinds of mechanical work. Bruce made a new cylinder head for the Ulster and his faith in Kiwi mechanics was to become a corner-stone of the team he built.

appointed crowd marshals and so watched the country's first International Grand Prix race for free at Ardmore airfield. Ken Wharton ran the fantastic, wailing V16 BRM from England. Stan Jones brought his Maybach Special from Australia, and a trio of Cooper-Bristols were also there, one driven by another Australian visitor, a nutbrown, black-haired Sydneysider whose name was Jack Brabham . . .

Until that time Bruce and his father shared competitive drives in the Ulster, but towards the end of 1954 Pop bought himself one of the first production Austin-Healey 100s to enter the country, ex-Ross Jensen. It was maintained alongside the two Austins, and Bruce's growing capabilities were proven when he set out to make a new cylinder head for the Ulster after the original had cracked. He cannibalised a replacement from a 1936 Austin Seven Ruby saloon, filled its combustion chambers with bronze and sculpted them to the required shape. Eventually his red-painted special Ulster could rocket through the flying quarter-mile at 87mph, and covered the standing-start quarter in under 20 seconds . . . His parents forbade him from continuing to drive the car to school.

He decided to sell it in August 1955 so he could buy a road car which he could also use in competition. He chose a Ford 10 Special, but never got on with it, and eventually took over Pop's Austin-Healey instead.

During the Ford Sp1 period, Phil Kerr had graduated from the Austin Nippy to a Buckler sports special. Another friend named Colin Beanland was running a hotted-up Ford Anglia saloon. In 1956 Bruce commenced a degree course at

Auckland University's engineering college near Ardmore airfield, where the annual NZ GP races were held. Pop entered the Healey there for the sports car race supporting that year's GP, but after another spell in hospital his doctor advised him not to take part. Bruce badgered his father into letting him take his place. Pop agreed and Bruce found himself practising at Ardmore, against Stirling Moss, visiting in a Porsche. The Healey developed gearbox trouble, Bruce worked his first motor racing all-nighter to put it right and drove in the race only for the head gasket to blow, causing his retirement.

Pop and Bruce did a deal whereby whoever was quickest in practice would race the Healey that day. The deal survived until another airfield race at Ohakea and there Bruce had already learned the way round in his Ulster. He was seven seconds a lap quicker than his father, whereupon Pop retired from driving and concentrated on acting as "team manager".

The Austin-Healey was progressively modified and Bruce notched some success in the summer races of 1956-57 until the hard-pressed engine threw a rod on the Ryall Bush road circuit at Invercargill down on the South Island.

Bruce was depressed. The broken Healey engine promised to be expensive to repair, but the bob-tailed Cooper centre-seat sports car which Jack Brabham had brought to Ardmore for that year's NZ GP meeting had been left behind for sale. The McLarens decided to buy it, selling both the Healey and the unloved Ford Special to cover most of the cost. It was their first 'real' racing car, and Pop, Bruce and Colin Beanland all set to work with a will to prepare the car.

Bruce raced it extensively and was writing regularly to Jack Brabham in England and Jack was helping the family sort out their new acquisition. Then in preparation for the summer season of 1957-58 Jack wrote suggesting that he should bring out a pair of Formula 2 Coopers with specially-enlarged Coventry Climax FPF four-cylinder engines, one for himself to drive in the NZ GP and following International series – and the other for Bruce . . .

At University, Bruce's studies were reaching their culmination. He sat his final exams and was being prompted to choose between formal careers as either a motor engineer or a civil engineer. But his enthusiasm was bound-up in the forthcoming race series, and Jack's arrival with the promised over-size F2 Cooper. The bob-tail sports was sold to Merv Neil to fund it, and Jack built-up two oversize basically 1500cc FPF engines – one for Bruce bored-out to around 1750cc and the other for himself bored and stroked (with a special crankshaft) to 2.2 litres.

In fact Bruce's single-seater debut came in Frank Shuter's supercharged 3-litre Maserati 8CLT. This fearsome front-engined straight-eight monster had four valves per cylinder and a separate exhaust primary for each exhaust valve, meaning there was a gleaming blued battery of sixteen pipes sweeping out from beneath its bonnet. The car had been built for Indianapolis postwar, but never raced there, fetching-up instead with Freddie Zambucka in New Zealand. After the extrovert Zambucka's death, Frank Shuter had bought it for an attempt on the New Zealand land speed record. Bruce was given the job of making the old Maserati a runner. He worked on it assiduously and tested the car at Ohakea, revelling in wheelspin up to around 140mph.

But even compared to that nothing could diminish the thrill of seeing Jack Brabham arrive with the two little rear-engined Coopers. Driving the new car for the first time in practice for the NZ GP at Ardmore Bruce placed second in the first race heat and then prepared for the GP proper. He was running the engine in gear, rear wheels off the ground on jacks, to warm the gearbox oil, when the transmission broke. Less than 30 minutes before the start Jack produced a spare gearbox and Bruce and his helpers worked feverishly to fit it. The organisers delayed the start as long as they dare, and Bruce dashed out just in time to see the smoke of the start drifting away on the breeze, joining-in half a lap behind the field. He took to the track and charged, but amidst all that excitement they'd forgotten to change the soft warm-up plugs for the race and he lost more time in a long pit stop to replace them. He restarted dead last again, but was forced to retire when the new gearbox tightened-up. The hastily-tightened bell-housing bolts had worked loose, letting all the oil drain away.

Through that season the New Zealand International Grand Prix Association had organised a 'Driver to Europe' scholarship, which would take the driver they nominated as the most promising local hope to England for a European season through the middle of that year. Before the NZ GP meeting the award lay between Bruce, Phil Kerr and Merv Mayo, and the night following the big race Bruce's bitter disappointment turned to joy as it was announced at the prize-giving that he had been selected. He was the NZIGP's first 'Driver to Europe'.

As a curtain-raiser to the trip he still had the local season to complete with the 1750cc Cooper-Climax. He was second at Dunedin and Teretonga, where a chunky young bank clerk from Timaru – filling-in spare time as freelance motoring correspondent for the local paper – introduced himself. His name was Eoin Young – nicknamed 'Buster' – and to him as to most New Zealand enthusiasts of his generation, Bruce was a star in the making. They would become firm friends and in later years once Bruce was fully established in Europe he invited Eoin to join him as helper/secretary/go-for. Eoin rapidly established himself as the Jackie Stewart of racing writers, a brilliant columnist for *The Autocar* and Bruce's best biographer. He would ghost Bruce's regular *From the Cockpit* columns for *Autosport* magazine, and later Denny Hulme's equivalent *Behind the Wheel* pieces.

After that Teretonga race meeting in 1958, Bruce took the Cooper to a hill-climb at Clellands not far from Timaru, where the car snapped a half-shaft on its second run and Eoin's furiously-driven Austin A30 salvaged a second in class behind a Cooper-Anzani. As he wrote in his memorial book *Bruce McLaren: The Man and his Racing Team* (Eyre & Spottiswoode, London, 1971) Eoin recalled: "That night Bruce and I went down to the local dance in his father's Jaguar and I introduced him to Pat Broad. Bruce asked if he could escort her home but she explained that she was sorry but she was going on to a party. We toured Timaru that night trying to find the party but finally gave up. The next day I tracked down Pat's telephone number and Bruce called round to see her. They were engaged after the 1960 GP at Ardmore and in 1961 were married in Christchurch."

On March 15, 1958, twenty-year old Bruce McLaren and his pal Colin Beanland – a year his senior – flew to Sydney on the first leg of their 'Driver to Europe' trip; Bruce having invited Colin to accompany him as mechanic and moral support for the tour to a strange land. They were taking the 1750 Cooper with them and would convert it back to 1500cc form in England. It had been shipped to Sydney loaded on the *Orantes* for the onward trip through the Suez Canal. They sailed safely from Sydney but when the ship put into Melbourne to load extra cargo Bruce found a letter waiting with the news that the NZIGP had arranged a start for him in a works F2 Cooper at Aintree in the April 15 '200' meeting. To arrive on time he'd have to leave the ship at Aden and take a 'plane. Down in the ship's hold there he carefully removed his specially-made clutch and brake pedals, unscrewed the St Christopher medal from the dash panel and made the dash for London.

Jack Brabham met him at Heathrow and took him to the Cooper works in Hollyfield Road, Surbiton, where he was introduced to John Cooper; in many ways a similarly sunny personality, puffing *bon mots* past his inevitable pipe. "Where's my car?" asked Bruce. John looked puzzled: "Your car? In that pipe-rack I reckon, Boy . . ." suggesting if Bruce wanted a car, he'd have to set-to and build it first.

But it was a leg-pull – the first of a million more – and 'Black Jack' had done a deal for £60 starting money from the Aintree organisers. Old Charlie Cooper, John's father and very much The Boss, wasn't so sure, and he insisted Bruce could only borrow a works car if he insured it first. The premium was fifty quid – so he was in profit from the beginning. He'd never look back. His maiden British race duly took place, but he suffered carburetion problems which left him ninth.

Since the latest 1958 Coopers ran coil-spring instead of transverse leafspring front suspensions, Bruce decided to sell his own car to the Australian-in-England

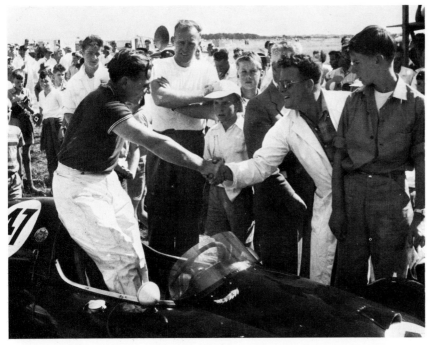

Teretonga Trophy, 1959; Bruce home here from his first European season having just beaten Jack Brabham's sister Cooper-Climax fair-and-square for the first time, staving off both Jack – who eventually finished third – and Ron Flockhart's works BRM. The silver fern on the scuttle is the New Zealand national emblem.

Count Steve Ouvaroff and buy one of the new cars in kit form in its place. He would build it himself in the gloomy Hollyfield Road workshops. The *Orantes* sailed in with the old car and Colin Beanland on board, the car went off to Ouvaroff and Colin helped Bruce build-up its replacement while the two Kiwis took a room in the Royal Oak pub just round the corner from the Cooper works. At one stage the works team had operated out of lock-ups in the yard behind the pub, connected to Cooper's by a footbridge which Charlie Cooper had thrown across the Tolworth Brook. The landlord of the pub only charged them for the room when they were there, and since most of that summer would be spent travelling it was a good deal. They had landed on their feet.

Colin bought a Mark I Zephyr to act as tow car and with a trailer borrowed from the factory they set out to learn about serious International motor racing. Highlights of the season included a minor F2 race at Brands Hatch where young Bruce beat Ken Tyrrell in a similar Cooper. The organisers of the German GP at Nürburgring ran a concurrent F2 class within their Formula 1 race and accepted Bruce's entry as a reserve. Bruce was disappointed, his heart set upon racing at the legendary 'Ring, until John Cooper assured him he'd make the grid because someone was bound to crash in practice "Just make sure it's not you, Boy" . . .

He showed his class in practice, qualifying on row four of the grid behind a couple of BRMs. One was driven by Harry Schell. John briefed Bruce that the Franco-American was one of the best starters in the business, "Just watch his rear wheels, Boy, and when he goes, you go. Never mind the flag, he'll watch it for you." Sure enough, young McLaren was fifth into the first corner with all the F2 field behind him. Phil Hill's powerful 1500 Ferrari moved ahead but when the Italian car's brakes began to fail Bruce was by and held his class lead to the finish. Up on the dais, garlanded alongside Tony Brooks – GP victor for Vanwall – one can imagine the pride he must have felt. This drive made Bruce's name in Europe and assured his future. Even old Charles Cooper was impressed. "That Jack Brabham's" estimation of the boy from New Zealand had been proved right, and after a rush back to England for the Brands Hatch August Bank Holiday Monday meeting next day, Bruce was regaled with an enthusiastic crowd roaring out 'Happy Birthday to You', led by John Bolster on the PA system. He was 21 that day. He'd come of age in more ways than one . . .

At the end of the season he took a 1960cc engine home in his F2 car to run in the New Zealand races, and clinched the national Championship with the combination. John Cooper had promised him a "probable" Formula 2 works drive for 1959 but through the English winter the Coopers decided with Brabham to concentrate solely upon their Grand Prix team for '59 when Coventry Climax would at last be supplying them with full-size 2½-litre Formula 1 FPF engines. They handed over their F2 operation in effect to Ken Tyrrell and Alan Brown, and when Bruce returned for his second European season John told him he'd be driving a third works F1 car, as team-mate to Brabham and Masten Gregory. "Will that be all right, Boy?" asked the pipe. Would it!

Bruce would drive the Tyrrell-Brown F2 cars in between GP commitments.

His first Formula 1 season is now history. He proved adept, quick to learn, rapid enough to be competitive and very reliable – an ideal cadet as Brabham went after the Championship and Masten Gregory's impetuous pace and showmanship at

On their way to glory; Jack Brabham leads his Cooper works team-mate Bruce McLaren through the Esses at Sebring, Florida, during the 1959 World Championship-deciding United States GP. Jack ran out of fuel on the last lap and Bruce went by to win. At 22 he was the youngest-ever winner of a World Championship-qualifying GP.

the wheel acted as a spoiler, aiming for fastest laps which at that time scored Championship points and so denied them to the opposition. As Masten's season was interrupted by accidents so Bruce took a more prominent role.

In the British GP he had a terrific battle with Stirling Moss' private BRP-entered BRM to finish third by half-a-car's length, no more, but thereafter he failed to finish a race until the Championship decider – the inaugural United States GP at Sebring, Florida, in December.

The title could go three ways. It lay between Jack Brabham, Stirling Moss driving Rob Walker's private Cooper, and Tony Brooks at that time driving for Ferrari. If Jack won, the title would be his. If Stirling beat Jack and set fastest lap, then Moss would be Champion. Brooks had the outside chance – he had to win with neither Jack nor Stirling finishing in the points to take the title.

Stirling's Colotti gearbox failed almost before his race had started, and Brooks was rammed by his team-mate von Trips, and rejoined only after a delay. This left the Coopers and Jack and Bruce in the box seat, leading 1-2. But with just two laps to go Jack ran out of fuel. Bruce dodged round the slowing Cooper and stamped on his brakes, looking across at his agonised friend and mentor, wondering what to do now? If he won, would Jack still be Champion? Brooks was still running. Jack waved him on, Bruce realised he was leading his first World Championship GP, he picked-up a gear, floored the throttle and hammered across the line with Trintignant's second Walker Cooper hot on his heels. Jack pushed his car across the line to finish fourth and salvage his first Drivers' World Championship title. Bruce was dazed and overjoyed at his first Grand Prix win, and at 22 he was the youngest-ever winner of such a race.

As Eoin Young wrote: "He was famous . . . but he did not really feel very famous. He was still working hard to make a success of his career and he displayed none of the trappings of a famous racing driver. He drove a Morris Minor he had bought from Betty Brabham, and he shared a little bed-sitting room in Surbiton with Phil Kerr" – Phil had been brought to England at Bruce's recommendation to manage Jack Brabham's new Chessington garage business – "The bathroom was on the landing to be shared with other tenants. Their daily menu included cornflakes and coffee for breakfast, lunch depended on where they were and whether they could afford it, and the evening meal was always at Nick's Café in Kingston down by the coal yards beside the Thames. Their standard order was sausages, bacon and baked beans for one and ninepence. They made themselves instant coffee when they got back to the bedsitter. By comparison Bob Cratchett had it made. On occasions they would be invited out to meals and the high point of the week, when they were at home, was a Sunday roast with the Brabhams."

Buying Formula 1 rent-a-drives were by no means as common then as they are today, nearly twenty-five years later. And being given a works drive at that time didn't go hand-in-hand with payment of a fair-sized fortune in annual fees. Bruce was a young top-flight racing driver who was brought up right. He'd have butter on his bread later. For the moment he was utterly unspoiled, getting by on margarine . . . It would always show, even in later years when fame and comfortable fortune came his way. One can think of few equally youthful drivers who make their way into Formula 1 today who would survive so well-adjusted . . .

During the European winter of 1959-60 Bruce and the new World Champion, Jack Brabham, ran their F1 cars in Antipodean events, where Jack won the NZ GP with Bruce on his tail and the New Zealander was soon to propose to Patty Broad. She accepted and would follow him to England in the Spring. Meanwhile Bruce and Jack and the Cooper works cars had appeared in Buenos Aires for the Argentine GP, opening the 1960 World Championship series. After the leading Lotus, the BRMs, Moss' Walker Cooper and Jack's works car all broke, Bruce emerged to find himself leading his second successive Grand Prix. And he won again, by nearly half-a-minute from Cliff Allison's Ferrari.

The threat of Lotus' new rear-engined Type 18 persuaded Cooper to invest in a crash programme to build an all-new car of their own for the European World Championship events. Bruce worked diligently on the design alongside Jack, John and Hollyfield Road Chief Designer Owen Maddock. When Owen was bogged down with demand for drawings, Bruce even pulled together his own draughting set and joined 'The Beard' – as popular Owen was known in the drawing office – to complete them.

Their new Lowline Cooper proved a huge success. Jack won no less than five consecutive GPs with it through the summer of 1960 to notch his and Cooper's second consecutive World Championship titles, matching only Ferrari, Mercedes-Benz, Alfa Romeo and Fangio before them. Quite good company . . . And Bruce was second at Monaco, where Jack crashed, and went to Zandvoort for his first Dutch GP – having been refused an entry the previous year – actually leading the World Championship, with his World Champion team leader yet to score a point. Bruce would place second to the Guv'nor at Spa and Oporto and he finished the season runner-up to him in the Drivers' Championship.

The 1960 season was the last of 2½-litre racing, and Formula 1 changed to restrict cars to a maximum 1½-litres unsupercharged from 1961-65. Cooper

Monaco, 1962 – Bruce in the Cooper-Climax T60 which he co-designed, on the way to scoring Cooper's final World Championship-qualifying GP victory for four long years. Later that season he won the non-Championship Reims GP in a sister car.

fortunes sagged during that first season of 1½-litre racing in '61 when Coventry Climax's new V8 engine was late completing and the team struggled with obsolescent four-cylinder FPF units against Ferrari's potent V6 and Porsche's worriesome air-cooled flat-fours.

Bruce drove Tommy Atkins' ex-works Lowline Cooper in British Interconti-nental Formula races. Over the winter of 1960-61 his fiancée Patty had come to England to work as a beautician, while Phil Kerr had bought a bachelor apartment for himself and Bruce which was luxury compared to the bedsitter. The Minor had been replaced by a brand-new 3.8 Jaguar saloon "with all the tweaks" and an E-Type rapidly followed. In November '61 Bruce and Patty were married in Christchurch, honeymooning in Fiji before returning home for the Antipodean summer-season races with the ex-Atkins Lowline.

By this time Jack Brabham had left Cooper's to set up his own team in partnership with an old engineering friend from Australia, Ron Tauranac. Ron had a grasp of suspension theory and chassis design belying his geographical isolation in Australia, far from the heartland of major-league motor racing. Through the 'fifties he and Jack had corresponded back and forth about Cooper developments, and many of Ron's ideas were built into the cars through Jack. Now that he had left the team Bruce became number one in his place, but Charles Cooper never recovered from what he saw as Jack's betrayal, and poor Bruce found himself shut out from the original design process – such as it was. Jack had left because he knew that Cooper had neither the knowledge nor the facilities to keep abreast of Formula 1 development, nor any longer to set the trends. The Formula 1 problem was becoming progressively more complex, and the solution demanded massive commitment and sheer tunnel vision on the F1 front more than ever before. An under-manned, under-capitalised production racing car company like Cooper wouldn't stand the pace, particularly while old Charlie was there, careful of every penny, resenting any and every expense.

Bruce had an uphill battle to fight for 1962 but he won it, with the new Type 60 Cooper-Climax V8 which incorporated several of his ideas with John's always friendly connnivance. The Lotus 25 monocoque released at the same time was a far more sophisticated solution, but the handsome T60 was good enough to carry Bruce to victory at Monaco and in the non-Championship race at Reims which followed. They didn't know it at the time, but Reims marked Cooper's last F1 victory until 1966, and the new 3-litre Formula.

Bruce ended 1962 third in the World Championship behind Graham Hill and Jimmy Clark, but the following year was punctuated by incidents. The new '63 F1 Cooper was a disaster in its first outings, and only slowly improved. Patty seriously injured her foot and ankle in a water skiing accident early-on in Australia, being clouted by the tow-boat propeller, and she suffered extreme discomfort for months before the bones set and wounds healed. In the midst of the new F1 car's problems John Cooper suffered a debilitating road accident on the Kingston Bypass in his twin-engined 'Twinny-Mini' prototype saloon car and, with Ken Tyrrell running the team in the field, Bruce then knocked himself out in a high-speed crash during the German GP when a rear suspension wishbone apparently broke, flinging him straight off into the hedges and trees. It was at about this time that he began to look for a way round the frustrations of being number one driver for the Cooper Car Company as their fortunes were in rapid decline, and he began talking to Teddy Mayer, and his race driving younger brother Timmy . . . A new future opened-up before them which would develop as related in these pages.

Wally Willmott had become Bruce's personal mechanic during this period. He was another Kiwi, who had made the pilgrimage to England in 1962 after completing a five-year apprenticeship as an auto electrician in Timaru, Eoin Young's home town. He was another part-time racer, having run his own Ford Spl and a 500cc Cooper-Norton. He and Bruce became very close, and Wally would invest endless hours of loving care in Bruce's Tasman Coopers on their

northern-winter trips back home. Bruce groomed Wally and Mayer mechanic Tyler Alexander as equals in his embryo team after their tragic but Championship-winning '64 Tasman tour. Wally finally left the team in 1967 to marry, and went off to live in Australia.

Once Bruce's team had found its feet, the accolades came Bruce's way, reward for dedication, commitment, almost unreal energy and skill. He and Teddy built one of the most efficient teams in racing, and Bruce's personal driving career was to include victories in the 1968 Race of Champions and much more important the Belgian GP, he came within a whisker of winning the '69 Italian GP and he starred in CanAm sports car racing, taking the Championship in 1967 and '69 with Denny Hulme his Kiwi team-mate second on both occasions and taking his turn as Champion, with Bruce runner-up, in 1968.

The end came with shocking suddenness at Goodwood, soon after 12.20pm, on Tuesday June 2, 1970. Goodwood had been closed to racing since 1966 but was still in regular use by most of the British-based racing car industry for test and development. The still beautiful, undulating Sussex course wound round the one-time perimeter track of what had been the wartime Westhampnett fighter base, a grass airfield still in use for club flying. The old pit line had been reduced to a ram-shackle corrugated iron shelter, the grandstands and advertising banners had long since been torn down, but this was McLaren's baseline course; still a fine test circuit and the yardstick by which they measured progress.

"It was a test day like any other", Teddy recalls, "Nothing special, Bruce was just checking out the new M8D car for CanAm that year. Denny had just been burned at Indy and Peter Gethin was due to try an F1 to deputise for him in the Belgian GP. I was in my office at the Colnbrook works. Then my 'phone rang, and they told me Bruce had been killed."

He had accelerated hard out of Lavant Corner, but for the pit-straight chicane the slowest on the course, and his big orange M8D had bolted for the open left-hand curve onto Lavant Straight which followed; 650-horsepower churning those fat rear Goodyears round, hurling-on the car like a shell from a cannon. Bruce had driven this way thousands of times before. But this time a pin securing his car's massive tail body section was not there and in the curve the panelling lifted, the airstream grabbed and ripped it off and yanked the rear wheels

momentarily clear of the road. Body gone, rear wing with it, the M8D left the road just after the curve and careered violently – far beyond 100mph – broadside into a concrete-reinforced earthbank protecting a one-time, long-abandoned marshal's post there on the infield. The impact was unsurviveable . . .

They took Bruce home to New Zealand, and he was buried at St Mary's Cathedral, Auckland, eight days later. His death was a national disaster. On June 24 a moving memorial service was held for him in London at St Paul's Cathedral. Sir Dennis Blundell, New Zealand High Commissioner, quoted Bruce's words on Jimmy Clark's death published in his *Autosport* column two years before:

"Too often in this demanding sport, unique in terms of ability, dedication, concentration and courage, someone pays a penalty for trying to do just that little bit better or go that little bit faster. And too often someone pays the penalty just for being in the wrong place at the wrong time when a situation or a set of circumstances is such that no human being can control them. However, that's the way it is. We accept it, we enjoy what we do, we get a lot of satisfaction out of it, and maybe we prove something, I don't know . . ."

His team would perpetuate his name.

At home in Walton, 1970 – Patty, Bruce and daughter Amanda.

Opposite: Wally Willmott, Tyler Alexander, Teddy Mayer (kneeling behind Tyler) and Bruce McLaren with the prototype M1A at Laguna Seca during the 1964 Monterey GP meeting.

Bruce's Michael Turner-styled M1B chasing the leaders at Laguna '66. Being outclassed by the big six-litre Lolas and Chaparrals determined the team to do better in '67.

Chapter 2
Teddy Mayer and his Men

"As a team manager straw boss Teddy is the best there is. He knows what he wants, is very determined and stays with it 'til he gets it. McLaren are the best; the most professional . . ."

Peter Revson, 1972

Previous pages: Team Founder – Bruce McLaren was for seven busy years the driving force behind the team which bore his name. Here he is in his 1968 M7A with which he scored his marque's maiden F1 victory on its debut and later added their first GP success in the Belgian race at Spa.

Opposite: Monaco '67 – Bruce ran this hybrid M4-based F2 car fitted with a 2.1-litre Tasman BRM V8 engine in the early-season F1 races and here at Monte Carlo finished very strongly fourth overall; the little car with its extra pannier fuel tankage was ideally suited to the tight street circuit.

Bruce's last World Championship points were scored in the 1970 Spanish GP here at Jarama where his works M14A finished second to Jackie Stewart's victorious Robin Herd-designed Tyrrell March 701. This car was heavily damaged in a first-lap collision next time out, at Monaco, and Bruce died soon after in the CanAm testing accident at Goodwood.

As so often, Bruce's close friend Eoin Young has put it into words best. Looking back on the formation of the team he wrote: "Bruce McLaren's racing team grew from humble beginnings around Bruce's talent as a racing driver, his reputation as a 'nice guy', and his ability to pick the right people to work with him. Running the *Zerex Special* with a three-man team, however, was a far simpler operation . . . than it was soon to become when the team shifted to larger premises with a higher rent, and employed more mechanics for the McLaren sports car project. At about this critical stage in the team's history towards the end of 1964, Teddy Mayer joined the company as a director bringing with him a welcome boost to the team's bank balance and the promise of increasing his own by applying his keen mind to the business of motor racing . . ."

Edward Everett Mayer was well-suited to the role of dynamic business manager, making the business work while Bruce and the technicians performed that function on the cars. As time passed Teddy's growing mechanical experience paid off, and he made himself responsible for race-engineering one of the team cars – making the technical decisions on set-up and adjustment as he saw fit to make the most of McLaren's chances in the field, while his long-serving American engineer friend Tyler Alexander or designer Robin Herd or Gordon Coppuck would care for the other team car. Along the way he won himself a reputation for engineering interference, a short-fused martinet, but he made the team work, and work well.

A compact man, small-featured, with a rather querulous attitude to the world at large, Teddy Mayer – or 'The Wiener' as he was sometimes known behind his back – came from a wealthy Pennsylvanian family background. Father was a stockbroker, and an uncle William Scranton, had been State Governor. Teddy's brother Timmy was 2½ years his junior, and both were bright. Teddy studied modern European history and political science, and went on to Cornell University for a law degree, taking a special tax law course for a year after he left University. Tim studied English literature, and both were interested in sports cars . . .

In 1958 they bought an Austin-Healey 100-6 and decided to try racing it. Teddy was and remains an avid ski enthusiast and he explains what happened: "I went down to Chile to teach snow skiing soon after we bought the car and Timmy started to race it. He got quite good, and when I returned from Chile we decided that I would help him run it as team manager and he would drive it . . ."

While Teddy continued his law studies motor racing was merely a time-consuming hobby, but it took increasing hold and by 1961 the Mayer brothers were involved in a three-car Formula Junior team which Teddy managed, running Coopers for Timmy, Peter Revson and an older friend named Bill Smith who was already a successful businessman in his own right. They all put money in the kitty and called themselves the Rev-Em Racing Team.

Through 1962 they ran the FJ Coopers in 16 races and emerged with the staggering record of 15 wins, 14 seconds and 14 thirds. Young Tim's talent and ambition brought him a test-drive from Ken Tyrrell's quasi-works FJ team in England and the brothers made the pilgrimage to the heart of International road

Timmy Mayer had proved himself an extremely capable racing driver when he won a Cooper works contract to join Bruce as number two in the 1964 GP team. First he and Bruce ran the new Bruce McLaren Motor Racing Ltd team's Tasman-special Coopers in the down-under series, January-February '64; as here at Teretonga Park, Invercargill – the World's most southerly racing circuit – where the 'McLaren Spls' finished in team order, first and second. Bruce would win the Championship . . .

racing in the summer of '63; Timmy to drive Tyrrell's Coopers and Teddy just to keep him company and see what serious motor racing was all about: "I had no specific job other than to try and further Timmy's career if possible, have a bit of a holiday, and try to straighten out in my own mind what I wanted to do . . ." He was 26, Timmy 23.

Their experience already extended to more powerful cars than the Cooper Juniors. They had raced a Lotus 23 sports car and graduated to Cooper Monaco sports-racers with big 2½-litre Climax FPF power units. Timmy had proved very competitive with the best in his class; names like Jim Hall, and Roger Penske . . .

Timmy's performances with the Tyrrell Coopers showed promise, although that season of '63 saw Lotus dominant with their Cosworth-tuned Ford engines, and the Cooper contract with BMC "was like running lead ballast" in the cars. At Tyrrell's recommendation, John Cooper was very keen on signing Timmy as Bruce's number two driver for the 1964 Cooper Formula 1 season. He would replace South African Tony Maggs, another Tyrrell Cooper FJ star who had graduated to works F1 driver for 1962-63, and who now wanted to join the Bowmaker Lola team alongside John Surtees. As a platform on which to build major Formula single seat experience the Tasman Championship of early '64 seemed ideal, and as described later in these pages Teddy and Bruce did the deal which would create Bruce McLaren Motor Racing Ltd.

Things went well in New Zealand, less so in Australia, until in practice for the Longford race in Tasmania Timmy crashed and was killed.

This was the cross-roads of Teddy's life. He was to alter the focus of his personal drive and ambition from furthering the career of one person to furthering that of the team; McLaren Racing.

"When I got back to the States after Timmy had been killed I was very upset, and I didn't know either what I wanted to do nor where I wanted to do it. I wasn't married, and I had no particular ambition in any one direction.

"I went away and did some skiing and just thought about life in general. I wondered if it was right to encourage young men to drive racing cars, with all the potential dangers that suggests, and concluded that they were free agents, they did it because they wanted to do it. Looking back now I can honestly say I've never, ever had to force a driver to drive. It's been quite the reverse. You have to say 'no' to drivers fighting to get into your cars, so there was no big problem there. Driving is something they do voluntarily. They like the experience, and the fame, adulation – whatever – that goes with it, even when they're starting, before they can earn money doing it.

"Bruce was in touch, and when he wanted to buy Mecom's *Zerex Special* he asked me to handle the deal, and then continuing this train of thought I figured that if I had a worthwhile contribution to make in terms of sound business control or sound engineering, then I should do so . . . It's what I knew, and what I was interested in most . . ."

Teddy drafted a proposal offering his services in a management capacity to the embryo McLaren team. Bruce at that time was confident his tiny staff could handle their current programme and wrote back suggesting Teddy might be able to work in America as an agent for the team.

"I replied that I didn't think that was a very suitable arrangement because I had to become completely involved full-time in racing or go back to being a lawyer. Finally we decided it would be a reasonable idea for me to join the team, and I wrote a synopsis of the team potential as I saw it. I felt there was a possibility of making some money after about three years, but I wasn't particularly convinced that it would be an instant success and I certainly wasn't convinced that it was an excellent financial investment. I didn't see it as a large loss either – in other words it was a purely speculative idea for both Bruce and myself. Bruce was hedging his bets by remaining with Cooper, and I was hedging mine by not making a large financial investment, and I could always go back to be a lawyer . . ."

Teddy returned to England in the late-Spring of '64, and in many ways he shook the tiny team rigid by taking it by the scruff of the neck, imposing discipline and forcing it to run with the accent on efficiency in all things. Their first dirt-floored workshop at an earth-moving equipment service centre in New Malden was hardly General Motors, but Teddy the martinet came close to running it with the same disciplines. He hated time-wasters and while British motor racing *à la* Cooper's was based very much on the old chums network, with a friendly sense of albeit-limited *mañana* where old-established suppliers were concerned, the American newcomer would not contemplate any such thing. If one company couldn't supply in time then he would find another which could, and Bruce – mindful of how long it had taken him to build-up his circle of valuable contacts in the UK racing car business – would often cringe as his new business partner roasted one of them on the 'phone. Almost unconsciously they worked-up a 'Bad Guy-Good Guy' double act. Teddy would prime the subject and lay the groundwork for a sense of genuine urgency which would pay dividends as smiling, sunny Bruce took over, lowered the temperature and charmed exactly what was wanted out of the supplier. By this time he would be well wound-up and determined to prove that his concern could do the job better than whatever rival "that little white-haired Yank" had been praising during his onslaught.

Today Teddy smiles slowly at the memory: "Yeah – we used the 'Bad Guy-Good Guy' thing occasionally, when it was right for the situation. It sure paid dividends, too . . ." and the smile becomes a chuckle.

But he also admits: "Bruce had been on his own in the world, away from family and schools, and University longer than I had and he taught me how to manage myself with regard to other people. On occasion I'd get locked into a clash of personality with certain members of the team, and Bruce would sort it out. I'd let go at someone and perhaps go too far. Bruce never did that. If anything he wouldn't let go often enough, and only in the last couple of years or so did he learn to get angry and chew people out when they deserved it. I think I learned from him to be more understanding, and he learned from me to be a bit harder. You've got to remember when we set out together we were both very young . . ."

Another youthful member of the team was former Rev-Em Racing Team mechanic Tyler Alexander; fair-haired, good looking, a kind of English schoolgirl's idea of the good-looking all-American college boy – and to become an invaluable member of the McLaren set-up.

He trained as an aircraft engineer with all the attention to detail and painstaking check-systems that entails, but after completing his two-year training course he didn't settle into a normal airline or aircraft industry job. He wasn't much attracted by normal work routines and motor racing began to appeal much more. He lived in Hingham, Massachussets, where most of his friends were interested in flying, but some were racing home-built special cars. One of them was named John Fields, and he decided to go road racing far more seriously, buying a 500cc Cooper-Norton which Tyler maintained and prepared for him. They raced the car through 1961 and won 15 of their 17 races in national 500cc events.

Around the race circuits they got to know Timmy Mayer and his elder brother, Teddy, who were racing their FJ Cooper. Often the air-cooled 500 and water-cooled FJ would meet in the same race, though in different classes. At the end of the season Timmy was serving his time in the US Army – spending much of it teaching English to local children in an Army school in Puerto Rico – and Teddy asked Tyler to take the family's Cooper Monaco down to Nassau for the Bahamas Speed Week, where Roger Penske would drive it in Timmy's place. Tyler did more service jobs for the Mayers until by virtual osmosis he became 'their' mechanic. There was no formal job offer, no acceptance, they just found themselves working together.

He then joined the John Mecom team to which Roger Penske sold his cars at the end of '62, working on the near-legendary *Zerex Special* centre-seat Cooper sports car which Penske's crew had converted from a wrecked Cunningham team F1. The authorities eventually banned the car, and it was rebuilt with conventional side-by-side seats either side of the cockpit centreline, and with main chassis longeron tubes re-routed to make this possible. It was still very light and rapid, and Tyler travelled to England with the Mecom crew to run Penske in the car at the August Bank Holiday Brands Hatch meeting of 1963, when Roger slaughtered a top quality field to win handsomely.

Teddy and Timmy Mayer and Timmy's wife Garrell were in England at that time, Timmy driving one of Ken Tyrrell's quasi-works FJ Coopers and the family sharing a rented house on an island in the Thames. Tyler met them again at Brands and decided to rejoin the old firm, resigning his place with Mecom and accompanying the Mayers to a race at Roskilde in Denmark rather than returning to the 'States. Bruce would come round to island lunch parties that Autumn to discuss prospects for the Tasman Championship with the Mayers. His own car was being built-up by his personal Kiwi mechanic Wally Willmott in Cooper's workshop, and Tyler joined-in to build the sister team car for Timmy. Tyler stayed with the Mayers and after Timmy's death continued with McLaren, becoming chief mechanic, engineer in charge of racing in all classes and eventually a director of the company. Through the late-'seventies he ran the USAC track racing operation in the 'States based at McLaren Engines Incorporated in the City of Livonia on the outskirts of Detroit. This subsidiary had been set-up to handle CanAm V8 engine development and preparation closer to the battlefield, obviating the transAtlantic gulf between race series and the engine workshop in one pokey corner of the Colnbrook works. Tyler ran his Indy and in the mid-'seventies a works-backed BMW saloon car programme from Livonia.

McLaren Engines' BMW contract was won in 1977 to develop and run a 320i Formula 2-engined saloon in Stateside IMSA and endurance racing. The first car was handed-over to Tyler Alexander's men after the Daytona race opening the '77 US season. Veteran David Hobbs was to be their regular IMSA driver while he was joined by Ronnie Peterson (a BMW works driver in Europe at this time), Sam Posey, Tom Klausler and Hans-Joachim Stuck in the longer-distance Internationals.

Late in July the little car won its first IMSA race outright by nine seconds in Atlanta. The turbocharged 320t version was first raced in April, running in both Europe and the US with development by McLaren. For 1978 the McLaren-BMW crew at Livonia was led by rugged English mechanic Roger Bailey – formerly Chris Amon's right-hand man and one of the few non-Italians ever to work as a Ferrari mechanic. The 320t was considerably lightened with extensive use of plastics in a new body, but up against full 3-litre Porches David Hobbs could win only two races, at Hallet and Sears Point, compared to his four victories (at Mid-Ohio, Sears Point, Atlanta and Laguna Seca) the previous year.

By the end of '78 the McLaren-BMW 320t was delivering something like 610-620bhp from 2-litres, and while peak torque of the basic atmospherically-aspirated F2 engine was 166.4ft/lbs, the 320t with its Garrett AiResearch turbocharger offered a whopping 353.7ft/lbs. . .

During 1978 turbo 2-litre engines were being developed by both Nicholson-McLaren in Hounslow, England, and by Gary Knutson in Livonia. Unfortunately it took time to learn the foibles of the in-line four-cylinder, and an astonishing difference in octane rating between Sunoco premium grade US fuel and the best European grade contributed to a disastrous sequence of piston failures. But the BMW connection was another valuable programme for McLaren as a group, and it brought them a potentially valuable first contact with Ronnie Peterson. . .

McLaren Engines' race programmes continued vigorously under Tyler's direction until the track-racing operation was shelved in 1980 and he was summoned back to the UK, where the Formula 1 programme was in deep trouble, and running out of steam . . . But this would only happen sixteen action-packed years after the team's creation.

Initially Teddy and Bruce each had about a half share in the team although outsiders were sometimes convinced Teddy was bank-rolling it all, some even thought he was one of the MGM Mayer family. But Bruce contributed capital, plus his own services as driver: ". . . which alone represented a considerable financial value, particularly in later years" as Teddy emphasises today.

In the beginning, the team had a Dunlop tyre contract born of Bruce's Cooper years, and of course they ran BP fuel with the fees and bonuses accruing, as Bruce did with Cooper. But through 1965 Bruce's increasing involvement with the Ford GT programme brought contacts with Firestone who were looking to find a way into International road racing to take on Dunlop and the biggest name of all – Goodyear. "Bruce's work with Ford was probably teaching him as much as he was passing back to Ford's engineers, particularly in the aerodynamic area, and then the Firestone contract starting with the '65 Tasman Championship came via the Ford programme. That contract plus Bruce's Ford involvement were instrumental in getting our own company going.

"Everyone got on well with Bruce. If somebody in the team or dealing with us in some way was unhappy then he'd be the guy to go to great pains to find out why. When we took the Tasman cars out on Firestone tyres we didn't realise just how important tyres were. That's when we got to know Bob Martin of Firestone who later became very familiar as their race-engineering chief over here, and he had a really hard time at first when our cars – which were designed around 13-inch wheels – wouldn't work at all well on the only tyres he could supply, which were 15s. Until that time we just thought tyres were tyres and it didn't make much odds what you were on, yet when we did get 13-inch Firestones we began to learn the difference. We didn't appreciate how it is today, if you're on the wrong tyres you might as well just stay at home . . .

"I didn't go down to the '65 Tasman races, I stayed here to get our new Feltham factory going but another big factor at that time was the sports car production deal we did with Elva Cars, a subsidiary of Lambretta-Trojan. They gave us a royalty on every car they built to our designs so that gave us a reasonable income with the Firestone testing contract, and a Ford contract to build a lightweight CanAm-type version of the Ford GT. We sold some special hill-climb cars that Bruce cobbled-up; we won some sports car prize money, and we would always sell any works cars we had no further use for. It was part of team policy – if it was standing still and not earning its keep, sell it."

When Bruce ended his long career with Cooper at the end of '65 he looked forward to running his own Formula 1 programme through '66. Choice of engine was the agonising problem, and after casting around the team chose a linered-down version of the quad-cam Indy Ford V8. It was a poor choice, as we shall see, though the Mallite monocoque car built to Robin Herd's design to carry it was quite good: "He was a bit green as a designer then, in that his things tended to be difficult to make, but they were certainly very sound structurally. Our main problems were with the choice of the Ford engine".

Yet the team had vast sports-racing experience of the lightweight alloy Oldsmobile F85 engine and it was this unit with which Jack Brabham and Repco of Australia dominated the 1966 World Championship, and then made it two in a row with Denny Hulme beating his team patron to the crown the following season. Why hadn't McLaren taken it on? Their experience of it should have given them a head start over Brabham: "We considered it, but the kind of modifications which Repco did were well beyond our resources, and I doubt very much if we could have done any more with it than we did with the Indy Ford. At the time I hoped we'd draw-in Ford with support beyond parts but that just didn't happen . . .

"I have a nasty feeling that if I hadn't urged the Ford engine more on financial than engineering grounds, Bruce would very probably have found some other solution to our engine problem, and it certainly couldn't have been worse than the one we actually chose . . ."

Through 1967 the team found its feet in Formula 1 with 2.1 BRM V8 and later

The management at Colnbrook '68; Bruce, Tyler Alexander, Teddy Mayer and Phil Kerr. Their combination of driving skill, technical ability, business sense and good old-fashioned dynamism made the team work, and work well.

full 3-litre V12 power, and for 1968 McLaren really reached maturity with the customer Cosworth-Ford DFV V8. Late delivery of the BRM V12 gave the team time and the opportunity to shake all the bugs out of their new M6A CanAm sports car early in the 1967 season, and so build the foundation of five years' extremely-rewarding domination of that North American race series.

"Initially we'd relied on the alloy Olds V8 far too long. Bruce in particular was convinced that light weight more than compensated for lack of cubic inches and outright power, but we soon found otherwise. When Surtees won the '66 CanAm series in his Lola he used an iron-block Chevrolet of 5-6 litres, and stretching our Olds to 4½-5 litres gave us more power but was too much for its bottom end. Through all our time with the Olds V8 we had little help from GM. Frank Ball, an Oldsmobile engineer, talked with us, but little more. When we decided to change to Chevrolet, GM helped a little, but with parts only, and then we won the CanAm Championship in '67 and that really helped a lot financially – it kept us afloat and supported the F1 programme. Effort on both was about equal, but one paid and the other didn't. If you can amortise overheads on two projects like that it helps a lot – one certainly secured the other in our case."

Teddy liked to get himself involved technically: ". . . because I was interested in it and because I felt I would be able to do a better job with the operational procedure if I knew what was happening technically. Usually I would set out the procedure as to how we would accomplish what we wanted to do, then Bruce and I would discuss it, and in many cases I would set out both the technical and operational procedures. This wasn't because I was qualified to do so, but because I liked setting-out procedures, and Bruce was often busy on other jobs and didn't particularly like putting things down on paper . . . Although he generally left operational procedures largely to me, he would correct my technical procedures a great deal and then he would proceed with the technical side and I would execute the operational procedure. It worked out very well . . ."

Phil Kerr joined the company to become joint Managing Director with Teddy after eight active and highly successful years building the Jack Brabham empire. Before Bruce's death he handled most of the team's administrative work and after that sad event he became more involved in policy making jointly with Teddy. Phil had been involved in persuading Jack Brabham to give Denny Hulme his real Formula 1 chance in 1965 at a time when some people – like Ken Tyrrell – still regarded 'The Bear' as being "too fat and lazy ever to make good". Phil looked after Denny's interests during his time with Brabham, and handled the deal which gave him the 1967 CanAm McLaren drive while on his way to winning the Formula 1 Driver's World Championship with the Repco-Brabhams. When Denny left Brabham to join Bruce's F1 team at the end of that season, Phil was in a difficult position having a foot in both camps, and he soon followed Denny to rejoin his boyhood friend Bruce McLaren at his team's Colnbrook works. Teddy initially concentrated upon the team's growing North American activities, while Phil ran the factory and looked after much of the Formula 1 programme.

Gulf Oil sponsorship had come for the CanAm and Formula 1 teams via the Ford programme, and Reynolds Aluminum followed, via an original introduction by arch-sponsorhunter Frank Williams who found that Reynolds – one of America's largest metals companies – had an interest in entering motor racing but knew they were far too big for him to handle. He introduced them to Bruce, Teddy and the team and as Teddy says "They were interested in doing something because we used aluminium and a small deal developed into a big one as we eventually race-tested their Reynolds 396 silicon-aluminium engine material in experimental linerless Chevvy engines . . ."

The old Firestone agreement had been replaced by Goodyear at the end of '66 and it was with Goodyear's encouragement that McLaren branched out to tackle Indianapolis in 1970. The Indy purse of almost $1-million was an irresistible attraction compared to Formula 1, but through the 'seventies as the Indy/USAC programme continued so Formula 1 finances inflated rapidly to match and then improve upon Indy's. "By 1976", Teddy points out, "the Indy purse was still around the million-dollar mark, and even by '78-'79 not much more. It shot up to around three-million by '83 but by that time we had long-since opted out, the effort and manpower expended in USAC was better-placed helping get us out of trouble in Formula 1. Apart from Indy the rest of the USAC series was bad news financially. The two other big 500-mile races at Pocono and Ontario, California, paid about a third of Indy-sized money, while the other series rounds were in effect just testing for Indy, the Big One . . ."

Through 1970-71 the BRM team had been sponsored by Yardley Black Label cosmetics. Towards the end their's was not the most happy relationship and Phil Kerr did a deal which brought Yardley's tasteful livery to McLaren's Formula 1 programme for 1972-73 with an option for a third season in '74. Gulf Oil's main interest was in CanAm and Indy, but they retained a small Formula 1 interest, their continued backing evidenced by orange patches on the cars' flanks.

In effective replacement for Bruce on the driver strength, Teddy brought in his one-time Rev-Em FJ team-mate Peter Revson, who had performed nobly for McLaren at Indy and provided their main opposition – Lola-mounted – in CanAm.

Unfortunately the early-seventies saw rapid inflation and Teddy found: "Though we had a very good relationship with Yardley we just could not afford to fulfil the deal for '74. The money they wanted to pay was just sufficient for one car and they were insisting we run two.

"Marlboro had taken over where Yardley had opted-out of BRM and they had a similar experience and now they were courting us, and asked if we'd be free to run with them for '74-75. . .

"To say that Yardley weren't happy with what was happening would be putting it mildly, and contractually we were sailing very close to the wind; that's true. They probably saw it as Marlboro poaching their team away from them, but they couldn't come up with an adequate budget for us to fulfil the deal. It was just an impossible situation. I was quite desperate to get the thing sorted out, dealing with Patrick Duffeler of Marlboro and Dennis Matthews who was MD of Yardley. He was a good man to deal with, tough but very fair, and eventually we did the deal whereby we ran a Texaco-Marlboro-sponsored two-car team for Denny and Emerson Fittipaldi, and Phil ran a parallel one-car Yardley operation with Mike Hailwood. Both were based in the works at Colnbrook, there was a lot of interchange between the races, and equipment was identical . . .

"The Texaco-Marlboro deal went with Emerson who was leaving Lotus. The choice was between us and Brabham, and for sure we didn't want to see him and that sponsorship going to Brabham. Jody Scheckter had driven for us the previous year and he'd had an altercation with Emerson when leading the French GP at Ricard. He'd led all the way, it was his first serious Grand Prix, and either Emerson tried to pass him in an impossible place or Jody slammed the door on him and Emerson went out of the race and almost turned over. The one proviso he made for joining us was that *no way* would Jody be in the team. He was perfectly happy for Denny to be in the second Texaco-Marlboro car, and Peter Revson staying-on in the Yardley car.

"Peter was signed-up, but that winter with all these deals going on he was increasingly sceptical how his one-car operation would work in practice. Mark McCormack – the management people – got him wound-up I think, and abruptly he went off to join Shadow instead.

"That was really difficult. Yardley had been mollified by still having Peter driving for them. They really wanted a top name driver or personality. Then Mike Hailwood wanted-out of his deal with Surtees.

"He said he always took a paper-back with him in the car so he'd have something to do when it broke down.

"John was very unhappy about all that, and when we moved factories I remember unearthing a huge pile of correspondence about it. Eventually we paid John a little bit of money and got Mike's services for Yardley. The two teams ran in parallel, trading technical information but very much in competition once the race began. It worked fine until Mike's crash at Nürburgring. Denny retired at the end of that year, and went home to New Zealand and Phil eventually followed him . . . leaving me to run the business on my own . . ."

Emerson won the Championship for the team in 1974, actually on October 6 which became a memorable date for another New Zealand member of the team, John Nicholson.

It was his 33rd birthday, it was the day on which he clinched the British John Player Formula Atlantic Championship driving the Lyncar special with his own version of a Cosworth-Ford BDA engine and across the Atlantic at Watkins Glen the World Championship titles had just fallen to Nicholson-prepared Cosworth DFV power . . .

Bruce had always favoured New Zealand mechanics joining his team. They had so little industry back-up down-under that Kiwi mechanics rapidly learned to be self-sufficient, and to develop a mechanical initiative which their British counterparts could seldom match.

Brought-up in Auckland, John had left school at 15 to take an apprenticeship in an automotive machine shop run by a friend of his father's. The company, L. H. Hayter, later Engine Rebores Ltd, expanded and John became a partner. A group named Motor Specialties took it over and John suffered the frustrations of being told by accountants how to rebuild his engines. Still business was good, and to promote the company's capabilities John began racing a Lotus 27 monocoque FJ car with 1500cc Ford engine. Until that moment he'd found little to interest him in motor racing.

A tough but taciturn character, he let the Lotus 27's performances speak for themselves during that Tasman summer of 1967-68. He would just unload his car, race it, load up again and trail home. It was low-key motor sport: "You know, the biggest race in New Zealand was the one to the pub . . ."

In late '68 he bought Graeme Lawrence's Brabham BT18, but was ready for change. He'd been in the same business for 11 years. He wrote to McLaren in the UK and received an answer from Phil Kerr, offering a post plus his air-fare from Singapore. He worked his way there as mechanic on Roly Levis' Brabham BT23C, via races at Mt Fuji in Japan, at Hong Kong and Singapore.

When he arrived at Colnbrook, the team was preparing to defend its CanAm titles. Engine specialist Gary Knutson had returned to Chaparral and George Bolthoff had been brought in to develop a CanAm Chevrolet ZL-1 V8. "George was a really good guy to work with. When I asked him how, he told me how. I didn't give any aggro, we worked long hours and I enjoyed every minute of it. It was fun . . ."

George went off to McLaren Engines in Livonia late in '69, John joining him there for the height of the 1970 CanAm season. Gary Knutson returned to manage the team's engine programme for 1971 and John's time was full "merely getting enough engines out the door each week". His own driving ambitions had been kept under control, grumbling round Goodwood hour after hour in the latest CanAm prototype running-in engines. But coincidentally during the winter of 1970-71 Cosworth announced their intention to relieve the workload of preparing all F1 DFV engines in the field at that time, and announced they would assist approved specialists in preparing the V8s away from Northampton.

Teddy asked John if he was interested in rebuilding the team's DFVs and he agreed: "If I ever wanted to be a racing driver, that decision screwed me for the rest of my life . . ."

Through 1971, when John bought a Formula Atlantic car to race on his own account, he tired of the cramped McLaren engine shop at Colnbrook. In 1972 March made him an attractive offer to run their new engine rebuild shop in Reading. In response Teddy and Phil Kerr made a counter-offer and on January 1, 1973, Nicholson McLaren Engines Ltd was born, taking residence in new premises the opposite end of the Heathrow runway at Hounslow. The company's DFVs became merely the visible tip of the ice-berg as preparation and modification work encompassed all kinds of other competition engines, and in addition to McLaren's F1 demands, John also supplied DFVs to other teams, including Lotus, Tyrrell and others. The company continued successfully far into the 'eighties, outliving the original team from which it had grown . . .

Back at the end of the '75 season, with very little positive warning, Emerson Fittipaldi abruptly left Marlboro-McLaren to join his brother Wilson's Brazilian-backed Copersucar effort. There was a lot of money there, but it was the end of Emerson Fittipaldi as a serious World Championship contender. "We had warning of his departure but never really thought it would happen. He was bloody good. He always kept his car out of trouble, you could virtually guarantee he would finish races; he was a terrific asset and when he felt it was really important to try hard he'd drive the best opposition into the ground. But through the summer of '75 he discussed retiring, and then decided not to, which was good news. Marlboro were in deep discussion with him for months about money.

"Then the Brazilian deal came up firm and he went for it. Just like that. One 'phone-call and he was gone; early-December and we were left high and dry without a number one driver. We were on the 'phone to James Hunt whose Hesketh team had just recently folded, within minutes of putting the 'phone down on Emerson, and within days he'd done a deal with Marlboro and he was in, alongside Jochen Mass who'd become number two when Denny retired. The rest is history . . . James was fantastic for us during '76 when he took his Championship and good again the following year once we got the M26 car sorted out, but it all went bad for James and us in 1978.

"We'd had a tough time and we managed to do a deal to bring Ronnie Peterson into the team. It had terrific potential but almost as soon as he signed-on he was

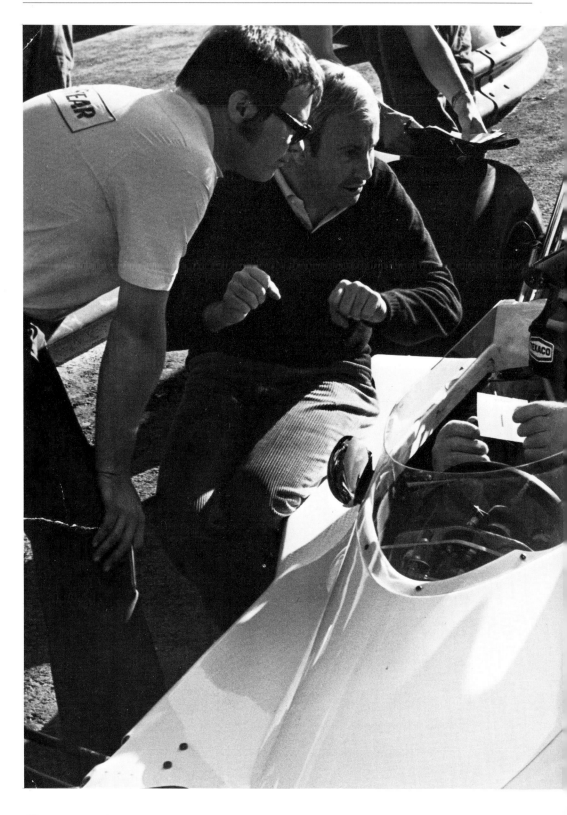

First time out in a McLaren at Ricard-Castellet during testing, winter 1973-74, Emerson Fittipaldi finds out about an as yet unpainted M23. Here he is checking tyre temperatures and car set-up with Teddy (left) and Gordon Coppuck – still wearing his Yardley-McLaren jacket from the previous season – on the right.

killed at Monza. That was one hell of a blow . . .

"We got John Watson and already for '77 the choice to replace Jochen Mass lay between Gilles Villeneuve and Patrick Tambay. Both were really hot prospects. We'd given Villeneuve his Formula 1 debut at Silverstone and he went well but spun several times while exploring just what the car could do, and what it couldn't. Tambay ran third at Zandvoort in the Ensign which was by no means a front-running car. Villeneuve looked like being bloody expensive in machinery, and I wasn't sure we could afford that. Marlboro liked Tambay, so did I and we took him instead. In his first few outings for Ferrari, Villeneuve looked every bit as expensive as I expected – it was only later he showed his real class . . ."

By the late-'seventies Team McLaren was in a vulnerable position, with new cars proving uncompetitive and drivers incapable of contributing very much to pinpointing the problems. Eventually Marlboro stepped-in to recommend a merger with Ron Dennis' Project Four team – eventually to replace Colnbrook's failing F1 designs with new engineer John Barnard's innovative carbon-fibre monocoque MP4.

The 'merger' took effect in the Autumn of 1980. Teddy describes how; "The first job was to make Gordon Coppuck's Lotus 79 copy M29 competitive" – Gordon maintaining it was more like a Williams – "and do new underwing floors for the M30 for the end of the season. But then we had the M30 written-off at Watkins Glen, and knew we'd have to do more work on the M29s for the first races of '81, before the MP4 would be ready . . ."

Through 1981 John Watson was able to prove that Barnard's MP4 could be competitive, and after finishing third in Spain and second in the French GP he continued the progression with a memorable, emotional victory in the revamped team's home Grand Prix, at Silverstone.

"I then saw the future as being quite bright. We'd won a race, which was the object of the merger. We began to think about building the strongest possible team for '82 and Niki Lauda was making noises about coming back from retirement. I'd talked to him about it several times in fact, and he'd driven Ron's Marlboro ProCar BMW M1s before his retirement so he knew the set-up, and Marlboro themselves were keen. We also talked with Nelson Piquet, Alain Prost and Gilles Villeneuve. All were very strong but in the end we took Niki – and at that time nobody could be sure he'd cut it . . . He more than proved himself . . ."

During 1982 Ron Dennis' vigorous behind-the-scenes negotiations with Akram Ojjeh's *Techniques d'Avant Garde* advanced technology concern and Porsche resulted in an exclusive deal which would bring McLaren International turbocharged TAG-Porsche V6 power late in 1983. It was a necessary move, for the indefatigable Cosworth-Ford DFV's competitive days at last seemed numbered with Renault, Ferrari, Alfa Romeo, BMW and Hart turbo engines all outpacing it wherever sheer power could tell.

The march of the turbo engine frankly worried Teddy; "Looking to the future it was clear that the cost of Formula 1 racing could easily become prohibitive with turbo engine development soaking-up funds. The development of Turbo cars had already priced our kind of CanAm out of existence. I had, and have, strong reservations about the future of specialised teams in Formula 1."

The season also saw the Project Four principals having fulfilled their prime ambition of winning Formula 1 races, now wanting to do their own thing, their way. They suggested buying-out Teddy's major shareholding in McLaren International, and it was a not too unhappy 'Wiener' who bowed-out of the organisation he had helped seed nearly twenty years before.

In temporary retirement from racing he still maintained his share in the totally independent McLaren Engines operation at Livonia, Detroit, in partnership with his old friend and former Rev-Em team-mate Bill Smith. For much of its career McLaren Engines had relied perhaps 80 per cent on race work, but into 1983 the emphasis had changed, and although deeply involved in the Buick Indy test programme the company was committed some 80 per cent to industry R&D work, the balance of its time occupied by oval track-racing Cosworth DFX turbo V8 preparation and rebuilding, maintaining BMW M1s for IMSA racing in the USA and also rebuilding Porsches for the same class. Gary Knutson and Wylie McCoy ran the place, with its six engine dynos running continuous reliability tests for industry when not involved with race work, and Tyler Alexander was there on the Buick project – Ron Dennis having also bought out his small share in McLaren International at the end of '82. Teddy also maintained a small interest in Nicholson-McLaren Engines and into 1983 was laying initial plans which could pull together part of the original McLaren team of the '60s for a new racing project of the mid-'80s . . .

Chapter 3
Ron Dennis – Regaining Glory

*"You can have all the money in the world, but without the
right designer you're just history . . ."*

Ron Dennis, 1983

In 1980 with encouragement from Marlboro – their mutual sponsors – Team McLaren Ltd and Project Four Racing Ltd merged to form McLaren International. The new company carried that honoured name into its third decade of Formula 1 racing. Project Four was described by Ian Phillips of *Autosport* magazine – a journalist very close to Formula 2 in which Project Four had found its feet – as "an ambitious, some might even have said flash, outfit which tasted success in other forms of racing but yearned for the challenge of Formula 1 . . ."

Ian highlighted how the merger brought together Teddy Mayer whom he rather arguably characterised as "perhaps one of Grand Prix racing's old school traditionalists" and Project Four's Ron Dennis: ". . . a mechanic turned ambitious team owner, never a motor racing enthusiast, but a man who had grown up with the commercialism and professionalism of the sport in the 1970s, somebody definitely attuned to the requirements of today's made-for-TV motor racing . . ." He added, perceptively: "The chemistry, said the cynics, was not right . . ." and so it would prove by the end of 1982 when Dennis finally bought-out Mayer's major shareholding and took executive control of McLaren International.

Ron Dennis had left school after taking his O-levels and started an apprenticeship with Thomson & Taylor, a famous name company in British motor-racing and motor-trading mythology, based just beyond the Brooklands Motor Course bankings at Byfleet. He took a Vehicle Technology Course while with "T&T"s as everybody knew them, and during this period they were absorbed into the fast-growing Chipstead Motor Group. This was an ambitious company in its own right, headed by Jonathan Sieff of the Marks & Spencer chain-store family, and amongst other acquisitions it took over the Cooper Car Company, and its Formula 1 team. This deal went through in the early part of 1965, and works drivers Bruce McLaren and Jochen Rindt became Chipstead men in that last full season of 1½-litre F1 racing. Chipstead saw no point in pouring money into development of new cars for just one last season's racing, so the Cooper-Climax cars of that year were very much low-budget also-rans. Cooper moved their team base from Surbiton to the old T&T building in Canada Road, Byfleet, where some of the Cooper old-sweats today recall "young Ron Dennis out the back in the car park, cleaning-up Moskvitches fresh from the docks".

Chipstead's Formula 1 sponsorship was dedicated to design, development and construction of the all-new Cooper-Maserati V12s for the new 3-litre Formula which took effect in 1966. Drivers were to be Jochen Rindt and Richie Ginther, although the diminutive little American was only on loan from Honda and would return to them later in the season when their own 3-litre challenger became available. In mid-season John Surtees fell out with Ferrari and Chipstead rushed him into a Cooper-Maserati cockpit alongside Jochen, and he would win the Mexican GP for them right at the end of the year.

Meanwhile Ron Dennis had been transferred to the team, and he attended his first GP as a mechanic on Jochen's car, aged 18½ . . .

At the end of 1967 Jochen moved to Brabham and Ron went with him as mechanic. He was competent and keen, and worked with Jack himself until the Guv'nor retired from race-driving and from his team at the end of 1970.

Ron Dennis: "I remember the sequence of events quite well. We were on the Canada, America, Mexico trip and in those days the cars went by road, so we had ten days holiday in Acapulco. Jack and Ron Tauranac had rushed back to England and left me in charge of everything including the money. I had to cash our prize money cheque at the Glen and look after it all the way to Mexico. At the time I already knew of Jack's intention of retiring and I remember lying by the pool and – although being slightly over-awed by the responsibility of looking after the money and the preparation of the cars – suddenly thinking in my naivety, here I am doing all that's necessary to run a team – there were no commercial sponsors in those days – and just drawing my salary for it. Why not do my own thing? . . ."

Neil Trundle had been chief mechanic on the Brabham Indy team, he joined Ron to set-up Rondel Racing for 1971, running a sparkling trio of Brabham F2s in their two-tone blue team livery.

Rondel Racing got under way in 1971 thanks – as Ron is quick to point out – to the generosity of several people: "Notably Ron Tauranac of Brabham who loaned us two chassis for the year, at the end of which we paid him the new price and carried the cost of depreciation. His generosity enabled us to earn a living and get into the business of running a team. We'd started the company with £2,000 and it might not have happened if we'd had to buy new cars right at the start . . . Then Mo Gomm of Gomm Metal Developments in Old Woking let us use space in his workshops as a team base. We bought our transporter on hire purchase.

"The French driver Bob Wollek had wanted a car and while we were building it Graham Hill walked into the shop. He'd just joined Brabham and there was some good-natured moaning about 'You rotten buggers, I join the team and you two leave it' but when he saw the F2 car we were building-up he said 'I'd like to drive that'.

"He didn't have an F2 deal that season, and Wollek only had enough money to do half the series so we talked to him and Graham eventually drove the first part of the season, and won for us at Thruxton which was a terrific start.

"Then the father of a girlfriend of mine, who owned quite a large antique shop, told me about a customer who was a dyed-in-the-wool car enthusiast. He introduced me and this was Tony Vlassopoulo who had considerable shipping interests at the time. He was interested in becoming involved and put in some capital, along with a builder/property developer friend of his named Ken Grob. And we began going places . . ."

The 1971 season with Graham Hill, Bob Wollek and Tim Schenken driving the Rondel Brabhams saw Tim take fourth place in the European F2 Championship, while in 1972 with backing from the French Motul Oil company Rondel ran four cars for Schenken, Henri Pescarolo, Carlos Reutemann and Bob Wollek. Their season was interrupted by Carlos' nasty accident at Thruxton first time out when he smashed his ankle, but he ended the season fourth in the Championship, like Tim before him.

For 1973 Motul-Rondel built their own F2 cars, designed largely by former British Aircraft Corporation/Brabham engineer Ray Jessop. They were not particularly successful though always impeccably, sparklingly prepared by Dennis and his men. Tom Pryce joined the team that year with support from businessman-club racer Chris Meek.

During that year Ron's ever-extending ambitions turned to Formula 1. A Motul F1 car was laid down by Ray Jessop but with the Yom Kippur War that October and the Arab oil embargo, western economies were plunged into crisis and during that winter it looked very much as though motor racing might grind to a halt in '74.

"Rondel was in quite good shape, but at that moment we had a considerable overdraft by the values of the time and with the oil crisis our backers just got

nervous. The Jessop F1 car was two-thirds built and Vlassopoulo and Grob were very fair but we decided to stop there. Rondel didn't go under. It just ceased operations, just like that . . .

"I didn't want to struggle into Formula 1 just anyhow, scurfing hopefully onto the back of the grid. Tony took the F1 and raced it into '74 as the Token with Tom Pryce driving, but meanwhile John Hogan of Philip Morris had approached me to run an F2 team for a couple of Ecuadorian hopefuls. Two Surtees cars had been ordered and I set-up the Ecuador-Marlboro F2 team . . ."

Drivers Faust Marello and Guillermo Ortega proved in fact to be no-hopers, and Tim Schenken was brought in to become the only graded driver to compete regularly in European F2 during that season of '74. His Surtees TS15A yielded the team's best result, second at Nogaro near the end of the year. The team was based in Germany at Mindenheim outside Munich, under an ex-Porsche mechanic while Ron operated from the UK, organising spares and so on.

"After that season I was determined to do my own thing again. Robin Herd of March suggested running one car for Vittorio Brambilla in F2. There was no specific sponsorship, I didn't have dreams of grandeur about running the team under my own name and I was kind of lying in the bath wondering what to call it when I thought of 'Project Three'. Project One had been Rondel, Project Two had been the Motul, now here we were with Project Three – that's how the Project teams came about . . ."

With Italian sponsors, Ron ran March 752s for Brambilla and Sandro Cinotto amongst others. As usual his workshops were spotless, the cars' preparation impeccable but the results didn't come. "We were still operating from Gomm's, but then for '76 we moved into Pool Road, Woking, into premises of our own, and set-up Project Four Racing with new sponsors to run semi-works March F2s. We won ourselves a reputation for operating cars effectively outside the factories, they gave us good deals and it all looked good . . . All the time we were building-up the assets of the companies; making real progress."

Project Four's first racing season of 1976 saw 18-year old Eddie Cheever running Ron's March with Ferrari Dino V6 engine until "We were able to repay Ron Tauranac's generosity by swopping from March chassis to his new Ralt

Ron Dennis (centre) flanked by his drivers, Niki Lauda and John Watson, studies qualifying times at Hockenheimring during the German Grand Prix meeting.

company's in mid-season and doing our bit to demonstrate how effective they could be. I like to think we helped Ralt to become a success for Ron, in just the way he helped us get under way with Rondel . . ."

Eddie Cheever and the Brazilian Ingo Hoffman drove Project Four's F2s in 1977 using BMW power, the young American-Italian driver taking second place in the European F2 Championship with Hoffman seventh. Come 1978 and Project Four's F2 operation reverted to March chassis as the BMW Challenge Team, Cheever and Hoffman taking fourth and sixth in the Championship. Former British Clubmans Formula driver Creighton Brown was running the ICI-sponsored F2 team at that time, and at Donington Park at the end of the season Ron approached him to suggest a partnership to further both their ambitions in racing. 'We'd been good friends, the partnership was logical. It gave Creighton more time to run his farming interests and at the same time raised his level of involvement with racing . . ."

So ICI Project Four came out for the '79 F2 season running March cars for Derek Daly and Stephen South, ending the season with Daly third and South fifth in the European title chase. Meanwhile Project Four had also been campaigning a Marlboro-backed F3 team in the British Championship which driver Chico Serra won for them. And BMW came up with their M1 coupe racing programme . . .

"BMW had produced the design and hoped to homologate the type for endurance racing, doing a production deal for the cars with Lamborghini in Italy. But then Lamborghini went belly-up and Bauer in Germany were originating the parts with nobody to put them together."

BMW did a deal with Osella in Italy and Project Four in Britain to assemble the cars for a series of ProCar M1-only promotional races supporting the year's Formula 1 race programme, with star drivers aboard. Both Osella and Project Four were commissioned to produce batches of 15 cars each, but the Dennis outfit completed their fifteenth at the same time as Osella delivered their third. Consequently BMW awarded Project Four a contract for ten more M1s and Marlboro sponsored the team in running a works car for Niki Lauda – which won the ProCar Championship.

By this time Ron Dennis' ambitions in Formula 2 and Formula 3 had been fulfilled. Stefan Johansson would win the 1980 British F3 title in a Marlboro-Project Four entry to add to Serra's '79 success and the only way forward was into Formula 1. "So I looked round for a genuinely top-class designer, and made a short-list of who they were. It was a *very* short list, and only John Barnard was available even though I asked Gordon Murray of Brabham and Patrick Head of Williams, just in case they felt like a move. If you don't ask, you don't get . . .

"Initially John didn't seem terribly interested in what I was saying, but when he appreciated he'd have virtually a free hand and I'd find the backing to pay whatever it cost, we started to go places. I showed him the Pool Road facility. There was an M1 in there and he picked up its carbon-fibre rear wing, and began studying it closely, weighting it in his hand. I didn't think much about it, just said something like 'Isn't it a nice part', but some time later John came back to me and suggested making a whole monocoque out of it. Ground-effect monocoques had to be slender and the reduction in cross-section made it difficult to maintain stiffness. Carbon-fibre is extremely rigid, and John said this is what we should do while I got my head down and tried to find the money to finance whatever it cost. At the time I envisaged a budget around £80,000. At that time you could build a car for £50,000 so I thought 'Surely that'll be sufficient' – and it wasn't, but we found the means to go ahead . . ."

The rest we know . . .

Ron Dennis describes himself as "an ambitious person"; positively bristles when well-meaning admirers and some not so well-meaning might remark "Didn't he do well, he was only a racing mechanic". Perhaps because of that background, which is *nothing* to be ashamed of, he has always tried that bit harder to progress further. Above all his obsession with cleanliness and sparkling presentation made his team and his cars stand out.

"In some ways I always felt I could have had a more academic career but my gut feeling was not for studying. I was never bonkers on motor racing either, but the supposed technical excellence of it always appealed. I was a mechanic working with my hands and deep down I resented it. But I thought it was good experience and it would stand me in good stead. I hated getting dirty and within half an hour of getting home at night I would be spotless . . ."

On his obsession with cleanliness: "I know I am an old woman about it, but I truly believe that there's nothing clever about an organisation which covers you in grease and sends you home stinking. Striving for this perfection might sound trivial, but it makes for a better environment and certainly helps when we bring sponsors to the workshop. The standards apply right through the company . . ."

Project Four through 1979-80 was a big operation ". . . and on paper it looked to have made a reasonable profit. But I reached the stage where none of our programmes was giving me more than money and not much of it for the effort. I'm not really motivated by money. I don't know what motivates me really, but after evaluating the situation we decided it had to be Formula 1 next. It was a challenge, and I didn't think it would be difficult to compete. If we had the best-looking team and were qualifying, that would be a reasonable target to aim for – and viable of course."

The carbon-fibre monocoque MP4 had a painful birth, and Ron Dennis' faith was shaken at one point when Gordon Murray of Brabham wished him luck with the idea: ". . . We've had nothing but trouble with the stuff", he said. It was already in production so it was beyond my control by then anyway. Luckily, I had one hundred per cent confidence in John . . ."

Not for the first time, nor the last, Ron had courageously set-up the programme before he was really convinced how he could pay for it all. Through the Spring of 1980 the rift between the FISA governing body and the FOCA (Formula One Constructors' Association) teams had widened and in an atmsophere of dispute, threat and counter-threat the future of World Championship Formula 1 racing looked rocky indeed. It was not a good time to go sponsor-hunting but ". . . Marlboro was always open to me because of the F2/F3/Procar programmes we ran for them.

"I did my level best to procure their F1 budget. It was the optimum to me" – he uses lots of words and phrases like that, straight out of the executive handbook – "Although I reckon I am a pretty good salesman it was a flyer for them. I had to persuade them it was going to be a very, very good car first of all. But convincing them to break the continuity of their involvement with McLaren was even more far-fetched. They had an investment in the name which had been very successful. They said it would be more desirable to incorporate our new car into their old structure . . ."

None of the principals involved either will or can recall who first suggested a merger between the two operations. It was a difficult yet extremely sensible and practical solution to the problem of a great team in technical decline, looking for a car, and an aggressively ambitious newcomer, painstakingly developing an innovative new car free of week-to-week calendar pressures but short of a sponsor. The merger brought Project Four's programme instant membership of FOCA with all the travel-arrangement, expenses, start, prize and bonus money advantages accruing plus access to McLaren's Cosworth DFV engine shop developments plus the accepted experience of Team McLaren men like Teddy Mayer and Tyler Alexander and the drawing office staff from Colnbrook.

Looking back on the merger three years later Ron Dennis recalls: "We had to form a new company and I felt it had to be a new kennel. I didn't want to sit in their kennel and I felt it wasn't big enough anyway." So after a lengthy search the new McLaren International HQ was opened in Boundary Road, Woking, Surrey Looking at the operation there in November 1981 Dennis remarked: "I am sure people still say it won't work with two managing directors and that Teddy and I won't get on. Sure, there's nothing like being one hundred per cent the boss, but there are more positives than negatives in our relationship, plus the fact that it would be almost impossible for one person to do the job as efficiently. The areas of overlap generally result in better decisions. Teddy and I get on very well . . . If there is any niggly frustration, what I like to think is our common denominator – intelligence – prevails and the problems are buried or have no significant effect . . ."

With John Barnard, Creighton Brown and Tyler completing the board, McLaren International came into being on November 1, 1980; the two merging companies having already cooperated on a crash programme to retrieve some semblance of McLaren competitiveness at the end of that season. They planned to start '81 with drivers Alain Prost and John Watson. Prost's debut season in Formula 1 had proved his class and he was *de facto* number one, no question. But despite his having signed a two-year contract with the team, he moved on after emerging thankfully little harmed from a huge shunt at Watkins Glen which destroyed his M30 car. "We still don't know if it was the car or him, but he attributed it to the car and said it was one accident too many, and he was off . . ." to join Renault.

Having two ready-made drivers had been another big advantage of the merger from Project Four's viewpoint, and losing Prost was a blow. Andrea de Cesaris, hard-driving Italian, took his place, Wattie retrieved his number one position and the Barnard-designed carbon-fibre MP4 became competitive in mid-season and with a little luck won the British GP . . .

One of the new regime's promises to Marlboro had been to put them back in the winner's circle within a year; something the marque McLaren hadn't achieved since the Japanese GP ending the '77 season. At Silverstone they proved as good as their word but as Ian Phillips emphasised: "It was curious to find Ron Dennis, five minutes after Watson's win, surveying Andrea de Cesaris' wrecked car on his own rather than soaking up the champagne with the rest of the team: 'It's not until the next day when I wake up and think 'that's another step achieved' that race results really hit me. Of course it was an emotional thing. It wasn't a personal triumph but a company and team achievement. It was what we had set out to do. Every employee gets a company document when he joins us saying in a nice way how we like to do things and trying to explain that it's not so much winning races that we are working towards but the manner in which we want to win them. You can live in motor racing a long time on image and pole positions, but you can't always be best . . ."

At the end of '81 McLaren International signed-on Niki Lauda to return from his self-imposed retirement from race driving to line-up alongside Wattie in 1982. It was a major coup for the former Cooper and Brabham mechanic's new team; convinced that Niki was the type of charismatic driver the public wanted to see, Ron declared at the announcement function: "Nothing has been paid to bring him back whatsoever. I truly believe that money has nothing to do with Niki driving the car, or for our team during 1982. We are paying him what we consider to be the going rate for a driver of his calibre and his value in respect of promotion for Marlboro. The figure is totally incidental, nothing to do with anything other than what we think is the going rate . . ."

He had pestered Niki to return: "I used to 'phone him periodically, sometimes every other month, sometimes every four or five months. Then I made a really serious attempt to talk him into it in mid-summer '81. Typically, he just 'phoned me one day and said he wanted to do it once he'd made sure all his responsibilities were being carried by other people." He tested an MP4 at Donington Park and Ron: ". . . knew ten minutes after he climbed out of the car . . . that he would come back."

In the background there was the long-term lure of an exclusive turbocharged engine deal which Ron had put together for the team. The days of the Cosworth DFV and normally-aspirated 3-litre engines in Formula 1 seemed clearly

numbered. Renault had led the way along the 1.5-litre turbocharged road, and after years of trial and tribulation they had begun winning. Now Ferrari had followed their lead with BMW supplying engines to Brabham, plus Alfa Romeo and the Toleman-Hart British team. Ron determined to find a turbo engine to ensure his new team's future, in his normal well thought-out and realistic manner: "John Barnard's philosophy, supported by all the directors, is that there is no current turbo that's got everything going for it. They've all got compromises and there is no room for compromise in Formula 1. At least, we don't think so. We certainly won't start with compromise although during development you sometimes have to live with it. To start with it, though, asks for problems . . ."

He talked to Porsche – arguably the world's finest automotive R&D people with a vast fund of turbocharged racing engine experience behind them, and asked if they would be willing to tackle such a programme. If they would, he would raise the funds to finance it. They nodded assent, and he began beating the bushes for backing and found it with the Ojjeh family's *Techniques d'Avant Garde* advanced technology trading company which as 'TAG' co-sponsored the Williams Formula 1 team. TAG Turbo Engines was set-up as an independent company to cooperate with Porsche upon presentation and promotion of their F1 turbo V6 which would carry their logo cast into its cam covers. The prototype engine was first unveiled to the press at the Geneva Motor Show in March 1983, and appeared in the suitably modified MP4s in the Dutch GP at Zandvoort on August 28, heralding a new beginning for Marlboro-McLaren.

Why Porsche? "Purely because we are convinced that they are the world's leaders in turbocharging technology. They've got more knowledge than anyone else on all the important systems which go with turbocharging such as fuel, ignition control and consumption. We just felt . . . that the issue would be won or lost on the systems as opposed to reliability. Porsche also have tremendous resources and we are quite convinced that they will be able to do the job much

faster than anybody else. Also they were prepared to sit down with our designers and design the engine as a complete part of the car. So many other companies wanted to produce an engine out of the blue and say here it is, it develops Xbhp – fit it in your car. Immediately we were in the area of compromise which we would not accept."

Was it difficult to persuade Porsche to do the job? "The first thing was to convince them that Formula 1 had a lot to offer them apart from the obvious. Secondly, and the real basis of the negotiations – and the most time-consuming – was to be able to make the project possible within their political structure and restraints."

While he was thinking and working hard and fast to unravel problems of financing the project, Porsche's engineers under Hans Mezger had already invested several months work in the project "as a result of a commitment from me that obstacles would be overcome".

With Niki Lauda in the fold and a Porsche turbo engine on the way the Ron Dennis ideal of a Formula 1 team seemed within reach.

For the future his ambitions were clear: "Winning races. Consistent winning of races, more than just four or five a year . . . the whole organisation has been structured to achieve that . . ."

The aims, twenty years after the original team's formation, had not changed – just the faces, the names and the approach were new . . .

Section I: The Men Behind McLaren

Chapter 4
The Designers

"What you have got to do is come up with a car that is slightly better than someone else's, and do it now. Get it done, get it done simply, get it done early. . ."

Bruce McLaren, 1970

The earliest McLaren cars were designed very much in the practical, workmanlike Cooper mould, with McLaren ideas incorporated where Bruce felt some small advantage could be gained. Robin Herd, a brilliant graduate engineer with a glittering career mapped out ahead of him at the National Gas Turbine Establishment – part of the British Royal Aircraft Establishment at Farnborough – joined the team at Feltham in 1965. His initial designs were based, naturally, upon contemporary aerospace structural technology and as we shall see caused some grief while being built. But they were as effective as their engines allowed.

Robin's aerospace background combined with Bruce's Ford GT experience to foster a growing interest in competition car aerodynamics. The monocoque M2A tyre-test vehicle built for Firestone in 1965 proved many ideas for Robin's first Formula 1 M2B design which would follow for '66, and one of them was a rear wing mounted above the tail. In testing at Zandvoort in November '65 they fitted this crude wing and Bruce lopped 3 seconds off his lap times. Without the wing his times grew by that same margin. Clearly there was enormous advantage to be gained there, but all evidence of the wing was then destroyed as the team determined to use it as their secret weapon for 1966. Robin recalled: "If the Indy

Design discussion at Colnbrook with Robin Herd, Bruce and Teddy checking points on a wind tunnel model of what would become the BRM V12-engined M5A for 1967. Robin went off to Cosworth at the end of the season; "to study at the feet of Keith Duckworth was too good an offer to pass-up". Bruce offered to treble his salary to keep him in the fold, but the Cosworth charisma was irresistible. Robin went on to found March Engineering which became the dominant force in the British production racing car business.

Ford engine had lived up to expectations you would have seen the M2B McLaren with a wing on the back . . ."

Early in '66 further testing at Riverside Raceway in California with the Indy Ford V8 engine revealed such multiple problems that planned tests of an advanced wing system had to be set aside. This time Robin intended to experiment with an adjustable rear wing. Another problem during that test session was Dan Gurney's presence on the pit counter as a fascinated spectator. Continued engine problems saw wing experiments set aside. They were not resumed until 1968 when the team at last had a truly competitive engine in the Cosworth-Ford DFV and Brabham and Ferrari led the way in adopting strutted wings on their cars at Spa. There, Bruce scored his first *Grande Epreuve* victory in his own car.

Wind tunnel testing proved a vital part of CanAm car development where the all-enveloping sports car bodyshells could harness such potent aerodynamic forces. The M1A with its Tony Hilder-styled body was a very attractive-looking car, but its gently-curved upper surfaces promoted terrific lift at high speed. The car was bullet fast along the straights, but hoiked itself up on tippy-toe and was not very quick round the corners.

The M1B sports-racers carried Michael Turner-styled bodies formed around wind tunnel results, and with their tacked-on spoilers were much more efficient. Robin realised very early on that it was difficult – indeed dangerous – to give too much credence to wind tunnel results without testing them full-size on circuit. Like many racing car designers before and since he appreciated that only if motor races were run in wind tunnels, the tunnel engineer would be king.

During development of the CanAm Championship-winning M6A in 1967 they ran at Goodwood with numerous pressure tappings on the inner and outer surfaces of the car and Robin rode shotgun to record the readings. He told Eoin

Goodwood again during the summer of '67 with the monocoque-chassis M6A CanAm car under development. Teddy chats with Bruce while Robin has a good look round the car, folder in hand, on the right. It was during this test series that Robin rode on – not in – the car to study suspension behaviour through a hole in the rear body panelling . . . and Bruce spun it.

Young of another test series in which he lay spreadeagled across the tail deck, watching rear suspension behaviour through holes in the body. Almost inevitably at one stage his legs slid across to pin Bruce's left arm in the middle of a corner and they spun viciously down the road: "Looking back . . . as the car got steadily more out of shape I'm surprised to recall a feeling of calmness rather than terror, and having enough time to convince myself that if Bruce couldn't get us out of this situation, nobody could. It was fascinating to see the combination of throttle bursts, steering movements and brake applications that sent us spinning harmlessly down the centre of the track. When the car stopped we both looked at each other and started hooting with laughter . . ."

Initial designs were laid down only after long and often heated discussion of basics between Robin and later his new assistant Gordon Coppuck, Bruce, Teddy, Tyler and Don Beresford who had joined to take charge of construction. Robin's initial tendency to over-complication was wrung out of the system by 1967 with the conventional aluminium monocoque M4A/B F2 series, the BRM V12-engined M5A Formula 1 and the extremely successful M6A CanAm sports cars. That winter he set down the M7A Formula 1 car to accept the team's first Cosworth Ford DFV engines for '68. Then came the offer to join Cosworth Engineering to produce a four-wheel drive car which would provide the traction necessary to make the most of the new V8 engine's power and torque. Robin accepted, and left McLaren to move to the Northampton engine factory. Bruce was hurt, but he would get over it . . .

Gordon Coppuck took over.

He was to become responsible for the majority of McLaren designs during the team's career. He was born in December 1936 and educated at Basingstoke Grammar School, about 15 miles from his home at Fleet in Hampshire. His early passion was motor-cycling. As a nine-year old spectator at a Hankley Common scrambles meeting he had his leg broken when a rider ran into the crowd. At school he was involved in a pilot scheme for part-Grammar/part-Technical education, and when he left at 15 he became apprenticed to NGTE at Pyestock near Farnborough. There he studied gas turbine installation and design, before spending two years' National Service in the Army, and then returned to NGTE where he met Robin Herd, at that time a youthful Senior Scientific Officer. Gordon did several jobs with him.

Meantime he'd entered motor-cycle competition. By 1961 he'd won an International Gold Medal in the Welsh Six-Day Trial and a First Class Award on the Scottish. He rode works Greeves, Triumph Tiger Cub and Cotton-Villiers machines in these trials. Now at NGTE, Robin had an ancient VW which he used in local restricted rallies. He saw the art of rallying as confined to the navigator's seat and used to 'hire' drivers to conduct his mathematical brain around the countryside. One weekend his regular driver couldn't make it, so Gordon was invited to take his place; "Anyone who can ride a bike must be a good driver". They finished second, but Robin didn't ask Gordon again . . .

Then at the end of '65 Gordon's interest in cars was kindled when Robin announced he was leaving NGTE to work for Bruce McLaren. Robin soon had need of another draughtsman, and asked Gordon if he would join them.

"I took two weeks' holiday to go and work with McLaren's who were still at Feltham then. They could see if I could do the kind of work they wanted, and I could see if I liked doing it. Then Eoin Young and Wally Willmott took me up to Colnbrook to show me the new works, and when they moved-in in December 1965 I joined them . . .

"I detailed Robin's stuff. He would describe the general concept of the car and I would draw and fiddle the bits to fit the other bits in the necessary order. I wouldn't take part in deciding the overall concept of the car. Then when Robin left I did a little bit on the M7A, revamping the suspension a little."

Gordon was a quiet, thoughtful character, and characteristically he wasn't sure if he was capable – after only two years' experience – of taking over responsibility

Bright-eyed Gordon Coppuck served his McLaren 'apprenticeship' under Robin Herd and eventually became chief designer and a director of the company. His cars dominated CanAm, Indianapolis and Formula 1 racing at various times through the 'seventies, bringing the team their multiple Championship titles.

for executing the designs which Bruce wanted, and he asked that somebody should be brought in "over my head . . ."

The choice fell on an outgoing Swiss-born ex-Lotus engineer named Jo Marquart. He had held a research post with the diesel engine company of Saurer and came from Winterthur near Zurich. He had wanted to work in the UK and his father – who was in the transport business – arranged a work permit with a friend who was Chairman of the Scottish Omnibus Company. Jo's real interest was in cars and he went to work for Lotus on the Elan Plus-2 and later under Maurice Phillippe's guidance on racing cars.

He and Gordon were the same age, 33, and the Englishman soon realised that in fact the Swiss brought-in over his head had little more experience than his own.

Between them they redesigned the victorious M6A CanAm sports car to produce the 1968 M8A: "Jo did the front half and I did the back. It was the first time I had experienced proper design responsibility and it was the same for Jo. We kind of felt our way for a while, and would always discuss ideas with Bruce, but we got more confident as we went along . . ."

Jo became Formula 1 designer to the team while Gordon worked on the M12 production CanAm car to be built by Trojan, the M6GT road version of the CanAm car – which was Bruce's pet project – and the M10 Formula A/5000 single-seater production model.

"I did the M10 pretty much on my own. Jo was very busy with the four-wheel drive M9A Formula 1 and at one point we had to have three jobbing draughtsmen in to do drawings for us. The M10 was the first car where I really decided concept things like roll-centres and so on, and then drew the suspension to produce the effects I wanted.

"At first for Formula A we said we'd just put a Chevvy V8 in the back of a modified M7, but of course it wasn't that simple. The Chevvy is much wider than a Cosworth and it can't be used as a stressed member in the same way. So I had to widen the monocoque and extend it rearwards to support the new engine. I thought the simplest and lightest way of doing it would be to extend it as far as the clutch bell-housing and link the sides there with a sandwich plate between the engine and gearbox. In those days the competition's monocoques used to go right the way back and link with a final diaphragm right over the transaxle.

"We then went on to make the monocoque stronger and stiffer than the M7, and built-in our early ideas on driver safety by forming the cockpit into a kind of self-contained cell. We took the monocoque side panels right up and over the top behind the driver's shoulders and this proved very successful. Bruce's own M7C Formula 1 car later used a similar monocoque and it was adopted for all subsequent designs in place of the basic M7 'bath-tub' type . . ."

Gordon detailed Bruce's M6GT Coupe but the team really wanted the CSI – the governing body of the sport – to allow them to include Trojan's CanAm sports-racing production in the necessary 50-off figure to allow homologation of the type for endurance racing and Le Mans. The authorities had done this for Lola, allowing them to include open CanAm T70s in their production total to homologate the roofed-in T70GTs for endurance racing, but paradoxically refused to play ball with McLaren: "We could have fought them, but we were plain too busy. Bruce ran one car on the road as a development vehicle before his death, but that was about it . . ."

The M9A four-wheel drive project was a costly flop. Teddy Mayer recalls it cost the team perhaps as much as a fifth of its total budget for 1969 "and that was just one car plus bits for more". The CanAm programme had brought contracts with GM's engineering division and Teddy had mentioned the four-wheel drive project to them: "One engineer named Jim Musser was a particularly bright guy who'd done a lot of experimental work behind the scenes with Chaparral. I told him we were doing a four-wheel drive car and he warned me right then that big tyres and wings had made 4WD nothing more than a big waste of time. We'd had other warnings too, notably from Tony Rudd of BRM who'd tested a 4WD car five years before, and I told Bruce what Jim Musser told me and hoped it would scotch the project, but it all went through and cost a bomb for zero return . . ."

Thereafter Jo Marquart progressed the M14A Formula 1 design for 1970 and Gordon was detailed to a new project; Indianapolis. "The original idea was to build a car which would be reliable, run fairly fast and make quick pit stops. We reckoned if we were running at the finish we stood a fair chance of winning.

"So we built a simple single-seater version of the CanAm car and chose an Offy engine because they were as reliable as the Ford V8s and quite usefully lighter. We added a suspension interlink on the rear to share the cornering workload between the tyres, and added a jacking system at the front, working on the spring abutments, so the driver could compensate as his fuel load lightened . . ."

The American establishment was very impressed with the M15s' debut at Indy, initially in testing before the snows came at the end of '69 then in the month of May for the 500-Miles race itself. The design won a special award from the Indiana Chapter of the Society of Automobile Engineers, but then the programme was fouled-up by Chris Amon's inability to adjust himself to the specialised driving demanded by Indy, and by Denny Hulme's severe burns suffered in testing. Peter Revson and Carl Williams took over for the race, Revvy retiring and Williams finishing ninth.

Gordon: "Despite all that, we'd learned a lot about Indy, and what we'd learned resulted in the M16 design for '71."

When Mark Donohue took out Roger Penske's customer McLaren M16 onto the Speedway on May 13 an expectant hush settled on crowd and pit crews. This had been the hot combination in testing thus far. When Mark zipped round the 2½-mile track in 49.73 seconds to smash the mystical 50-second barrier for the first time and average a staggering 180.977 mph, the place just erupted.

The Penske people were elated and so were the Gulf-McLaren crew who had built Donohue's car as their first-off M16 in the winter. The news was telexed to Colnbrook and Gordon managed to unwind a little and feel assured that he had been on the right track with the wedge-shaped, bewinged new car. That weekend works driver Peter Revson underlined that fact by stealing pole position with a four-lap average of 178.696 mph from Donohue's initially fastest 177.087. Denny Hulme unsettled himself with a huge high-speed spin early in the month, but qualified fourth fastest behind Bobby Unser's intrusive Eagle, with 174.910mph.

Gordon's name instantly became one to conjure with at the Speedway – home of so much myth-making – and since most engines were pretty even, it was clearly McLaren chassis power and their ability to put power down onto the track surface which had established such shattering superiority.

By this time McLaren's standing in North American racing could not be higher. Their CanAm cars had a stranglehold on the big-money sports car series. Their Formula A/5000 cars had been the things to beat in their class. And now USAC oval-track racing lay at their feet. They didn't win at Indy, but their's were the cars to beat – and the designs to copy, as many USAC constructors realised . . .

Jo Marquart had left at the end of 1970, possibly feeling not as confident of the team's future after Bruce's death in testing that June as he had been with Bruce secure by his shoulder. He was going to set-up the Huron racing car concern, and later moved on to GRD.

Ralph Bellamy, ex-Brabham designer, took his place, working on the Formula 1 M19 as described later in these pages, and the M21 Formula 2 car. The M19 uncovered deep problems with rising-rate suspension geometry and its management, but Ralph left at the end of '71 to return to Brabham. Gordon was alone in charge of the McLaren drawing office.

He began work on the M23 Formula 1 car, drawing upon Indianapolis M16 concepts with the wedge-form monocoque and hip-mounted radiators. "We had taken an M16 tub and a Cosworth rear end from the M19, sat them down on the workshop floor, looked at 'em, thought about them, and weighed them, and all the answers told us the right thing. Do it. So we did, and the M23 came into being."

He eschewed the advantages of inboard front brakes as "marginal" and settled on an uncomplicated, practical concept, exquisitely executed in the best McLaren traditions. His services to the company were recognised at this time as he was made a Director at the start of '73, and the M23 would become one of the all-time classic Grand Prix car designs, bringing McLaren drivers two World Championship titles, in 1974 and 1976, and accumulating victories on the road in 18 Championship-qualifying Grand Prix races . . .

Such success owed much to painstaking preparation and continuous development.

A major role was played in this area by Team McLaren chief mechanic Alastair Caldwell. He carved himself a reputation as "a prickly bastard", abrasive, opinionated, brutally outspoken. He blamed this partly on over-exposure to Denny Hulme, but he was a native tough guy. One colleague recalls how "Alastair could put your back up just by the way he'd say good morning . . ." another characterised him as "The kind of guy whose aim in life is to own a brand-new Mercedes, but until he gets it hates anybody driving one . . ."

Many aspects of the Caldwell story are typical of what made so many fine Kiwi mechanics who found a home with Team McLaren. His father David was a Scots-born vet in Sheffield post-war who emigrated to New Zealand in search of a new life in 1949. Alastair was six, the youngest of three sons. He was a rebel. Father's ambition was for his boys to win University degrees. At 14 Alastair put

Ralph Bellamy and Denny Hulme pictured with the prototype M19A upon its release to the press at Colnbrook in February 1971. Ralph's rising-rate suspension system for this car offered immense theoretical advantages which unfortunately could not be harnessed in practice. Even so the M19 would come good and serve the team for more than two seasons.

into execution a carefully-conceived plan and ran away from school in Hamilton and eluded his father's pursuit for six months before returning to the fold. If he didn't want to stay at school, he must at least learn a trade. Alastair ". . . thought the least evil would be a motor mechanic – I didn't want to be anything, but a motor mechanic would do". He began an apprenticeship in the garages of the New Zealand Post Office, learning about all manner of vehicles in a very short time.

He'd been at school with other racing enthusiasts, like 12-year old Howden Ganley, Jimmy Palmer whose father raced Cooper-Bristols, Pete Kerr, Johnny Muller and Ross Greenville. Pete became Jochen Rindt's chief mechanic with Roy Winkelmann Racing – the dominant F2 team of the '60s – and moved on to March and Shadow. John Muller made it to the top as a racing mechanic, had his fill and retired. Ross Greenville came to England to make his name as a racing driver *á la* Bruce himself, but crashed a Gemini heavily at Aintree, lost a foot and any chance of a viable racing career. Alastair's brother Bill was also interested, and he began racing an Austin-Healey. At that time in the early-'60s, Howden had a Lotus 11 and Greenville an FJ Lotus 18. Alastair accompanied Howden to the South Island to race the 11 at Christchurch, and caught the racing bug.

Brother Bill was at University but worked nights as a very successful dance hall promoter and pop-group manager to finance his own racing, progressing to a Lola sports-racer, then an FJ Brabham. Alastair at 19 had an A-grade mechanic's ticket, a wife (Jean) and an unbelievably well-paid – £25 a week – job in a Wellington garage. He moved to work for Bill Hannah, former mechanic to another NZIGP Driver to Europe scholar Angus Hyslop, at Havelock North, and prepared Bill's Brabham on its trailer out in the vegetable patch.

Early in 1965 they took the car to the International meeting at Teretonga Park outside Invercargill. During the race the throttle spring fell off, the throttle jammed open and Bill crashed fatally, the car also killing two spectators on a sheep truck parked as a temporary grandstand.

Alastair blamed himself for the disaster. Understandably it turned him off racing. He was 22, a garage foreman and eager to get into business on his own, but his youth was against him where the oil companies were concerned. They refused to back him in a garage business. " 'Come back when you're 25' they said. I said I'd go to England and go motor racing instead . . ."

He flew in to Heathrow and banged on the McLaren Racing door at Colnbrook and announced he was a mechanic, did they have a job for him? Bruce gave him the chance, and he grasped it with both hands. He figured that hard work would be his best chance to establish himself and so he talked to no one, watched all that happened around, and beavered, hard . . .

"I sussed out the stars in the workshop. There was Wally Willmott who was a descending star and Tyler Alexander who was a rising star. He talked a lot and was very abusive to the senior management which amazed me . . . but the place was very happy, very well run, run by enthusiasm . . . Bruce was always excited about the new gearbox or the new wing and he was always down there, giggling. It was a great atmosphere . . ."

He worked by his own admission ". . . balls to the wall for six months. Literally, I never had a day off for six months. Tyler worked very hard and I was the only guy who could match him. He would start at 8.30 and so did I. He would finish at 2.30 in the morning and he would have to *tell* me to go home. Everyone else would be long gone. I *knew* that this was telling . . ."

His first race was the '67 Italian GP at Monza with the M5A-BRM. Mike Barney told him to drive the transporter and follow him, not realising Caldwell had no HGV licence and had never handled such a large truck in his life. "I knocked down a couple of railings but nobody noticed, and then I drove the damn thing to Dover . . ."

He became properly established in the team, his mechanical abilities impressing management and work-mates alike. His wife and two children arrived from New Zealand 36 hours before he was due to leave for Kyalami: "It was snowing, cold. I'd never been so cold before. We had no central heating in that grotty little maisonette. The fact that she didn't leave me astounds me now . . ."

The blow of Bruce's death at Goodwood in June 1970 was almost too hard to bear. Alastair was there with the F1 M14A: "That nearly made me quit again . . . Bruce was more than just a friend of mine, it was all very traumatic. I was broken up – the whole place was broken up. We didn't go to Spa, just cried for a week or so. I thought of going home then . . . but decided to stay. Basically it was because I couldn't afford the fares and I was too proud to ask my father for the money. We decided to hang on and make enough . . . at the end of the season I said I was off and they gave me some more money . . ."

Looking back on Bruce's death, Alastair told Eoin Young: "There was a marked change in the management after that. Teddy changed a lot. He learned to become more amenable, he could no longer be the little bastard because that wasn't going to work, so he had to change. Phil Kerr provided a good stabilising influence and Denny was very good. He was a rock. He had to change as well because he could no longer be a bastard either; he had to come down . . ."

Alastair had been Denny's mechanic, now he was made Racing Manager with responsibility for both F1 cars and – when Denny retired and Phil Kerr followed him back to New Zealand – he became Formula 1 Team Manager. This entailed paper work, administration, bookings of flights and hotels, which held little appeal, but as Teddy emphasises: "Alastair's mechanical aptitude was of immense value to the team. Sure he upset a lot of people, most of the time, but his technical input was invaluable, it really was, and his ruthless control of preparation on the cars gave us the reliability to win Championships . . ."

The six-speed McLaren transaxle and the innovation of the weight-saving air starter were both Caldwell developments: "When I worked on my first Hewland FG gearbox in '68 I thought you could put six speeds in there. I mentioned it to somebody and they said we don't need them anyway. I had the six-speed gearbox running at the end of '74 when Emerson was with us. I thought it was a bloody good idea but nobody else did, so it didn't get done. Money was tight even though we'd won the World Championship; our most successful year was our worst year financially. By the end of 1975 the financial climate had changed, and we decided to do it properly. When it worked it made me more confident of my ability to do those sort of things, so I decided to have a crack at the air starter as a personal project . . ." And it proved so successful it became a universal feature throughout major-Formula racing. Alastair Caldwell played a crucial role in McLaren's heyday of success until the start of 1980 when he moved on to Brabham – where his abrasive character did not sit well – and then on to lesser teams in Formula 1. His part in the McLaren story should never be discounted . . .

Between 1972 and 1975 Gordon was assisted in the Colnbrook drawing office by John Barnard and Dave Quill. John learned a lot before moving on to work with Vel's Parnelli Jones Racing in the 'States. He would later replace Gordon as chief designer of McLaren Formula 1 cars . . .

By the end of 1975 the M23 series had been racing for three seasons and Gordon, Teddy and the rest of the team were convinced it had reached the end of the road. It had always been McLaren policy to build long-life designs with great development potential, but it had become evident that Emerson Fittipaldi could not get near Niki Lauda's Ferraris. Gordon: "We'd convinced ourselves we couldn't beat Ferrari because of their extra horsepower, and we knew continued development had put the M23 well over the weight limit. We were still the only team to run with Ferrari late in the year but we couldn't beat them, and so I started to lay down a lighter and more aerodynamic car for the coming season – the M26.

"But no sooner had we started than we lost Emerson and won James for '76 and he promptly sat the M23 on pole in Brazil and South Africa, split the Ferraris at Long Beach and was super-fast in Spain. His ability to out-qualify the Ferraris was promising enough, but in Spain – despite all the aggro when we got ourselves disqualified – we knew we'd made a better guess than most at the effect of new airbox and wing regulations . . . Suddenly the M26 didn't look so necessary and it became a low-priority project. Then Niki had his accident at Nürburgring and we set the M26 aside and threw everything behind the M23 . . ."

What should have been an obsolescent car went on to take the Drivers' Championship for James Hunt, although Ferrari still beat McLaren in the Constructors' competition.

And the M23 went on into '77 because wet weather untypically disrupted winter testing of the M26 at Ricard and then the new racing season had begun again, the calendar unrelenting as always . . . James Hunt damaged M26/1 severely in pre-race testing at Kyalami ". . . and we were in the situation we least wanted of having to develop a new car during the height of the European season".

The M26 was successfully developed as a Grand Prix winner in Hunt's hands and through the winter of 1977-78 tests at Ricard saw one car running with revised hip radiator ducts fared back between the rear wheels into end-plate rear wing supports. This was part of a long-term concept study for the intended replacement M27, but as the M26s entered their first full season's use so the M27 project was set aside. It was a non-ground-effects design, and as Lotus showed the way ahead with underwing sections boxed on either flank of a very narrow centre monocoque chassis to generate downforce beneath the car, so Wolf and others were quick to follow, and McLaren trailed that way too.

Gordon had begun to suffer from the years of intense pressure. McLaren lagged further behind during 1978, James Hunt being blamed by the team's management for "stroking it", or "not trying", or "not having his heart in it any more". Looking back in 1983 Gordon Coppuck thinks differently: "I think James was trying like hell, at least for the first half of the season, but towards the end he did get discouraged and we weren't making real progress . . ."

James Hunt was pure competitor. He attacked all sports to win. Winning was all that mattered and with McLaren lost against the new ground-effect cars, winning became unattainable.

Teddy believed Gordon was tired, worn down by the fierce calendar pressures involved in design and engineering responsibility for the Formula 1 M26s and the

USAC oval-track M24Bs then being campaigned in the 'States with Cosworth DFX turbocharged engines. The new ground-effect M28 for 1979 was a catastrophe for which Gordon carried the can. "It was too big, too heavy and too slow in a straight line – the first car when originally built was also nowhere near stiff enough . . . it was just a bad time . . ."

To drag themselves out of trouble Gordon hastily laid out a replacement car, the Williams-like M29 but with the team relegated to the uncomfortable position of mere also-rans after so many years of continued success internal frictions and clashes of personality became ever more disruptive.

The team had always included a number of extremely strong-minded individuals. Indeed it had been formed around some of them, and through the late-'70s those who could shout loudest or most persistently usually had their way. Outsiders would look sympathetically at quiet, popular Gordon and wonder how he could bear-up under what they saw as increasing "design by committee" at Colnbrook. Teddy always had a strong influence upon design, sometimes right, often wrong. Both he and his designers admit he "developed a strong reputation for interference". Teddy understandably defends his interference as justified and productive, others don't see it that way to the same extent. Tyler was another with emphatic ideas on the way to go, although he spent most of his time in the States at McLaren Engines, running the USAC programme, and Alastair Caldwell played a very significant role, Gordon freely acknowledging that ". . . he made some very positive contributions".

But a team which has fallen off the tightrope of competitiveness in Formula 1 always suffers agonies trying to regain its footing, and McLaren's writhings were unexceptional. Teddy played a major role in the final stages of M29 development and in conception of the M30 which replaced it, and neither car was very startling, whereupon the McLaren International merger with Project Four Racing was effectively imposed by Marlboro, and one of Project Four designer John Barnard's conditions for (in effect) returning to the fold was that his responsibilities should be undiluted, and that Gordon should have no place in the revamped team.

Two years previously, the author had been talking to Gordon in his Camberley home, sitting around the dining table, with a characteristic framed portrait of Bruce smiling down from the wall. We'd been talking about the problems the team had suffered during their Championship year of '76, the Spanish disqualification, the Monza sample analysis which claimed they were burning illegal fuel. Gordon had glanced up at Bruce's portrait and said flatly: "At McLaren's we have never looked for the kind of tricks which give you short-term advantages. We are in motor racing for a lifetime. With us it's a life commitment . . ."

Now his life with the team was at an end, he acted on a consultancy basis race-engineering the Formula 1 March and developing their 1981 F2 production cars, then went into partnership with March F2 team manager John Wickham to found their own team, Spirit Racing. By 1983 he was back in Formula 1, with the turbocharged Spirit-Honda . . .

John Barnard, born in 1946, began his working life with GEC in North Wembley after studies at the Watford College of Technology and Brunel. He designed machines for making electric light bulbs, a remarkably complicated procedure. But it was good grounding, for he was involved at all levels from original drawing, through prototype manufacture to development running ready for production.

His hobby was tinkering with road cars seeking ever-higher performance. He started with an Austin A35 when he'd just turned 17. His father had refused point-blank to let him buy a 100mph special, so he acquired the A35 instead and fitted an Arnott supercharger . . .

"Frog-eye Sprites were the thing of the time but the A35 would blow the pants off them, until you wanted to stop. It was a good introduction to what happens when you do it wrong . . ."

An Aston Martin DB2/4 later occupied much of his spare time. It threw a rod, repair of the original engine was too expensive so John fitted instead a Chevvy V8 with Borg-Warner 'box. His motoring and motor racing interests flourished until one day he wrote to Lola and McLaren asking if they had any jobs available. He went to Colnbrook to see Jo Marquart and was advised to start work on Formula Fords and suchlike before setting his sights on a Formula 1 team. "Then I went to see Eric Broadley at Lola and in a brief conversation he listened to what I wanted to do and said 'Fine, start in the drawing office'. I was in . . ."

Starting in late '68 he made the most of Lola's virtual British polytechnic of racing car design, which would also throw-up talents like Patrick Head, whose Williams cars would win two consecutive Formula 1 Constructors' Championships. John became responsible for Lola's minor-formula designs, Fords, Supervee etc. Into the '70s he was largely responsible for the Lola T280 and T290 sports cars using Cosworth-Ford DFV and 2-litre in-line four-cylinder engines and worked extensively on the Jackie Stewart T260 CanAm car which frightened the mighty works McLarens on occasion. By 1972 John wanted to join the top echelon of design for Formula 1 or USAC oval track racing, and a place became available at McLaren:

"I became sort of number two to Gordon Coppuck. My first job was on the M23 which was in quarter-scale outline when I arrived. There was a mock-up chassis under way of jigging but no proper tub drawings, so I started doing them, apart from the front bulkhead which Dave Quill drew. It was fairly complicated, with aluminium outer skins and glass inner sandwich around the radiator ducts which had foam filling injected to form the new deformable structure requirement. The chassis was fairly elaborate and very strong. It worked well . . ."

John and Gordon got on well but the junior man could not tolerate as the more equable Gordon could, McLaren's committee-style design; "with some bright' spark on the factory floor insisting you should do it his way. For my money if you are Chief Designer the people making the bits should do just that, unless you make an obvious mistake or there's some bloody good reason you can't do something that you haven't recognised . . ."

He designed the ill-fated McLaren M25 Formula 5000 car, virtually an M23 with the Chevvy stressed-mounted at the back through a special water pump casting and with just two low-level torque tubes bolted to the tub: "Denny tested it right near the mark first time out, but the tub lay on the toilet roof for about two years after that while the legal side wrangled away over it . . ."

A deal to buy it had ended in litigation.

What interested him more was increasing feedback from McLaren's USAC operation: "On the later M16B, C, C/D and 16E with the new tub I became more involved. I completely redrew the M16 tub front to back for the 16E because over its long development life all sorts of nasties had grown inside to support various mods. It had grown weight and complication, so it was time to re-do the design, save weight and stiffen it up. We kept the outer skins, but all the innards were revised . . ."

Mechanic Hughie Absalom had joined Parnelli Jones' team in California along with Jim Chapman who had been with Lola on CanAm when John started there. Jim called and invited him to come over to replace former Lotus engineer Maurice Phillippe, who was returning to England – eventually to take over design of Tyrrell's Formula 1 cars. John arrived in Torrance, California in July 1975 and worked briefly on the team's Lotus 72-derived Formula 1 car driven by Mario Andretti before concentrating on the VPJ6 track car, producing the highly successful VPJ6B with Cosworth DFX turbo power thereafter. But at the end of '77 the under-financed, over-stretched team collapsed and driver Al Unser contacted John and explained that Jim Hall of Chaparral sports car fame was interested in producing a new USAC car, would Barnard pencil it for them? John proposed a Lotus 78-type ground-effects car, preferring to design and build it in England; "there are more specialised skills that we need there . . ."

McLaren International Engineering Director, John Barnard, made his name at Indianapolis and became one of Formula One's leading designers in the '80s.

While his wife Rosemary stayed in California to wind-up their affairs, John flew home to set-up the new Indy Chaparral programme. He designed it in his dad's front room at his home in North Wembley, helped by Gordon Kimball who'd worked with him at Parnelli's and who would subsequently return to the US to design Pat Patrick's Wildcat USAC cars. Wind tunnel testing of the new car was conducted in John's head, using some test figures which Patrick Head shared with him from Williams F1 testing.

The new Chaparral 2K was built in England by Bob Sparshott's B&S Fabrications company which ran Brett Lunger's private McLaren M23 and M26 cars in Formula 1. Al Unser led Indy in the car before its gearbox failed, but John Barnard's delight became embittered by the media's adulation of Jim Hall's "latest brilliant design", whereas the ambitious Englishman had emphasised in the original agreement that he should be given proper credit for the car. He was anxious to make his mark to further his career, and now felt cheated. "Within the trade everybody knew who'd done the car, where and how, but I suppose I was trying to build myself a future and I was a bit sensitive about not getting the credit for it . . ."

His last job for Hall was a set of sliding skirts to fit the two complete Chaparral 2Ks and spare chassis built by B&S Fabs. Thereafter he freelanced on some work for Hector Rebaque's private Formula 1 team, until "late in November '79 Ron Dennis of Project Four called me. I didn't know him at the time, but I'd been talking to Patrick Head, saying that I wasn't sure what to do next, and he mentioned that Ron wanted an F2 car designed. We got talking, and Ron explained that it wasn't an F2 car he was after, it was Formula 1!"

Ron Dennis was by no means a design engineer, and here John saw his opportunity to make his mark, without Ron being able to "swallow me up" as Jim Hall had done: "In fact it helped him to blow my trumpet a little to show credibility . . . What was impressive to me was that he was prepared to appreciate the necessity for serious research before proper design could begin – and this was the birth of the Project Four car, the MP4/1 . . ."

He began his investigations in December '79 and in search of enhanced chassis rigidity with minimum weight looked at carbon-fibre: "It had already been used for skirts and odd bits; McLaren used it for under-bodies, and somebody there knew an expert at British Aerospace who invited us round one day and we saw what it could do. The BAC contact fired me up, gave me an insight into what carbon-fibre could do, its properties and potential.

"How you can make a racing car out of it takes longer, that's difficult, because you need to know what you can do with it, and what you can't, before you begin serious design . . . You have to consider how you are going to mould it, and how you are going to join it. It's a completely different material from steel and aluminium which we all knew about . . ."

In the first few months of 1980, Ron Dennis and his Project Four partner Creighton Brown did their sums and appreciated the investment necessary to launch their new designer's brainchild. They studied ways to generate sufficient funds. They had a long Formula 2, 3 and BMW ProCar association with Marlboro, and through them thoughts turned to amalgamating the promised potential of the new project with the old-established track record, experience and standing of Team McLaren, who by this time were in deep, deep trouble in Formula 1.

John admits he was anti-merger: "My initial reaction was that we would just be engulfed by McLaren. I couldn't be as susceptible as Gordon had been to design by committee" – the very idea grates on him – "but then discussions came down to the amount of influence each of us would have on the project, and I was so far down the road towards the carbon-fibre car I was reluctant to let it go . . ."

Before the merger, whatever Team McLaren's principals had been told, just a few MP4 parts had been made, including the monocoque moulds. After the merger John returned to Colnbrook before the new McLaren International HQ had been finalised in Boundary Road, Woking, Surrey. John found himself Chief Designer in Gordon Coppuck's place, resisting input as one might expect given his outspoken position on "design by committee" from Teddy and Tyler and others.

"At Colnbrook I got in briefly on the M30. We made underbodies for it based on MP4 research, which – umm – meant compromising the design to make them fit. But at Italian GP time we did make some improvements to the basic car with new ride heights, rake angles and so on, working with just that little extra bit of knowledge you gain from serious wind tunnel testing, we used the Southampton University tunnel with its rolling-road surface . . ."

Meanwhile dismay was growing around problems in building the innovative MP4. "There had been no enthusiasm in this country for building our carbon-fibre monocoques, the big people capable of doing the job didn't have the capacity for such specialised work. Our reception was very dispiriting.

"Then a friend in the 'States, Steve Nichols, who had been Gabriel damper chief on Champcars, gave me a name at Hercules Inc, who were interested in all kinds of carbon-fibre applications. One Friday I got back from another abortive trip to a UK company and Ron called these Hercules people on the 'phone. He eventually got the chap who could say 'yes' or 'no' and Glory Be, he was interested . . . So we went over to Salt Lake City to see him and his R&D people who were willing to have a go. So they came to mould our tubs, and we assemble cars around them here in Woking . . ."

John was accompanied on initial visits to Hercules Inc by BAC carbon-fibre engineer and stress expert Arthur Webb who acted as consultant to the new team, and John and his colleagues – Alan Jenkins, Steve Nichols (ex-Gabriel), and draughtsmen ex-McLaren/Colnbrook Colin Smith and Mike Locke, all grew in confidence as the MP4s were built, developed and raced their way to competitiveness – taking the McLaren name far into the '80s . . .

Section II: Racing World-Wide

Chapter 1
Early Days

*Starting right; Tasman Championship '64: "I've heard
people saying that my team is over-staffed and over-equipped
(we have five engines, four transmissions and spares for the
spares) but it is certainly paying off . . ."*

Bruce McLaren

When Jack Brabham left the Cooper team to set up his own racing operation at the end of 1961, Bruce McLaren inherited Jack's position as Cooper's number one driver. He won the Monaco and non-Championship Reims GPs in 1962, but the '63 season was a difficult one. John Cooper was badly hurt in a road accident in May and Bruce was knocked unconscious when his car uncharacteristically broke and he crashed in the German GP in August. Yet he had actually led the World Championship briefly after second place at Spa, and although he placed third at Monza he described the year as "disastrous for me . . . Since that brief spell at the top of the Championship ladder after Spa I only finished two races". Plans for an ultra-modern monocoque F1 Cooper had been dropped, and Bruce finished sixth in the Driver's Championship.

He was frustrated by Cooper's slowing rate of development and his own lack of success. Eoin Young wrote: "People were beginning to comment on the dimming of the McLaren star, and there were those who blamed Bruce for Cooper's lack of success . . . He felt he knew what had to be done, but it was becoming increasingly difficult for him to have his suggestions acted upon . . ."

While John Cooper had always found ways of financing development, since his accident his energies had waned and his father Charles hated spending money. Bruce wanted to build a pair of special single-seaters for the new 2½-litre Tasman Formula races planned for New Zealand and Australia that winter. He suggested running them as Cooper works entries, but Charlie would not have it. He believed the regular F1 cars would do the job. Bruce was sure they would not. He wanted a brace of special new lightweights to make the most of the regulations. His works team-mate Tony Maggs was leaving, to be replaced by Timmy Mayer. Plans were laid for Timmy to accompany Bruce down-under but he was unknown there and Charlie had his doubts. He said bluntly that if there were any problems with entries and adequate appearance money he would cancel the whole project.

At this early point Bruce opted to go it alone. With Timmy's elder brother Teddy he set-up "Bruce McLaren Motor Racing Ltd" to run the cars he wanted the way he wanted. Teddy contributed his pool of Climax engines from Timmy's Monaco sportscar programme, and with help from Wally Willmott and Tyler Alexander the two special cars were built at Cooper's. Tyler was amused by the dark and gloomy works. It did not impress as "high-tech" . . .

The two cars drew on contemporary Cooper F1 thinking, though with reduced tankage, cockpits just 25-inches wide and with stressed-skin steel panelling stiffening the centre-section there. Radius rod rear suspension – unusual for Cooper – was actually drawn from Owen Maddock's intended system designed that year for his still-born monocoque. The 2.5-litre Climax FPF four-cylinder engines drove through Cooper/Colotti five-speed transaxles. The prototype was complete and on test in September '63, and the team made its debut at Levin, New Zealand, on January 4, 1964. The dark green cars with their Kiwi silver stripes were beaten by Denny Hulme's latest Brabham, but finished 2-3, Timmy leading Bruce home.

Timmy Mayer pulls on his goggles during initial tests at Goodwood, November 1963, with the brand-new 'Bruce McLaren Motor Racing' Cooper-Climax Tasman Spl. The slimline cars used stressed-skin panelling to stiffen the spaceframe chassis amidships and were powered by 2.5-litre Climax 4-cylinder FPF engines.

In eight attempts, Bruce had never won his home GP. Now Wally and Tyler painstakingly prepared the new Coopers. Bruce's engines were converted from 2.7s by shortening the stroke to give a stronger unit than a normal 2.5. Jack Brabham had done the same, having bits made by Repco in Australia, while Bruce's conversion set came from England. Now they found his engine's pistons gave too low compression. A replacement set was hurriedly fitted. They had to be run-in before the GP. Only place available was Auckland's Western Springs cycle track, and Bruce grumbled dizzily round, three laps a minute, for an hour and a half to do the job.

Timmy led the race initially from Brabham, before Jack, then Bruce forged ahead. Jack crashed and Bruce won at last from Hulme and Timmy. At Wigram and Teretonga, Bruce beat off Jack's Brabham before the move to Australia where the new team's luck slumped. Bruce and Timmy were beaten home 2-3 at Warwick Farm. Timmy lost the lead at Lakeside when his engine blew, leaving Bruce to finish only third behind Youl's Cooper and Hulme.

Last race of the series was held on the bumpy public road course at Longford, Tasmania. There in practice Timmy Mayer's car went out of control under braking after a hump-backed bridge. It smashed into two trees. The impact was unsurviveable. The car was sheared in two and Timmy died . . .

Next day Bruce drove an understandably muted race. He finished second to Graham Hill's private Brabham, and became Tasman Champion.

Eoin Young: "The die was cast. He had proved to himself that he knew enough about racing now to build his own cars and run his own racing team. Racing was beginning to get exciting again. The old challenge had returned . . ."

Bruce: "I like to feel that the combination of driver and car is important. I'm sure Jack Brabham feels the same way and that's why he is building his own car. By winning with one's own car, both other drivers and other cars have been beaten . . . The usual ambition once a person becomes serious about motor racing is to be a works driver. This is the pinnacle of GP racing, but one can go beyond it, full circle. The normal beginning is driving one's own car . . . Now I enjoy nothing better than running my own cars again . . ."

He would continue as Cooper's number one driver for two more seasons, but 1964 also saw him signed as race and test-development driver for the Ford GT programme, and his own team would progress at a frantic rate.

Initially, they would concentrate upon 'big-banger' sports-racing cars. The class had caught hold in America where Bruce had had his first experience with Briggs Cunningham's ex-Le Mans Jaguar 'E2A' in 1960. Subsequently he had raced Cooper Monacos there, and had met a clean-cut, ambitious young American driver, a rival of the Mayers, named Roger Penske.

Although he had a comfortable background – his father was vice-president of a Cleveland metals distributor – Penske had always been encouraged to work to support his hobbies. He raced Maseratis and Cooper Monacos and had shown a flair for attracting commercial sponsorship, notably from DuPont chemicals.

Back in 1961, Briggs Cunningham had ordered a new production F1 Cooper T53 for veteran Walt Hansgen to drive in the US GP. The car was chassis number 'F1/16/61' and Walt shunted it heavily in the race. Roger bought the wreck as it lay, and that winter saw his mechanic Roy Gaine working on the frame in their garage at Newtown Square, Pennsylvania. He added body outriggers either side and a vestigial 'passenger' seat in one of them, beside the still central driver's cockpit, the car emerging with wheel-enveloping bodywork made by the Molin body shop up the road in Wayne, Pa as a centre-drive sports-racing car. Roger added the ex-Indy, 2.7 Climax engine which Jack Brabham had used to win the important *Los Angeles Times* GP race at Riverside the previous October in Hap Sharp's old Monaco. He checked with US authority throughout the car's construction and emerged convinced it was legal. Opponents in the 1962 Fall series of West Coast professional sports car races would not see it that way as their regular either-side-of-the-centreline two-seaters struggled in his wake. The *Zerex Special*

as the car was known won at Riverside and Laguna Seca before the storm broke, the CSI in Paris demanded of the American authorities how "a car not conforming with Appendix C has been allowed to compete in an International race for sports cars?" and in early December the car was banned.

As always Penske was prepared. He had bought Bruce's works Monaco T61M and raced it in the Nassau Speed Week that December under Texan oilman John Mecom's colours. Mecom also bought the *Zerex*, and during 1963 it was reworked, its single-seat frame top rails cut and re-routed to provide a full-width two-seat cockpit, and in Mecom pale metallic-blue and white livery Penske drove it with continued success in USRRC events. He also brought it to England, and won the Guards Trophy race at Brands Hatch easily. After Nassau in December '63 the old car was set aside at Mecom's, with a crated 3.5-litre Oldsmobile F85 V8 engine in one corner, waiting for somebody to find the time to fit it.

This engine was a lightweight alloy-block unit mooted by GM but abandoned when problems in the casting process made it unviable. It weighed little more than the 2.7 Climax 'four-banger' but offered an extra 40-50 horsepower. In such a lightweight car its power-to-weight promised to be very competitive with larger cars using larger cast-iron Detroit V8s.

Before taking off for the Tasman tour at the end of 1963 Bruce had already planned a *Zerex*-type sports car of his own for '64, intending to use the Climax FPF

First win – Bruce in the still Climax-engined ex-Mecom/Penske Zerex Special, at the Aintree '200' meeting, 1964. Basis of the car was a 1961 F1 Cooper, rebuilt twice by Roger Penske and by this time brought-up to International Appendix 'C' form by Bruce's team.

engines left over from the Tasman programme. A chassis was made, but Teddy Mayer, Tyler and Wally saw the power of Chevrolet and Ford's V8s at Nassau and were convinced that was the way to go. A 2.7 Climax could not cut it.

With the shock of Timmy Mayer's death still fresh, Teddy was recovering in America during March 1964 while in England Bruce pondered his future. The new 1-litre F2 class looked promising, perhaps his new team should build a car for it, but Wally Willmott suggested sports cars as more lucrative, with potentially greater custom. The US professional races and amateur market both showed promise. They talked it over. Enthusiasm grew. Bruce telephoned John Mecom, wanting to buy his Scarab-Chevrolet. Not for sale. What else could he offer? The *Zerex* was available. Big-banger sports car racing was about to take off in the UK. Lotus were building the Ford V8-powered Type 30. Roy Salvadori was having a 5-litre Monaco-Maserati put together. Bruce was interested.

He called Teddy and asked him to handle the Mecom deal. The purchase went through, complete with the spare Traco Engineering-tuned 3.5 Olds V8 and Tyler took delivery in Pensacola, Florida, right after the USRRC race there on April 5. Bruce had entered it for the Oulton Park national in England only six days later. Tyler rushed it to New York in a day and night's drive to catch a jet to London. Meanwhile Bruce had rented workshop space in a dirt-floored shed shared with an earth-mover servicing outfit in New Malden, near Surbiton and the Cooper works. There Tyler and Wally had just a day to convert the *Zerex* to Appendix C form with spare wheel and luggage space, before the now green and white-painted car could commence practice at the Cheshire circuit.

After all that effort Bruce retired with mechanical failure, but one week later he won the supporting sports car race at the Aintree '200' meeting, beating Clark's debutante Lotus 30. Next day he was at Le Mans, giving the Ford GT its bow.

Two weeks later the 2.7 Cooper-Climax, as the *Zerex* was now known, won at the important May Silverstone meeting. *Motoring News* managed to call it the 'Cooper-Redex-Special' which was original. Bruce held off Salvadori's fearsome new 5-litre Monaco-Maserati . . .

Next day the ageing car was stripped at New Malden and its frame hacked apart. Bruce had found it had the torsional rigidity of a wet bus ticket, and this was to be put right, and the 3.5 Traco Olds was to be fitted. Bruce went off to Monaco for Cooper and Nürburgring for Ford while Tyler and Wally worked to make and fit an entirely new chassis centre-section, working from a wire model. The Olds V8 was mounted, driving through the trusty Colotti Type 21 gearbox from the sole surviving Tasman car. Target date was June 6, and the Player's '200' at Mosport in Canada. There was no time to make a properly manifolded exhaust system, so the car ran near-vertical stack pipes, protruding through its rear deck.

Eoin Young: "The chassis was completed on a Sunday morning so Bruce decided it should be painted there and then . . . I was despatched to find a tin of paint and I finally returned with a tin of garden gate green unearthed in a handyman's shop that was just on the point of closing. The colour was appalling, but it was paint and when we had finished the frame gleamed bright green. It cried out to be called the Jolly Green Giant. It was also the *Zerex Special* re-framed and re-engined but for various reasons Bruce decreed it should be known officially as the Cooper-Oldsmobile . . ."

Charles Cooper had never forgiven Jack Brabham for leaving to set up his own team, and now he regarded Bruce's extra-mural activities with ever-increasing suspicion, and Bruce had to protect his F1 drive . . .

The revamped car was flown out to Mosport for Bruce's first-ever Canadian appearance. He promptly won both 100-mile heats. It was a marvellous debut.

Back home the F1 season reached its height and Ford took Bruce – unsuccessfully – to Le Mans. The team moved from "the incredible slum-like conditions in the tractor shed at New Malden" into what Eoin's press release described fulsomely as "a spotless new 3,000 square foot racing workshop" in the Belvedere Works behind a new shopping centre at Feltham, Middlesex.

There the Cooper-Olds was prepared for the August Bank Holiday Guards Trophy race at Brands Hatch which it had won in Mecom form with Roger Penske driving the previous year. Bruce made it two in a row, leading from start to finish and setting a new lap record. Some of his team had just moved into a huge rented house in Surbiton which they called 'The Castle'. That night they had an uproarious 'Castle-warming' highlighted by a mediaeval joust between Bruce and Graham Hill, clad in glass-fibre suits of armour with mock swords and lances. Jimmy Clark joined in, fetching Graham a supendous whack with a sword he had found, not appreciating that his sword was real, and Graham's helmet was not!

At Feltham, Bruce, Teddy, Wally, Tyler and Eoin were joined by ex-Cooper draughtsman Eddie Stait while Cooper's former Chief Designer Owen Maddock worked for them on a freelance basis. They were laying down an all-new Oldsmobile-powered sports-racing car of their own design, and a new Tasman special was being progressed for the January/February '65 series.

On August 29, Bruce ran the Cooper-Olds in the Tourist Trophy at Goodwood, qualifying on pole and leading a terrific battle with Clark's Lotus 30 before incurable clutch-slip sidelined him after only 16 laps. He still set a new record lap.

In September the new McLaren-Oldsmobile Mark 1 was complete and out on test at Goodwood. Its shapely aluminium bodywork had been designed by Tony Hilder, formerly with Specialised Mouldings and made by the two-man Robert Peel Coachworks, on the Thames towpath at Kingston. It clothed a simple low-slung spaceframe welded-up from round and square-section mild steel tube with alloy-sheet stress panels bonded and riveted in place to stiffen the undertray and lateral bulkhead areas. Oil and water ran through the main-frame longerons. Front suspension used narrow-based lower wishbones and very wide-based upper wishbones with the rear pick-ups close to the dash panel. At the rear, reversed lower wishbones and single top links were used, with twin parallel radius rods running forward to the frame. Armstrong co-axial coil-spring/dampers appeared front and rear, with screw adjustment for ride height. Anti-dive angle was built into the front wishbones to prevent pitch-down under braking. Camber and wheel alignment were fully adjustable front and rear. Girling 11.5-inch diameter disc brakes were used up front, 10.75-inch at the rear. The prototype rode on Cooper cast spoked wheels but Owen Maddock was designing the definitive original McLaren four-spoke cast wheel; strongest of its type at that time.

This new Mark 1 McLaren was uncomplicated and light, and the team felt confident it could be competitive with its light but powerful Traco-Olds engine. Teddy was offering good money for F85s from scrapyards across America, and in California Jim Travers and Frank Coon of Traco Engineering were developing a 4.5-litre stretch to replace Bruce's 3.9. Using 48 IDA Weber twin-choke carburettors, Bruce had around 310bhp in the prototype and he promptly sliced three whole seconds off his Goodwood lap record. It looked promising, and the new Hewland HD transaxle seemed efficient and reliable.

The car was sprayed in New Zealand national colours of jet black with a silver stripe, and its race debut came again at Mosport in the Canadian GP for sports cars on September 26, 1964.

Bruce: "It meant more to me and my team members than any other race . . . It was the first race with the car that we built ourselves from the rubber up and we were delighted with its performance and potential. We didn't win, but we certainly didn't leave Canada with our tails between our legs . . ."

Jim Hall's 5.5 Chaparral-Chevrolet automatic transmission car took pole position, outgunning the McLaren debutante, but the Texan crashed early on and Bruce led until the throttle linkage fell apart and lost him four laps. He hauled back to third at the finish, and for the first time a lap record fell to "McLaren (McLaren)". There would be more, but not yet a while . . .

Traco's big 4.5 V8 went in for Riverside in October, but after taking an early lead a hose blew-off. Bruce confessed he could not complain. He had made the fitting himself, and it did not have a beaded end. After the delay he charged back

McLaren Racing at Belvedere Works, Feltham, show off Tony Hilder's quarter-scale model of the first car to be totally designed and built by the new team in their own premises. Studying the M1A maquette here are Bruce (left) flanked by Wally Willmott, Bruce Harre – shortly to become a Firestone tyre technician – Howden Ganley – destined to become a Formula 1 works driver in his own right; and Eoin Young – later journalist and motoring publications/ memorabilia broker; five Kiwis going places . . . Meanwhile in the workshop behind them the prototype M1A chassis was taking shape.

Bruce testing the prototype M1A sans body enters the Goodwood chicane, late-summer 1964. The idea was to sort-out the chassis before adding the aerodynamic forces generated by the aluminium body panelling. Note the top-ducted radiator, spare-wheel mounting and front suspension with the forward arm of the bottom wishbone anchored well forward on the frame, the transverse top link behind the coil-spring/damper unit and long top rod trailing back towards the dash panel.

The Garden Gnome goes for a ride – Denis Jenkinson of *Motor Sport* was World Champion Sidecar passenger riding with Eric Oliver in 1949. Here during M1A testing '64 he climbs aboard for a ride round Goodwood with Bruce. Wally Willmott, Tyler Alexander and Teddy Mayer look on. The car is now fitted with its aluminium body-panelling and carries the team's Michael Turner-designed insignia on the nose. Scrawled on the driver's door was 'Strong Traco Eng. Mother'; homage to the Traco-Olds V8 engine.

up to third, only for the hose to blow-off again. At Laguna Seca more hose trouble dropped him from Heat 1, and an improperly heat-treated gear failed in Heat 2. Bruce flew to Mexico for the F1 GP, then back to London, to sign a contract . . .

The team had considered putting Mark 1 into production for customer sale. It would generate much-needed revenue, but they concluded the sheer logistics and investment in both capital and manpower would be beyond them. Then veteran constructor Frank Nichols came by for a chat. His ailing Elva Cars company had gone into liquidation three years before, but had been taken over by energetic Peter Agg's Lambretta-Trojan Group. Re-formed as Elva Cars (1961) Ltd it had a good established production factory in Rye on the south coast, and a worthwhile share of the small-capacity sports car market. Now Frank suggested that he should build customer McLarens, guaranteeing the team a royalty on each car sold. He introduced Bruce to Peter Agg and they signed the agreement on November 21, 1964, the first 'McLaren-Elva-Oldsmobile' to be displayed at the forthcoming London Racing Car Show, in January.

Teddy Mayer: "It was a very good deal for us because while it left us free to get on with prototype design and racing as we wanted, it gave us three things; a royalty on every car sold, exposure of our name and our skills, and perhaps most important of all it introduced us to the disciplines of proper engineering practice with proper drawings for everything we did. Until that time we'd kind of muddled-through, Cooper-style I guess, making things first and maybe drawing them later, if we could find the time. Now we had to do it right . . ."

Of course there were problems, for while Elva built their first cars, McLaren's men were away racing, only Teddy staying in the UK to mind the shop.

For the new year's Tasman Championship, Bruce built an improved Cooper-Climax T79 for himself while his old '64 car was fettled-up for his works F1 team-mate Phil Hill to drive. They were just about ready to go when through his Ford contacts Bruce won a lucrative test and development contract with Firestone tyres. His cars were to run exclusively on Firestone rubber, the Akron company being anxious to tackle Dunlop's road-racing monopoly outside America. The money was good, assuring the still-infant team of further income, but the initial effect on Bruce's defence of his Tasman title was disastrous.

The Coopers had been designed to run 13-inch wheels and Dunlop tyres. Firestone had no 13-inch sizes available and a last-minute change to 15-inch wheels and Firestone Indy tyres shot holes in the cars' intended suspension geometry. Bruce and Phil struggled against poor handling throughout the series until the final round at Longford where Bruce finally managed to win, beating Graham Hill's private Brabham, and Phil was third. This was Firestone's first road-racing 'GP' victory; the McLaren deal had begun to pay off.

Back at Feltham the team's staff had grown to 18, two new offices had been built and the drawing office enlarged. The prototype Mark 1 was dedicated to Firestone tyre testing and experimental work. Jim Hall's automatic transmission Chaparral had impressed Bruce deeply. He discussed a similar system with Tony Rolt and his engineers at Harry Ferguson Research, and in three months a Teramala patent torque-converter and two-speed gearbox system was constructed for the Mark 1 cars to test. In parallel with this work, Elva Cars loaned the team a 2-litre Elva-BMW Mark 8 for young Chris Amon to campaign as works driver. He would also double as second-string McLaren test and race driver.

The team was energetic, and ambitious, and Teddy was determined the bills should be paid. They took on anything "which was in our line and which promised to show good profit . . .". Bruce worked closely with Ford Detroit engineer Roy Lunn on their GT programme, and towards the end of 1964 they discussed building a lightweight open version of the Ford as a Group 7 sports-racing car. Ford's FAV production plant at Slough was full to capacity, and McLaren had the know-how and the specialised facilities required to do the job. Bruce was a trusted member of the Ford team and Ford contracts always paid very well indeed . . .

So McLaren were presented with a standard GT40 racing coupe chassis with

Friendly Bruce – always ready with a smile even in adversity – British GP practice, Brands Hatch 1966. The engine here is the under-powered Serenissima V8 and Bruce managed to take sixth place for his marque's maiden World Championship point. His Chris Amon-style helmet was worn in deference to John Frankenheimer's MGM film crew. The helmet pattern had been adopted for the hero in the Grand Prix film script. It was all income . . .

Overleaf, above: The first American CanAm champion was Peter Revson here in his works M8F at Riverside during the 1971 Los Angeles Times GP. This was one of the most handsome of a big, brutish beautiful breed – the McLaren-Chevrolet sports-racing cars.

below: Indy winners '76 – Johnny Rutherford's 'Hy-Gain' McLaren-Offy M16E settling into one of the banked turns during what proved to be the shortest Indy 500 on record; flagged off after only 102 of the scheduled 200 laps due to heavy rain. This time 'JR' had made sure he was in the right position as the clouds lowered and the rain came down.

7-litre engine, and ex-Chaparral engineer Gary Knutson was put in charge of development, working with a skinny New Zealand mechanic-cum-hopeful racing driver named Howden Ganley. The Ford was converted into an open roadster and the steel monocoque radically reconstructed with aluminium skins. Officially the car would be known as the 'Ford GTX' when it appeared in the North American Fall series, 1965, but the McLaren boys christened it *'Big Ed'* after Ford's comically catastrophic Edsel project, and it stuck . . .

While *'Big Ed'* was going together behind a security screen at one end of the McLaren works during 1965, the M1A original McLaren-Elva-Oldsmobile design was uprated with a revised spaceframe chassis and all-new bulbous body styled by motor racing artist Michael Turner as the prototype M1B, to make its debut in the same North American race series . . .

At Rye 24 production M1As were completed, some with 4.7 Ford V8 power as an alternative to the standard 4.5 Traco-Olds. It would soon become apparent that the Olds was just too small. There really was no substitute for cubic inches . . .

All this work demanded more design brain, and it was provided by youthful Robin Herd who joined the team to opt-out of a highly-promising career as a senior scientific officer working on the Concorde SST project at the National Gas Turbine Establishment centre at Farnborough. Robin was enthusiastic, imaginative and highly qualified with a brilliant double-first engineering degree from Oxford. He and Bruce pooled their creative abilities through the summer of '65 looking beyond the sports cars to the new 3-litre Formula 1 which was to replace contemporary 1½-litre GP racing in 1966.

Bruce was still Cooper's number one, teamed with new boy Jochen Rindt through that season of '65, but things had changed at Surbiton. Old Charles Cooper had died suddenly the previous October. His son John, still suffering the after-effects of his road accident, wanted to be free of the commercial worries of running the business. In May '65 he sold out to the Chipstead Motor Group, who held the British Maserati concession amongst others, and since there was no point in building all-new F1 cars for that final season's racing Bruce and Jochen had a thin time, Chipstead conserving their money and energies for an all-new 3-litre car for '66. Bruce's mind was made up in any case, he would build and race his own F1 cars that year, if only he could obtain suitable engines from somewhere. Coventry Climax were not going to build a 3-litre engine. BRM were but it would not be ready until later in the year. Maserati's V12 would be exclusive to Cooper. Jack Brabham – ironically – was having a 3-litre version of the lightweight Oldsmobile F85 made in secret by Repco in Australia. Bruce's Ford links seemed the best bet. Their four-cam Indy V8 was a pure-bred racing engine with all kinds of potential. If it could be reduced from 4.2 to 3-litres it might just suffice . . .

So McLaren's major effort was concentrated upon the sports cars for the new season, with the Ford GTX progressing profitably on one side and the longer-term F1 project on another.

The '65 sports car season commenced in England with a supporting race for the Formula 2 Senior Service '200' at Silverstone on March 20, but torrential rain wrecked the meeting and the sports car race was abandoned after only 18 of the scheduled 25 laps and the F2 feature race was cancelled. Jimmy Clark won in the Lotus 30, but even he had spun. Bruce spun and dropped to midfield and Graham Hill in John Coombs' first customer McLaren-Elva-Oldsmobile Mark 1 found his engine drowned-out, refusing to run on both banks.

At Easter Monday Goodwood Bruce was second, struggling with rain tyres while the rain held off and Clark romped away to a really convincing Lotus win. A few days later, testing at Oulton, Chris Amon shattered the lap record using the Ferguson automatic transmission in the works Mark 1. Bruce's enthusiasm was fired and he raced the system there in the Tourist Trophy one week later. But practice was punctuated by a transmission oil-seal failure, then a broken con-rod, and with a fresh engine for Heat 1 of the race he led as John Surtees' new Lola hit trouble but soon transmission fluid was leaking again and he had to stop. Tyler and the crew stripped the unit and rebuilt it on the pit counter in time for Heat 2, Bruce set out from the back of the grid, charged up to second on Clark's tail, broke the lap record, then retired as the engine oil pressure zeroed. The auto torque converter was making the engine run too low in its rev-range and pre-ignition was causing the engine problems. Development looked expensive, other avenues showed better potential, so McLaren's automatic transmission project was regretfully shelved . . .

On May 15, Silverstone saw Bruce and Surtees locked in combat, lowering the lap record repeatedly until John's big red Lola failed with just three laps to run. Bruce won, with the new lap record of 1:31.6, 115.03mph, to his name.

Whit-Sunday Mallory saw the first customer McLaren-Elva-Olds victory as Graham Hill won Heat 1 in Coombs' grey car, still resolutely on only seven cylinders. A rocker had broken, and he could not start Heat 2.

Bruce had a new 5-litre Traco-Olds V8 fitted for the Player's '200' back at Mosport where he led both heats until first boiling brake fluid then a broken gearbox put him out. At St Jovite-Mt Tremblant Chris Amon drove in Bruce's absence at Monaco and he beat Hap Sharp's Chaparral for the team's first '65 win.

The crew journeyed down to Indianapolis to watch the Indy '500' and attended Teddy's wedding at Litchfield, Connecticut. July 3 found them back at St Jovite-Mt Tremblant where the Labatt '50' fell to Bruce despite Jim Hall misjudging his braking in the Chaparral and ramming the McLaren's tail.

The team opted-out of the British GP meeting supporting race at Silverstone. After earning dollars in Canada the start money offer of £5 per lap completed was not at all attractive . . .

On July 24 at Silverstone the 52-lap Martini Trophy saw the 5-litre Mark 1's UK debut. Bruce was to have driven, but in Friday practice a carburettor fuel union worked loose, spraying fuel over the engine bay, and his neck. He was wearing a nylon rally jacket and no gloves and when the fuel ignited he was painfully burned as the nylon melted into his overalls. Chris Amon took over for the race, starting in the repaired car on the back of the grid after only two morning acclimatisation laps. Surtees' 6-litre Lola-Chevrolet led from pole but in only four laps Chris was on his tail, breaking the lap record and then inheriting the lead when the Lola broke – again. He won handsomely, at 108.48 mph.

Bruce was delighted for his young team-mate, but only two days later something failed on Mark 1 during tyre testing at Brands Hatch and the car turned sharp right on the straight, lost a wheel against a bridge support and sprayed pieces over 200 yards of track before coming to rest. Chris was driving, and emerged unhurt apart from a cut on his nose where he had banged it as he dived under the dash.

On August 30, his birthday, Bruce ran the rebuilt Mark 1 in the Guards Trophy at Brands Hatch but Surtees' 6-litre Lola-Chev was far too strong, and Bruce could not improve on second place. Six McLaren-Elvas were present – Bruce's 5-litre ZF-gearbox works car; a 5.5 Chevrolet version for the American former Monaco-Ford driver George Wintersteen; two 4.5 Oldsmobiles for John Coundley and Graham Hill (Coombs' car), and two 4.7 Fords for David Prophet and no less than Dan Gurney. Clearly the 6-litre Lola-Chev was too powerful for the McLaren. Bruce and the team drowned their sorrows that night in the Contented Plaice, Kingston. It was his birthday, after all . . .

By this time their single-seat prototype was ready and running. In retrospect Robin Herd observed: "On our initial design we erred . . . and tended towards technical ingenuity and bullshit rather than race-winning engineering . . ."

They had been attracted to the rigidity offered by an aerospace material – a composite laminate of special 26-gauge aluminium sheets bonded over an eighth-inch sandwich filling of end-grain balsawood. It was made by William Mallinson & Sons, and was known as Mallite. It had been developed for the floors and panelling in aircraft cabins, had the same tensile strength as plain 20-gauge sheet in the same aluminium alloy but offered considerably enhanced stiffness, especially in torsion.

Now the new M2A single-seater built essentially as a Firestone tyre test vehicle, was based upon a rolled-Mallite monocoque with inboard-spring rocker-arm front suspension and conventional rear, and 4.5-litre Traco-Olds V8 engine, driving through a Hewland HD5 transaxle. The car was intended to test tyres and prove the Mallite structure and systems in preparation for the forthcoming F1.

One week after news of the M2A broke in September '65 the Michael Turner-bodied M1B was announced, this improved design to be productionised by the Elva Cars subsidiary of Lambretta-Trojan and sold in the USA as the McLaren-Elva Mark 2 through 1966.

Bruce took the prototype to St Jovite-Mt Tremblant on September 18. The Laurentian circuit had just been extended from its original 1.6-miles to 1.8 but in practice the M1B's crank broke splitting the block and transmission case, so he non-started. Surtees' Lola won again. Canadian Ludwig Heimrath's production M1A was fourth, Charlie Hayes' broke its suspension.

The following weekend the Canadian GP was held at Mosport where Surtees was badly hurt during practice after suspension failure on his Lola. Bruce took pole and Chris Amon made his debut with 'Big Ed' – the lightweight 7-litre Ford GTX. Bruce won Heat 1 from Jim Hall, they had a terrific battle in Heat 2 which

Bruce tops Paddock Hill at Brands Hatch in his works McLaren-Elva-Oldsmobile M1A during the 1965 Guards Trophy meeting. The team still hunting for a finalised livery were running the cars brick-red with twin pale stripes at this time.

Testing, always testing; Bruce hustling Robin Herd's Mallite monocoque M2A Firestone tyre-test vehicle into Paddock Hill Bend at Brands Hatch, Autumn '65, booting it through on the 4.5-litre Traco-Olds V8's torque. This was the car rigged with an experimental rear aerofoil device which instantly gave it 3 secs per lap improvement at Zandvoort that November. (below) The wing set-up gauge attached in the works. The idea was set aside and half-forgotten for more than two years. Robin Herd: "Good Lord, was it that long? Just put it down to incompetence and short memories . . . we were fully-extended on other ideas".

the Chaparral man just won, by 1.8 secs overall, Bruce being classified second on aggregate, Hayes fourth and Bud Gates' customer car 16th. Heimrath broke his M1A's suspension while Augie Pabst's new car caught fire and was destroyed.

Phil Hill took over the M1B with Teddy and the crew in attendance for Seattle's North-West GP. He was second in Heat 1 and then lost a lap with a sticking throttle in Heat 2, finishing 11th. Hayes ended the day fourth on aggregate.

Bruce was in Holland with the Mallite M2A and the old Mark 1 sports car, tyre-testing for Firestone, missing Laguna Seca where Hayes was third in Heat 1 only to lose control, clip a barrier and survive a 180-degree roll-over in Heat 2 after which the M1A landed wheels-first with very little damage! Richard Macon, Mike Goth and George Wintersteen salvaged minor placings for the marque.

Bruce had been conserving his team's energy and resources for the all-important *Los Angeles Times GP* at Riverside on October 31, running M1B with bigger brakes and wider front tyres. He was leading handsomely when a tyre began to deflate. He had to change it, finishing third ahead of Hayes, Chris in '*Big Ed*' and Macon.

In December it was Nassau for the Bahamas Speed Week on the Oakes Field aerodrome course. Bruce ran M1B and Chris '*Big Ed*', practising with a new Ford automatic transmission although the normal manual box was refitted for the main Governors' Trophy race, which Bruce led from lap 2 and won handsomely, despite a late misfire. The GTX broke its final-drive. Unfortunately BOAC had mislaid the team's spare Traco-Olds engine, so Bruce had to run the misfiring Governor's Trophy-winning unit in the Nassau Trophy race, a pit stop discovered water on the spark plugs and he retired.

Both McLaren drivers started the Formula Vee race, a knock-about Nassau tradition, and they finished 1-2, Amon ahead. Bruce: "It was apparent how much we had taught him this year . . . Just before we climbed into the cars Chris wandered over and said 'You know how I was here last weekend and you weren't? Well, I had time to try both cars and I put the best engine in the best chassis, and you've got what was left over!' And then he pulled on his goggles and they started the race . . ."

Back in England the team had out-grown Belvedere Works and after a long hunt Teddy had discovered a suitable new home in Davids Road, Poyle Trading Estate at Colnbrook, a couple of miles from the end of the Heathrow runways, deafeningly under the direct western flight-path. Two factories here would share the team's home for 14 momentous years.

Just before Christmas '65 the new Formula 1 M2B was shown to the press at Colnbrook, along with Bruce's pet single-seater, the remarkable M3 'whoosh-bonk car' . . .

Section II: Racing World-Wide

Chapter 2
Into Formula One 1966-67

*"We were all very young, some of us greener than the others,
but it was a terrific time, learning at a fantastic rate as we
went along . . ."*

Robin Herd, 1983

The Formula 1 prototype was another Robin Herd Mallite monocoque design which was probably a considerable technical success for it was torsionally one of the stiffest open cockpit racing cars ever built at that time. The M2A had already covered over 2,000 test miles by December 17 when the almost complete F1 prototype was unveiled with its reduced-capacity Indy Ford V8 quad-cam engine.

The M2B's monocoque hull was formed by sheets of Mallite rolled to form D-section side-boxes enclosing the fuel space and bonded to fabricated sheet steel bulkheads and inner panels. There were four of these boxed hoop bulkheads; at the front suspension, the scuttle, behind the seat and in line with the final-drive at the rear suspension pick-ups. A special two-part Shell resin was used to bond the Mallite panels to the bulkheads and to the sheet steel inner panels. Avdel rivets clamped the panels together to form a secure bond during the 45-minute curing process. All joints were sealed to make the internal fuel cavities leakproof, though later cars would use rubber bag tanks.

Suspension was conventional with inboard coil/damper units at the front and parallel radius arms at the rear. Girling discs resided within the cast-magnesium 13-inch road wheels though 15-inch would be used at some circuits like Spa. Water and oil pipes ran along the top of the chassis, and hot air from the radiator was ducted out through the top of the nose section.

Back in April '65 the team had had a design discussion about 3-litre F1 engines, and the Ford had been selected largely because they felt Ford *might* take a financial interest if it looked promising. "We got some back-door advice from them" Teddy Mayer recalls, ". . . but it never went further than that. We were on our own . . ."

They appointed former BMW and Daimler-Benz engineer Klaus von Rucker to study the engine conversion from 4.2 to 3-litre form, but little was done and as the project lagged so Gary Knutson took it over and shipped it out to Traco Engineering in Culver City, California. Five 1964 Indy-Ford V8s had been purchased, and by December two were running on Traco's test-beds; one with an ultra-short stroke and unchanged bore, the other with a less-short stroke and reduced bore. The engines were tested in the car at Riverside in February '66, but unrealised at the time the basic head form of the Indy engine was not amenable to 3-litre conversion and where the big 4.2 standard unit gave a reliable 470 bhp at Indy, and McLaren hoped for 335bhp in F1 form, the reality was around 300bhp on a good day, with enormous bulk and weight to be accommodated – even though the huge engine was not, in fact, quite as heavy as it looked . . .

The 'whoosh-bonk' spaceframe car meanwhile was a production special intended for sprint and hill-climb use. Bruce had tenacious energy when he dreamed-up a pet theory. In face of total opposition from the rest of his team he would still follow them through. Sometimes he would have the last laugh – other times he would grin, admit defeat, and surrender. But he could generate faith in such projects amongst his men, and the whoosh-bonk car came from his insistence that "You can take the suspension off the sports car – whoosh – knock-up a chassis and – bonk – there's the car".

Eoin Young, Teddy Mayer, Wally Willmott and Bruce himself show off the prototype M2B Mallite McLaren-Indy Ford V8 at Colnbrook ready for the 1966 3-litre Formula while Denis Jenkinson chats with Gregor Grant (founder-editor of Autosport) beyond, Mike Kettlewell of Gregor's magazine looks on and Mike Twite of Motoring News quietly studies the car's front end. All the trouble would be found in the engine-bay . . . That same day Bruce's prototype 'whoosh-bonk' spaceframe M3 was half-completed in a corner of the 'shop.

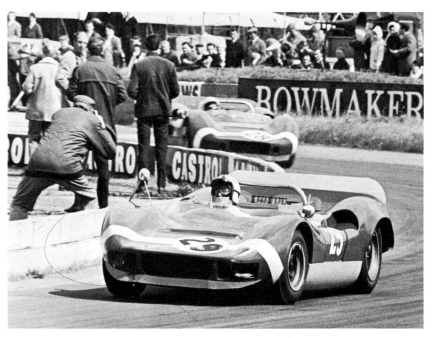

Patsy Burt and her racing and garage manager Ron Smith were old friends, and Bruce built the first M3 as it became known for her, Bruce designing it as he went along to pick-up the sports car suspension. John Thompson welded-up the frame and in two weeks the car was ready for a body to be made, sitting on trestles with a 4.0 Traco-Olds engine and ZF gearbox. Three were built, for Patsy, for Swiss hill-climber Dr Harry Zweifel, and for MGM who wanted a high-speed camera car to film John Frankenheimer's awful epic *Grand Prix*.

Into 1966 Bruce passed-up the Tasman Championship and spent February in California testing the M2B and Ford's J-car for Le Mans. Meanwhile KarKraft had reworked '*Big Ed*' to long-distance roadster form, and Ken Miles/Lloyd Ruby drove it to victory in the 1966 Sebring 12-Hours. There is a story that the half-day grind around bumpy Hendrick Field ended with '*Big Ed's*' wheelbase shortened by an inch due to the aluminium chassis crumpling. Officially the car was then broken-up, but it seems in fact to survive today, in the US, the owner's evidence of its identity being very strong.

At Colnbrook three M2Bs were laid down, though only two would be completed and two M1Bs were prepared for Snetterton's G7 race on Good Friday, opening the new 1966 season. One was the '65 prototype, the other brand new with 13-inch wheels for Bruce. Chris Amon led him into second place behind Denny Hulme's big 6-litre Sid Taylor Lola in Heat 1, and was second again in Heat 2 while Bruce dropped out with no oil pressure. The team did not bother with the sadly downrated TT at Oulton Park, where Coundley's M1A was fifth. Keith St John, Frank Gardner (Alan Brown's car) and Prophet in M1Bs all figured, poorly.

At May Silverstone, Chris had a 5-litre wet-sump Olds engine, Bruce a 4.5 after his 5-litre had run a cam bearing in practice. Denny Hulme won again, going away, the twin red M1Bs 2-3, Prophet's new car eighth.

Then came Bruce's Formula 1 debut in his own new car, at Monaco on May 22; the McLaren marque's GP baptism. The Ford V8 with its huge Hilborn fuel injection stacks looked immense in the tail of the white M2B with its broad green stripe and its exhaust note was simply ear-splitting, racketing back from the walls all around. But only 300bhp over a narrow rev band was unhelpful with the ZF gearbox in four-speed form and Bruce admitted immediately "it looks as though we're going to have to make some fairly drastic moves in the engine room". In the

race an oil-pipe union came undone in the nose, gushing oil into the cockpit and onto the road. Bruce retired before the expensive engine let go.

The annual sports car trip to Canada followed; St Jovite-Mt Tremblant first where Bruce won the Labatt '50' but, Chris' engine ran its bearings. At Mosport for the Players '200' Bruce won again from Lothar Motschenbacher's M1B and Chris, with John Cordts' customer car fifth for a McLaren 1-2-3-5 success. Ludwig Heimrath and Rick Muther placed well in Heat 2 with their customer cars.

The Formula 1 Ford engine had been withdrawn for further development after that harrowing exhibition at Monaco and Count Volpi's Serenissima concern in Italy offered instead their Alberto Massimino-designed sports car-derived V8, then being developed by Alf Francis. Serenissima wanted F1 exposure and McLaren wanted an engine. It gave no more than maybe 260bhp, but it was an engine, and the race M2B was hacked about with the rear monocoque horns either side of the engine bay cut down to accommodate the new engine's side exhausts, whereas the Ford's had been in-vee.

The M2B-Serenissima was taken to Spa for the Belgian GP and disgraced itself. It refused to run properly in practice, then finally chimed-in on all eight only to run its bearings within half a lap. There was no spare and no alternative but to non-start in the GP. Phil Hill drove MGM's M3 camera car on the opening lap, tailing the field as they tore into a rainstorm around Burnenville and his footage showing the ensuing carnage and conditions is amongst the best in the movie.

The McLaren drivers had their year made for them at Le Mans, where Bruce and Chris shared a 7-litre Ford GT Mark 2 and won. It was by far the biggest race either of them had ever won; by Bruce's judgement.

In July they returned to St Jovite, this time with a 5.4 Chevrolet engine in the M1B replacing the little but light Oldsmobile and offering 100bhp more. Teddy Mayer: "We should have made the change sooner". Bruce: "I guess we were wrong to stick with the Oldsmobile for so long . . . In the early stages of sportscar racing, development of tyre and transmission wasn't up to the stage where 500 horsepower could be used reliably. Now I think it is . . ." Lothar Motschenbacher's 5.0 M1B-Olds was the weekend's major opposition as Bruce won comfortably.

Back in the UK, Group 7 sports car racing was in its last season, despite immense promotion from the circuit owners it had never attracted the size of crowds they hoped for, and now the sponsoring fuel companies had to make the choice between G7 and F2, and preferred the single-seater class. In North America the situation was very different, for the US and Canadian clubs had combined to found the Canadian-American Challenge Cup series of races taking in the regular Fall sports car classics as they had become . . .

The McLaren team had planned to run a second F1 car for Chris Amon, but the engine situation never allowed it. Consequently he was entered in the sports car race supporting the British GP at Brands Hatch, and in a torrid drive he had the nose smashed on the opening lap, tore back through the field from dead last to challenge Hugh Dibley's big Lola-Chev for the lead, and was run off the road by Dibley at Druids Hairpin on the last lap. He recovered to finish third behind Skip Scott's M1B-Ford. Scott's blue car was one of a pair bought by American entrant Bill Kay for him and Peter Revson, but poor Kay suffered a fatal heart attack just a couple of weeks before the GP. His cars would be taken over by George Drummond and run for Scott and Revson in the inaugural CanAm series.

In the British GP itself the M2B-Serenissima behaved well, though Bruce was not delighted with its handling, and after a fine start he ran in the top six briefly. It felt good to be back. But he was on rain tyres on a drying track, and fell back before finally finishing sixth and scoring his marque's maiden World Championship point through reliability, not strength . . .

The works M2Bs went to Croft for an August sports car race but both drivers opted-out in torrential rain, then came the Guards Trophy back at Brands Hatch. Bruce and Chris had identical M1Bs for the first time, allowing set-ups to be transferred direct one to another. Both were 5.4 Chevy powered with stiffened chassis and Koni dampers, but Bruce made the wrong tyre choice. The sky was threatening before Heat 1, he started on wets but the race stayed dry and he floundered after sharing fastest practice time with Surtees' Lola. Surtees led Chris home, Bruce was lapped. For Heat 2 he fitted dry tyres, led handsomely until the heavens opened, then slithered straight into the bank, smashing his car's nose, splitting its radiator. Surtees led Chris home again; Lola first, McLaren second.

The F1 programme was set aside waiting for the revamped Ford V8's return for the lucrative US GP at Watkins Glen in October. Meanwhile the CanAm Championship began at St Jovite on September 11 where Surtees' Lola again dominated, Bruce and Chris 2-3. At Bridgehampton, Gurney's Lola beat the McLarens, this time Chris ahead 2-3. At Mosport Amon led McLaren 1-2 until both were put out by minor collisions while lapping slower cars. At Laguna Seca in round four Bruce finished third outclassed by the Chaparrals of Phil Hill and Jim Hall. Bruce believed his mistake was in underrating the Chaparrals, regarding them as the best cars despite Lola's successes. The Texan machines used aluminium-block Chevrolets out the back-door at GM, saving perhaps as much as 200lbs compared to McLaren's iron-block units which had grown from 5.4 to 6-litres after the first round. The smaller Chevy gave some 470bhp, the 6-litre on fuel injection nearer 570. In Canada the good-handling M1Bs had made time through the corners, lost time on the straights, and a big effort was made for Riverside. Bruce took pole, but ran into ignition problems and retired, Chris lost a disappointing seventh place when his engine blew. The CanAm finale came at Stardust Raceway, Las Vegas on November 13, where Surtees won race and title with Bruce second and Chris' gearbox broke. Mark Donohue's Penske Lola took second place in the Championship with Bruce third and Chris sixth behind the Chaparral drivers. Other McLaren placings were Chuck Parsons (8), John Cannon and Peter Revson (9=), Earl Jones (13), Masten Gregory and Lothar Motschenbacher (14=).

At Watkins Glen the M2B reappeared with the re-worked Ford engine and in a race of attrition it inherited a fifth place finish for two more Championship points. Then in Mexico for the final GP of the year it blew and the programme was at an end . . . They would find a better engine, somewhere . . .

The team did not go to Nassau, but Peter Revson shone there in the Drummond Racing M1B-Ford, leading the major race much of the way before losing his brakes but inheriting third when Hap Sharp's Chaparral crashed on the last lap. Skip Sott, Sam Posey and Billy Foster each drove customer McLarens.

With this difficult and often disappointing season at an end the team at Colnbrook studied options for '67. Bruce decided in favour of BRM engine power. They were building a 3-litre V12 essentially for sportscar use but it would be available for F1. With the death of British Group 7, McLaren also planned to build a car for the new 1600cc F2 class coming into effect in the new year, and pending delivery of the V12 engine a ballasted 2.1-litre F2 would be used in Formula 1. And on the sports car front defeat by Lola in the CanAm series had stung, and careful plans were laid for vengeance in '67 . . .

Meanwhile, what became of the early single-seat McLarens? The tyre test Mallite monocoque M2A was sold in 1967 to English club driver John Ewer. He fitted a Cobra engine and ZF box and he and Sid Fox raced it briefly before it was sold to Robert Ashcroft, who gave one Peter Gethin the drive. Tony Dean won with the car at Rufforth then M2A was sold to Welshman Dave McCloy. He crashed it heavily at Oulton Park. It was rebuilt, raced rarely through '68 then appeared once in Formula 5000 in 1969. That November children throwing fireworks apparently ignited McCloy's garage, and the first McLaren single-seater was destroyed.

Of the three M2Bs built, Bruce's Monaco, Spa and Brands Hatch car was chassis 2, the Watkins Glen and Mexico mount chassis 1, originally used only for testing. In 1968 all three chassis were sold as a job lot to Ken Sheppard to carry the age-old Coventry Climax *Godiva* V8 engines, the total stock of which Sheppard had also acquired, from Paul Emery. M2B/2 was fitted with one of these engines and did half a lap of the Silverstone paddock in May. Keith St John was to drive M2B/1 with 4.5 Olds V8 power in F5000 at Brands Hatch at Easter, 1969, but decided against it when he saw the car . . . Today one chassis survives with the Donington Collection near Derby, England. The others are still about. . .

Of the 'whoosh-bonk cars', Harry Zweifel's M3A/1 was hill-climbed extensively by its owner and by Peter Bonner, M3A/2 was sprinted and hill-climbed for several seasons by Patsy Burt, eventually with Chevvy V8 power, and M3A/3 – the 4.7 Ford-engined MGM camera car – was sold via John Ewer to David Bridges. It was driven for him in *Libre* events by Brian Redman, before being sold to Robin Darlington. David Prophet took it out to South Africa where he sold it to Bob Olthoff when the 1968 national Championship there was extended to include Formula A cars with Formula 1. Olthoff also had an M1 sports car, and the ex-MGM machine raced two seasons in South Africa before selling to Fred Cowell.

During the early months of 1967, Bruce was deeply involved with Ford's J-car and Mark IV GT development aiming at winning Le Mans for the second time. Meanwhile at Colnbrook Robin Herd's M4A F2 car took shape, to be announced in February for production in Lambretta-Trojan's new factory at their 10½-acre Croydon site, the old Elva plant in Rye being superceded. Mallite had proved difficult to work and to obtain, and the M4A was a comparatively simple bathtub monocoque device skinned in 20-gauge dural sheet with conventional outboard spring suspension. Fuel was carried in two 10-gallon tanks flanking the cockpit and a further 5-gallons were housed in the seat back structure. Girling disc brakes were used, 10.5in diameter and the 13-inch McLaren four-spoke cast wheels had 7in wide front rims and 10in rears. Power came from the new Cosworth-Ford FVA 1600cc twin-cam, which in effect formed one half of the forthcoming DFV V8 Formula 1 engine. In its first season this GP unit would be exclusive to Team Lotus. For 1968 Ford would make it generally available for customer sale. In the M4A the FVA four-cylinder engine drove through a new Hewland FT200 five-speed transaxle. The car scaled 928lbs, just 2lbs over the F2 minimum weight. An initial batch of ten cars was to be laid down, five bound for the US and Formula B racing while the McLaren works intended to use two. There was talk of converting the basic design to 1-litre F3 form. From Trojan the chassis cost £2,450.

Meanwhile sports car racing had died in the UK, but Bruce, Robin Herd and his assistant Gordon Coppuck were brain-storming out a brand-new CanAm car with the rest of the team, and an all-new monocoque F1 design was on the stocks for BRM's forthcoming 3-litre F1 unit.

To keep the team in Formula 1 meanwhile, an M4A was modified with the rear of the monocoque cut away to accommodate the 280bhp 2.1-litre BRM V8 engine, originally developed from the old 1500cc F1 World Championship engine for Tasman racing. The car was ballasted to the F1 minimum, fitted with extra pannier fuel tankage and Bruce made his debut in the handsome little red-painted M4B special in the Brands Hatch Race of Champions as listed in our Racing Record appendix, see page 249. Bruce was fourth in Heat 1 but missed a gear, over-revved and blew the engine starting Heat 2. He was fifth in the Oulton Park Spring Cup, fifth again at May Silverstone and delightedly fourth in the Kiwi triumph at Monaco, when Denny Hulme won for Brabham, Chris Amon was third at the start of his career as a works Ferrari driver and Bruce was fourth with the M4B special. The little car was just about tailor-made for the Monte Carlo streets and Bruce could easily have been second but for the battery running flat, forcing a pit stop. At Zandvoort Bruce ran onto an oil slick at the long Huzaren Vlak corner on lap 2 and crashed quite heavily, writing off M4B's suspension although the monocoque escaped unscathed.

He shared a Mark IV Ford at Le Mans with Mark Donohue, finishing fourth after numerous problems, in what the Ford team rated as his best drive for them. Dan Gurney offered him the second Eagle-Weslake V12 F1 ride pending arrival

Robin Herd's neat bath-tub monocoque M4A Formula 2 car for 1967 was almost the complete antithesis of the Mallite M2B F1, with practicality and simplicity now the keynote. Here in the Colnbrook works the prototype is on its ear for final plumbing, showing off the open-topped monocoque layout and off-the-shelf Cosworth FVA 1600cc 4-cylinder engine, while during initial tests at the FVRDE's Chobham military-vehicle

test-track Bruce discusses skid-pan running with Robin and Wally. Car builder Don Beresford looks on (right) while Nigel Bennett of Firestone (bespectacled) simply looks frozen stiff. The car has prototype aluminium body sections fitted, replaced by glass-fibre mouldings when put into production by Trojan for F2/3 and North American Formula B.

of the BRM V12 engine for his new McLaren M5A car, and Bruce drove the Eagle in the French, British, and German GPs.

Meanwhile Bruce was engaged in Formula 2, the team's second 'works' car going to John Coombs who had lost Graham Hill's services to Lotus, and replaced him with Piers Courage. A production car sold to Frank Lythgoe Racing for Alan Rollinson to drive. Bruce only ran a truncated season, but quite enjoyed it, placing fifth at Snetterton on his debut and at Zolder, second at Rouen where the likes of Jimmy Clark and Jack Brabham fell over each other leaving him to whistle unscathed through the wreckage, third at Crystal Palace, fourth at Silverstone and sixth in the Eifelrennen at Nürburgring. Piers led him home there, was second at Zandvoort, third at Hockenheim, and fifth at Crystal Palace. That winter Bruce drove a works BRM in the Tasman Championship and Piers Courage proved newfound maturity and stature in his M4A, driving very well in that series to win a new F1 ride the following year.

But it was McLaren's return to CanAm which would show the way forward. During March 1967 there was debate at Colnbrook about a new Group 7 design. They decided to do their own engines instead of relying on outside suppliers. They chose basically Bartz-modified Chevrolets assembled by themselves and incorporating their own ideas. Lucas fuel injection was fitted, most of the work being done by Gary Knutson and Bruce himself. A transmission choice had to be made between the ZF 5DS25 GT40 'box and the Hewland LG five-speed. The new British 'box won. The old Firestone deal had been replaced by a more lucrative contract with Goodyear. Both British and American-made Goodyears were available, the former proving ideal for single-seater racing, the latter for the sports cars.

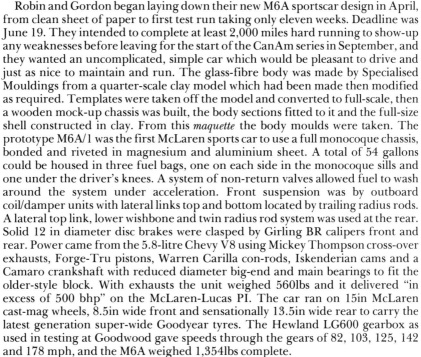

The handsome but hefty M5A-BRM V12 during its startling debut race, Canadian GP, Mosport Park, 1967 when Bruce looked set to win until the battery boiled dry and lost its charge because the alternator had been omitted to save weight. The car was red with a silver stripe edged in green. It sold later to Jo Bonnier and subsequently became a vertically-mounted wall adornment in his Lausanne art gallery. Today it survives in Sweden, owned by Gunnar Elmgren, PR of Svenska Renault.

Robin and Gordon began laying down their new M6A sportscar design in April, from clean sheet of paper to first test run taking only eleven weeks. Deadline was June 19. They intended to complete at least 2,000 miles hard running to show-up any weaknesses before leaving for the start of the CanAm series in September, and they wanted an uncomplicated, simple car which would be pleasant to drive and just as nice to maintain and run. The glass-fibre body was made by Specialised Mouldings from a quarter-scale clay model which had been made then modified as required. Templates were taken off the model and converted to full-scale, then a wooden mock-up chassis was built, the body sections fitted to it and the full-size shell constructed in clay. From this *maquette* the body moulds were taken. The prototype M6A/1 was the first McLaren sports car to use a full monocoque chassis, bonded and riveted in magnesium and aluminium sheet. A total of 54 gallons could be housed in three fuel bags, one on each side in the monocoque sills and one under the driver's knees. A system of non-return valves allowed fuel to wash around the system under acceleration. Front suspension was by outboard coil/damper units with lateral links top and bottom located by trailing radius rods. A lateral top link, lower wishbone and twin radius rod system was used at the rear. Solid 12 in diameter disc brakes were clasped by Girling BR calipers front and rear. Power came from the 5.8-litre Chevy V8 using Mickey Thompson cross-over exhausts, Forge-Tru pistons, Warren Carilla con-rods, Iskenderian cams and a Camaro crankshaft with reduced diameter big-end and main bearings to fit the older-style block. With exhausts the unit weighed 560lbs and it delivered "in excess of 500 bhp" on the McLaren-Lucas PI. The car ran on 15in McLaren cast-mag wheels, 8.5in wide front and sensationally 13.5in wide rear to carry the latest generation super-wide Goodyear tyres. The Hewland LG600 gearbox as used in testing at Goodwood gave speeds through the gears of 82, 103, 125, 142 and 178 mph, and the M6A weighed 1,354lbs complete.

Teddy had long been unhappy about the team's colours. They had changed from dowdy British Racing Green to black and silver, red with pale stripes, and now he fell for a bright yellow-orange papaya shade, prompted by Jackie Epstein's Lola T70 "which would show up like a beacon on TV". Once racing began with the M6A the team found slower drivers were instantly aware of that wicked orange flash in their mirrors.

Bruce had long been in discussion with fellow New Zealander Denny Hulme about joining his team, and Denny signed on with Goodyear backing for CanAm and their partnership would extend to Formula 1 for '68 when Denny would move from Jack Brabham's team.

The prototype M6A was ready on target and Bruce ran it in as usual unbodied, believing despite some of his colleagues' doubts that this enabled him to set-up the chassis devoid of aerodynamic factors which could be added later. There was one aerodynamic factor, the radiator ducting, built into the car and on that first Monday's testing Bruce lapped in 1:16.2. During the second test week the body was added and Bruce lapped consistently around 1:14.5. Both Bruce and Denny drove later, getting below 1:14 while Denny was quickest at 1:13.4. They also ran 200 miles on the rough Snetterton track and nothing broke . . .

A series of air-pressure taps were rigged on the body and Bruce drove at around 150mph with Robin crammed in the passenger seat recording pressures. Denny's M6A/2 was to be maintained by Don Beresford and Barry Crowe and after a brief Silverstone shake-down in which it lowered his own Lola-Chev lap record he ran further at Goodwood and declared "She'll be right" and left development as it was.

The CanAm Championship would begin shortly, but first let us look at the McLaren M5A, built for the BRM V12 engine. The car was on test at Goodwood with the M6A in August, the monocoque having been ready and waiting since February. It was very much in the M4A/B mould but where the F2 car had a squarish tub the F1's was more rounded to accommodate the extra fuel load. The monocoque section curled 360-degrees above the driver's shins, while leaving the area above his knees open for ease of maintenance. Behind the seat-back section twin monocoque legs extended either side of the engine bay. There were only two bulkheads at either extremity to pick up suspension and steering while strong-points were built into the tub to accept radius rod and wishbone loads. The driver's seat back stiffened the tub to some extent but had a large access hole to clear ancillaries on the front of the engine. The instrument panel had little structural role. Rubber fuel bags were housed within the aluminium side pontoons, the 'wheelbarrow arms' alongside the engine, a section beneath the driver's knees and lay in a tray above his legs. Total capacity was 42 gallons. Suspension followed previous McLaren wide-based practice. The front cast hub carriers were unusual in having a steel steering-arm plate bolted on rather than an integral cast-in component. Small F2 sized disc brakes hid within the 13-inch wheels, only concession to extra load being an eighth-inch extra thickness. Bruce was always notably light on his brakes, and when Denny began driving the M6A the sports car's braking had to be uprated. The BRM V12 engine was claimed to deliver 370bhp at 9,750 rpm, and it drove through a five-speed Hewland DG.

After a 30-mile shakedown test at Goodwood the car was rushed out to Mosport for the inaugural Formula 1 Canadian GP on August 27. The engine as delivered proved a little longer than anticipated and items like the water pump and distributors projected into the cockpit. To save both space and weight, but mainly a few pounds weight, the alternator was omitted. The Varley battery was laid on its side under the driver's seat, with the oil catch tank above it. During the race the oil tank filled and heated-up which did not do the battery any good. It rained for the race and in slick conditions Bruce ran with the leaders before spinning. He recovered and chased hard to regain lost ground while others suffered. He was second, chasing Denny's Brabham hard when the road began to dry. Clark retook second for Lotus and the BRM engine began misfiring, oil surge was losing oil pressure and Bruce realised the battery was running flat, causing the misfire. Without the alternator it was not being charged, so he had to stop for a fresh battery, eventually finishing seventh. But it had been a very promising debut, if only the Goodwood test had revealed that blow-by gases were feeding the catch tank to boil the battery dry he might well have won . . . Deleting the alternator still gripes Teddy Mayer. Even fifteen years later he grimaces when reminded of it: "It wasn't very bloody bright, was it . . ."

A week later the CanAm Championship opening round was run, but then back at Monza for the Italian GP Bruce qualified M5A on the front row and with 20 laps to go he and Surtees' revamped Honda were on their own ready for a final dash to the flag when a BRM cylinder liner shattered. BRM had found another 19bhp in the engine and Bruce at last looked like regaining his former stature.

During scrutineering officialdom worried about the M5A's colour, red with a silver stripe edged in green in deference to New Zealand. There were mutterings about respraying it green for Great Britain, but when Bruce ran so quickly in practice the 2-2-2 grid was hastily re-arranged 3-2-3 and it seemed suspiciously as though this was intended to place a red car on the front with Lotus and Brabham's green front-runners; red being Italy's racing colour, and Ferrari being slow.

At Watkins Glen for the US GP the diff gave trouble in practice and Bruce over-revved his precious V12 engine, then spun in the race and knocked-off a hose on a high kerb. In Mexico the engine again proved its thirst for oil, and Bruce stopped as the pressure zeroed. But there was still oil in the tank. Bruce: "I think the oil pump is weak on suction. This afterwards bit is the most harrowing part of motor racing – 'Now why should that have ever happened?' . . ."

For 1968 a new Formula 1 era would begin with acquisition of the Ford-Cosworth DFV V8 engine. For the moment it is time to concentrate upon Group 7 sports-racing cars, and McLaren's five-season heyday in CanAm.

Chapter 3
CanAm – The Bruce and Denny Show

"At times I'm really lost for an answer when people ask me about dominating CanAm. It isn't really for us to answer such questions. All we've been doing is getting on with the job of going racing . . ."

Bruce McLaren, 1969

1967

1 — Road America, Elkhart Lake, Wisconsin — September 3

For the M6As' debut Bruce qualified on pole only to run bearings in the race, Denny led from start to finish of the 200 miles and won handsomely from the Donohue and Surtees Lolas, and Hall's Chaparral. The production M1C-Chevrolets of Scott, Jerry Hansen, Skip Barber and Bud Morley were 5-6-7-8. One report read ". . . the two bright orange-yellow cars made a brilliant head to the long row of 32 starters . . ." – 17 of them were McLarens, the above cars and those of Chuck Parsons, Don Morin, John Cannon, Ludwig Heimrath, John Cordts, Brett Lunger, Brook Doran, Jerry Entin, Richard Brown, Gary Wilson and Ron Courtney apart from the finishers.

2 — Chevron GP, Bridgehampton, New York — September 17

Denny again, flag to flag with Bruce completing the team's first CanAm 1-2, humbling the Lola T70s again. They qualified 1-2 on the grid, Denny on pole. Chuck Parsons was sixth, Barber ninth, Brown and Heimrath 12-13. The 30-strong field included 14 McLarens, these entries plus Scott, Mike Spence in Eustace Soucy's ex-Amon '65 car, Morley, Morin, Lunger, Cordts, Jerry Alderman and Peter Revson. Ventilated disc brakes had been adopted on the M6As, 1 1/8-inch Girlings at the front and 13/16in Kelsey-Hayes rears. They also had cable-released 5-pint reserves of engine oil on board due to the Chevrolet's thirst for the amber fluid.

3 — Players '200', Mosport Park, Ontario — September 23

Denny's hat-trick despite a late-race excursion at Moss Corner which he attributed to a suspension problem troubling him for 20 laps. With bodywork crushed onto the left-front wheel he set out on the last lap and a half, but burst the tyre and limped home, still first with Bruce second a half-minute adrift. He had his own dramas – starting a minute after the rest of the field due to a leaking fuel bag which had to be changed in a last-minute pre-race panic. Mike Spence was third, a lap adrift – Denny was already virtually assured of the CanAm title. Scott and Cordts finished 7-8, Brown tenth, George Eaton 13th and Barber 15th. The 28 starters included 14 McLarens, Heimrath, Cannon, Parsons, Lunger, Dave Causey and Courtney in addition to the finishers. Thus far Team McLaren had won $60,000 from the series . . .

4 — Monterey GP, Laguna Seca, California — October 15

Bruce won from pole position, while Denny's progress faltered in his quest for four in a row when his engine blew on lap 81 of the 106. Bruce set fastest lap, broke the lap record and lapped second-place man Jim Hall's Chaparral 2G. There were 32 starters, only 11 of them McLarens. John Cannon's was seventh, others driven by Spence, Parsons, Scott, Morin, Jim Adams, Bill Amick, Jerry Entin and Brett Lunger. The team had rented a workshop in Long Beach close to Champion

Spark Plugs' dyno facility. Their two tons of spares seemed inadequate, with first bigger brakes, then stronger fuel bags, heavier half-shafts and stronger rear wheels being ordered on the 'phone from Colnbrook. Denny's tub was carefully examined for damage after Mosport but was judged unharmed. Large new Goodyears junked the original axles and stronger components were fitted for Laguna. They had four fresh engines, Denny's race unit giving 514bhp, Bruce's 516. The race was run in blistering heat and was torture for cars and drivers alike.

5 — Los Angeles Times GP, Riverside, California — October 29

Dan Gurney's new Gurney-Weslake headed Ford V8 put his Lola on pole and Jim Hall's improved Chaparral gave Bruce fits before the M6A won by only 3 secs. Denny's car suffered front bodywork damage from a tyre marker thrown into his path by Parnelli Jones' Lola. The damaged bodywork was cut away but he was black-flagged with insufficient bodywork to qualify as 'safe'. Spence was fifth, Morin, Cannon, and Parsons 10-11-12, Scott 14th and Entin 16th. There were 39 starters, 13 McLarens; the works and finishers' cars, plus Jay Hills, Jim Adams, Amick, Jim Paul and Ron Herrera.

6 — Stardust GP, Las Vegas, Nevada — November 12

Mark Donohue's Lola led with a half-mile to go, ran out of fuel and John Surtees' sister car snatched victory. Bruce started the race with oil and water mixing in his engine and little hope. Within a few laps he was out. Denny had a tyre deflate and changed it, charged back through the field and looked likely to take the honours when his engine blew spectacularly right in front of the grandstands. If it had held together he would have added the CanAm title to his Drivers' World Championship, just sealed for Brabham in Mexico City. As it was Bruce took the title; "It's not the way I would have chosen, but I can't really complain. In the six CanAm races our team collected six fastest laps, qualified six times on the front row, took five pole positions, and won five races . . ." The 30 starters included 11 McLarens; Spence was third, Entin and Cannon 7-8, Parsons 10th. Scott, Herrera, Wilson, Paul, and Morin joined the works M6As in retirement.

Denny Hulme said of the M6A "The beauty of it is that you can toss it about like a single-seater" – it would enter, negotiate and leave corners in almost any attitude at will. Journalist-driver Jerry Titus commented "It handles like a sophisticated go-kart". Bruce felt its great advantage over the opposition was in the slower corners. It certainly did its job brilliantly, and Bruce commented in his regular *Autosport* magazine column: "Trying to learn how to go motor racing properly over the last couple of years has worn us down nearly to our knees, but the 1967 CanAm series stood us back on our feet again, and now we're going to try even harder . . ."

If his opponents had had a crystal ball, they would have trembled . . .

————————— 1968 —————————

For their defence of the CanAm Challenge title in 1968, McLaren had produced their M8A while Trojan had productionised the victorious M6 design as the customer M6B. With an infinitely more serious Formula 1 programme on their hands advance work on the M8A could be neither as extensive nor as painstaking as on the '67 car. Just five days before the cars were due to leave by air for the opening round, neither was complete. But the first prototype had already completed 500 miles of Goodwood testing in chassis form and with an old hack M6A body. Bruce had lapped in 1:13.4 untroubled.

The M8A was 25lbs lighter than its predecessor and was to carry a new 7-litre McLaren-Chevrolet engine with 100bhp more than its '67 counterpart. Main difference between the two designs was that the M8A carried its engine as a stressed part of the chassis structure, whereas the M6A's had been unstressed. Overall the new car was some 4ins wider and 4ins lower than the M6A, the extra

Denny Hulme demonstrating the simple but lovely lines of his works M6A-Chevrolet V8 during the 1967 CanAm series which the papaya-liveried McLarens utterly dominated – founding the legend of the Bruce & Denny Show, and more than compensating for the team's disappointments with the M1Bs during the 1966 series.

width accommodating 30 gallons of fuel each side.

The monocoque chassis was skinned in L72 aluminium alloy sheet with a magnesium floor, terminating in a ⅜in thick magnesium sheet rear bulkhead from which Gary Knutson's McLaren-Lucas fuel-injected 620bhp Chevvy engine was hung on tubular frames, 1½ins lower than before. Drive was through a Hewland LG600 gearbox with BRD frictionless roller-spline half-shafts to 15in wide rim McLaren cast wheels. Suspension layout and geometry was derived from M6A practice, but the car used giant new 11⅞in front and 11½in rear ventilated disc brakes, the discs being fully 1 1/16in thick. To improve driver vision the whole Specialised Mouldings body was smoother-shaped with less pronounced front wheel humps. A shallow full-width rear wing was fitted, Bruce hoping no additional spoilers would be necessary once an optimum angle had been pre-set.

Design responsibility for the M8A was Swiss engineer Jo Marquart's, working directly with Bruce. Six mechanics would travel with Teddy and the team drivers; three from the engine division in California and three from Colnbrook, including Tyler and Cary Taylor who had been Denny's F1 mechanic with Brabham the previous year.

Hardly a Mickey Mouse driver, nor a Mickey Mouse car; Bruce and Tyler with the 1968 CanAm Championship-dominating McLaren-Chevrolet M8A. It was Denny's turn for the title that year.

1 — Road America, Elkhart Lake, Wisconsin — September 1

Tyler flew in with the two new M8As which breathed potential with their glittering finish. Gary Knutson arrived from California with three new 7-litre aluminium-block Chevy engines with their impressive foot-tall injection stacks. Shelby American fielded two production M6Bs with 7-litre aluminium-block Ford V8s for Peter Revson to choose between, and Roger Penske produced his dark-blue pin-striped M6B for Mark Donohue — the ex-McLaren M6A he had raced earlier in the year's USRRC events having been sold to Jerry Hansen. Lothar Motschenbacher had driven a Lola the previous year, but now had an M6B with Gurney-Weslake Ford engine on carburettors. Jo Bonnier's Ecurie Suisse fielded a new M6B.

Team McLaren had uncharacteristic practice problems, ending with an eight-page checklist, three more than '67's. The race was run on a wet track, Denny started with dry tyres, led to the finish despite a broken rocker arm leaving only seven cylinders operative, and Bruce was second, trouble-free, heading a marque 1-2-3-4-6 from Donohue, Revson and Motschenbacher, who set fastest lap . . .

1 – Hulme M8A; 2 – McLaren M8A; 3 – Donohue M6B; 4 – Revson M6B Ford; 6 – Motschenbacher M6B-Ford; 8 – George Eaton M1C; 9 – John Cordts M1C; 15 – Candido Damota M1C; 18 – Jo Bonnier M6B; 20 – Ron Courtney M1C; *DNF* – Heimrath M1C; Leonard Janke M1C; Hansen M6A-Ford; Richard Brown M6B; Gary Wilson M1B; Ralph Trieschmann M1C.

2 — Bridgehampton, New York — September 15

Great battle for the lead between the works cars, Jim Hall and Donohue which saw the M8As break, the Chaparral slow and the Penske M6B winning. Dan Gurney debuted his lower, sleeker, lighter 'McLeagle' M6B using titanium suspension and exhausts to save weight, small 5.3 Gurney-Weslake Ford V8 engine and compact Hewland DG300 gearbox. Combustion gas blow-by was the McLaren engine problem, pressurizing the small sump, blowing out lubricant and eventually making them blow. 1 – Donohue; 3 – Motschenbacher; 5 – Richard Brown; 6 – Gurney M6B-Ford; *DNF* – Hulme, McLaren, Courtney, Revson, Bonnier, Eaton, Damota. Bruce set fastest lap.

3 — Klondike Trail '200', Edmonton, Alberta — September 29

A change in piston rings helped Team McLaren to another 1-2 in the new series, Denny winning from Bruce, 10secs behind. Donohue was third, a half-minute adrift. It was a race of attrition on a slippery track and only twelve cars finished. Jerry Titus joined the series in an M6B with 'small' 6-litre Chevy V8 on Tecalemit-Jackson PI. 1 – Hulme; 2 – McLaren; 3 – Donohue; 7 – Wilson; 10 Eaton 5.3 M1C-Ford; 12 – Cordts M1C; *DNF* – Gurney; Revson; Motschenbacher; Titus M6B; Roger McCaig M6B.

4 — Monterey GP, Laguna Seca, California — October 13

It rained and rained, Lord didn't it rain and John Cannon in a veteran 6.0 M1B-Olds was on the best rain tyre combination and he won sensationally while the stars spun and stopped repeatedly for clean goggles and adjustment.

1 – Cannon; 2 – Hulme; 3 – Eaton; 4 – Motschenbacher M6B-Ford; 5 – McLaren; 6 – Titus; 8 – Donohue; 12 – Revson; 17 – Rich Galloway M6B; *DNF* Gurney; Jim Paul 5.5 M1C; Hansen.

5 — Los Angeles Times GP, Riverside, California — October 27

Bruce led all the way in a processional race to win for the second successive year with only Donohue still on the same lap as he took the flag. Denny damaged his car's body as in '67 but was allowed to continue this time, Jim Hall's Chaparral suffered brake failure. Bruce had dinged Denny's car during pre-race testing, Don Beresford refabricating part of the tub before the race.

Bruce again, demonstrating the sleek lines of the stressed-engine M8A on the way out of Laguna Seca's Turn 6 during the Monterey GP CanAm round, October 13, 1968. The Gulf-McLarens were virtually uncatchable; they would improve for '69 . . .

Gulf

GOOD YEAR

LAREN CARS   *Bruce McLaren*

LOCKHEED

Gulf

Denny led the Championship with Bruce and Mark Donohue tied on points behind him. If anything happened to Denny's M8A at Las Vegas either of the others could steal it . . .

1 – McLaren; 2 – Donohue; 4 – Motschenbacher; 5 – Hulme; 6 – Cannon; 7 – Hansen; 8 – Swede Savage M6B-Ford; 9 – Brown; 13 – Titus; *DNF* – Eaton; Bonnier; Herrera; McCaig; Paul; Galloway; Hills; Revson.

6 — Stardust GP, Las Vegas, Nevada — November 10

Denny won the race and the Championship for Team McLaren's second in a row, while chaos erupted on the first corner with a multiple accident in which Bruce's car suffered body damage. Donohue's Championship hopes evaporated as the Penske McLaren refused to start on the line. Dan Gurney pressed Denny. In the closing stages Motschenbacher's M6B suddenly slowed on its way to the pits and Jim Hall's following Chaparral tripped over it in a terrible accident which destroyed both cars and severely injured the Texan driver-constructor.

In the final CanAm reckoning Denny was Champion with 35 points and $40,000 winnings from Bruce on 24 and $26,460; Donohue third with 23 and $16,700. 'The Bruce and Denny Show' had staged a triumphant return . . .

1 Hulme; 3 Titus; 6 McLaren; 7 Eaton; 8 Bonnier; 9 Brown; 11 Leonard Janke M1C; 14 Hills; *DNF* – Motschenbacher; Revson; McCaig; Cannon; Savage; Hansen; Paul; Donohue *DNS*.

1969

After two years with McLaren, Gary Knutson returned to Chaparral in 1969 and another American engineer named George Bolthoff took over preparation of the team's engines. The new year's CanAm Challenge defender was a reworked version of the M8A known logically enough as the M8B, three were built, one of them on an existing M8A tub. Main external change was the cut-back front wheel arch form with a tapering trailing edge to improve streamlining, while a strutted rear wing acting direct upon the rear hub carriers was acceptable to the CanAm clubs, although banned from Formula 1 by this time. The team was sponsored by Goodyear, Gulf Oil and Reynolds Aluminum.

In a discussion with Bruce at the end of the season the author was told how "We started testing in January for the new series, using Denny's '8A as a test-bed. We did a very large test mileage before shipping three new M8Bs for the series . . . two new cars and the spare was Denny's '8A suitably modified. It was an 11-race series which sounded more daunting but in fact we had quite an easy time of it, and the series wasn't really something you could get your teeth into. In practice Denny and I would occasionally have a go and get quite fast, but in most of the races we were gone after the first six laps, and there was no one in sight . . ." In 1983 Teddy Mayer can look back and say simply "The M8B with the wing acting direct on the rear uprights was probably the most effective race car we ever built . . ." The series shaped up like this . . .

1 — Mosport Park, Ontario — June 1

Bruce and Denny started from the front row and finished a fifth of a second apart 1-2, with John Surtees third in Jim Hall's Knutson-tuned M12 production McLaren, these new customer models mating the full-length monocoque of the successful M6A/B series with the '8A suspension, the engine remaining unstressed. All the leading cars used aluminium Chevrolet block V8s. McLaren users included Dan Gurney with the uprated McLeagle M6B handicapped by Ford's decision to suspend development of their projected 7.5-8-litre CanAm engine, leaving him with a 5.6 unit and approximately 100bhp handicap. Lothar Motschenbacher and Canadian George Eaton ran private M12s, but like the Hall team had received their cars very late. There were five other M6Bs and five still older McLarens in the race, including Dave Billes' M1C driven by John Cordts,

entered at the very last moment when a scrutineer friend told him there was only a thin field. It paid off handsomely.

1 – McLaren M8B; 2 – Hulme M8B; 3 – Surtees M12; 4 – John Cordts M1C; 5 – Jacques Couture M1C; 7 – Oscar Kovaleski M6A; 8 – Rich Galloway M6B; 9 – George Eaton M12; 10 – Leonard Janke M1C; *DNF* – Gurney M6B; Richard Brown M6B; Motschenbacher M12; Jerry Crawford M1C; John Cannon M6B.

2 — Labatt Trophy, St Jovite-Mt Tremblant, Quebec — June 15
Denny evened the score, winning from Bruce while opposition came from Surtees and Motschenbacher. Surtees and Bruce became involved in a collision under a yellow flag, John retiring and Bruce's throttle return later playing up. George Eaton proved himself a serious contender and John Cordts kept up well in Roger McCaig's M6B, deputising while the owner was indisposed. There were 20 starters, 12 of them McLarens.

1 – Hulme; 2 – McLaren; 4 – Motschenbacher; 5 – Cordts M6B; 6 – Fred Baker M6B; 7 Eaton; 9 – Jacques Couture M1C; *DNF* – Surtees: Jerry Titus M1C; Ford, Brown; Galloway; Kovaleski.

3 — Watkins Glen, New York — July 13
Run in a combined meeting with the Watkins Glen 6-Hours World Championship endurance round, this event saw the debut of several new cars, including Chris Amon's CanAm Ferrari 612 with 6-litre V12 engine. But McLaren led Hulme all the way though Chris was third after a battle with Surtees' Hall M12. "Four Grand Prix stars putting on such a performance will save CanAm" read one report. Twenty-five cars started, ten of them McLarens.

1 – McLaren; 2 – Hulme; 4 – Eaton; 11 – Kovaleski; 12 – Surtees; *DNF* – Motschenbacher; Fred Baker M6B; Cordts; Brown; Galloway.

Cutaway wheel-arches and the strutted rear wing identify Denny Hulme's 1969 McLaren-Chevrolet M8B, shown here in the opening round at Mosport Park. The CanAm series had been extended to incorporate 11 rounds, ostensibly to loosen McLaren's stranglehold. They responded by winning all 11 ...

4 — Klondike Trail '200', Edmonton, Alberta — July 27

The big V12 Ferrari 612P stirred some real life into CanAm at Edmonton where Amon led some of the way despite various woes and eventually finished only 5secs behind Denny's victorious M8B. Bruce went out with piston failure early on. George Eaton was spectacularly third with a flapping rear tyre, while Surtees' exotic new Chaparral 2H – which he was later to describe unequivocally as "the most frightening and diabolical device it's ever been my displeasure to sit in" – was delayed by a broken throttle spring. Only 17 cars started, seven finished.

1 – Hulme; 3 – Eaton; 6 – Kris Harrison M1C; *DNF* – Roger McCaig M6B; McLaren; Duane Williamson M1C; Galloway; Motschenbacher.

5 — Buckeye CanAm, Mid-Ohio, Lexington — August 17

Strongest opposition yet, Donohue's new Penske Lola, the Ferrari, Chaparral and a new Group 7 Porsche but it all fizzled away and Denny won again while Bruce suffered an oil pump failure near the end, unwittingly running the last 17 miles with no oil feed at all. "Hey!" he yelled at the Gulf Oil man, "It'll run fine *without* your oil . . ." Everyone was casting covetous eyes at the team's shrouded spare car on its trailer.

There were 22 starters, ten McLarens.

1 – Hulme; 2 – McLaren; 6 – Eaton; 9 – Brown; 11 – Williamson; 12 – Kovaleski; 13 – Harrison; 15 – Cliff Apel M1C; *DNF* – Motschenbacher; Cannon.

Many covetous eyes had been cast on the team's spare M8B during the early races of the 1969 CanAm series. Here at Michigan International Speedway Bruce leads Denny with Dan Gurney in the loaned spare breasting the rise in their wake. The McLaren team operation became the watchword for smooth efficiency; Mercedes-like to US eyes, they proved themselves unbeatable.

6 — Elkhart Lake, Wisconsin — August 31

Bruce's turn to win, Denny second, Chris Amon chasing in the Ferrari until its fuel pump failed. Mario Andretti appeared with a massive iron-linered, alloy-block 8.1 Ford V8 in an ex-Shelby M6B modified to carry the engine "big as *Quo Vadis*". He complained it accelerated so fiercely he had trouble reaching forward for the gearchange. He set third-fastest practice time but the engine's torque ripped out the drive-train and rear suspension and he did not start. Penske withdrew from CanAm, saying his current organisation did not have the necessary capacity with USAC and TransAm saloon car commitments. There were 34 qualifiers including Andretti, 15 McLarens.

1 – McLaren: 2 – Hulme; 6 – Motschenbacher; 7 – Brown; 8 – Kovaleski; 10 – Harrison; 11 – Apel; 12 – Dave Causey 7.0 M6B; *DNF* – Harvey Lasiter M1C; Spence Stoddard M1C; David Hobbs M6B (ex-Bonnier, Ford); Galloway; Williamson; Eaton.

7 — Inver House Scotch CanAm, Bridgehampton, New York — September 24

Dull race in dull, cool weather, Denny ahead of Bruce at the finish, Porsche third with Siffert, Motschenbacher's M12 fourth and three-times lapped. Surtees featured strongly but briefly in Hall's M12, the Chaparral 2H having been set aside, and Amon's Ferrari broke. Twenty starters, nine McLarens. At midday during practice the team went water-skiing, Teddy staying behind just in case anyone should run fast enough to cause alarm . . .

1 – Hulme; 2 – McLaren; 4 – Motschenbacher; 8 – Brown; 9 – Janke; 10 – Harrison; 12 – Bill Wonder M1C; *DNF* – Surtees; Eaton.

8 — Michigan Raceway, — September 28

Jack Brabham qualified the spare works M8B, then Dan Gurney took it over for the race, started from the back of the 27 car grid, passed 12 of them on lap 1 and caught Bruce and Denny. The three finished 1-2-3, Bruce, Denny, Dan . . . Domination . . . Surtees was ill, Andrea de Adamich drove Hall's M12, trailing Eaton until the Canadian was delayed by a puncture and oil leaks. The Ferrari broke its engine in practice and did not start, Dan's own McLeagle suffered likewise. Dave Causey's M6A was the ex-McLaren '67 Championship winner, later used by Donohue to win the USRRC for Penske, and by Hansen.

1 – McLaren; 2 – Hulme; 3 – Gurney M8B; 5 – Andrea de Adamich M12; 8 – Eaton; 9 – Causey; 10 – Hobbs; 12 – Brown; 13 – Harrison; 15 – Galloway; 16 – Frank Kahlich M1C; 17 – Bill Wonder M1C-Ford; 18 – Janke; *DNF* – Apel; Motschenbacher; McCaig.

CanAm winner – a works McLaren – of course!

Classic lines – "The best car we ever built I would think" according to Teddy Mayer; Bruce in his 1969 CanAm Championship-winning M8B.

9 — Monterey-Castrol GP, Laguna Seca, California — October 12

Chris Amon's Ferrari went wrong again, so Bruce loaned him the spare M8B, he started from the back of the grid, stopped to replace a body panel, worked his way into sixth place then the diff failed. The Chaparral 2H returned but died on the first pace lap and Jack Oliver made his debut with the Autocoast Ti22. Oh yes, Bruce won, and Denny was second. As always in California the field was large, 31 starters, 16 McLarens.

1 – McLaren; 2 – Hulme; 4 – Mario Andretti M6B-Ford; 6 – Cordts M6B-Ford; 8 – Motschenbacher; 9 – Galloway; 10 – Brown; 11 – McCaig; 13 – Stoddard; 14 – Harrison; 15 – Lasiter; *DNF* – Gurney; Eaton; Monte Shelton M1C; E. Haga M1C; Amon.

10 — Los Angeles Times GP, Riverside, California — October 26

It looked as though Team McLaren was set not only to achieve a highly lucrative hat-trick of CanAm Challenge titles but might even do it with a whitewash this year, winning every round. Denny dominated utterly, lapping all opposition, Bruce's luck ran out when he was holding second as a rear wishbone broke, he charged up a bank and struck and injured an unfortunate marshal, who would recover. The M8B was severely damaged around the tail. Thirty-six qualifiers, 15 McLarens.

1 – Hulme; 3 – Andretti; 4 – Gurney M6B; 8 – Brown; 9 – McCaig; 10 –Stoddard; 13 – Monte Shelton M1C; 16 – Motschenbacher 18 – David Hurley M1C; 19 – Harrison; *DNF* – McLaren; Eaton; Cordts; Galloway; Janke.

11 — Texas CanAm, College Station — November 9

Bruce took an unexpected and unplanned victory to clinch his second CanAm Championship title when Denny's engine blew while leading. It was Bruce's sixth win in the series, having been second three times and retiring twice. Denny had won the other five races for a McLaren whitewash of the series, adding five second places, this his first retirement. Both scored twice as many points as their nearest challenger, Chuck Parsons driving his Lola. Andretti beat the M8Bs for pole with his 8.1 Holman & Moody M6B-Ford but his engine failed him, as did Amon's in the Ferrari.

1 – McLaren; 2 – Eaton; 6 – Motschenbacher; 7 – Causey; 9 – Janke; 10 – McCaig; *DNF* – Hulme; Andretti; Cordts.

1970

For the 1970 CanAm Challenge Trojan's latest production McLaren was numbered M8C – virtually the M12 with M8-style bodies – while the latest development of the works team theme would be known as the M8D. The FIA had forced more strict wing rules upon the liberal North American clubs, and they were re-written to ban any aerodynamic device above the wheel centreline being connected to the suspension. Nor could any "forward facing gap located in the airstream" have a roof higher than 80cm – c. 32 ins – above the bottom of the chassis. The M8Ds prepared at Colnbrook on new chassis used 4in wider tracks than the preceding M8Bs, and low-level rear wings mounted between upswept flaired fins above either rear fender. In testing, engine man George Bolthoff had found the latest 8-litre 700bhp Chevrolet engine too unreliable, and the M8Ds would run 7.5s instead, they said. It was while testing the prototype at Goodwood on June 2, that Bruce was killed.

Team McLaren responded by confirming their entry in the Challenge, with one car for Denny, whose hands were yet to recover fully from burns sustained at Indianapolis, and the other for Bruce's stand-in. Peter Gethin, fresh from McLaren dominance in Formula 5000 on both sides of the Atlantic, was brought in to the Formula 1 team in Denny's place during his recovery, and with Bruce's loss, Dan Gurney re-emerged in Formula 1. Both would also find places in the

CanAm team as it found its feet again . . . Dan appearing alongside Denny, still favouring tender new skin on his hands, in round one at Mosport Park only two weeks after the Goodwood tragedy.

1 — Labatt's Blue Trophy, Mosport, Ontario — June 14
Three M8Ds had been completed so two were available at Mosport where Denny and Dan Gurney arrived to drive them. Two M8Bs from '69 had passed into private hands, continuing Team McLaren's policy of selling anything saleable once it was of no further use to them. Lothar Motschenbacher had the car based on an M8A tub and used as the team spare before Bruce raced it to clinch his title at Texas in the final round. The machine he had crashed at Riverside had gone to enthusiastic Oscar Kovaleski. John Cordts and Roger McCaig ran new M8Cs, the ex-Hall/Surtees M12 went to Jerry Titus and the ex-Eaton car to New Zealander Graeme Lawrence, while Bob Brown had acquired the ex-Gurney 'McLeagle' M6B. Dan took pole from Denny, Jackie Oliver's new Autocoast Ti22 split them in the race and then took the lead when an incident aggravated Denny's already painful hands. Into the closing stages it lay between Oliver and Gurney but with 14 laps to go they found Motschenbacher in their path, Gurney got by but Oliver could not. He tried three times, felt he was being baulked and finally barged by, contact sending the M8B off course into a frighteningly fast accident from which Motschenbacher was lucky to emerge unscathed. Each driver protested the other's actions, but Gurney was away to win, from the Autocoast. There were 28 starters, 15 McLarens.

1 – Gurney M8D; 3 – Hulme M8D; 5 – McCaig M8C; 6 – Gordon Dewar M6B; 10 – Rainer Brezinka M1C; *DNF* – Motschenbacher M8B; Bob Brown M6B; John Cordts M8C; Ron Goldleaf M6B; Oscar Kovaleski M8B; David Hurley M1C; Graeme Lawrence M12; Bill Wonder M1C; Jerry Titus M12; Leonard Janke M1C.

2 — St Jovite-Mt Tremblant, Quebec — June 28
Again Dan took pole from Denny, and driving easily despite an off-song engine he won from Motschenbacher's rebuilt and healthy M8B after Denny's car had overheated into retirement. Oliver qualified third fastest but his car was destroyed in a backwards flip on the opening lap, when the airstream got under its nose and lifted it on the humped straight. Lawrence's M12 was caught in the incident and he retired. A dull race thereafter . . . Twenty-two starters, 13 McLarens.

1 – Gurney; 2 – Motschenbacher; 4 – Brown; 5 – McCaig; 6 – Kovaleski; 7 – Titus/Peter Revson M12; 9 – Cliff Apel M6B; 10 – Horst Petermann M1C; *DNF* – Hulme; Cordts; Dewar, Goldleaf; Lawrence.

3 — CanAm Trophy, Watkins Glen, New York — July 12
Denny was back. His hands hardening-up he took pole from Dan Gurney, and led from start to finish. Dan held second until overheating dropped him back. Jackie Stewart made his debut with the absorbing new sucker-system Chaparral 2J but retired, and Peter Revson's works Lola looked strong until delayed. Team McLaren fitted 1969-spec Type '430' motors of 7.0 rather than 7.6-litres while the big '465s' were returned for analysis of their overheating tendency. With long-distance cars in the field from the Watkins Glen 6-hours the previous day, there were 35 starters, only 11 of them McLarens . . . Five Porsche 917s were in the top seven places . . .

1 – Hulme; 8 – Brown; 9 – Gurney; 12 – Kovaleski; 18 – McCaig; *DNF* – Cordts; Motschenbacher; Lawrence; Apel; Goldleaf; Krank Kahlich M1C.

4 — Klondike Trail '200', Edmonton, Alberta — July 26
Dan Gurney's contractual obligations with Castrol clashed with McLaren's arrangements with Gulf. Teddy Mayer "It seemed as though we could work it out amicably and in fact the sponsors concerned were very good about trying to make

it work, but it became obvious that Dan couldn't fulfil his Castrol obligations in a Gulf car and Gulf team, and very regretfully we had to part . . . We brought in Peter Gethin in his place. And he did far, far better than I thought he would . . ."

The stocky Englishman had shone in Formula 5000 McLarens but before appearing at Edmonton had driven no more than 15 laps in Group 7 machinery, and those at low speed. Now he was thrown-in at the deep end to learn all about the M8D and CanAm competition. The cars were back on 465 engines, exhaustive analysis failing to reveal any clue to the overheating problem. Consequently the car systems had fallen under suspicion, and radiator cores were thickened and airflow ducting modified to improve cooling. And Gethin took second fastest practice time behind Denny and they finished 1-2 in the race, in team order. It was a thin field, and a thin race; 22 starters, half of them McLarens.

1 – Hulme; 2 – Peter Gethin M8D; 3 – Motschenbacher; 4 – Brown; 8 – McCaig; 9 – Janke; *DNF* – Dick Losk M1C; Dewar; Shelton; Cordts; Lawrence.

5 — Buckeye Cup, Mid-Ohio, Lexington — August 23

Denny won from Peter Revson after a terrific drive by the American in his works Lola T990, which battled with Gethin and Motschenbacher. The German-American dropped back with failing brakes, Gethin's engine was unhappy from the start and eventually failed. Graeme Lawrence finished his first race of the series. Twenty-six starters, 12 McLarens. And Motschenbacher bumped Revson and Gethin into the second row of the starting grid, lining up beside Hulme . . .

1 – Hulme; 3 – Motschenbacher; 6 – McCaig; 9 – Gethin; 12 – Lawrence; 14 – Brezinka; *DNF* – Tom Dutton M6B; Dewar; Goldleaf; Janke; Kovaleski; Kahlich.

6 — Road America, Elkhart Lake, Wisconsin — August 30

Peter Gethin loyally finished second behind Denny Hulme and was elevated to win this CanAm round when Denny was disqualified. He had spun and stalled 13 laps from the end. Marshals pushed him clear of the track and reported he used the push to restart, so all laps completed after that push were disallowed. Peter waited for him to come up behind, and waved him by into the 'lead'. Denny was classified 15th. Motschenbacher suffered a mechanical failure, lost a wheel and effectively wrote-off the ex-works M8B. Revson's Lola qualified second fastest alongside Denny and held third until a tyre deflated. Thirty-two starters, 12 McLarens. David Hobbs took over the ex-Hall M12, Jerry Titus having been killed in a TransAm accident.

1 – Gethin; 6 – Brown; 8 – Lawrence; 10 – Goldleaf; 11 – Apel; *DNF* – McCaig; Hulme; Motschenbacher; Kovaleski; David Hobbs M12; Tom Dutton M6B; Kahlich.

7 — Road Atlanta, Georgia — September 13

Back home at Goodwood Denny had been testing the 'M8E' prototype for the 1971 series, 4ins narrower than the '8D with a simple rear wing deleting the side farings and saving 22lbs weight. Suspension geometry had been revised but Teddy announced "We'll only race it this year if the competition gets really strong . . ." It looked to be happening at Atlanta where the M8Ds were out-qualified by Vic Elford making his debut in the Chaparral 2J sucker car with its fan-induced skirt-contained under-car low-pressure area glueing it to the road. But Denny led the race, until he came up to lap a group of back-markers on lap 10 and rammed the tail of Gary Wilson's Lola T163. He limped his tattered M8D into the pits to retire. Gethin led, struck unsignalled oil and crashed into the bank, limping his tattered M8D into the pits to replace the nose. Revson's leading Lola crashed, Bob Brown smashed his faithful McLeagle against the wreck. Peter regained the lead in his repaired works car but after further troubles lost his gears and was out. Tom Dutton crashed his M6B heavily and in a repeat of the Revson/Brown incident Ron Goldleaf's sister car slithered into the wreck. Someone claimed there was $2-million-worth of damage done that afternoon . . .

Tony Dean won, in his humble Porsche 908. Motschenbacher raced his elderly M12. Thirty-one starters, 14 McLarens.

3 – Motschenbacher; 4 – Kovaleski; 5 – McCaig; 7 – Gethin; 9 – Lawrence; 11 – Brezinka; *DNF* – Brown; Dewar; Dutton; Apel; Hulme; Dick Smith; Goldleaf; Wonder.

8 — Minneapolis Tribune CanAm, Donnybrooke, Minnesota — September 27

After Atlanta, Colnbrook built-up a new M8D for Denny from the fabled M8E. Denny explained: "The E was a D tub with B suspension and body, and last week they just took the D tub out of the E, put on 4inch wider track suspension and body to suit". It was plated 'BM 8D/4'. Revson's Lola was on the front row again, on pole! Denny beside him had an easy race to win once Revvie's throttle spring broke. Amon pressed hard in the brand-new March 707. Chaparral missed the race, Peter Gethin was dutifully second from fourth place – out-qualified by Amon – on the grid. Twenty-six starters, only nine McLarens. Vic Elford drove Frank Kahlich's ex-Bonnier '68 M6B.

1 – Hulme; 2 – Gethin; 6 – Motschenbacher; 11 – Lawrence; 12 – Kovaleski; 13 – Dewar; 15 – McCaig; 18 – Brezinka; *DNF* – Elford M6B.

9 — Monterey-Castrol GP, Laguna Seca, California — October 18

Denny and Peter qualified again on the front row, but Jackie Oliver gave Hulme a tough battle for the lead in the best CanAm race since round one at Mosport. Gethin, between them, spun off on oil out of the race. Thirty-two starters, 13 McLarens.

Denny's engine was a new Reynolds unit with pistons running direct in the linerless block. Motschenbacher had a new M8C and turned his M12 over to Tony Adamowicz.

1 – Hulme; 7 – Adamowicz; 10 – Lawrence; 11 – McCaig; 14 – Ed Leslie *DNF* – Motschenbacher; Hobbs; Smith; Gethin; Losk; Dave Selway M1C; Brown; William R. Cupp M1C.

10 — Los Angeles Times GP, Riverside, California — November 1

The Chaparral, the Lola, Peter's second McLaren all broke, the March was slow but Oliver pressed Denny hard as the M8D number one won again. But Elford's Chaparral, despite a storm about its legality, took pole by two seconds, Denny second, Peter *sixth* quickest behind Revson, Oliver and Amon, being troubled by understeer throughout practice. Dick Smith's M12-derivative was tee-boned at speed by Cannon's Agapiou-Ford and was burned out, Smith escaping little harmed; the week before, his house had also burned down . . .

Twenty-nine starters, thin field for Riverside, ten McLarens. Denny was Champion, 132 points, $50,000; Motschenbacher's rugged series yielded second place, 65 points, $35,000 and Peter was third, 56 points, $26,000. Dan Gurney's brief appearance netted him seventh place in the standings, 42 points, $12,000 . . .

1 – Hulme; 5 – Motschenbacher; 6 – Brown; 7 – Adamowicz; 10 – McCaig; 11 – Hills M6B; 15 – Skelton M1C; *DNF* – Gethin; Kovaleski; Lawrence.

──────────────**1971**──────────────

The new year's production CanAm car from Trojan was designated M8E, the works cars taking the designation M8F. Gordon Coppuck had lengthened the wheelbase 3ins since 1970, the monocoque was more robust and the rear brakes had gone inboard. The body shape was little changed, although aerodynamic fences now ran full length either side of the shell, climbing into tail fins to carry a broad rear wing. Engine size was up to 8.1-litres and they were now prepared again by Gary Knutson, back from his second sojourn with Chaparral. They ran Reynolds Aluminum blocks, and delivered a claimed 740bhp. Rear rims were no less than 17ins wide. Peter Revson had joined the team for USAC racing and

CanAm 1970 – parade lap at Laguna Seca with the works M8Ds of Denny Hulme (5) and Peter Gethin (7) on the front row showing the way to Peter Revson's Lola, (26), Jackie Oliver's Autocast (22), Chris Amon's March (77) Bob Bondurant and the two works BRM P154s . . .

would also partner Denny in the big Group 7 sports cars. Denny's 1970 M8D was sold to Tony Dean, and Peter Gethin's to Lothar Motschenbacher. Amongst the customer M8Es, that delivered to American Racing Associates with 8.1 V8 was to be driven by Vic Elford, German driver Franz Pesch hoped to have one, and others went to Roger McCaig, Bob Bondurant, Gary Wilson and Fred Parkhill. Bob Brown was out again in his M6B Spl 'McLeagle', other McLarens being handled by Bill Wonder (M8C), John Cordts (M8C), Oscar Kovaleski (M8D), Rainer Brezinka (M6B), Cliff Apel (M6B), Charlie Kemp (M8C), George Drolsom (M8C) and Tom Dutton (M6B). By this time Group 7 racing had a foothold again in Europe with the rather thin, generally Porsche-dominated Interserie, and M8Es were being campaigned in it by Sid Taylor (driver Peter Gethin), Ecurie Evergreen (Chris Craft), Gesipa Rivets (Willi Kauhsen), Team VDS (Teddy Pilette) and Gelo Racing (George Loos). Main opposition in CanAm would come from Jackie Stewart in a brand-new, carefully-developed Lola, and it was quick.

1 — Mosport Park, Ontario — June 13
Stewart's Lola took pole from Denny with Peter Revson third-quickest, and it led the race until its gearbox failed, Denny's waiting game paying off, as he won from his new team-mate. Motschenbacher was third in his ex-works car while his team's brand-new M8E was modified with his spare D-type rear suspension. Both wore ultra-light honeycomb bodypanelling and the E/D was entrusted to Bob Bondurant. Tony Dean had hurt himself in an F5000 crash, and his ex-Hulme M8D was driven by Chuck Parsons. Tom Dutton's Atlanta-damaged M6B from 1970 had been re-chassised with an M12 tub; Frank Kahlich ran his old M6B. Twenty-four starters, 14 McLarens . . .

1 – Hulme M8F; 2 – Revson M8F; 3 – Motschenbacher M8D; 4 – Bob Bondurant M8E/D; 5 – John Cordts M8C; 6 – Bob Brown M6B; 11 – Dutton M6B; 13 – Stan Sparkowicz M6; *DNF* – Kahlich M6B; Brezinka M6B; Wonder M8C; Kovaleski M8B; Kemp; Rudi Bartling M1C.

2 — St Jovite-Mt Tremblant, Quebec — June 27
Denny took pole from Stewart's Lola and led the race but he felt sick and was growing sicker. Exhausted and gasping for air with his visor open, Denny had to give best to the World Champion who won for Lola, to a huge cheer. It was a CanAm sensation, McLaren beaten. Peter Revson was unable to help. Only 23 starters, 13 McLarens.

2 – Hulme; 3 – Revson; 4 – Parsons M8D; 5 – Motschenbacher M8D; 9 – Dutton; 12 – Brezinka; 14 – Wonder; 15 – George Drolsom M8C; *DNF* – Bondurant; Brown; Cordts; McCaig; Goldleaf.

3 — Road Atlanta, Georgia — July 11
With Coca-Cola sponsorship in addition to Goodyear-Gulf-Reynolds, Peter Revson won the first American round in the 1971 Challenge series starting from second-quickest time beside Hulme, who was handicapped by insufficient brakes during the race. Stewart led before retirement in the Lola. Peter used a Reynolds linerless engine for the first time in the series. Twenty-five starters, 13 McLarens.

1 – Revson; 2 – Hulme; 3 – Motschenbacher; 4 – Adamowicz (Kovaleski M8B); 7 – McCaig; 8 – Dutton; 9 – Kemp; 16 – Drolsom; 17 –Elford (Roy Woods Racing M8E); 19 – David Hobbs (Dean M8D); 20 – Wonder; 21 – Bondurant; 23 – Kahlich M6B.

4 — Watkins Glen, New York — July 25
Jackie Stewart started from pole and led again but Peter kept him in sight and took the lead when the Lola punctured. Denny, convinced his engine was not pulling properly, was never a factor. He stopped to replace a broken wheel, thereupon broke the lap record on his fight back. The field was packed with endurance cars, from the 6-Hours the day before. Peter ran a linerless block engine, out to

8.3-litres.

1 – Revson; 2 – Hulme; 5 – Adamowicz; 8 – Elford; 12 – Cordts; 14 – Brown; 15 – Dutton; 16 – Bondurant; 18 – Charlie Kemp M8C; 23 – Apel; 25 – McCaig; 26 – Hobbs; 27 – Motschenbacher.

5 — Mid-Ohio, Lexington — August 22
The works cars qualified side-by-side at the head of the grid but both broke in the race, the Lola lasted and Stewart won. Denny broke a UJ cross in Turn 1 on the opening lap, spun and was rammed by Dave Causey's Lola T222. Peter led unchallenged by Stewart who was anxious to conserve his car on the bumpy course. With the lead out to 20secs Peter had an identical UJ failure to his team-mate's with only 8½-laps remaining. Denny's car ran an 8.1 V8, Peter's a 7.9. Twenty-seven starters, 13 McLarens.

3 – Adamowicz; 7 – Revson; 8 – Dutton; 11 – Sparkowitz; 13 – McCaig; 15 – Kemp; *DNF* – Motschenbacher; Drolsom; Elford; Brown; Bob Nagel M12; Hulme; Bob Klempel M1C.

6 — Road America, Elkhart Lake, Wisconsin — August 29
Denny started on pole from Jack Oliver's Shadow, Stewart on row 2 and Peter at the back of the grid with no practice time due to USAC commitments. He reached second place after 11 race laps and when Denny's engine broke Peter won, Stewart retired, Oliver delayed by punctures. Twenty-three starters, ten McLarens. Denny's M8F rebuilt with outboard rear brakes.

1 – Revson; 3 – Elford; 4 – Motschenbacher; 7 – Dutton; 9 – Drolsom ; *DNF* – Sparkowitz M12; Hulme; Adamowicz; Kahlich; Greg Young M8E/D.

7 — Donnybrooke, Brainerd, Minnesota — September 12
The M8Fs headed the grid, Peter on pole but Stewart's Lola led for 2½ laps before 'Revvy' found a way by and drove away to a most convincing victory. Stewart was delayed by a pit stop to investigate a strange vibration and Denny, conserving high engine temperatures, drove home second. Twenty-four starters, 13 McLarens. Peter clinched McLaren's fifth title in the six years of CanAm racing.

1 – Revson; 2 – Hulme; 3 – Young; 4 – Elford; 8 – Brown M8E; 12 – Dutton; 13 – Sparkowitz; 14 – Drolsom; 15 – Fred Parkhill M8E. *DNF* – Wilson M12; McCaig; Motschenbacher; Apel M6.

8 — Edmonton, Alberta — September 26
Peter sat on pole, Stewart led 67 of the 80 laps but Denny won his first CanAm round for three long, dry months. Jackie's Lola had slowed with a rear suspension problem and eventually spun, allowing Hulme into the lead. Peter started 11 laps late when a 3/8in bolt dropped down an injection trumpet. Skullduggery was suspected but could not be proved. It was removed and Peter finished 12th. Twenty-two starters, half of them McLarens.

1 – Hulme; 6 – Cordts; 7 – Motschenbacher; 8 – Parons; 9 – Drolsom; 10 – Wilson; 12 – Revson; 13 – Losk; *DNF* – Dutton; Brown; McCaig.

9 — Monterey Castrol GP, Laguna Seca, California — October 17
The M8Fs on the front row again, Peter on pole, and he won despite some controversy. He was black-flagged for dropping oil as he started his last lap, but ignored it and drove on. But at the end of the lap he was not given the chequered flag. Jackie Stewart was, after completing 91 laps instead of the scheduled 90. Peter drove into the winner's circle, his car smoking heavily, its tail and exhaust dripping oil. Lola entrant Carl Haas protested Revson's disregard of the black flag, but the stewards decided to let the finish stand, as at 90 laps, though they fined the winner $250. Denny was third, on the same lap as his team-mate and Stewart. In pre-race testing Vic Elford ran the Roy Woods M8E with ex-works M8D body panelling though the standard narrow M8E tracks, and crashed it

backwards into a bridge abutment at around 100mph. He emerged virtually unscathed, but the car was destroyed. Woods bought Tony Dean's M8D, rebuilt since its Mid-Ohio shunt to D specs but with a production M8E tub. Vic found it much more to his liking with its wide-track stability. Thirty-two starters, 15 McLarens.

1 – Revson; 3 – Hulme; 6 – Motschenbacher; 7 – Adamowicz; 10 – Parsons; 12 – Dutton; 14 – Hills; 15 – Wilson; 16 – Drolsom: *DNF* – Brown; Elford; McCaig; Ron Stafford M1C; Gary Burke M1C; Chuck McConnel GP7.

10 — Los Angeles Times GP, Riverside, California — October 31

Both M8Fs ran sleeveless 8.3 V8s, the Roy Woods team ran George Follmer in their M8D and the M8E was rebuilt around a fresh tub for Sam Posey. Denny took pole by a whole second from his team-mate, he led from start to finish, Jackie Stewart receding in second place until the Lola's engine failed. Peter drove conservatively to finish second. Tom Dutton placed 11th to complete nine finishes from ten starts – virtually a CanAm record for a privateer. For everyone else it was a normal CanAm; they all broke down. Twenty-nine starters, 13 McLarens.

1 – Hulme; 2 – Revson; 4 – Posey; 5 – Parsons; 7 – McCaig; 8 – Wilson; 9 – Follmer; 10 – Kemp; 11 – Dutton; 12 – Sparkowicz; *DNF* – Adamowicz; Hills, Motschenbacher.

1972

"People are saying that this year's first CanAm round is going to be like an old Western movie, with just us and Porsche facing one another down the main street; and when that's over, there's only going to be one of us left for the rest of the series . . ."

Gordon Coppuck was commenting on prospects for the 1972 CanAm series. Porsche were coming in with a turbocharged G7 version of their thunderous flat-12 *Typ* 917 long-distance and Interserie cars. They had toyed with CanAm before, the 917/10 turbo was going to be something far more serious, and Roger Penske was to run the team, with Mark Donohue as driver, and other cars with less works support would be sold. I was at Weissach studying Porsche developments one day that May when Donohue appeared in the incredibly scruffy turbo-development hack. I described and photographed the car for the US weekly *Autoweek*, and heard later that Roger Penske himself had gone ape, as "some spy" had pre-empted his plans for a sensational US press launch. Porsche had invited us to Weissach in sweet innocence.

McLaren had been testing their answer to the turbo Porsche threat at Silverstone and Goodwood, Gordon's M20 marking a new beginning after the long and supremely-successful M8 series had reached its worthwhile development limit in the M8F the previous year.

He had three main aims; first to produce another CanAm winner in a neater package; second to achieve a low polar moment with most of the car's mass concentrated well within the wheelbase; and third to insulate the cockpit more effectively from radiator heat, to give the drivers a more comfortable time.

Consequently the new M20 had a marked 'coke bottle' planform, widest across the cockpit where the fuel tankage was concentrated in two sill tanks and for the first time a seat-back tank. Total capacity was 79 US gallons, the seat-back tank helping cool the driver. But main move here was to mount the radiators on either hip, behind the cockpit. A longer cast bell-housing between engine and Hewland gearbox extended the wheelbase 2ins from the M8F's 98in figure, effectively pushing the 8.1-litre engine mass further forward within the wheelbase.

Without radiators in the nose, Gordon took the opportunity to mount a wing or 'dive-plane' between the forward extremities of the front fenders, balancing its effect with a full-width rear wing in end-plate fins on the tail. Air ducting sunk into the doors fed the hip radiators either side just behind the cockpit, large-area oil coolers using the same intakes. But for detail geometry changes, suspension was

identical to the M8F's but for the first time loads were fed into localised steel inserts on the aluminium-sheet monocoque, instead of into full-width steel bulkheads front and rear. The engine was of course semi-stressed, steadied on the rear of the tub by tubular A-frames either side.

Team organiser Phil Kerr had done a much-publicised deal for Jackie Stewart to join Denny Hulme in the team, but he missed mid-season F1 races with ulcer trouble, opted out of the CanAm drive and at Mosport for round one, the Western shoot-out, Peter Revson filled the breach . . .

CanAm '71 with Denny's M8F showing off its wing fences under heavy pressure from Jackie Stewart's L&M Lola T260 at Laguna's Turn 9.

1 — Mosport Park, Ontario — June 11

Donohue took pole in Penske's *Panzer* on its race debut but Peter was alongside in M20/3 and Denny right behind in M20/2. Neither car was behaving well, leaping around over the bumps, suffering too much understeer and displaying poor brakes. But after the Porsche lost its lead with induction system problems and three laps in the pits it was Peter who took the lead. Denny was second with a very sick engine, and by repeatedly breaking the lap record Donohue looked set to catch him. Peter re-took the lap record from Donohue and was leading comfortably just two laps from the end when his engine plumed smoke and his hopes were dashed. Donohue was on the same lap as Denny and closing fast. Had the race been two laps longer he might well have won, as it was, the M20 notched victory on its debut. But the writing was on the wall . . . A number of other CanAm Porsches started the race, taking a 4-5 finish for Milt Minter and Peter Gregg. Roger McCaig's McLaren M8FP was a production version of the 1971 Champion car, pleasing his team no end. Greg Young ran the ex-Hulme M8F, Francois Cevert due to join his team at Atlanta. Lothar Motschenbacher ran his '71 ex-works M8D virtually unchanged while his M8E/D was sold to Steve Durst. Gord Dewar returned with a previously unraced M8C in D-type bodywork. Only 18 cars started a race whose regulations permitted 35 – nine of them were McLarens.

1 – Hulme M20; 3 – Revson M20; 6 – Motschenbacher M8D; 7 – Durst M8E/D; 8 – Dewar M8C/D; 11 – Bill Wonder M8C; 13 – R.D. Klempel M1C; *DNF* – Young M8F; McCaig M8FP.

2 — Road Atlanta, Georgia — July 9

Atlanta again saw its share of mayhem. Jackie Stewart had decided finally to withdraw from his planned McLaren drive, and Peter replaced him formally. In testing pre-race Donohue crashed horrifically in the Penske Porsche turbo, destroying it. George Follmer was enlisted to race Penske's turbo spare – the pre-season test car. Denny had been testing too. Spacers increased the M20's front track 1.8 ins, longer rear suspension links spread the wheels 2 ins. The original nose brake cooling ducts, shadowed by the wing, were blanked-off and new ducts cut in the outer wedges. The rear wing was outrigged, this mod eventually going onto Peter's car as there was no time to make him wider rear suspension before the event. Greg Young's team entered their ex-Revson M8F unmodified for François Cevert, Stewart's F1 Tyrrell team-mate. McCaig had crashed at Mosport, his M8FP's tub had been rebuilt. John Cordts appeared in the ex-works, ex-Dean, ex-Woods M8D now owned by Overhauser. Cevert enlivened practice, 2 secs faster in the M8F than Revson had run the previous year. Peter had a monstrous practice engine blow-up, scattering hot fragments as he skated, wheels locked, many a yard. Denny took pole from Follmer, Peter and Cevert on row two. On lap 5, chasing Follmer hard, Denny's M20 reared-up into a 180mph back-flip and was totally destroyed. The hard-headed Kiwi was knocked unconscious but emerged after a rest in hospital with no serious harm, perhaps thankfully he could not recall the accident. Peter witnessed it all, his M20 having stopped at the spot two laps earlier with an ignition problem. He helped extract his team-mate from the wreckage, then fixed his own engine, rejoined the race and set a new lap record before retiring finally with no oil pressure. Untroubled, Follmer gave the Penske Porsche turbo its maiden CanAm victory. Cevert's debut ended in engine failure after a fine run, Greg Young was second. Twenty-five starters, 13 McLarens.

2 – Young; 6 Motschenbacher; 10 – McCaig. *DNF* – Hulme; Revson; Cevert; Durst; Dewar; Devine; Wonder; Drolsom; Klempel; Cordts M8D.

3 — CanAm Challenge Cup, Watkins Glen, New York — July 23

In nine days the team built-up the prototype M20 as a new race car for Denny, incorporating the Atlanta lessons, wider front track using long wishbones instead of spacers, both cars now with the outrigged rear wings. Tom Dutton ran Drolsom's M8C, Kovaleski had sold his ex-works M8B to TransAm racer Warren Agor, who fitted an iron-block 7-litre for his CanAm debut. In practice Denny found his head buzzing under cornering G, a legacy of the Atlanta incident. He and Peter still qualified on the front row, Revvie on pole. Follmer's Porsche was in deep trouble, and Denny was right enough on the day to lead Team McLaren's first 1-2 of the series. Twenty-two starters, nine McLarens.

1 – Hulme; 2 – Revson; 3 – Cevert; 7 – Motschenbacher; 13 – Dutton; 14 – Agor. *DNF* – Young; Durst; McCaig.

4 — Mid-Ohio, Lexington — August 6

By race time Peter's rear wing was forward in its original position, otherwise the M20s were unchanged. The weather chopped and changed all race, Denny made five tyre-change stops and finished fourth, Peter's car ran poorly and failed. Gary Wilson rejoined the series with the ex-McCaig '71 M8E and Alan Johnson of SCCA fame made his debut with the ex-Woods M8E. Dewar's M8C received a Porsche-style nose. Though ungainly he claimed it won him an instant 4 secs per lap . . . Follmer took pole from the M20s . . . and beat them. Jackie Oliver's Shadow was second, Minter's Porsche third . . .

4 – Hulme; 7 – Dewar; 8 – Wilson; 9 – Agor; 11 – Cevert; 12 – Kahlich M12; 13 – Alan Johnson M8E; 16 – McCaig M8F; 17 – Klempel M1C; 19 – Durst; 20 – Drolsom.

5 — Road America, Elkhart Lake, Wisconsin — August 27

Denny took pole convincingly – by almost 3 secs – from Cevert's Young American team ex-works M8F, and led handsomely only for ignition failure after 12 brief laps to put him out. Peter missed much of practice; he was at Ontario, California qualifying for the USAC 500-miles. He then started down the field, only for a slipping clutch to prevent him running higher than fifth before retirement. Gulf McLaren's iron grip on CanAm was loosening. The old reliability had gone. Follmer's Porsche turbo won, Cevert's sick M8F was second. No less than thirty-three starters – 18 McLarens. Motschenbacher was recovering from an F5000 accident, hiring his car to Brett Lunger. Dave Causey drove the ex-Gurney ex-Bob Brown 'McLeagle' M6B special, and George Drolsom ran the Burmeister M8C, Tom Dutton being given the ride for the rest of the series.

2 – Cevert; 5 – Young; 6 – Wilson; 9 – Agor; 10 – McCaig, 11 – Cordts M8D; 12 – Brett Lunger M8D; 13 – Drolsom; 15 – Wonder; 16 – Durst; 17 – Peter Sherman M12; 18 – Dave Causey M6B; 20 –Klempel M1C: *DNF* – Dewar; Revson; Kahlich; Hulme; Ed Felter M8E.

6 — Donnybrooke, Brainerd, Minnesota — September 17

Mark Donohue was fit enough despite a still-damaged knee to drive a new Penske Porsche alongside George Follmer and they qualified 1-2 and the Gulf-McLarens were really struggling. Personnel problems did not help. Both cars ran drilled brake discs instead of grooved, rears outboard to insulate them from gearbox heat. Both cars had their rear wings mounted more neatly 6ins further outboard and wore Porsche-size giant Goodyears, 2ins wider and larger in diameter (28ins) than previously, Denny's on 19in rims, Peter's on 17s. His engine blew mightily at 7,000rpm in top, around 195mph, on the long Donnybrooke straight in practice. Denny was growling bearishly about turbocharger boost screws and teams who could summon up an extra hundred horsepower by a turn of the screwdriver . . . In race morning warm-up with a fresh engine Peter equalled Follmer's front-grid qualifying time. The race began with a fearsome Porsche-McLaren duel, Donohue, Denny, Follmer, Peter – Denny was comfortable on Donohue's tail when his block split and he was out. Peter clung on behind the Porsches until lap 25 of the 70, "it felt like a valve had dropped" he reported from the passenger seat of a marshal's car. But at top speed Donohue burst a tyre, Follmer led but ran dry of fuel on the final lap. Cevert tore by to victory, in the year-old ex-works McLaren . . .

Jerry Grant appeared with a 1968-chassised M8, serialled an M8D but carrying M8F bodywork. Warren Agor passed his M8D over to TransAm associate Kent Fellows, replacing it with a new production M8F. Hans Wiedmer from Switzerland appeared with his M8F and local driver Jerry Rosebeach produced the ex-Craft ex-Brown M8E.

1 – Cevert; 5 – Cordts; 6 – Motschenbacher; 7 – Felter; 9 – Sherman; 12 – Rosebeach; 13 – Ole Thornsjo M12; 14 – Fellows; 15 – Agor; 16 – Causey; 18 – Dutton; 19 – Wiedmer; 20 – Young; 21 – Revson; 24 – Durst; 25 – Wilson; 26 – Grant; 27 – Hulme; 28 – Kahlich; *DNS* – Dewar.

7 — Edmonton, Alberta — October 1

Porsche regained their grip; Donohue won, Follmer dropped to third with a puncture, but Denny led the first 31 laps, Peter had two stops and Cevert lost third when a half-shaft broke. The M20s ran detuned engines in search of reliability. Greg Young's engine blew in practice, the transmission seized and his McLaren flipped at almost 200mph. The driver was shaken but miraculously unharmed, as was George Follmer whose Porsche passed beneath the somersaulting M8F . . . Twenty-one starters, 11 McLarens.

2 – Hulme; 6 – Revson; 7 – Motschenbacher; 8 – Wiedmer; 11 – Dutton; 12 – Cordts; 13 – Agor; 15 – Cevert; 17 – Wilson; 18 – Dave Morris M12B; 20 – Kahlich.

8 — Monterey GP, Laguna Seca, California — October 15

George Follmer could clinch the CanAm title for himself and the Penske Porsches at Laguna, and he did so. Mark Donohue started from pole and led virtually the whole way, just rolling it off at the end to let his team-mate take the flag first. Penske were in the position Gulf-McLaren had enjoyed for five years past. The race was over as such just after half distance, when both M20s retired. Jackie Oliver's Shadow went very well, splitting the orange cars and Cevert started from the back of the grid, finished third. Denny's hopes failed with a cam-drive chain, Peter's with his transmission. Indy Rookie-of-the-Year Mike Hiss drove the Jerry Grant M8-hybrid ex-Donnybrooke, Chuck Parsons took over McCaig's M8FP, Mark Waco the ex-Kovaleski M8B. Steve Durst heavily damaged his M8E/D in practice. Thirty-three starters, 17 McLarens.

3 – Cevert; 10 – Wilson; 11 – Motschenbacher; 12 – Bill Cuddy M8E; 13 – Robert Peckham M8C; 15 – Mark Waco M8B; 17 – Wiedmer; *DNF* – Revson; Hulme; Hiss; Cordts; Durst; Dutton; Parsons; Felter; Kahlich; Agor.

9 — Los Angeles Times GP, Riverside, California — October 29

Denny qualified brilliantly on the front row, and the promise of a real race between the Porsches and the M20s looked bright, the four cars astonishingly close on times. But Denny's engine went off song, he dropped back and eventually retired. The Penske Porsches led Peter's car but his engine was also faltering. Follmer was able to return the Laguna favour, and roll it off to let Donohue move ahead, but Mark had a tyre deflating and stopped to change it. Follmer unexpectedly took his fifth win in the series and Peter was second in Gulf Team McLaren's final CanAm appearance – 45secs behind the new sophistication . . . Fifteen McLarens in the field, Cuddy withdrawing his M8D after a heavy practice accident.

2 – Revson; 7 – Hiss; 11 – Peckham; 12 – Kahlich; 13 – Dutton; 15 – Fellows; 18 – Wiedmer; 20 – Hulme; 22 – Wilson; 23 – Cevert; 26 – Motschenbacher; 27 – Felter; 31 – Parsons; 32 – Cordts; 33 – Waco.

Denny was runner-up in the Challenge points standings, with 65 compared to Follmer's title-winning 130, Mint Minter (Porsche) was third with 65, Mark Donohue fourth with 62, Cevert had 59 and Revson 48 . . . Second and sixth for the five-times Champions . . . There would be no more works McLarens in CanAm racing – they could not match Porsche's investment in turbocharged engine technology.

Teddy and Phil Kerr announced at the end of that year that Team McLaren could not compete effectively with Porsche on grounds of prohibitive turbo technology development costs, and there were no works McLarens in the 1973 CanAm series. Roy Woods had bought the ex-Revson M20 and entrusted it to David Hobbs with Carling Black Label beer sponsorship. David drove well throughout the series but could only salvage seventh overall in the final standings; the best McLaren behind six turbo Porsches.

Three McLarens were campaigned by the big-money Commander Motor Homes team, including an M20 rebuilt from Denny's '72 Atlanta wreck and fitted with a twin-turbocharged dual-fuel injection system 465 cubic inch (7.6-litre) Reynolds-Chevrolet V8 engine for Mario Andretti. One injection system was boosted by the turbochargers, the other naturally aspirated to give an effective rev band between 4,400 and 6,800rpm. At 6,600rpm they claimed to have seen 1,200bhp on the test-bed, with torque over 1,000ft/lbs. A Weisman transaxle was used, carrying copy-cat McLaren M20 suspension now hung on its casing.

The team's hip-radiatored CanAm McLaren M20 of 1972 could not hold off the turbo-Porsche challenge and at long last the marque's grip on the North American Championship was broken. Denny Hulme and his team-mate Peter Revson – seen here – fought a valiant rearguard action but the M20 was to be McLaren's last CanAm contender.

Additional cooling radiators were required, and Andretti's Firestone contract proved a further handicap. The car was no Porsche-beater.

The team's ex-works M8F and customer Trojan-built M8FP were driven by Milt Minter, Danny Hopkins, Bob Brown and John Cannon during the series, while Scooter Patrick campaigned another ex-works M8F owned by Herb Kaplan's US Racing Team, and John Cordts went well in Bill Overhouser's M8D, amongst the usual bevy of US and Canadian club racers.

By 1974 the CanAm series was Shadow-dominated, the Penske Porsches having retired with Mark Donohue (temporarily in his case) after dominating the '73 season, and the series as a viable International Championship was dead. Its heyday as "The Bruce and Denny Show" was now mere fond memory.

Interserie

In Europe an attempt had been made to set-up a similar Group 7 sports-racing car series to CanAm, starting in 1970 with a few pilot races in which British clothier Alistair Cowin ran his club-racing McLaren M6B/M12 hybrid to finish fourth in the *Challenge International* at Dijon, David Prophet's M12 was second at Magny-Cours, and Chris Craft's wailing Cosworth DFV V8-engined M8C – owned and entered by Ecurie Evergreen – won the Swedish Grand Prix outright at Karlskoga.

For 1971 an Interserie Association was formed, based in Stuttgart, to promote the new series, but they could not attract enough money to make the series genuinely viable and attractive, and the basic ingredients emerged as three

Porsche 917 Spyders, four CanAm McLaren M8Es, a BRM P167, March 717, a 7-litre Ferrari 512M 'special' plus a handful of others. Nine races were planned, only seven took place, and while Leo Kinnunen dominated in his Porsche 917 Spyder, Peter Gethin was runner-up in Sid Taylor's Castrol-sponsored McLaren M8E with 8.1 Chevrolet V8 engine. Chris Craft's Ecurie Evergreen M8E ran a 7,6-litre engine, and he was second in the opening round at Imola where the Sid Taylor car was unable to appear.

At Zolder for round two Gethin won easily, while Teddy Pilette effectively wrote-off the Belgian Team VDS M8C when a rear wishbone broke. Derek Bell deputised for Gethin – racing in Formula 1 – at Hockenheim and won easily while Pilette emerged in a brand new M8E replacing the Zolder wreck. Craft won in Alain de Cadanet's Evergreen car at Norisring where wealthy German privateer Georg Loos was fourth in his 8.1-litre sister car, and at Keimola in an eight-car field Gethin was second, having to start from the back of the grid. Bell retired the Taylor car back at Hockenheim for the final round, while Taylor's team had taken on the BRM P167 alongside their M8E and it won the race, driven by Brian Redman.

In 1972 another poorly-supported Interserie was Porsche dominated, again by Kinnunen. Teddy Pilette's VDS McLaren M8F ran with a turbo-charged 7.6-litre Chevvy engine – the jovial Belgian describing its handling always as "Terrific" by which he meant a combination of terrible and horrific . . . Denny Hulme had tested the car for the team at Goodwood, and the weighbridge showed VDS's creation to weigh no less than 500lbs more than Denny's '71 M8F, and only a quarter of that excess could be traced to turbocharging gear. Georg Loos chose between his Porsche 917 Spyder and M8F during the series while Franz Pesch drove a sister Gelo Team M8E. Helmut Kelleners ran a Weisberg-sponsored 8.1-litre M8F and Rieger campaigned a 7.6 M8C.

For 1973 it was the same old story, Leo Kinnunen and Porsche taking the Interserie Championship for the third consecutive season. Helmut Kellener's backers had acquired the ex-Hulme McLaren M20 from the '72 CanAm Championship defence while with Colnbrook out of sports car design Trojan had no production cars to offer for the new year. Kelleners eventually set the M20 aside to join the Porsche *Panzer* Division, while the old Kelleners M8E was hired out to Michel Weber, and Englishman Kaye Griffiths ran his similar car on occasion. As in CanAm, it was no contest . . . and the series lay down and died.

Chapter 4
The Indy Cars

On Johnny Rutherford, twice works McLaren Indy winner:
"After winning the race in 1976 and then completing only
one lap in 1977 he said; 'Oh well, Chicken one day, feathers
the next . . .' "
Indianapolis 500 Year Book, 1978

When McLaren signed with Goodyear in 1967 they were told that the tyre company regarded their sponsorship partly as an investment in a future Indianapolis programme. Firestone had dominated the Indy track classic since its inception in 1911. Goodyear was altogether a larger concern, but lacked the competition-bred image of Firestone. They had moved into competition in the late-'fifties in stock car and West Coast-type sports car road racing, and through the 'sixties showed increasing interest in attacking Firestone's prestigious Indy bastion.

It was under Goodyear's auspices that the catastrophic Shelby American turbocars had been built for Indy '68 to be driven by Bruce and Denny Hulme. The cars were under-powered, under-developed and the legality of their engines became suspect, and virtually overnight during qualifying the project was abandoned. It was Bruce's first experience of Indy, but Denny had been there the previous year when he finished fourth in Smokey Yunick's Ford V8-engined Eagle. After the Shelby turbocar's withdrawal he took over a works Eagle entered by Dan Gurney, and finished fourth again. Denny was also Eagle-mounted in 1969, but retired with clutch trouble, being classified 18th. He ran as high as second, while Bruce and the team were at Mosport in Canada listening to the radio commentary: "and when Denny was up in second place and then dropped out, we kind of looked at each other and said 'To hell with it, let's have a go and build a car for him . . ." as Teddy recalls.

The final decision was taken in July '69 and at Colnbrook Gordon Coppuck set about design, basing the USAC single-seater on CanAm sports car experience in general tub layout and conception, intending to use what had become the dominant engine – a 2.65-litre Garrett-turbocharged Offenhauser four-cylinder.

The prototype M15 as the new type was known, was completed early in November '69 and rushed to Indy, because Bruce wanted to test there before the onset of winter. "I don't believe in arriving at Gasoline Alley on May 1 with an untried car . . ."

Once again the M15 was essentially a very simple machine. The broad monocoque tub was skinned in 16-gauge Reynolds Aluminum sheet over three sheet-steel fabricated bulkheads and terminated just behind the cockpit where the Offy engine was bolted to two engine bearer plates on the rear bulkhead with two A-brackets running along either side of the crankcase to pick-up on the special magnesium bell-housing which had been made to unite the tall American engine and the Hewland LG500 four-speed gearbox.

Rear suspension was carried on the gearbox in similar fashion to the M8-series CanAm car's, with conventional single top links, reversed lower wishbones and twin radius rod layout, while at the front McLaren's usual single lateral links with radius rods trailing to pick-ups on the monocoque flanks were retained. The steering box was mounted behind the driver's feet and as on the CanAm cars the radiator was slung in an integral aluminium sheet outrigger doubling as an accident impact absorber.

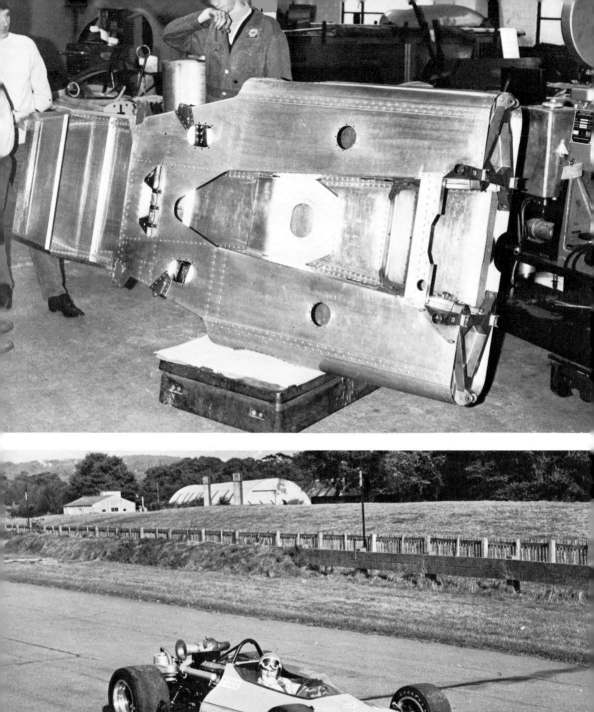

The Goodyear safety fuel cells tucked within each sill totalled 68 US gallons capacity, this fuel load dictating the broad flat profile of the car. Fuel consumption was predicted to be around 2mpg, and Avery Hardoll spill-proof aircraft fillers were mounted on each sill tank. Lockheed disc brakes were fitted all round and McLaren-designed BRD half-shafts were used. The brake pedal was interesting, almost 6 ins wide because Denny favoured left-foot braking at Indy, allowing him to maintain engine revs with his right foot and so minimise throttle lag with the turbocharged engine.

USAC regulations specified that the suspension components, anti-roll bars and roll-over bars should be made in chrome-moly SAE 4130 material. Wheel sizes were restricted to 10in wide at the front, 14ins rear. The Offy engine delivered around 650bhp at 9,000rpm on Hilborn fuel injection and weighed 475lbs. Its purchase price alone was £10,500 ... The new McLaren weighed-in around 1,350lbs, 30lbs over the minimum weight limit. Weight distribution was approximately 30:70 front:rear.

The new prototype was completed exactly a week after the Riverside CanAm race and Colnbrook reverberated to the deep-throated boom of the Offy engine being run-up in the workshop. The age-old engine line, based on a 1931 design, caused some amusement. One wag talked of painting a sign on the rear of the monocoque: "1970 Stops Here!"

Next morning the M15 was at Goodwood, where Denny discovered all about turbo engine throttle lag on a road circuit, and smartly spun off. Bruce clinched the CanAm Championship the following weekend at College Station, Texas, while the M15 had been flown to Indy. The drivers Bruce, Denny and Chris Amon arrived there on the Monday morning, and spent the week testing extensively. The Indy practice of only allowing one car out on the circuit at a time during testing hampered their running, but Denny lapped at 168mph and Bruce was quickly up to 162. He commented: "Two months ago we were saying 'Right, remember now, it's just another race . . . but there's never been a single race that we've got this excited about . . .'"

By the time the prototype and two race cars had been prepared for the qualifying month of May at Indianapolis the following year they had a rear tyre load-sharing interlink system and driver-controlled front ride-height jacks built-in, the latter idea being to adjust settings as the hefty fuel load burned-off. Gordon Coppuck recalls: "We had added bits and pieces and ended-up with cars about 100lbs over the design weight. Even so, they were the lightest cars at Indy. But we were strangers there. You're up against USAC drivers who go there perhaps several times a year testing, and who know the circuit. They know which months it's good and which months it isn't, and can say with absolute assurance 'It's going to be a slow day'. They could do this while we could have been there on a slow day struggling to make the cars go fast and getting nowhere. We could only be guided by their experience and what they were prepared to tell us. Bobby Unser in particular was quite helpful. He was quicker than we were during that first November test, but he gave us confidence, we weren't on a wild goose chase . . ."

The American track-racing establishment was extremely impressed with the finish and turn-out of the new McLaren, as their CanAm road-racing compatriots had been before them. But Chris Amon found himself unable to adjust to the specialised technique of driving at Indy. Teddy Mayer: "He was man enough to say 'I'm not enjoying this – I'd rather not try to qualify' and he gave us the chance to find a replacement. Then Denny got burned . . ."

The M15s had snap-down caps covering their fuel fillers, but USAC insisted they fit an extra spring to help it flip open at fuel stops. Ironically, vibration in the car at speed caused this spring to flip-open the cap at speed, whereupon the airflow drew out raw fuel . . .

Denny saw the droplets coursing up his windscreen like rain and at the next turn, as he stamped on the brakes, fuel gushed forward from the flapping left-side filler, whipped up in the airstream and sprayed back over the engine where the red-hot turbocharger casing flashed it into flame.

Methanol burns invisibly. At 180mph Denny only knew of searing heat. The harder he braked the more fuel fed the fire. He feared an explosion. His hands were burning, his leather gloves shrinking, clawing his fingers as he punched at his harness buckle. The onboard fire extinguisher went off in a blurr of white, without notable effect, and the windscreen was crumpling down, melting . . .

The car was down to around 70mph, Denny standing in the cockpit. Then he jumped trying to clear the rear wheel. The fire tender raced down the infield verge chasing the car, but Denny's overalls were still burning. Helpers couldn't see it. At last both fires were extinguished, the rugged New Zealander having suffered deep burns on his hands. Eoin Young: "Sitting up in hospital in Indianapolis, coming and going with the pain-killing drugs, his hands, feet and left forearm caked in white tacky dressing like icing, Denny was still able to chat and titter when Bruce and others in the team called to see him each day. The burns were extremely serious and there was the unspoken chance that he would lose some fingers on his left hand. Bruce was terribly concerned at his condition, their closeness in times of trouble showing through as clearly as it had when they travelled together between races like a couple of kids out on a treat . . ."

Bruce and Teddy had the immediate problem of replacing Amon and Hulme as drivers. Peter Revson and Carl Williams were available and took the rides, Peter running well before retirement and Williams finishing ninth.

Back home, immediately after the race, Bruce died at Goodwood.

His team carried on, as did their Indy-racing programme, for while the annual Memorial Day 500-Miles was the most prestigious race on the USAC calendar it was just one of a whole Championship Trail series. Team McLaren would concentrate on only the major races, like Indy and later the Ontario (California) and Pocono 500s which joined it, while other teams would take McLaren cars into a full track-racing season. In later years McLaren tackled the whole series too.

In September '70 the inaugural California '500' was held at Ontario Motor Speedway. Peter Revson qualified his Gulf-McLaren M15A on row four while Gordon Johncock qualified one of the other two team cars which he had just acquired post-Indy on the following row. Peter ran second, then took the lead when Al Unser's Colt crashed. But in his final pit stop the M15A's engine refused to restart, and a coil-change cost several laps. Gordy Johncock finally finished fourth, Peter frustratedly fifth.

Towards the end of that USAC season McLaren thought about the new year. Gordon Coppuck: "We had learned a lot about Indy, and started to think about the new year. By the end of July '70 the wedge-shaped Lotus 72 was going extremely well in Formula 1, and we concluded that that was probably a very good basic design for an Indy car. We weren't convinced that it was right for a GP car" Ralph Bellamy – Gordon's ex-Brabham co-designer at Colnbrook was completing his M19 at that time – "but for Indy we thought it must be a dead cinch . . .

"Your aerodynamic forces are very constant at Indy, with only about a 60mph difference in running speed at each corner; you're doing about 210mph on the straights and 150mph through the corners. We decided on these basic parameters for our design at the end of July, and then at Ontario "– for the California '500' with the M15s – "our car was second-lightest to Johnny Rutherford's modified '68 Eagle. That was a warning to us to keep to the design weight.

"I started drawing in September. We took our time building proper race cars without bothering with an initial prototype, and the car was ready in January . . ."

Shown to the press at Colnbrook in January '71, the McLaren M16 looked sensational. The hip-radiatored wedge-nosed car was based on a tapering monocoque skinned in 16-gauge L72 Reynolds Aluminum sheet. The door-stop glass-fibre nose cone contained nothing more than fire-extinguisher and master

Denny Hulme, CanAm Champion 1968, in the gleaming papaya-liveried works Gulf-McLaren M8A; here thundering over the rise at Riverside during the Los Angeles Times GP.

Overleaf: Texan speedway star, Johnny Rutherford, fisting his works McLaren-Offy M16E round the scarred shallow banking, Phoenix, Arizona 1976.

1972 'Indy 500' line-up. Bobby Unser's bulky but blindingly-fast new Eagle on pole, flanked by the McLaren M16Bs of Peter Revson (centre) and ultimate winner Mark Donohue in the Penske Sunoco Special on the outside.

'Gatorade' livery made the works M16E a startling sight when it first appeared in 1975. Here is Johnny Rutherford leaving a margin of safety between himself and the barrier at Phoenix early in the year. The M16E was largely the work of John Barnard during his first spell with McLaren. The combination missed out at Indy this year when the race was flagged-off early due to rain while 'JR' was running second.

cylinders. The radiators were steeply raked forward on the rear of the tub within shaped intake ducts, the left-side matrix for water only, that on the right being a thinner block with an oil-cooler section ahead of it. The fuel load of 62½ Imperial gallons was also centred well within the wheelbase to promote a low polar moment of inertia, and the 2.65-litre turbo-Offy engine was again slung semi-stressed on the rear of the truncated monocoque, and steadied by tubular A-frames either side as on the M15.

To clear optimum airflow to the hip radiators the front suspension featured inboard coil-spring/damper units operated by fabricated top rocker arms, with wide-based wishbone location down below.

At the rear the usual single top link, reversed lower wishbone and twin radius rod system was retained, with the M15-originated interlink between the inner pivots of the top links. As all the turns were left-handers this inter-connection reduced the camber change on the inner wheel as the car rolled, improving traction. In practise the right wheel affected the attitude of that on the left, but not vice versa.

The 700bhp 4-cylinder Offy engine drove through a three-speed version of the Hewland LG500 gearbox, preferred to the normal Indy two-speeder as the extra lower gear gave improved acceleration from pit stops and at the end of yellow-light periods. Lockheed 'twin-pot' calipers clasped 11.9-inch diameter outboard front discs, shrouded deep within new four-spoke cast wheels, 15 inches in diameter with the regulation maximum 10in front rims and 14in rears. Drivers were to be Denny Hulme and Peter Revson . . .

The M16 wedge shape was highly penetrative, ideal for continuous high-speed running. The team had found on their CanAm cars that it was one thing to achieve a high degree of aerodynamic down-thrust from their body shape and quite another to balance it adequately front to rear. The M16 shape gave a large degree of downthrust at the front, and it had to be balanced with a large wing on the back and a great deal of work ensured good airflow round it. The canard fins either side of the nose worked purely as trimming devices. A special manifold was cast to drop the turbocharger as low as possible out of the airstream.

The engines came from Herbie 'Horsepower' Porter who maintained Goodyear's float of tyre-test and race Offies, with Gary Knutson tweaks.

Gordon's suspension system provided a slight rising-rate effect on bump. "With conventional systems you always get a falling rate – less resistance the further the wheel gets deflected. A damper inclined at, say, 45 degrees, loses about 5 per cent mechanical advantage say as it gets to full bump. On the M16 it was very easy to make it gain about 5 per cent, so we got 10 per cent mechanical advantage on the front suspension as a whole. This isn't to be confused with Ralph's rising-rate linkage on the Formula 1 M19; he made advantages of 100 per cent. Nevertheless, 5 per cent increase is better than a 5 per cent decrease . . ."

The race cars were built religiously down to 1,370lbs, 100lbs lighter than the M15s, and the team believed they should have at least a year's development in the design. It was to prove successful far beyond that . . .

Late in 1970 Roger Penske and Mark Donohue had come to England to look at possible CanAm contenders. On the flight over they discussed what they should do if they couldn't find a competitive car. Mark was keen to try USAC oval-track racing. They had done some already with Lola cars, and had planned a new one with Eric Broadley of Lola but while in England stopped off at Colnbrook "to say hello". They knew Teddy would not sell a CanAm car to his greatest potential rival, but McLaren were still Indy underdogs, and might be willing to sell a customer M16A.

Mark Donohue: "The minute I saw it, I knew they already had a better package than what we were discussing with Eric . . . They had obviously learned a lot about wings in Formula 1 and were applying that knowledge to Indy – as we were planning to do. But they had gone further, by making it a clean complete package, whereas our Lola conversion would have been cobbled together. I quietly

PETER RE
INDIANAPOLIS MO

ON & CREW
R SPEEDWAY · 1970

Revvie's ride – after Chris Amon found himself unable to adapt to the specialised driving style demanded by left-turn only Speedway racing and Denny Hulme was burned in pre-qualifying practice, Peter Revson and USAC specialist Carl Williams took over the two race McLaren M15s. Revvie shone. Here he is, flanked by Cary Taylor, George Bolthoff, Tyler Alexander, Bruce and 'Hughie' Absalom. Note the top-ducted nose, massive aircraft-type fuel fillers in the monocoque flank, voluminous separate oil tank slung beside the engine bay, smoothly integrated cockpit surround-cum-rear wing moulding, and the prominent turbo-charger mounting.

marvelled at their guts, to come up with such a new concept, and it inspired me even more to go USAC racing . . ."

Teddy Mayer: "The minute Roger saw it he said 'Build me one', so he took the prototype and they helped with early development . . ."

In January '71 the prototype was taken to America and tested by Denny and Peter Revson at Ontario, California, then loaned to Penske for Donohue and engineer Don Cox to continue testing at Phoenix, Arizona. It would become the dark blue and yellow-liveried Sunoco Oil-sponsored Penske entry for Indy, while the later cars ran as the works' Gulf-backed entries sprayed papaya.

Tyre testing at Indy in March, Donohue ran 172mph, 1mph faster than everybody else. The opposition complained the engine was too exposed and that wings weren't allowed. They were not *per se*, but the M16 wing was formed into the engine cowl, USAC's chief technical inspector looked at it and declared it was within the rules, as were the nose canards, being part of the bodywork.

"At that point" Mark commented in Americanese "the McLarens obsoleted every other car at the track . . ."

In May he was instantly quick, lapping at 178mph. Al Unser's previous year's pole had been taken at only 170! Neither works driver was as quick, Donohue and Cox had more experience of setting-up the M16 at that point. Penske asked Mark to share figures with Teddy Mayer: "This is a long-term deal, and if you make him mad now it's gonna mean trouble later". Thereupon the M16 programme became a truly cooperative effort.

Mark finally got up to 181mph in testing, and then his car wasn't quite right as he ran his qualifying attempt and clocked a disappointing 177mph, still fast enough for pole but beatable. When Teddy asked why so slow Donohue responded honestly that the track was so hot the car was oversteering too much. He suggested less wing incidence on the nose of Peter's car, and in the middle of his 'pole-sitter's interview' a roar from the crowd and excitement from the commentator announced Revson on pole, 178.696mph. Teddy said he'd done the opposite to what Donohue advised. Mark didn't believe him . . . Denny qualified fourth at 174.91mph.

In the race Donohue just drove away into the middle-distance from the start. Revson the often arrogantly outspoken easterner from a wealthy background was not well accepted by the USAC fraternity at that time. Donohue was better liked, and the way Peter handled his pole position adulation irritated both Mark and Bobby Unser whose Eagle joined the M16s on the front row. On the pace lap Mark and Bobby alternately accelerated and decelerated in formation, leaving Revson out of step. To keep them in line he had to back off or accelerate and follow their lead. Donohue: "Finally we got round to the front straight and Bobby and I gave it a big blast with our motors – and backed off immediately. Peter charged ahead . . . then looked back and saw he was too far ahead. He backed off just as our blower pressure was coming up, and as we crossed the startline – all three abreast – we were going about 60mph faster than he was. It was timed perfectly. He never knew what hit him . . ."

Mark led for 61 laps, until his gearbox broke. Teddy Mayer: "We'd had specially hardened diffs made for the cars but Roger wouldn't use them, and that's what broke . . ." Mark left his car against the inside wall near the pit entrance, and later in the race Mike Mosley crashed against the outer wall at Turn Four and flamed his way down into this parking area, virtually destroying the M16. Revson unaccountably lost confidence in his car's handling and dropped back despite all entreaties from his pit crew, and later could not attack Al Unser's winning car, worn out by "heavy steering". Denny retired with split water lines.

The Penske car's tub was rebuilt on the Colnbrook jigs in time for the inaugural Pocono '500' in July and there it qualified on pole and won handsomely in the home state of Penske Racing and Sun Oil. At Michigan Mark won again.

The rest of that season had seen Mark running well at Trenton in April until his Penske M16A was sidelined by clutch failure. In May the M16s had been totally

dominant. By the time of Pocono in July they had to run hard to stay ahead and by the time of the California 500 in September they were surrounded by near-equals. Penske ran Mark's car there with its rear wing moved some 8-inches further back, but in qualifying the engine broke. The replacement broke again, and a third was damaged in an uncharacteristic spin into the wall. Still Mark took pole at 185.004mph. Denny's works car was dogged by engine trouble and he gave up all attempts to qualify, sitting out the race in Gulf's air-conditioned motor home and not bothering to rush to Italy in time for the clashing GP at Monza. Gordy Johncock moved over from his private M15A to the works M16, supporting Peter Revson whose sister M16 qualified on the front row. But both works cars went out with turbocharger failure. Mark dominated until he missed his pit signals and ran out of fuel. It was the nadir of the Penske-Donohue partnership's career . . .

For 1972 new M16Bs were built with deeper-chord front and rear wings, bobbed nose to allow the rear wing to move further back within the maximum length, and a bullet-faring on the induction plenum chamber. Penske bought two, one for Donohue, the other for Gary Bettenhausen. Initially the cars were little better than the M16A, but while Penske ran a full USAC series, Team McLaren concentrated on the major 500-milers; Indy, Pocono and Ontario.

Dan Gurney's new Eagles were the cars to beat that season, and at Indy speeds soared into the 190mph bracket with Bobby Unser's Eagle taking pole at a stunning 195.940. Peter was alongside him on 192.885. In the race they became the third and fourth retirements; Donohue's M16B was third fastest qualifier on the outside of the front row at 191.408mph and he ran a reliable race to inherit the lead 13 laps from the finish when Jerry Grant's 'Mystery Eagle' made an unscheduled pit stop. Donohue and the Sunoco Penske-McLaren had won the Indy '500'.

His victory confused him. He always believed in 'the unfair advantage' – the title of his excellent biography – and always tried to outer-engineer his opposition before the race began. This time Penske put him into the race with a more modestly-boosted engine than his major rivals, looking for reliability. The approach paid off and the marque McLaren had won Indy at its third attempt.

*Trend-setter –
Gordon Coppuck's
McLaren-Offy
M16A set new
standards at Indy
first in the hands of
Penske Racing and
Mark Donohue,
then driven by Peter
Revson and Denny
Hulme for the
Gulf-backed works
team. Here is
Denny's car,
showing off its
slender
wedge-shaped
monocoque and
nose section,
far-out-rigged rear
wing-cum-engine
cover, lowered
turbocharger
mounting, nose
canards and hip
radiator pods. Note
the left-side only
mirror, Denny was
prepared to cover
those diving inside
him . . . anybody
trying to sit him out
round the outside
would be on their
own.*

INDIANAPOLIS

IIS HULME

AOTOR SPEEDWAY 1971

That magical front-row line-up for the '71 Indy 500, with Peter Revson's works Gulf-McLaren M16A on pole on the right, Mark Donohue's sister Penske Racing Sunoco Special M16A next up, and Bobby Unser in Dan Gurney's Olsonite-sponsored Eagle on the outside. Mark and Bobby ganged-up on Peter at the start, and it was not to be the works' driver's day. Mark led until his uncatchable M16 broke, later to be written-off where it lay parked by a crashing car.

United States Auto Club

Certificate of Performance

The undersigned Certify in the name of the
United States Auto Club
that

McCLAREN SPECIAL

ON MAY 15, 1971, DRIVEN BY PETER REVSON, ESTABLISHED A NEW FOUR-LAP QUALIFYING RECORD IN THE CHAMPIONSHIP DIVISION OF 3:21.46 FOR AN AVERAGE SPEED OF 178.696 MPH ON THE 2½-MILE PAVED INDIANAPOLIS MOTOR SPEEDWAY, INDIANAPOLIS, INDIANA.

President   *Director of Competition*

Gary Bettenhausen's second Penske M16B was classified 14th and the number two works car entrusted to USAC veteran Gordon Johncock was 20th after a late 26th place qualification at 188.511mph.

The rest of the '72 season saw the Penske cars placing 2-3 at Milwaukee where Gary Bettenhausen led Donohue most of the way only for Mark to stage his final charge too late to catch Bobby Unser's victorious Eagle. The Penske M16As were run as on all the short 1-mile ovals, with oil coolers in the nose spoiling their sensational lines but improving balance and cooling.

Flooding caused by Hurricane *Agnes* postponed Pocono, while at Michigan Unser's Eagle took pole at a staggering four-lap average speed of 199.778 mph. Gordy Johncock was second quickest at 198.129, but the race was red-flagged after a ghastly accident in which Penske McLaren driver Gary Bettenhausen's brother Merle wrote-off his Grant King-built M16-copy Kingfish, severing his right arm in the impact. Gary immediately withdrew from the race to accompany him to hospital, and after a 90-minute clear-up the race was restarted, with Gordy taking the lead. A dense swathe of oil was then dropped on the track which caused another stop, but under the yellow flag preceding that hiatus the works M16 trailed blue smoke, and retired.

Pocono's 500 was run a month late. Gordy led in the works car, Gary Bettenhausen led in Penske's, but both Revson and Johncock works cars lost engines, Bettenhausen lost sparks and the first McLaren finisher was Salt Walther, eighth. During qualifying Peter had aborted his first day's run when he felt droplets of water spraying the back of his neck. They came not from the car's systems but from a leak in a plastic bag of ice-water which the mechanics had just placed on the fuel pump to prevent possible vapour-locking . . .

Soon after Pocono, Gary Bettenhausen broke his arm in an August sprint car race, and Penske offered his place to Englishman in America David Hobbs, but he couldn't take it due to contractual clashes.

At Ontario Jerry Grant's meteoric Eagle took pole at 199.6mph, Peter qualified at 194.5 and Gordy at 194. George Follmer appeared in Roy Woods' ex-Penske McLaren but suffered engine trouble, and Roger McCluskey actually won the rain-interrupted race in Lindsey Hopkins' ex-Revsion '71 M16A. Gordy Johncock led much of the way and was lying fourth after his final pit stop with those ahead of him still to make their's when a tyre burst and he crashed heavily. Peter's engine blew-up. Mike Hiss drove the Penske car and finished second though lapped according to the official charts, while Penske claimed he had in fact won and the race ended in controversy.

For 1973 McLaren laid down six M16 Cs. The vestigial headrest of the M16B had grown into a full-length cover smoothing airflow back onto the rear wing, and new truncated radiator hip ducts replaced the earlier tapered-back type. A new cockpit surround was fitted, featuring a rounded planform like the new F1 M23's in place of the square-cut M16 original.

Teddy had signed Johnny Rutherford to join Peter Revson in the works team.

Johnny's M16C took pole for the Indy '500' at 198.413mph and was essentially the quickest at the Speedway, but a front wheel hung-up at one refuelling stop, fuel wept from a breather and brought him the black-flag, then the engine plenum chamber split to lose boost pressure . . . He finished ninth in a race which was turned into a nightmare by a series of horrendous accidents, an early halt called by driving rain, and a restarted second section next day. Peter qualified only tenth at 192.606mph and crashed on the third race lap in Turn Four where track conditions had changed from causing understeer to oversteer pre-race, and later claimed Swede Savage's life in another ghastly accident which befell his Eagle.

Gordon Johncock actually won in another Eagle, and veteran driver Roger McCluskey was third in Lindsey Hopkins' ex-works M16, subsequently going on to win the Michigan 200, and place second in the Milwaukee 150, Pocono 500 and Ontario 100. McLaren designed a composite suspension system for this car to mate the C-type geometry to the old A-type hull.

Gary Bettenhausen was fifth in both Indy qualifying and the race driving Penske's M16C, while other McLarens in the race were John Martin's unsponsored M16B (qualified 24th, finished eighth), Bobby Allison's new Penske M16C (started 12th snapped a rod bolt on the opening lap), and the unfortunate Salt Walther whose Dayton-Walther M16B started 17th but became involved in a horrifying startline collision which sent his shattered car pin-wheeling down the straightaway, inverted and blazing furiously. Walther survived to race another day, but spectators were burned by scattering fuel, and vast damages suits were served.

McLaren victories during '73 included Johnny Rutherford's two at Ontario (a 100-miler) and Michigan, while Gary Bettenhausen won the Texas 200 for Penske. At the end of that season Gulf Oil withdrew from sponsorship of the

works USAC team . . . and Penske left USAC racing in favour of NASCAR.

Donohue had won Indy in 1972, perhaps the 'even' year of 1974 would serve McLaren well?

After the holocausts of '73, USAC regulations had been revised to accommodate fuel more safely within the monocoque away from that vulnerable right-side, up against the retaining wall, and with a 15ft maximum length restriction to limit wings so reducing maximum cornering speeds. The new car was designated M16C/D with a more abbreviated nose, a true M23 cockpit surround topping the flat hull, and an F1-style monocoque-pillar rear wing mount carrying a pronounced banana-section airfoil. The engine cowl was swept-down short of the wing while the C-type abbreviated radiator pods were retained on either hip.

Johnny Rutherford missed first-weekend qualification for the front of the grid, so qualified late in 25th place on the grid at 190.446mph demonstrating the slash in speeds brought about by the new regulations, and the race ended with Johnny victorious and McLaren's even-year charm had worked.

David Hobbs took the second M16C/D works car to qualify ninth at 184.899 mph – slower than his team-leader but on the favoured first qualifying weekend rather than the second. David's Carling Black Label beer-sponsored car finished a fine fifth, though four laps adrift. It was a great year for the works team . . .

Other Indy runners '74 included Jim Hurtubise's reworked *Miller High Life* beer M16B which classified 25th after a 32nd lap piston failure; John Martin's *Sea Snack Shrimp Cocktail* M16B/C which finished 11th; Mike Hiss' 1973-built Penske M16C/D which started third at 187.940mph but was flagged-off 14th; Salt Walther's M16C, 17th after piston failure; and Gary Bettenhausen's Penske *Score Special* M16C which was the race's second retirement on only the second lap, with valve trouble.

Johnny's '74 season with the McLaren also yielded victory in the Ontario 100, Pocono 500 and Milwaukee 150.

For 1975 yet more modification was made to the now five-year old M16-series with the M16E detailed at Colnbrook by Gordon's assistant John Barnard as the Chief Designer was fully committed to Formula 1 development. The M16E featured a lengthened wheelbase with new parallel lower link rear suspension. Lloyd Ruby was brought in to handle the second works M16E alongside Rutherford, the cars respectively finished in white, red and blue *Allied Polymer Group*, and green, white and orange *Gatorade* livery. The race was called at 174 laps due to heavy rain, and Bobby Unser's works Eagle was declared winner, with Johnny's M16E second. Ruby's luck hadn't changed – he was always one of the unluckiest of USAC drivers – and he posted the second retirement of the race when a piston burned on lap seven.

Salt Walther's M16C posted the first retirement of the '500' with ignition failure on only the second lap and he took over team-mate Bob Harkey's similar car to finish tenth, highest McLaren finisher behind Rutherford. Penske's M16C/Ds were driven by Tom Sneva and Bobby Allison, the former's *Norton Spirit* with pillar wing mounting qualified fourth fastest at 190.094 mph but was destroyed in a fearful mid-race collision. His team-mate Allison's car used a tubular-strutted wing and was placed 25th after breaking its gearbox. John Martin's old car was seventh and last McLaren runner, placing 26th with punctured radiators.

Johnny Rutherford won for McLaren again in 1976 – even-numbered year again . . . his works *Hy-Gain*-sponsored M16E qualifying on Indy pole at 188.957mph with Tom Sneva alongside on the front row in Penske's latest M16C/D update. Fastest man on the Indy grid, however was Mario Andretti whose Penske *Cam-2* M16C/D qualified on the second weekend, and therefore ineligibly for pole, at 189.40mph for 19th place on the grid. The works car radiator pods were flared again after their square-cut truncated form of '75, and in the race Johnny established a decisive lead after a stop to trim the nose 'foils and

Right:
1974 was McLaren's year at Indy; here Johnny Rutherford's works McLaren M16C/D showing-off its M23-derived mods during a scheduled pit-stop – note the revised abbreviated nose cone to allow the rear wing to be mounted further back within the maximum overall length, and the pit-to-driver intercom aerial mounted on the tub deck just below the race number. Out

···THE WINNER···
·JOHNNY RUTHERFORD·
NDIANAPOLIS MOTOR SPEEDWAY 1974·

on the pit lane after the race the victor shows his delight. Now the completely redesigned engine cowl and separate pylon-mounted rear wing can be seen.

145

change the right-side tyres which "made the car suddenly come to life". When pouring rain halted the shortest Indy '500' on record after only 102 of the scheduled 200 laps, Rutherford had notched his second '500' victory in three years. Al Loquasto had two M16B-variants available to him for the race and qualified one *Frostie Root Beer Spl* at 182.002mph for 24th place on the grid. Tom Sneva was the coming man of USAC racing in Penske's second '76 Indy McLaren M16C/D running *Norton Spirit* livery and he qualified on the outside of the front row at 186.355mph and was sixth as the race was flagged-off.

But the historic M16-series had run to its end, and for 1977 a new M24 USAC car replaced it. Back in 1971-72 an M16 Indy car had been analysed with an F1 M19 Cosworth engine rear-end and running gear. Gordon and the team "just loved" the result and this exploratory exercise thus prompted the Formula 1 M23 design which brought McLaren two road racing World Championships. When Cosworth introduced their USAC-racing 2.65-litre turbocharged DFX version of the 3-litre F1 V8 it showed immense promise. McLaren adopted it in place of the Offenhauser four-cylinder which was at long-last obsolescent, and Gordon produced his M24 chassis design as virtually an M23-DFX revised to match USAC regulations.

The first M24 was completed during 1976, and the second was delivered to Penske Racing during that season. In 1977 the M24-Cosworth DFX cars became front-line equipment for McLaren's now *First National Citibank Travellers' Checks* – sponsored programme, and for Penske. The cars combined pure M23 engine mounts with heavier monocoque skins and bulkheads within the F1-type deformable structure-protected monocoque tub, plus M16E-style suspension.

In the first four races of that year, Johnny Rutherford took pole, led two and won one while Andretti in Penske's second-delivered car was the first driver to crack the 200mph lap speed barrier at Indianapolis, while Johnny set a new lap record at 200.624mph. He suffered bitter disappointment as the car's gearbox failed in the race as first retirement. The Penske McLaren M24s were both considerably modified by Roger's English chief engineer Geoff Ferris, effectively as rolling test-beds for the prototype Penske USAC car.

Tom Sneva put his Penske-McLaren on pole at Indy, Andretti was on row two, Rutherford on row six and four other McLarens on the grid. Sneva placed second, his brother Jerry's old M16E-Offy was tenth while Andretti, Al Loquasto, Cliff Hucul and European visitor Clay Regazzoni all retired M16s.

During the '77 season Tom Sneva and Johnny Rutherford had both won 200-milers at College Station in Texas and Johnny also won the Phoenix 150.

For their eighth attempt at Indy in 1978, Team McLaren arrived with Johnny Rutherford – for the sixth successive year – as their number one driver, chasing his and the team's third '500' victory. They had won Indy twice and the Penske-McLarens had their '72 success. McLaren cars had been on pole four times, with all the attendant prestige. Since Rutherford had joined Team McLaren in 1973 they had finished either second or third in the USAC National Championship every year, and had a total of 14 race wins to their credit.

Now team manager Tyler Alexander had two M24s at Johnny's disposal – one of the previous year's M24s updated as an M24B and another brand-new car, the seventh M24 to be built. The B-type was lighter than the original version, with its oil cooler resited horizontally on the left side of the gearbox.

Meanwhile Jerry O'Connell's Sugaripe Prune Racing team were running one of the previous year's M24 chassis to be driven by veteran Wally Dallenbach. Dayton-Walther Racing returned with their ex-Penske M24s for Salt Walther to drive, and Graham McRae attempted to qualify an older M16C/D with Offy power. Jerry Sneva ran one of Bill Freeman's much-modified M16B-Offies, similar to Jerry Karl's, and Canadian Cliff Hucul ran another Offy-powered McLaren, an M16C/D.

Rutherford qualified fourth fastest while the new Penske PC6s of Tom Sneva and Rick Mears shared the front row with Danny Ongais' Parnelli, all Cosworth

DFX-powered. Dallenbach was seventh, while Walther, Hucul, Karl and Jerry Sneva also made the grid. But Johnny lost much time in the pits with engine trouble and finished well back, 13th. Dallenbach's was the best McLaren finish with sixth place although his car was actually lying silent, out of fuel after 195 of the 200 laps.

Johnny's '78 works team season was highlighted by a win at Michigan, and he was second at Pocono, Milwaukee and College Station before winning again in the Phoenix 150. Wally Dallenbach's M24-DFX was a model of consistency during the year, with a string of 3-4-5 place finishes.

For the 1979 '500', amid great controversy, American track racing split into two factions and USAC introduced turbocharger boost-regulating valves which severely restricted engine power. There were two McLarens to be reckoned with at Indy; the works M24B sponsored by Budweiser beer for Johnny Rutherford and O'Connell's *Sugaripe Prune* M24 now driven by USAC Champion Tom Sneva. Works M24Bs used new monocoques with a new slimline wedge nose, and Sneva

was blindingly fast in his progressively modified M24. Roger McCluskey ran Warner Hodgdon's ex-Penske M24. Four Offy-engined M16-series cars attempted to qualify, but only Cliff Hucul's made the grid. Sneva lined-up on the centre of the front row with 192.998mph against poleman Rick Mears' Penske PC6 on 193.736. Rutherford's best was 188.137mph, on the centre of row three. Roger McCluskey's M24 joined-in on row nine. Tom Sneva seemed assured of a sixth place finish until something broke only 12 laps from home and he crashed heavily, without injury. Johnny's works car suffered a gearbox failure which saw him lose more than 30 laps in the pits, finally placing a poor 18th. McCluskey's was the best-placed McLaren, 13th . . .

Tom Sneva's Penske Racing McLaren M24-Cosworth DFX shows off its unmistakable F1 M23 ancestry as it barks away down the Indy pit-lane '77. Sneva became a pillar of McLaren's oval-track racing achievement in the late-'70s/early-'80s.

Al Unser set the pace and looked like winning in Jim Hall's bright-yellow Chaparral 2K partial ground-effects car. It was designed and built in England under the direction of Gordon Coppuck's former assistant at Colnbrook – John Barnard. His was a new talent in the making . . . to McLaren's eventual advantage.

The 1979 season was notable for Tom Sneva's performances in his Jerry O'Connell-owned Sugaripe Prune-sponsored M24-DFX, maintained by Jud Phillips and his crew. The bright yellow car was second at Atlanta, and Michigan, third at Trenton, while Johnny's works M24B salvaged thirds at Phoenix and Michigan and fourth at Ontario, still emerging as usual fourth in what was now the USAC/CART National Championship.

By 1980 Team McLaren was out of Indy, after nine seasons' works team participation. The Formula 1 team was trapped in uncompetitiveness, and now the USAC operation folded due to lack of sponsorship. It was decided to shut

down the American track-racing operation to concentrate on Formula 1 and rumours of at least two years had become reality just before Christmas '79. Johnny took his services to Jim Hall's Chaparral team.

During 1980 'Snively' Sneva's performances with O'Connell's three-year old McLaren M24 were terrific. He was second in the season-opener at Ontario before attacking Indy with O'Connell's brand-new Phoenix ground-effect car. But after qualifying, while searching for more speed, something broke and the car demolished itself against the wall. They were left with a guaranteed starting place but the car which had won it was history. So they fell back upon *Ole Hound* as the faithful M24 was known, but this meant Sneva must start last on the grid as the rules dictated, losing his fourth-row place. The twice pole-position driver was in unfamiliar territory back there . . .

In the race he enhanced his terrific reputation as a charger by mixing it with the front-runners before half-distance. He finally took the lead for a few laps – the first time anyone had done that from starting 33rd at Indy – before surrendering to eventual winner Johnny Rutherford's Chaparral. Sneva's 33rd to second place finish was another Indy first. Billy Engelhart qualified 22nd in the M24 which was now being entered by Beaudoin Racing and finished 11th. Jerry Karl's elderly M16E-Chevrolet, modified by his crew with ground-effects pannier-sections, was classified 21st after clutch failure ended quite a good run.

'Snively' went on to take third at Pocono, fourth in the road race at Watkins Glen and a couple of sixths, all in *Ole Hound*. For the end of the season a fresh Phoenix was ready, and the old McLaren was taken on again by Gary Bettenhausen's younger brother, Tony Jr.

Only three McLarens attempted the 1981 Indy classic, Tony Bettenhausen Jr taking out the ex-Sneva M24 (Tom's second place '80 car), while Vern Schuppan ran his own M24B, and Jerry Karl replaced Jerry Sneva in the M16E-Chevvy after Sneva Jr had been disqualified from Indy for the year when a bolt was found jamming his engine's pop-off valve shut to maintain illegal boost pressures. Schuppan drove a wonderful race, hardly out of the top ten all day and eventually placed third, one lap down on the winner. Bettenhausen was seventh and Karl 15th.

Into 1981 the few remaining McLarens in the USAC/CART oval-track series had been generally well outclassed by the new generation ground-effect cars. But Tony Bettenhausen's seriously under-budgeted M24 performed extremely well, finishing second in the Michigan 500 and bringing him sixth place in the National Championship. The last National Championship round of the year was the Miller High Life '150' run at Phoenix, Arizona, without a single McLaren in the top twelve, the last oval-track McLaren result being Bill Tempero's twelfth in his stock-block M24-Chevrolet in the Copa Mexico road race at Mexico City, on October 18, 1981. In 1982 not a single McLaren would feature in the top twelve; their time had passed . . .

Chapter 1
The Orange F1s 1968-71

*"We have chosen to enter the most prestigious and widely
publicised classes of international racing because we believe
that a sponsor's exposure is proportional to the status of the
events in which the team paticipates."*

McLaren promotional leaflet

Into the winter of 1967-68 Bruce looked back on his team's maiden CanAm success, and attributed it "mainly to the BRM engine for our Formula 1 car arriving so late. This meant that our whole factory was able to concentrate on the CanAm cars, and we put a lot of time and effort into them. Ford probably spent far more money and had more people working on their cars, but none of the other specialist teams was able to put anything like as much effort into it. Now we're approaching Formula 1 that way with five new Cosworth engines . . ."

The new Ford-backed Cosworth DFV had set new standards in the works Lotus 49s through the second half of 1967, and now for '68 the V8s were available to other teams at £7,500 a throw. The M5A-BRM had run well in the wet but was outgunned in the dry even by the Brabhams, which supposedly had no more than 340bhp. The new Cosworth-Ford delivered a minimum 408.

Denny Hulme had been signed-on with help from Goodyear and Gulf Oil, and Bruce counted prospects for the new year in the order "five Cosworth engines, Denis Hulme, and after that a chassis to put between him and the engine – that's about third in importance as I rate it at the moment. I think we can knock up a chassis that will work fairly well . . ."

As can be seen in the Racing Record Appendix, the team opened the season with the lone M5A entered for Denny in the South African GP. He finished fifth. After the experience of over-complication and perhaps excessive attention to theory with the Mallite cars, the M4-5-6 cars of 1967 had proved the value of simplicity and carefully-conceived practicality. Now the new M7A for the DFV engine was a logical development from the BRM-powered car although the cockpit-enclosing monocoque structure had now been abbreviated to open bath-tub form like the M4A. Robin Herd had pencilled the monocoque before announcing he was going to join Cosworth Engineering in Northampton to design an all-new four-wheel drive car for them to race in '69. Bruce had shared all his knowledge and design philosophy with Robin who although clearly a brilliant engineer had been very green in racing reality when he had joined the team. When Robin left Bruce felt very hurt. He felt he was taking too much of the team's know-how with him to a potential competitor. Eoin Young: "Strangely enough it was the same sort of hurt that Bruce could not understand with Charles and John Cooper when Jack Brabham left the team at the end of the 1961 season." Some people gave as much to a team during their time with it as they took away when they left . . . Gordon Coppuck noticed how Bruce was reluctant to share confidences with him after Robin's defection. Gordon had followed Robin to the team from NGTE. Perhaps he would also follow him out of the team? As the months passed, confidence grew.

When Robin left Bruce was largely responsible for the suspension geometry of the new M7A design, which Gordon detailed. Robin's aluminium-skinned monocoque tub was shaped over three bulkheads, the structure being an open-topped 'bath-tub' with glass fibre body panelling above the driver's legs and round the cockpit. The bulkheads were complex 20-gauge steel fabricated box-sections, one sited right at the front to carry the front suspension and

New start – for 1968 the team would use the new Cosworth-Ford DFV V8 engine and Robin Herd designed M7A cars to carry it. Here Bruce checks set-up points with Don Beresford for the prototype monocoque on the chassis jig; rolled skins are about to be rivetted and bonded onto these exquisitely-fabricated bulkheads and shaped floor panel. In early '68 the Colnbrook racing 'shop would look like this, with bathtub monocoque M7A showing off its DFV engine on the trestles (left), M6A CanAm car back from the races at right, and redundant M5A with its full-length monocoque extending either side of the engine bay beyond.

steering, the internal centre bulkhead provided anchorages for the front suspension trailing links and the rear bulkhead behind the seat carried the fully-stressed DFV engine and provided pick-ups for the rear suspension radius arms. Skins were mainly 22-gauge L72 aluminium alloy sheet with some 20-gauge, magnesium-sheet being used for small flat panels. The inner skins were flat sheet, bonded and rivetted to the rolled outer panels. McLaren set great store by their glueing process, using rivets virtually just to provide clamping pressure while the bond cured. Thus far the process had proved extremely resistant to cracking around the rivet holes and fatigue life was very good.

The monocoque side-boxes contained 11-gallon FPT rubber fuel bags running full-length, with a further 9-gallons in a tank behind the driver's seat panel, and 9-gallons more in a bag contained within a glass-fibre moulded scuttle attached to the tub above the driver's legs. Around 32 gallons was considered sufficient for most GPs, so the scuttle tank would be run almost empty most of the time. Bruce's suspension derived from the M6A, using upper and lower single lateral links with trailing radius arms at the front and single lateral top links, reversed wishbones and twin radius rods at the rear. Outboard coil-springs with co-axial Koni dampers were used front and rear. New front uprights had been cast, still with the separate bolt-on steering 'arm' plates of the M5A which enabled it to be removed and packed-up easily to alter steering geometry. The rear suspension picked up on mounts attached to the Hewland DG five-speed transaxle. The DFV was attached to the rear of the truncated monocoque by four ⅜in bolts, though the top magnesium plates on the cam-covers merely bolted onto the upper face of the tub instead of being slotted into the rear bulkhead as on the Lotus 49.

CanAm experience had high-lighted the different driving styles of Bruce and Denny. Bruce could always set-up a car to handle as he liked, and it would suit Denny too, but while Bruce drove very smoothly, rolling progressively onto the brakes and changing down smoothly then accelerating hard out of the turns, Denny braked desperately late and liked to tweak the car's tail out of line and slide through the turns, a technique to which his Brabham-Repco responded well. Denny also confessed freely to being "hard on gearchanges" and his M6A's had to be strengthened in the CanAm series.

The M7A's brakes were unusual for a British F1 car in being by Lockheed instead of the almost universal Girling set-up. They had produced a new 10½in diameter ventilated disc and caliper. At that time ventilated discs were unusual in F1. Lotus had tried them and suffered problems with cracking as they cooled too well and heated rapidly. McLaren's discs were well-buried within the wheels and they expected more-constant temperature characteristics.

McLaren cast four-spoke 15inch magnesium wheels were used. Water cooling was by large Serck radiator outrigged ahead of the front bulkhead, hot radiator air being exhausted upwards through glass-fibre ducts formed into the very shapely nose body section. Oil-cooling was by radiator stayed above the gearbox, the cylindrical dry sump oil tank being slung alongside it. Water pipes ran externally either side of the tub.

Continuing their policy of selling their redundant cars, McLaren let the M5A-BRM go to Jo Bonnier's Ecurie Suisse. Bruce's '67 F2 M4A had already been sold to Jim Palmer for the Tasman Championship, and a new M4A was to be campaigned by fellow Kiwi Graeme Lawrence as a semi-works car in the European season.

Bruce drove for BRM in the Tasman Championship in January/February, winning at Teretonga but never happy with the design, and preparation of his car. He wrote an uncompromisingly harsh report on the cars for BRM patron Sir Alfred Owen's consumption, startling the team's management with its abrasive tone. Bruce was not like that, was he? . . . They were most surprised, but when his car did not even have an oil pressure gauge fitted as standard and he had to test with a hastily piped-up gauge lying in his lap his feelings can be imagined . . . Bruce was delighted when Piers Courage won Longford in his M4A.

Two weeks later the two papaya-coloured M7A-DFVs made their debut in the Brands Hatch Race of Champions, Bruce in the prototype M7A/1, Denny in M7A/2, and Bruce started from pole, led start to finish and set a new lap record. It was the perfect motor racing performance; Denny was third; a fantastic debut.

Astonishingly it was Bruce's first single-seater win at Brands Hatch since 1958 when he first appeared in the UK with a private F2 Cooper.

The McLaren drivers then flew to Indianapolis for Goodyear tyre tests with the Ken Wallis-engineered Shelby American gas turbine four-wheel drive cars which they had signed to drive in the USAC 500-Miles track classic that year. But the cars were bad and became worse as the race approached at the end of May, and when Bruce began to suspect the legality of Wallis' turbine engine he became most unhappy with the whole set-up. Goodyear pulled the plug and the cars were withdrawn pre-race.

Meanwhile Bruce had also been involved in the Ford Dagenham P68 long-distance project, developing and racing their Len Bailey-designed Cosworth DFV-engined Coupe. In its debut at Brands Hatch for the BOAC 500 he led the early stages before retirement. "I left the track early and I was driving home when I heard the news that Jim Clark had been badly hurt in a crash at Hockenheim . . . suddenly the elation was gone". Back home he heard Jimmy had died. He was stunned. If Jimmy could die every racing driver's vulnerability was brought home to them . . .

In May at Silverstone the M7As had their second race, Denny qualified on pole from Mike Spence's BRM and Bruce, and the orange cars finished 1-2 for their second consecutive victory – 100 per cent success. Bruce: "I pulled alongside

First of many; imagine Bruce's jubilation as he flings his arm straight and high to greet Charles Greville-Smith's chequered flag to signal the brand-new McLaren M7A's debut victory in the Race of Champions, Brands Hatch '68.

Denny as we cruised back to the pits on the slowing-down lap and he pointed to his goggles . . . In the early stages Graham Hill saw him doing something odd . . . he thought Denny was picking his nose, and he thought that was *really* relaxed! But in fact a stone thrown up by Mike's BRM had knocked a plastic lens out of his goggles and clobbered him on the head as well."

For the Spanish GP at Jarama Bruce's M7A was rigged with pannier fuel tanks either side. Teddy Mayer: "It was one of his theories which once he became convinced of he would pursue to the bitter end. He found the M6A had handled better than the M7A and had this thing about it being something to do with the widespread fuel load within the wheelbase. The panniers were an attempt to produce a similar effect in Formula 1 . . ."

The McLarens both ran well at Jarama despite Bruce sliding off into the catch-fences on oil in practice, Bruce was third when his engine's oil pressure fell too low to make finishing worthwhile. These DFVs were expensive. He retired. Denny was left second behind Graham Hill's leading Gold Leaf-backed Lotus. He lost second gear for the last ten laps, and finished second. It could have been a McLaren 2-3 finish in a thin field, the team were very much front-runners with their new cars. The Gold Leaf cigarette brand sponsorship of Lotus fascinated Bruce and Teddy. If they could pull off a deal like that for their own team it would make all kinds of sense. At that time, in 1968, the Gold Leaf Team Lotus deal using the whole car for brand advertisement was an F1 innovation. The days of Formula 1's major sponsors being oil companies like Esso, Shell and BP were drawing to an end. Non-automotive industry sponsors would enable major-league road racing to flourish like never before . . .

At Monte Carlo Denny's car ran a short 'Monaco-nose' to avoid traffic damage, Bruce's ran unchanged. They qualified in midfield but on the opening lap Bruce slid wide leaving the tunnel and clipped-back a wheel against the Armco. Scarfiotti virtually stopped his Cooper-BRM in avoidance, the unfortunate Jack Oliver – in his debut GP for Lotus – arrived at speed, had nowhere to go, and ripped two wheels off his own car against the crippled and now severely crumpled M7A. Denny had an unhappy race handicapped by massive understeer. He stopped to have a new half-shaft fitted and only just completed the requisite 90 per cent of full distance to qualify as a finisher – fifth and last.

The spare M7A/3 tub was built-up for Bruce at Spa, 'sans panniers', but neither McLaren had sufficient stability for their drivers' peace of mind in practice, though rain in second practice left Denny on row two, Bruce behind him. The Belgian GP often produced sensational last lap finishes for it was a long race with cars and fuel capacities stretched to their limit. Denny led until a half-shaft failed, and Bruce was second behind Jackie Stewart's Tyrrell-Matra. But starting his last

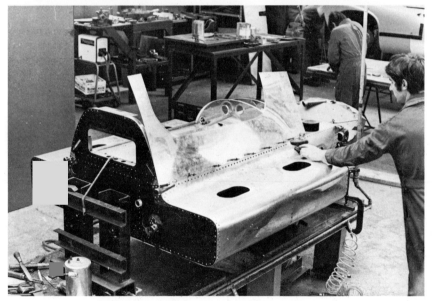

Bruce had a theory that the sports cars handled better than the single-seaters, perhaps something to do with their fuel load being spread wide across the car's track. Here are two attempts to match the phenomenon; the Lancia-Ferrari like panniers at Jarama '68 on the true bath-tub monocoque M7As, and the integral pannier tanked M7B under construction for Bruce in '69. Note how the M7As had detachable glass-fibre mouldings to form the entire upper 'body', whereas the later M7B is being built-up with a fully-stressed structure extending into the roll-over bar area behind the driver's head and over the dash-panel and scuttle above his legs. These were features borrowed from the Formula 5000 M10A which itself drew on M5A practice, to form a 'survival cell' for driver protection. High design integrity was always a McLaren virtue.

lap Jackie wheeled into the pitlane, his engine had begun to starve, he needed more fuel. Bruce yowled downhill between pits and grandstand, unknown to him, taking the lead. Ending that lap he took the flag with a cheery wave. Second was good enough after an unpromising start which had seen him badly boxed-in. Spa was nearly nine miles round, not a circuit on which to make a slowing-down lap, so he braked hard, turned in behind the pits and tried to drive back through the paddock to his transporter. He was puzzled by the sight of his crew leaping around behind the pit barrier as he took the flag, now people seemed unusually excited in the paddock. BRM Chief Mechanic Cyril Atkins ran up and told him "You crossed the line number one!" Bruce's race number was five. Then Cyril bawled "You've *won*! Didn't you know?"

It was sweet. Bruce's first *Grande Epreuve* victory in the car carrying his own name, and his first since Monaco '62, six long years before, in his Cooper days.

The team experimented with alternative Hewland ZF and American Weismann diffs, and the M7As' original Detroit half-shaft UJs were replaced by heavier BRD shafts and joints. Wide and narrow track suspensions were tried, Bruce finding the wider form better-suited to the crucial winding backstretch at Zandvoort where one and a half days' testing was completed before the Dutch GP. It was a wet race in a wet year, Denny's ignition drowned early on – he hated racing in the rain – and Bruce arrived at the end of the long straight on lap 20, braking for the 180-degree Tarzan loop and his front wheels locked. As he pumped the brakes

the car speared straight on, plucked down a catch-fence and thudded into the sand, out of the race.

The French GP was run at Rouen, McLaren adding strutted wings like those introduced by Ferrari and Brabham at Spa above the engines. Persistent understeer had dogged the cars. Now the front suspension had been modified by lifting the inner top link pick-up and lowering the outer bottom link pick-up to raise the roll centre and alter the camber change graph. After its Zandvoort excursion, Bruce's M7A/3 had reinforcing rivetted within the monocoque as its outer skin had been creased.

Both drivers were looking forward to the race, but rain teemed down and neither M7A had been set-up on rain tyres. There had not been practice time to scrub them in. Neither could feature in the race, they changed wet tyres but Bruce had one fitted with a leaky valve and had to stop again. Salvaging fifth and seventh places was regarded as good fortune. at least both cars finished.

The British GP at Brands Hatch saw three M7As present, Bruce's

ETT

Championship challenger; Bruce in his M7A clipping the apex of the Eau Rouge Raidillon at Spa-Francorchamps on the way to his unknowing Belgian GP victory, '68. It was the first World Championship-qualifying victory for his team, and the last of Bruce's own driving career. The cars ran as clean and slippery as possible here, while Brabham and Ferrari wore embryo strutted wings. The McLaren lead in wing technology of 1965 had not been exploited.

157

Denny Hulme defending his World Championship title in the French GP at Rouen-les-Essarts' Nouveau Monde hairpin '68, showing off the M7A's ugly right-side only long-range tank and initial strutted wing form, also special rear wheels compared to the familiar Owen Maddock-originated McLaren four-spoke cast design up front.

Monaco-shunted prototype having been entirely re-skinned, though it retained the original front suspension geometry and ran 13-inch front wheels. Denny retained his Weismann diff but was dogged by drive-shaft failures during practice. Black clouds threatened at the start and Bruce started on wet tyres, Denny on dry. Rain held off and Bruce was condemned to shuffle round and finish seventh while Denny might have been third but for bending a selector fork in his gearbox, allowing second gear to jump out. Ickx's Ferrari took the place, Denny was fourth. More alarmingly neither McLaren could compete with the latest high-winged Lotus 49Bs.

Nürburgring's German GP was the wettest yet, with thick swirling mist adding to the problems. Neither McLaren featured, Denny seventh, Bruce 13th, very unhappy. The season was falling apart.

At Colnbrook concentrated effort had produced the M8A CanAm title defenders, now the CanAm series had the team commuting across the Atlantic between GPs. There was little opportunity to try anything special on the M7As for the Italian GP at Monza in September, but winning in CanAm had raised morale, and running wingless the M7As were very fast on the Autodrome's long straights and open curves. With some 1500 miles of Goodyear tyre testing behind them at Goodwood, Denny had fixed ideas on the rubber he wanted, and it paid off. Bruce was to race his prototype with its 13in front wheels, Denny stuck to his regular M7A/2 and the spare car, number 3, was checked-out briefly in practice having been fastest of all round Goodwood. Dan Gurney's Eagle project was running out

of engines, time and money. There was a chance he would take out the spare McLaren for the race, but the Milan club did not have a formal entry and refused to accommodate the suggestion.

Bruce made the most of a multiple slipstream in practice to put himself on the centre of the front row, second fastest qualifier, Denny two rows behind him. Bruce made a superb start and had a comfortable lead until he slowed at the scene of an accident and his pursuers closed the gap. Stewart's Matra and Jo Siffert's British GP-winning Walker team Lotus 49B closed with him, Denny closing fast. The usual Monza slipstreaming battle began, raging until Bruce's car began to snake in the *Parabolica* 180-degree turn before the pits. He could smell oil smoke, and it slowly dawned on him it was his oil leaking onto the left rear tyre. He made a quick exploratory stop but nothing instantly repairable could be found and after one disconsolate lap he retired to watch Denny! He battled on, outlasted Stewart and Siffert, and his M7A survived to win comfortably, at an average 145.4mph.

Bruce: "Denny's a funny guy – he always knows when he's going to win a race. There have been three occasions this year when Denny has said 'Don't worry – it'll be all right'. One was Silverstone, the other Elkhart Lake and then Monza . . ."

The North American GP tour began at St Jovite-Mt Tremblant, in Canada, scene of so much McLaren sports car success in their four seasons' racing. After Monza the team spent two days in England before Bruce and Denny flew out for the Bridgehampton CanAm round, then the Canadian GP. The spare car was ceded to Dan Gurney to complete his season now that his Eagle F1 project had run out of steam. He ran it as an Olsonite McLaren with sponsorship from toiletware manufacturer Ernie Olson, his USAC backer. If he'd had his way the car would have been resprayed dark blue, but Bruce would not let him, so orange it remained. Dan responded by qualifying faster than either works driver. But the race developed with the McLarens well placed in the following group while Chris Amon's Ferrari led. But by lap 70 of the scheduled 95 all serious competition had failed, and Denny led Bruce in a Team McLaren 1-2. Dan Gurney's car retired with overheating. With his two consecutive GP victories, Denny was now tied with Graham Hill at the top of the Drivers' World Championship, with Stewart within striking distance, six points behind.

At Watkins Glen for the US GP it was not McLaren's weekend. Denny ran very competitively on Hill's tail in the opening stages before spinning off and crushing a brake line in the rough. He stopped for the problem to be located and the line isolated. He rejoined on three brakes while a replacement line was made up in the pits. A second stop had the line fitted and he went out again but in the closing stages a gearbox output shaft broke in the 90-degree right-hander after the pits. It was the left-hand shaft and with drive on only the right rear wheel the car lurched into an electrifying spin, crashing heavily to rest beyond a deep drainage ditch which wrecked the monocoque. Bruce's car ran out of fuel due to a blocked tank breather and Gurney's race ended with a puncture.

Stewart had won the GP and now the Drivers' Championship would be decided between Denny, Graham Hill and Stewart in the final remaining round, three weeks hence at Mexico City. The team had to give Denny their best shot in defence of his title, and there were 19 days in which to fly the car to England, rebuild it, and fly it back to Laredo, Texas, to meet the transporters carrying the circus cars down into Mexico for the GP. Mexican import restrictions and particularly their demand for prior-notice of import meant that missing the rendezvous would mean no car in Mexico, for no alternative import arrangements could be guaranteed in time. They had to meet the transporter train, or forget it . . .

The wrecked M7A was collected from Watkins Glen at 8pm the Tuesday after the US GP, and reached Colnbrook at mid-day Thursday. Fifteen days left. Mike Barney, team mechanic and a man who had worked with Bruce since his Cooper days in 1959: "We started right away to strip suspension, motor, cooling and fuel systems from the tub, then to strip the damaged panels from the bulkheads, make new panels, pick-up all the rivet holes in the undamaged bulkheads on these new panels, realign the bulkheads on the jig, do a dummy assembly run prior to bonding and riveting, then finally bond and rivet – leaving off the outer skins to facilitate protective taping of all internal rivet tails to prevent any from puncturing the fuel bags . . ."

They finished this monumental job at around 3am the following Tuesday, before setting about re-assembling the car with a new suspension set, having a new oil tank made by an outside contractor and finally repainting as necessary. "All this, mark you, at a time when most of our acknowledged ace chassis builders, sheet-metal workers, paint sprayers and managerial types were gadding about the US on the more lucrative CanAm series . . ."

The car was completed two weeks to the day after its accident – nine days after its arrival at Colnbrook. The only feasible route to Laredo was by air to New York, on to Los Angeles where the CanAm team would have transport waiting, then by road into Texas. Mike Barney and Alan McCall flew to LA, but fog caused the 'plane carrying the car to divert to San Francisco. Two days left, and now 1,900 miles to drive? They had been assured it was impossible to freight the car in closer to the rendezvous, now someone suggested flying it from 'Frisco to Dallas. Of course that was possible, the incredulous McLaren mechanics were assured. Midnight the following Tuesday, a week after the rebuild had been completed, Mike and Alan in Dallas, hiring a truck for the 600-mile freeway drive to the rendezvous. They managed it in 9½ hours, not knowing that the transporter convoy they had to meet had spent that same night in Dallas, leaving about an hour later and tracking them all the way. In Laredo the wild-eyed McLaren mechanics could not find anyone at the customs office who knew where the convoy "was waiting". When the convoy arrived they did not bother to inform anyone of their presence and Mike and Alan did not find them until mid-afternoon next day. It took a mere five minutes to load the rebuilt car into its allotted place . . .

This is a typical Formula 1 tale, repeated a dozen times over by any experienced Grand Prix team. The effort behind putting a star driver on the grid before the public eye is unimaginable by anyone who does not appreciate the demands of the motor racing life.

It had been a very full 19 days, but Bruce and Denny appeared fully-armed for practice and it was obvious the latter was really going for his second consecutive Championship title. Siffert and Amon occupied the front row after practice, Graham Hill and Denny 3-4, Gurney next up in his All-American Racers'-entered M7A/3, Stewart and Bruce each a row down behind him.

But Hill took an instant lead in his Lotus 49B from Stewart, Siffert and Denny. He could not keep touch with the leading trio and on lap 10 in the corner opening onto the pit straight a damper apparently broke and the car abruptly smeared itself off the barrier, plucking away both left-side wheels and slithering to rest just beyond the pit exit-road on its belly, a fuel line rubbed-away on the road surface and fire growing from friction sparks. Denny bounded clear as the fire-crew doused the blaze in a smother of white extinguishant. Mike Barney: "So that was it for the year, nothing left to do but pack up the rubbish and go home . . . at least we tried . . ."

Bruce retrieved Colnbrook honour by splitting the Lotuses to finish second behind new World Champion Graham Hill and ahead of his team-mate Jack Oliver, after Stewart's Matra had failed and Jo Siffert had dropped back. Marque McLaren finished runners-up in the Formula 1 Constructors' Championship. It had been their first full Formula 1 season. It was a great achievement, despite their dashed hopes in Mexico.

The M7As were good, workmanlike cars. They were compact and fast but mid-season performances had been disappointing with the inevitable concentration of effort upon CanAm preparations and it was only from Monza on that Denny had been able to mount his late run at the Championship. The production of a newly-competitive Goodyear tyre was undoubtedly highly significant in their change of fortune, and their reliability factor of 65 per cent including Dan Gurney's outings at St Jovite, Watkins Glen and Mexico City spoke highly for the team's painstaking preparation. They made 32 starts and finished 21 times and ran Hill and Lotus agonisingly close for road-racing's ultimate honour. Team McLaren had properly come of age, only four-and-a-half years after building the first car under their own name.

1969

For 1969 Bruce was enthused by the prospect of four-wheel drive in Formula 1. His enthusiasm pushed McLaren's M9A 4WD project through, Jo Marquart being responsible for the design. Bruce was not alone in his enthusiasm. Colin Chapman of Lotus followed the same path, as did Matra in France and also Robin Herd now with Cosworth. All were looking for better ways of harnessing their new V8 engine's horsepower. Every one of these cars would represent an expensive and time-consuming dead-end. The advent of strutted aerofoil aids to traction effectively side-stepped all 4WD's theoretical advantages. In road racing drivers would find they could not accustom themselves to the power understeer induced whenever a worthwhile share of engine power was directed through the front wheels. To retrieve some steering feel the only option was to reduce the share of power being fed to the front, and then one ended-up simply with a conventional rear-wheel drive car, carrying well over 100lbs extraneous weight in the complex transfer gearbox, forward prop-shaft and front final-drive and half-shaft arrangement. In comparison strutted wings represented negligible extra mass to be accelerated, braked and cornered, while their dynamic download effect imparted immense extra tractive capabilities to the road wheels. Once the tyre companies had produced rubber capable of handling that demand, conventional rear-drive cars streaked ahead.

BRM had researched Formula 1 4WD as far back as 1964. Teddy Mayer: "When Tony Rudd of BRM heard we were building a four-wheel drive car he said to Bruce: 'Have you tried fitting a hundredweight sack of cement in your car?' No, Bruce hadn't. 'Well have you tried setting-up your brakes so they bind all the time?' No, Bruce hadn't. 'Well have you tried de-tuning your engines to run only 300 horsepower?' No, we hadn't tried that either. And Tony said 'Well you might just as well, 'cos that's what it's like with four-wheel drive . . .' I dread to think how much that project cost us – I would guess it was about £70,000 at a time when that represented about a sixth of our total budget . . ."

After the Mexican race at the close of the '68 season one team M7A had been rebuilt and sold to Basil van Rooyen in South Africa, another followed, being displayed at the London Racing Car Show then shipped to Kyalami for 1200 trouble-free miles tyre testing. A third car, the M7B was built-up with integral pannier tank sections either side, Bruce having that pet theory about spreading the fuel load widely across the width of the car to help load-up the big wheels and tyres in corners. They had also had a lot of fun researching wings, running on the road, on the works Minivan . . .

Colnbrook test-rig – where strutted wings were concerned, McLaren soon caught up. This is the works Minivan, rigged for aerodynamic testing . . . Nothing if not practical . . .

Jo Marquart's ill-fated McLaren M9A four-wheel drive car in its only race – driven by the unfortunate Derek Bell – in the British GP that July. The car was a super-expensive waste of time, just as many friends advised the team it would be . . . It survives today in the fabulous Donington Collection near Derby, England.

Testing at Goodwood and Kyalami produced tall strutted rear airfoils which Denny and Bruce raced in the South African GP. At Brands Hatch for the Race of Champions the same cars also used strutted front wings during practice, but discarded them as untested before the race. At Silverstone for the International Trophy, Denny retained his usual M7A/2 while Bruce appeared in his new Gordon Coppuck-designed F5000 monocoque-based M7C – with the chassis plate 'M7A/004' attached. In effect it was an M10A F5000 tub with the engine-bay horns amputated to allow conventional DFV mounting, and would become his regular car. For the Spanish GP at Barcelona both M7s, Denny's A-type and Bruce's C, wore larger-rim reduced-offset front wheels largely to lighten steering effort.

They planned to introduce the M9A 4WD car at Zandvoort in June but it was not ready in time. Meanwhile the CSI had arbitrarily banned high-strutted wings at Monaco and all teams now sought the most effective method of carrying regulation low-level wings. At Zandvoort both regular McLaren M7s carried broad trays around and behind the engine to generate download, while front rim widths were now up from 9ins to 11. Colin Crabbe's Antique Automobiles team had acquired the slab-tanked 'M7B', with which Bruce had commenced the season, for their driver Vic Elford, and they were learning rapidly how to make it perform. It was a huge improvement over their old Cooper-Maserati T86.

Meanwhile at Colnbrook the M9A was hastily completed, in time for the British GP at Silverstone. The design was unusual in that whereas Lotus's Type 63 4WD monocoque extended either side of the Cosworth engine to the extreme rear of the car, and Matra's MS84 had a full-length spaceframe, the M9A still employed the DFV engine as a fully-stressed chassis member, bolted onto the rear closing plate of a conventionally truncated monocoque nacelle.

The engine was turned about-face with its power take-off just behind the driver's back, the transmission lying within the tub just behind his seat. He was placed far forward in the car, with one half-shaft enclosed within a tubular extension of the bevel-housing passing over his legs. He had to thread his feet under this shaft to locate the pedals, well ahead of the front axle line.

The transmission housing was McLaren-designed, only the ten pinions of the Hewland DG300 five-speed gearbox being of outside manufacture. The gearbox's primary shaft was hollow, with a quill-shaft from the twin-plate clutch passing through its centre from back to front, where the inner and outer shafts were splined together. A layshaft pinion drove through an idler gear to a straight-cut gear on the centre differential. This was a McLaren component, based broadly on Ferguson's design. A centre torque-split device had been made to divide power flowing to front and rear bevels. These were mounted on the car's left side, with propeller-shafts connecting to the centre diff and torque-split. Thick, heavily-ventilated disc brakes were mounted inboard on the half-shafts fore and aft to allow use of small 13in diameter road wheels. Front and rear suspensions were similar with double wishbones and inboard coil-spring/damper units, though the rear system added long bottom radius rods to react driving torque against the tub. It was a neat, tubby little newcomer, and of course being a McLaren it was exquisitely made and finished.

Bruce tested it at Goodwood first time out: "One of the things that will determine the performance of any of the new 4WD cars will be the ability of the driver to adapt to it. It just doesn't go round corners the same way as the conventional 2WD cars. An excess of power doesn't make the rear wheels break away – I don't know whether that's good or bad! It rained late that afternoon . . . I thought this would be my chance to try to lose control with it on one of the slower corners where there was plenty of road . . . I went in slower than usual, locked hard over and floored the throttle at the same time . . . all the car did was rocket-on round the corner . . . very disconcerting . . ."

But it was heavier than a 2WD car and would obviously take a lot of getting used to. Having built it, they suddenly weren't sure it had a future. Peter Gethin was to have driven it in the British GP in support of Bruce and Denny's regular M7s, but

he was racing the Church Farm team's F5000 M10A in America, so Derek Bell on leave from Ferrari took over instead. Elford appeared in Crabbe's M7B, and the race saw the M9A spin early-on due to a deflating tyre and soon retire after a nasty moment when a rear suspension component broke. Derek posted the second retirement of the race. The M9A test programme continued, briefly, but it was never to race again, and survives today as a silent exhibit in the Donington Collection of Single-Seater Racing Cars near Derby, England.

For the German GP, Bruce's M7C wore 13-inch front wheels with suspension geometry altered to suit and reinforced rear radius rod pick-ups since one had shown signs of incipient failure. Denny's faithful M7A was similarly improved. On the opening lap of the race Mario Andretti's 4WD Lotus 63 bottomed and left the road, losing two wheels against a wooden post. Poor Vic Elford hit one of the bounding wheels in Crabbe's M7B and was injured in a terrible crash which wrote-off the private McLaren.

Later in the season the cars were regaining their competitiveness on new Goodyear tyres, as at Monza where Bruce was fourth in a fantastic slip-streaming quartet at the finish, only 0.14 second behind Stewart's winning Matra, and an inebriated national newspaper motoring correspondent blundered into the mechanics' hotel room that night, and relieved himself over one of them ... Larger wings and brass radiators were fitted for the Canadian GP, the latter in expectation of high ambient temperatures, and the cars retained their Monza long-range right-side fuel sponsons. The same cars were run in the US and Mexican GPs, Goodyear's latest tyres giving Denny a staggering advantage in the final race enabling him to win handsomely, scoring McLaren's only victory of a hectic season – including as it did a full CanAm series of no less than eleven races. Concentration upon the abortive M9A 4WD project had compromised development of the M7s until the CanAm race programme intruded, and while Denny suffered reliability problems with his M7A, Bruce was at least theoretically better-off with his M7C and his finishing record was very good until Watkins Glen, when the engine blew on the warming-up lap and Mexico, where again it quit before the race began. Tyres played a decisive role. Firestone and Dunlop were ahead in the dry early in the season, until Goodyear's new G18 and G20 compounds dominated the final rounds. McLaren was also one of the happiest teams in Formula 1 with few internal squabbles, and Bruce finished the season third in the Drivers' Championship behind Jackie Stewart and Jacky Ickx (with Brabham that season) despite failing to win a GP all year. Denny won one, but early-season tyre troubles and later poor reliability restricted him to sixth in the table. The team took fourth place in the Constructors' Championship.

1970

In January 1970 the expected rear-wheel drive replacement for the faithful M7-series cars was introduced at Colnbrook. Known as the M14A it was improvement by evolution not revolution. The basic monocoque was effectively a simplified M7C, with 18-gauge aluminium skins bonded and riveted over fabricated mild-steel bulkheads. Where the M7-series' front suspensions had featured rear-facing links which demanded an extra internal monocoque bulkhead to provide anchorage, the M14A's ran ahead of the axle line to provide better lock and to increase the available length of fuel tank bay within the tub. Anti-roll bars were now tubular as on the CanAm cars to save weight. Front uprights were completely new, further reducing unsprung weight. At the rear inboard brakes were used. Coil-spring/damper units were all outboard, as before. Large 15-inch wheels were fitted, enabling 11.66in x ⅞in front brake discs with Lockheed twin-pot calipers to be buried within them at the front, while the 10.90in rears nestled against the Hewland transaxle cheeks. The monocoque wrapped 360-degrees into a robust stressed section in the scuttle area, just ahead of the dash-panel, while a detachable Specialised Moulding glass-fibre panel closed the open tub section ahead of that, with a separate nose cone which was wider and flatter than the M7A's enclosing the enlarged but lightweight aluminium water radiator up front. The team retained four of their 1969 Cosworth DFV engines and ordered two new ones. Two new M14As were taken to Kyalami for the South African GP in March, with M7A/2 as spare. A third M14A was to be completed later in the year. The old M7C had been sold to John Surtees, now operating independently and deep into construction of his own F1 car. He had the McLaren sprayed red with a white arrow down its nose and fitted with adjustable-width split-rim wheels as used on his TS5 Formula 5000 cars.

The Goodyear runners picked-up at Kyalami where the '69 season had ended, Jack Brabham winning in his brand-new monocoque Brabham BT33 while Denny finished second. The three Kyalami McLarens were joined for the Race of Champions by the faithful M7A/2 works entry for Peter Gethin, just reward for his previous year's F5000 dominance in the M10A model. Bruce crashed his car and it was rebuilt in time for the Spanish GP at Jarama, around a new tub, and with smaller front brakes and 13in wheels.

An interesting newcomer to the team was Andrea de Adamich's M7D – a new car built for a fee on the old jigs to accept an Alfa Romeo 3-litre V8 engine. This sports-car derived power unit promised to have very good torque, which should have made it ideal for the tighter circuits like Jarama and Monaco, and Alfa Romeo were keen to have a toe-hold in Formula 1, but as the team discovered individual units were to vary hugely in power output, torque characteristics, and standard of preparation when delivered from Alfa's Autodelta competition subsidiary. Andrea would have his work cut out just to qualify . . .

The team's second 'cadet driver' Reine Wisell made his bow in the GKN Trophy, Silverstone, with M7A/2 while Gethin drove his Sid Taylor F5000 M10B in the combined-Formula race. Denny was not impressed with 13in front wheels and at Monaco both mainstream F1s were back on 15s and new front uprights had been made.

Before the Belgian GP, Denny's hands were burned at Indy and Bruce died in the CanAm testing accident at Goodwood and team entries were withdrawn from the Spa race, along with Surtees' for his M7C as he was still dependent to some degree upon Colnbrook factory assistance.

They were back in harness for the Dutch GP at Zandvoort, where Dan Gurney was entered to drive M14A/1, specially modified to accommodate his lanky frame, and Peter Gethin drove Denny's regular car. Denny was present, but was preserving the tender new skin growing on his burned hands after the opening CanAm round the preceding weekend had caused it to lift and blister. A brand-new M14D had been completed for De Adamich and his Alfa Romeo engine, and Surtees' M7C reappeared. Unfortunately Peter was trapped into an understeering slide during the race and speared straight on into a bank, crumpling his loaned M14A's tub quite seriously. The team's main priority pre-French GP at Clermont-Ferrand was to convert the M14D to Cosworth power for Denny's return, while Andrea fell back on his M7D, neatly rigged with additional fuel tankage in readiness for a long, thirsty race. The Italian preferred the well-sorted M7D's handling, but it was heavier than the later version. Dan Gurney's car carried an enlarged wing, fitting neatly above the engine with a cutaway for the rearmost injection trumpets. Surtees withdrew due to engine shortage, his new F1 TS7-DFV nearing completion for a British GP debut. Cosworth were suffering the effects of a suspect batch of crankshafts, causing a chronic shortage of raceworthy DFVs for their customers.

At Brands Hatch, this shortage left Gethin without a drive, while Denny and Dan Gurney drove their M14s and a new spare tub was not yet available as a complete car. Andrea ran his M7D. Denny's hands were much improved, but one would still blister after a long drive. For this reason he was the only runner to use Goodyear's G20 tyres rather than the stickier new G24s. He would just bite his lip and bear the pain in his hands, though he sat slumped in his cockpit long after the finish, until they lifted him out . . .

Before the German GP, Gurney's contractual clash between his Castrol commitments and McLaren's to Gulf Oil came to a head. Therefore at Hockenheim Denny was joined in the team by Peter Gethin, Denny's car using the new Zandvoort-replacement M14A tub and Peter taking over the Kiwi's Brands Hatch machine. The M14D was rebuilt with the Alfa engine for Andrea.

Back at Colnbrook an entirely new 16-gauge skinned M14A tub was being completed, and this emerged as a complete car in time for the Italian GP at Monza, where Peter Gethin drove it, carrying chassis number '1' on its plate – the third car to do so that year. Denny was back in his original car there, the new one at Hockenheim being held back ready for the North American races. The team ran both their Alfa Romeo-engined cars at Monza, the M7D for 'Nanni' Galli and the M14D for Andrea. Jo Bonnier had acquired the ex-McLaren ex-Surtees M7C with its bullet-nosed pannier tanks, but neither he nor Galli could qualify.

By the end of the season the marque had failed to score a single GP victory for the first time in three years, and the curtailment of the tyre-test programme in mid-season, Denny's Indy burns and the brutal loss of Bruce himself had torn the heart out of their year . . . But they had survived, that was what mattered . . .

1971

The M14-series cars had not proved very successful, and for 1971 ex-Brabham designer Ralph Bellamy worked on a Formula 1 replacement, while Gordon Coppuck concentrated on Indy and CanAm. Ralph's new M19A was shown to the press one morning early in February '71.

The car was wider and longer than previous F1 McLarens, and to concentrate the fuel load around the centre of its wheelbase Ralph had adopted what he called "the Coke bottle shape, like a Matra" with the low-built tub swelling pregnantly around the cockpit. The wheelbase had been stretched to 8ft 4in from the preceding M14's 7ft 11in to enable more fuel to be housed between driver and engine in the rear of the tub. This was itself the usual beautifully-crafted structure built under the control of Don Beresford and Leo Wybrott in their prototype shop. Its outer skins were rolled from malleable NS4 aluminium-alloy sheet into voluptuous multiple curves shaped over internal steel bulkheads. The outer skin was in new-regulation 16-gauge thickness to resist impact penetration.

Glass-fibre body panels were made by Specialised Mouldings; a shapely top-ducted nose cone around the conventional radiator, and a large centre pillar-mounted rear wing with trailing-edge flap. The Cosworth DFV engine bolted-up against the monocoque's rear closing bulkhead in the usual way, and the engines were this year prepared and assembled by John Nicholson in his workshop within the factory.

It was the M19A's suspension which aroused most interest. Ralph had mounted his Koni coil/damper units inboard front and rear, attached to chassis pick-ups at their feet and coupled to short actuating rockers at the top. These rockers were fabricated from steel sheet and were linked to push-rods mounting low on the suspension arms. The geometry of all this push-me/pull-you arrangement was such that the springs were deflected by an accelerating degree the more the suspension deflected.

In other words a small initial movement of the road wheels would induce a small initial compression of the spring and its co-axial damper, but as the wheel moved as much again, the coil/damper unit was compressed rather more still. This gave the effect of a soft and supple suspension in initial movement, progressively hardening-up the more the wheel was deflected – it was rising-rate suspension.

Looking back on the M19A, Ralph Bellamy tells it this way: "I'd actually been detailed to help Jo Marquart to design a new F1 car for 1971. The project had only just begin when Jo told me quietly he would be leaving McLaren to start the Huron project. So we changed roles, with me in charge of the new F1 and him as my assistant because naturally he spent most of his time thinking about the new Huron. Then he left soon after, and I was officially given first design responsibility for the M19 . . ."

The new car ran its first tests on February 16 and looked promising although it was obvious that the drivers and Alastair Caldwell's mechanics would take some time to learn how to interpret what it was trying to tell them, and how to set it up. The prototype M19A-1 was taken to Kyalami for Denny Hulme to drive alongside Peter Gethin's M14A in the South African GP. To general amazement – and with the McLaren crew virtually hugging themselves in gleeful disbelief – Denny got into the lead and was holding off a frenzied closing drive by Mario Andretti in the Ferrari into the closing stages. Denny: "It would have become a very wide McLaren if he'd caught me".

But then the dream exploded with only four laps to run; Andretti rushed up over the hump past the pits ahead of the McLaren. The M19A's rear end had suddenly begun to steer. A bolt had fallen out of the suspension, but Denny was able to bring it home sixth.

Bellamy: "It was a bolt attaching a radius rod to the back of the tub. Just one of those awful things that can happen – at least it didn't send him off. But that was a

Memorable debut – Denny Hulme in the prototype M19A leading the 1971 South African GP at Kyalami before a rear suspension bolt broke and dropped him back. The M19-series suffered a chequered career after running into development problems with the Ralph Bellamy-designed rising-rate suspension system. By 1972 the M19s in Yardley livery would be formidable Formula 1 competition.

bitter disappointment. It would obviously have been great to win my first race with my new car".

In World Championship races that season the two regular cars M19A-1 and M19A-2 carried Denny to fifth in the Spanish GP, fourth at Monaco and 12th at Zandvoort where the second car emerged for Denny, and where Peter Gethin in M19A-1 was 15th though not covering sufficient distance to qualify as a finisher. He was ninth in the French GP, then Jack Oliver took over '1' for ninth in Austria and Mark Donohue took it into a tardy third place ahead of Denny's M19A-2 in the Canadian GP at Mosport. Mark's car was painted Penske dark blue with sponsorship from Sunoco Oil. In the US GP David Hobbs was tenth with Penske's car, just behind Peter Gethin now driving for BRM, while Denny crashed '2'.

It was again by no means a good year for McLaren. Their best showing even in non-Championship races was Denny's third in the Questor GP at Ontario Speedway, California, immediately after Kyalami, and after those heady early races the M19As' season fell to pieces.

Ralph: "The rising-rate suspension offered many theoretical advantages but in practice worked well enough on the front of the car and less well at the back. Trying to sort it all out and set up the system so the driver felt happy and could understand what was going on proved rather tricky . . ."

Gordon Coppuck, recalls that Goodyear changing tyre sizes in the middle of the M19As' development really fudged the issue, but Ralph feels the emphasis lay elsewhere: "The system wasn't beaten by changing tyre sizes but by my lack of knowledge. In early 1971 F1 cars ran into severe vibrations from the rear tyres which nobody understood. We now know that vibration occurs when the suspension is actually working well and the tyres are generating sufficient grip to distort severely. This we didn't understand . . ."

"Tyre vibration was BAD. To get rid of it was GOOD.

"We found that by fitting much stiffer rear springs, tyre vibration was eliminated, and what we were actually doing was reducing rear grip. The combination of variable-rate suspensions and hard springs was then found to be hopeless, but we didn't realise it until a test session with Mark Donohue at Silverstone showed that the rear suspension behaved in a strange way. We decided to try a conventional suspension the next day at Goodwood. When we did that, the car was improved. We then looked back over the records, and found that Denny had given us the same clues, but we hadn't interpreted them correctly . . ."

Mark Donohue had run a Penske Formula A car in the Questor GP and had gone well, and Roger began thinking of running him in Formula 1 in the Canadian and US GPs ending that season. The obvious car choice was McLaren. Roger and Teddy did the deal and in effect Donohue bumped Peter Gethin out of the team. But in mid-season, with the M19 so confusing its creators, Teddy and Tyler Alexander invited Donohue to test it and see if he could find some answers. He later recalled: "This was their first season without Bruce McLaren, and they seemed to have a need for a good driver-engineer . . . The car seemed to be understeering, but when we changed springs and anti-roll bars, nothing happened. It was just totally unresponsive. It didn't make any difference what we did – it always felt about the same. Sitting still it was soft enough to push up and down, but on the skidpad it acted as though the suspension was locked."

Eventually it was suspected that no matter how-soft springs were fitted, at the end of their rising-rate travel their rate would approach infinity. The front suspension was an integral part of the car, but the rear was on a removable cross-member. This could be easily changed, and it was there that rising-rate and extreme stiffness could cause oversteer on hard acceleration out of a corner, as the car squatted down. At the front, rising-rate characteristics combated bottoming when braking or cornering but Mark couldn't see great advantage at the rear, and it seemed he was right. But two weeks of testing yielded little further progress.

Penske took his M19A to Mosport two weeks before the Canadian GP but Donohue suffered a brake failure early on and crashed over a bank. Damage was

The team suffered the loss of Bruce's engineering input 'from the cockpit' and Mark Donohue of the Penske team was able to help out in that respect. Here he is in the Penske Racing/Kirk F. White Sunoco Oil-sponsored M19 during his F1 debut in the Canadian GP meeting, Mosport Park '71; Teddy thoughtful by the blue and yellow car's shapely flank.

not too major and it was then that the car was resprayed Penske-Sunoco blue and yellow while being rebuilt. Mark's third place in the race was scored in heavy rain and he was unimpressed both with the car and with his performance in setting-it up and driving it. He tried a non-rising rate front suspension in testing at Watkins Glen which was no better. A Trenton USAC race was rained-off and postponed to clash with the US GP, so Penske driver David Hobbs took the M19A instead and finished tenth. Donohue later came to believe that the M19's basic problem had more to do with poor wing forms than trick suspension . . .

During the winter of 1971-72, Ralph Bellamy left Colnbrook to rejoin Brabham, then on to Lotus with whom he would play a considerable part in the development of the ground-effect Lotus 78 and 79 in 1977-78.

Meanwhile Phil Kerr was in discussion with new sponsors for the team's Formula 1 programme. Yardley Cosmetics had made the most of two fairly trying years with BRM through 1970-71. Now their hard-nosed MD Dennis Matthews drove a hard bargain with Phil for prime McLaren sponsorship through the next two seasons, with an option for a third season in 1974. Goodyear and Gulf were co-sponsors, Gulf-orange side flashes appearing on the cars' finalised livery, with the Yardley white, black, gold and brown design dominating.

Chapter 2
The Yardley Years 1972-73

*"Yardley-McLaren as the F1 team is known, have a
reputation for being one of the most popular and charming
crews on the Grand Prix scene, in fact, just like Bruce
McLaren . . ."*
Alan Henry, Motoring News, July 13, 1972

The two M19As were run unchanged into 1972, the team coming to grips with them at last on improved tyres and wings, rising-rate front suspension, constant-rate at the rear. Peter Revson joined Denny in the F1 team, and he took M19A-1 as his regular car, Denny retaining M19A-2 in which he won at Kyalami.

A new lightened car designated M19C-1 (ostensibly last of the series to be built) was completed for Denny to drive in the Race of Champions. When Peter was absent at Indy, Brian Redman was called-in to drive the second car at Monaco, finishing fifth, At Whit weekend the Penske-McLaren M16B won Indianapolis, Jody Sheckter's works M21 F2 car won at Crystal Palace and Denny won the minor Oulton Park Gold Cup in M19A-1. Brian Redman crashed M19A-2 seriously in the French GP meeting at Clermont-Ferrand and the car was rebuilt around a brand-new tub. It appears that the shunted original was subsequently rebuilt and used to assemble a show version, renumbered as a replica: 'R4' according to 1980s M19A-2 owner Ken Moore.

The McLaren 'Coke bottle's best result apart from the Kyalami victory came in the Austrian GP at Osterreichring with Denny and Peter second and third in pursuit of Fittipaldi's dominant Lotus 72. Denny drove 'C-1 and Peter 'A-2 which itself had been rebuilt by this time around that new, simplified and lighter monocoque.

Vindication: back at Kyalami in '72 with the works M19A in Yardley livery, Denny leads Jackie Stewart's Tyrrell and the rest of the pack and won after coming so close the previous year only for his prototype car to fail.

Jody Scheckter's works Impact Group-sponsored F2 McLaren M21 en route to victory at Crystal Palace, Whit weekend '72 when Denny Hulme's M23 won a minor F1 race at Oulton Park and Mark Donohue's Penske Racing M16 won the Indy '500' – a great weekend for McLaren. The M21 was scheduled for Trojan production but the F2 market was thin and the tub design eventually formed the basis of Trojan's own F5000, marking the end of a long and successful association with McLaren.

Old M19A-1 was reworked with 49 gallons fuel capacity for the Rothmans 50,000 *Formule Libre* race at Brands Hatch, over 118 long laps of the GP circuit, and while Fittipaldi won again, Brian Redman finished second against a disappointingly thin field.

The team finished the season strongly, and at Watkins Glen young Jody Scheckter made his Formula 1 debut in 'A-1, running again teamed with Brian Redman in the final Brands Hatch Victory Race.

McLaren re-entered Formula 2 during this season with a brand-new full-length monocoque Ralph Bellamy-designed Cosworth FVA-engined car known as the M21. Impact Holdings, a garage group, had come forward with sponsorship and their one-car quasi-works programme demonstrated 22-year old South African driver Jody Scheckter's remarkable skills.

It was an expensive car to build but was immaculately maintained and prepared in the best McLaren traditions. Unfortunately it proved unpredictable, handling well on some circuits, poorly on others, and Jody lacked the experience to sort it out effectively. His best performance came in the last International F2 race to be staged at London's Crystal Palace parkland circuit, where he won handsomely. His was clearly a star talent in the making. But this was an expensive programme for Colnbrook, with little return, and by mid-season it was already known they would not continue into 1973. Trojan, however, had plans to put the F2 car into production. It didn't happen . . .

1973

The ageing M19s soldiered-on into the beginning of the 1973 season, but revised Formula 1 regulations demanding 'deformable structure' fuel tank protection within the chassis were to take effect from the Spanish GP, starting the European season on April 29.

Gordon Coppuck was completing his deformable structure M23 design to replace the M19s, while they contested the South American GPs commencing the new World Championship calendar. In South Africa, Denny gave the wedge-shaped new car its debut, qualifying on pole and leading sensationally until a puncture delayed him to finish fifth, while Peter's 'C-1 and Scheckter's 'C-2 respectively finished second and retired; Jody winning the drive on his home soil.

On March 18, 1973, Scheckter drove Denny's old 'C-1 in the Race of Champions at Brands Hatch, but contrived to crash it fairly gently at Druids Hairpin. Two M23s ran in the International Trophy race at Silverstone, and then came the Spanish GP and the old M19s were no longer eligible for Formula 1 since they lacked the new deformable structure tank protection. They passed into private hands, for conversion to Chevrolet V8 power and Formula 5000 use.

In its final form through 1972 the M19-series had handled very well but suffered from being relatively slow in a straight line. It was also overweight. Good-handling when achieved was attributed to the rising-rate front suspension and use of big wings, while low straight-line speed was blamed on induced drag from those wings and high profile drag from the bulbous shape.

The new M23 was Gordon's first Formula 1 design, deriving directly from the Lotus 72-prompted Indianapolis M16s. Suspension was virtually identical to that used on Denny's M19 as in the Brazilian GP. The deformable-structure monocoque tapered in planform, profile and section at the front, and the new hip-mounting pods for the split radiators were integral, unlike the detachable pods of the M16 track cars. These broad ducts provided an initial form of deformable-structure defence, the second line – sheathing the internal rubber fuel bags – was produced by double-skinning in 16-gauge aluminium alloy sheet sandwiching an injected foam. Development of this construction method had taken some time, but it was to prove extremely effective.

The M19-series' rising-rate front suspension was altered only in detail, retaining plain wide-based bottom wishbones, and twin-plane triangulated upper rocker arms formed by four tubular components. These rocker arms' inboard extensions actuated separate rocker links through pull-rods. The rockers then reacted against the top of the near-vertically mounted coil-spring/damper units.

Rear suspension was conventional, with adjustable top links, reversed lower wishbones and twin parallel radius rods. Reducing fuel load made a far greater percentage load difference on the front suspension than on the rear, so the rear suspension's rising rate system was much simpler, being confined to coil-springs tailored to become progressively coil-bound from the bottom end. Rack-and-pinion steering had been re-sited directly behind the top front wishbones to limit airflow disturbance towards the hip radiator ducts, and the links operating the front anti-roll bar were also enclosed for the same reason. The driver sat further forward than before, in a cockpit which Denny described as "the smallest we have ever had on a McLaren – so small that we now have a detachable steering wheel to help us get in and out. The reason for the slimline office is to bring the monocoque in very narrow and get the air passing back to the radiators."

Oil coolers sat behind the water radiators in the side-pods and the whole layout was extremely neat and tidy, with the dry-sump oil tank concealed within the tub ahead of the left-side cylinder bank, and a centre fuel cell between the tub's rear closing plate and the driver's seat. Wheelbase was 1in longer than the M19s in final form. Transmission was by McLaren's faithful Hewland FG400 transaxle.

Both Hulme and Revson were looking forward to the lower cockpit temperatures promised by the hip-radiator mounting. It had worked on the M20 CanAm cars "which was a big factor because it meant you never had to combat heat exhaustion in addition to everything else on the race track. Another plus is that with the fuel and oil tanks repositioned between us and the engine we will be effectively insulated from the heat of the engine . . ."

The new car ran 65-70 laps initial testing round Goodwood before being flown-out to South Africa for further testing at Kyalami prior to the Grand Prix. In its first day it ran faster than the M19-series' best-ever time after two years' development. Denny found the car far more controllable and predictable than the older cars: "It oversteers and stays out there in a nice comfortable slide. This may have been one of the reasons it was so fast around Goodwood . . . it didn't oversteer then go back to neutral; or understeer, back to neutral and oversteer again as the M19 did on occasion . . ."

Another sparkling Kyalami McLaren debut was made by Denny's M23 here in 1973 when the rugged Kiwi started from pole position and looked all set to win for the second successive year only to be delayed by a puncture. He managed to salvage fifth place while team-mate Peter Revson was second in an ageing M19.

In the heat of Kyalami the oil coolers were removed from the pods and re-slung either side of the gearbox but the car was very quick, and Denny took his first-ever pole position in a GP. He led the race but an early-lap collision had sprayed the roadway with debris and the M23 picked-up a puncture. Jody Scheckter was driving the spare M19 on his home soil and he sailed by to lead briefly before Stewart's Tyrrell rushed ahead. Back in the race, Denny was astonished to see a great plume of smoke streaming off his left front tyre every time he turned right. Presuming it too was deflating, although its profile looked stable, he made a second stop and had the wheel changed although it was not punctured. Revson's M19 finished second and Jody was fourth only four laps from home when his engine failed. Denny was way behind after his delays but salvaged fifth.

Throughout the '73 season the M23s were to qualify in the first three or four on the GP grids, and three of the new cars were available for the first deformable-structure GP at Barcelona's Montjuich Park circuit on April 29. At Zolder for the Belgian GP Denny's M23 carried a Graviner life-support system for the first time, a breathable air-supply piped into the driver's helmet and triggered in case of fire. Peter crashed his car as the track surface broke up, and Jarier's March later inflicted further damage on the parked car as he fell off . . .

The American was committed to a USAC race the same weekend as the French GP at Ricard and Scheckter rejoined the team for his M23 debut. He promptly out-qualified Denny, on the centre of the front row splitting Stewart's Tyrrell and Fittipaldi's Lotus, and led from flagfall until just 12 laps from the end when he had a controversial tangle with the Brazilian's black Lotus and both were forced to retire. Emerson was incensed by Jody's tactics but all who saw it believed it was a pure 50:50 incident, one of those things which will happen in a hard-fought race.

At Silverstone the team's brand-new articulated transporter disgorged the three Yardley M23s for Denny, Peter and Jody to drive; Ronnie Peterson's Lotus took pole from the senior McLaren pair with 'the boy' on row three. Ending the first lap Jody was waved ahead of his team-leader in hot pursuit of Stewart, Peterson and Reutemann's Brabham when he possibly hit a slick of oil or water left on Woodcote Corner from cars on the starting grid. On cool tyres, and full tanks, the South African's M23 drifted wide, put two wheels on the outside verge and snapped into a graceful half-spin, careering across the track to smash its nose on the pit-wall, after Peter's M23 had clipped-off its rear wing . . . Denny got through, but chaos erupted in his wake as a huge multiple accident engulfed the pack. Nine cars were eliminated.

Ninety-minutes later, the red-flagged race was restarted, and after a battle between Stewart and Peterson had ended with the Scot spinning off, Peter and Denny came to the fore, sandwiched the Swedes' Lotus and finished first and third; it was McLaren's first victory in their 'home' Grand Prix and Peter Revson's first-ever at this level; the first for the M23.

A brand-new M23 was completed as spare for Zandvoort to replace M23/3 shunted at Silverstone, and this car was driven by Ferrari refugee Jacky Ickx as a one-off guest appearance for the team, in support of Denny and Peter, in the German GP. Ickx knew the Nürburgring better than almost any other driver in Formula 1, and his knowledge helped him to finish third, behind the Tyrrells of Stewart and Cevert. Gordon had developed a new revised-geometry suspension set for the cars but testing at Silverstone proved inconclusive and the M23s were unchanged for Monza's Italian GP.

The M19s had gone well at Mosport '72 and for the Canadian GP there Peter qualified his M23 on the front row of the 2-2-2 grid alongside Peterson's pole-position Lotus, with Jody's sister car third fastest and Denny rather disgruntled, seventh. Heavy rain just before the start forced virtually everyone to fit wet-weather tyres, and Niki Lauda showed his class by leading in his Marlboro-BRM for the first 20 laps, until the circuit dried. There followed a spate of tyre-change stops to fit slicks, and almost simultaneously a collision between Scheckter's M23 and Cevert's Tyrrell brought out the pace car to slow the field.

'Fletcher flies' – Jody Scheckter, nicknamed 'Fletcher' by James Hunt after the youngster in 'Jonathan Livingstone Seagull' who tried to fly before being fully-fledged and enjoyed a long string of spectacular accidents because of it – led the French GP '73 from the start to within a dozen laps of the finish in his works M23. Here he is showing the way to reigning World Champion Emerson Fittipaldi's Lotus 72, shortly before they collided putting Emerson out of the race. The Brazilian was most displeased and when negotiating for a place in the new Texaco-Marlboro McLaren team for '74 he stipulated there should be no place for Scheckter. He went to Tyrrell instead, and ran Emerson very close for the World Championship.

Disastrously it led the wrong car, not the race leader, and from that moment lap-charting went to pieces in the control tower and along the pit row, and only after hours of post-race confusion was Peter Revson confirmed as winner of his second GP of the year in his 'YardleyMac'! Denny was in trouble with punctures from the warming-up lap and never featured.

Jody's collision had mangled M23/2's left-front corner and wrenched one side-pod upwards. The damage was repaired in McLaren Engines' facility at Livonia, Detroit, prior to the US GP at Watkins Glen, where Denny and Peter finished 4-5 and the South African went out when a rear wishbone broke, and he spun – this time harmlessly – to rest.

Chapter 3
Marlboro McLaren – World Champions

*"Now I can say I am certainly with the best team in Formula
One. Perhaps the car is not the best, I can't say for sure, but
the team is fantastic . . ."*

Emerson Fittipaldi, 1974

For 1974 the Texaco-Marlboro McLaren team was born, with Emerson Fittipaldi replacing Peter Revson who had gone to the American-financed Shadow team. Denny stayed on as Emerson's team-mate, while Phil Kerr's Yardley-McLaren team continued as a one-car operation with Mike Hailwood ex-Surtees driving.

McLaren's new line up made its race debut on January 13, 1974, in the Argentine Grand Prix on the Number 15 circuit of Buenos Aires Autodrome. Emerson qualified on row two, Denny alongside Mike Hailwood in the Yardley car on row five. Their red-and-white M23s were brand-new cars, chassis M23/5 and 23/6 with Mike the Bike inheriting the rebuilt prototype M23/1 from the previous season, while spare car M23/4 lay crated as a Texaco-Marlboro stand-by.

Major modifications had been made for the new season, the race-prepared cars featuring revised weight distribution after winter tests at Ricard, with a lengthy bell-housing spacer between engine and gearbox to move the rear axle further back, lengthening the wheelbase by 3ins. Rear track had been widened 2ins and geometry changes made to improve traction out of slow corners. Emerson had been responsible for the bulk of the winter testing, Denny as always content for someone else to do the work, and in the Buenos Aires paddock the Brazilian 1972 World Champion bubbled with unmitigated delight at his new team and car. He covered more practice laps than anyone else – 97 – and hurled the new M23 round with controlled forcefulness. But as the race started a plug lead came off and he stammered into the pits to have it replaced. Hailwood collided with Regazzoni's Ferrari but bounced clear and continued, while the ensuing chaos behind sent Revson's new Shadow straight into retirement. Emerson hared back into the race but managed to knock off the main ignition switch which was mounted on his McLaren's steering wheel. Assuming further electrical trouble he parked and slung off his safety harness before spotting his error. In an instant he had fired his engine again and then prudently returned to the pits for his harness to be cinched-up tight, an impossible task for the driver unaided . . .

Meanwhile, Denny was enjoying himself. His M23 was hurtling through the long fifth-gear loop at the end of the straight faster than anything else, and he closed on the leading bunch, then began picking them off, one-by-one. Reutemann was leading his home GP in the Brabham and was far ahead, Denny second. Around two-thirds distance the Brabham's airbox began to come apart, but although he had lost 200 rpm on top speed Reutemann was sitting on a 30 second time cushion from the Marlboro-McLaren. Just near the end it all went bitterly wrong for the Argentine driver. A plug lead came adrift from the distributor and his engine stammered onto seven cylinders. Denny began reeling him in, and on the penultimate lap his No '6' appeared in the lead to record the new team's first victory on their debut. Mike's Yardley car had a radiator punctured by a flying stone and he had to roll-off the revs to maintain safe temperatures, but survived to finish fourth.

In Brazil, the red-and-white cars had new optional higher radius rod pick-ups fitted, and more attention was paid to securing plug leads . . . The Yardley car had a dam across its chisel nose. Emerson qualified on pole and led from lap 16 to 32 whereupon the race was flagged to a halt due to heavy rain and he had won – two in a row for the Marlboro-McLarens; Mike was fifth, Denny way back after a puncture on the rolling lap, soft Goodyear tyres 'going off' during the race and a pit-stop to fit fresh.

Emerson stayed-on in Brazil for the minor non-Championship F1 race at Brasilia, in which his São Paulo-winning M23/5 started on the front row, out-qualified by Reutemann's Brabham, but won handsomely from Scheckter's Tyrrell after the Brabham's engine had blown. Three races, three wins for the team. The Brabham BT44 was quicker, but McLaren preparation and competitiveness had paid off.

The long-wheelbase form of these '74 M23s allowed the rear wing to be mounted as far back as possible from the aerodynamic disturbance created by the front-end of the car, although new restrictions for this season had seen it brought forward 10-inches from its '73 position, but only relative to the rear wheels as the new regulation demanded. Increasing the rear track also served to clear airflow under the wing's working undersurface, and for the Race of Champions at Brands Hatch a new rear wing mounting appeared which was so ingenious several other teams looked at it covetously. Another Brands Hatch innovation was the use of a slender 'winkle-picker' wedge nose carrying longer, high-aspect ratio canard wings either side. Both front and rear 'foils used an exaggerated banana section. Denny and Mike Hailwood drove their regular cars, while Emerson fell back on the ex-Revson 23/4 spare. The race was run in heavy rain. Emerson lay second initially behind Reutemann's Brabham until a tyre began to deflate and he placed third. Mike was a distant fourth with inoperative clutch release and Denny as always showed his hatred and disgust for wet-weather racing, made three pit stops complaining of oil on his visor, and came nowhere . . .

Peter Revson was sixth in his Shadow. A week later, testing at Kyalami, a mechanical failure pitched his car into the Armco barriers, and he was killed . . .

There Denny tried his M23/6 originally in '73 trim, complete down to the original wheelbase, rear track width, old nose-cone, older-style wing sections and 26 inch outside diameter rear tyres. But the car destroyed its Goodyears and felt awful. On the second day's official practice M23/6 was on Brands Hatch settings, like Emerson's '23/5 and Hailwood's Yardley '23/1. The taller, newer 28-inch outside diameter Goodyears promoted better stability and traction, and older-style broad nose-cones replaced the 'winkle-pickers'. Mike had finished third.

Back home the International Trophy at Silverstone fell to James Hunt's Hesketh, Marlboro-McLaren running Denny in old M23/4 and Phil Kerr's Yardley team the brand-new M23/7 for Mike Hailwood. Both went out early after qualifying side-by-side on row two, and Mike lying second as the race began.

Gordon had all five M23s at Jarama for the Spanish GP set up in short-wheelbase form with alternative monocoque pick-ups for the rear radius rods in an effort to isolate optimum anti-squat characteristics. Denny's M23/6 had five alternative lower and three upper pick-ups, while Mike's spare Yardley M23/1 was in standard form as a baseline for comparison. Ferrari's new pairing of Niki Lauda and Clay Regazzoni finished 1-2 in their flat-12 312B cars, Emerson finished a solid and reliable third after showing no serious challenge for the lead, and Denny was sixth.

The Belgian GP was run at Nivelles near Brussels, and with the M23s all in long-wheelbase form Emerson became the first driver of the season to win two GPs, fighting off a strong Ferrari challenge to do so. Denny was sixth and set fastest lap, and Mike had been running fifth until two laps from the finish when fuel pick-up problems dropped him back.

McLaren was the most numerous marque at Monaco, where Emerson's regular M23/5 appeared with a short bell-housing spacer between engine and gearbox, Denny's M23/6 a long spacer and Mike's M23/7 a medium-length one. Each used

*Overleaf:
Emerson winning
the Brazilian GP at
the start of his '74
season with
Marlboro-McLaren
– second race,
second win. Here
the revised M23
shows off its new
red, white and black
livery and revised
suspensions.*

179

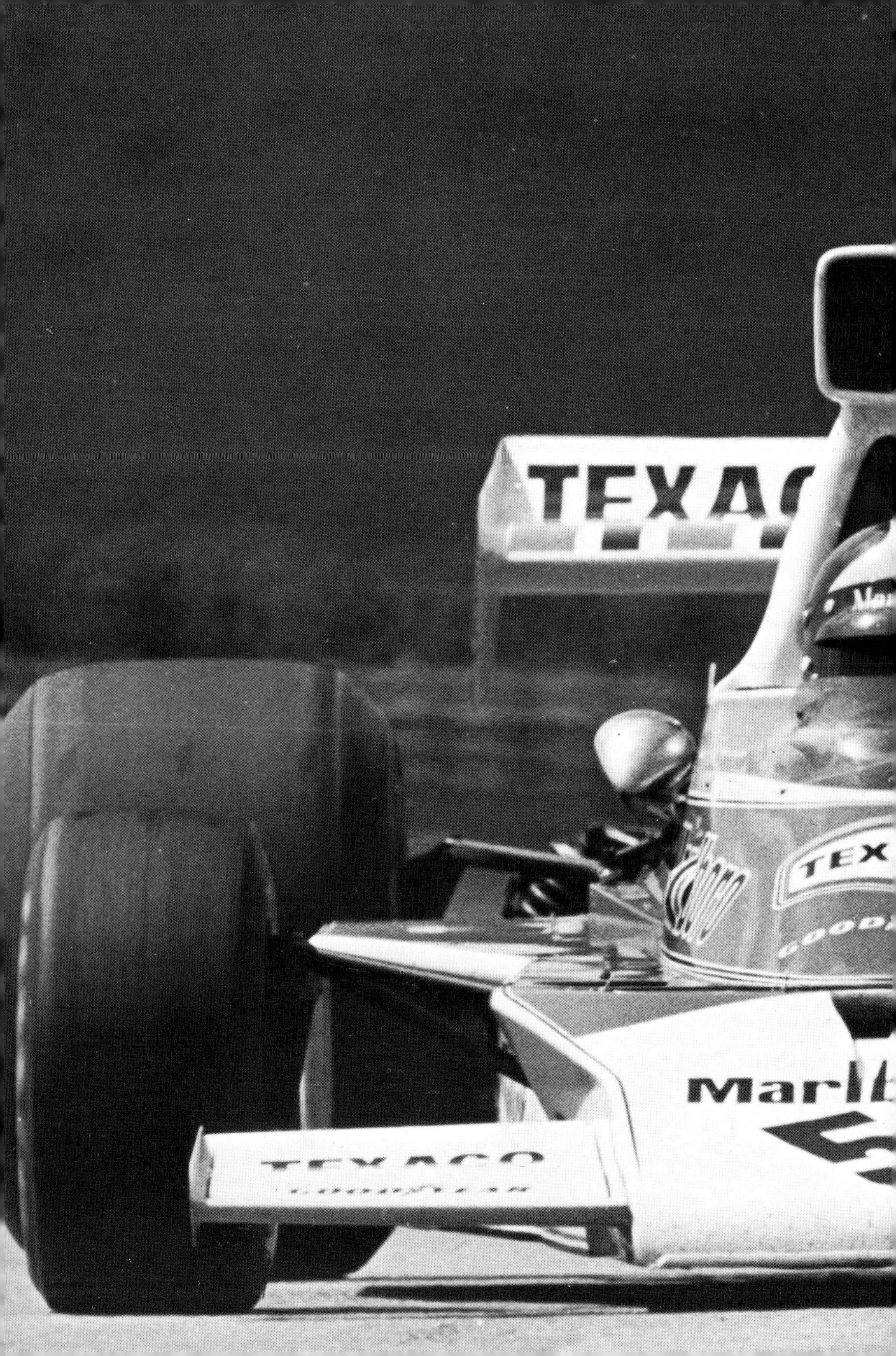
TEXACO

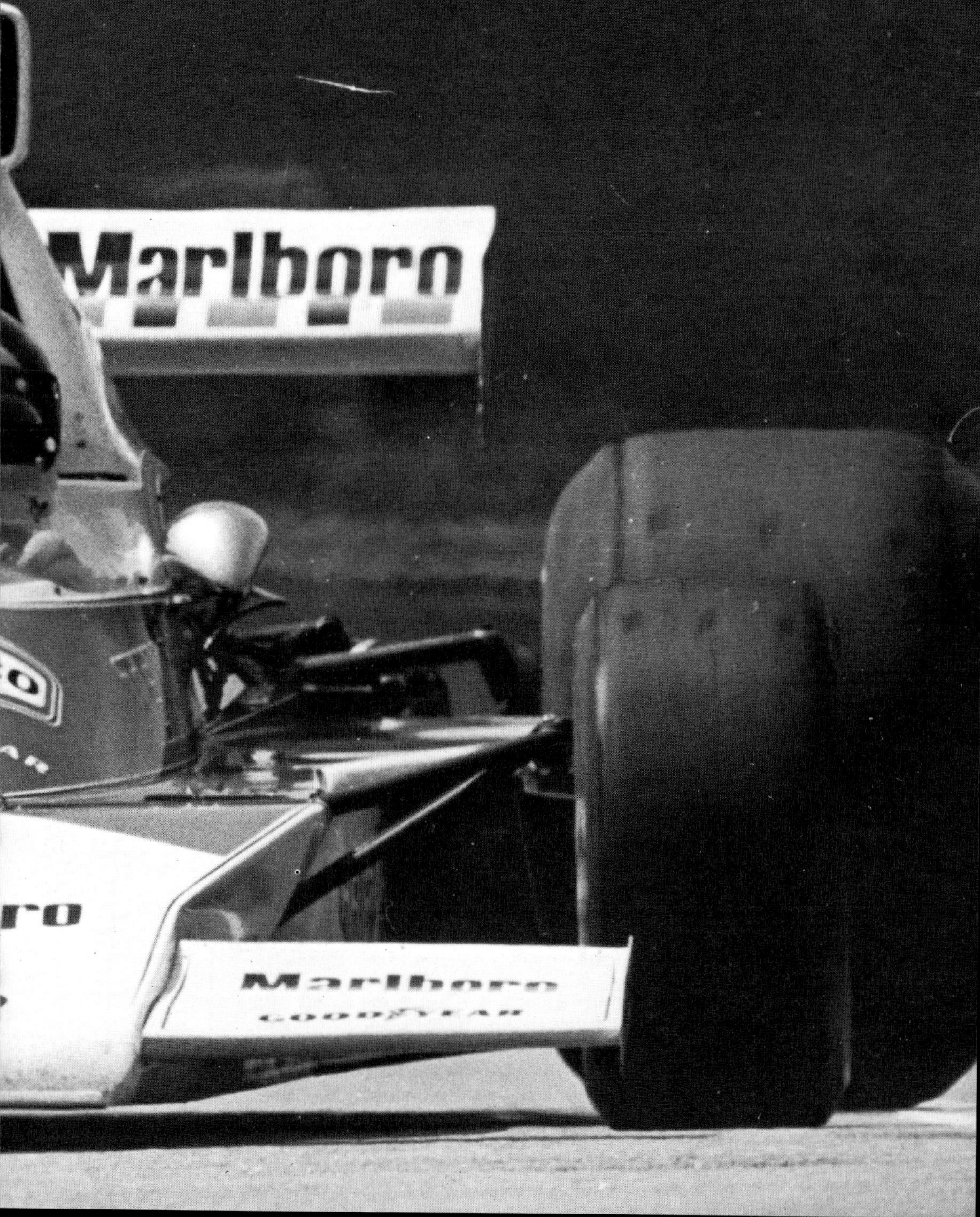
Marlboro
Marlboro
GOODYEAR

Battle of the Champions at Nivelles in the '74 Belgian GP, with Emerson's M23 just holding off comingman Niki Lauda's Ferrari 312B3 to notch another victory on his way to the year's Drivers' World Championship and McLaren's first Formula 1 Constructors' title after ten years' endeavour.

the winkle-picker nose cone and long canard wings, Emerson's having the extra feature of vertical sighting masts on the canard wingtips so he could place the car more accurately around the twisty Monte Carlo circuit. Mike raced his older car while Emerson fought against a bout of 'flu, feeling weak and shivery all weekend. Denny went out in a first-lap multiple collision on the climb towards the Casino, and Mike clanged into the barrier at Massenet after hitting spilled oil. Emerson was a muted fifth, but was still accumulating World Championship points, and still led the title standings.

The damaged cars were repaired at Dijon during tests for the French GP there later in the year, then the team hauled north for the Swedish round at Anderstorp. The Tyrrell team dominated there, Jody Scheckter scoring his first GP victory with team-mate Patrick Depailler on his heels. The Marlboro-Team Texaco M23s ran in long-wheelbase form, while Hailwood's Yardley M23/7 used the medium spacer, M23/1's matching its red-and-white sisters. Mike went out early with a fuel leak, Denny had a suspension collapse and Emerson drove steadily home fourth, three more points for the accountant . . .

At Zandvoort, Emerson and Mike finished 3-4 behind the Ferraris, and at Dijon-Prenois for the French GP the M23s appeared with new slimline, large-profile engine air-boxes to improve airflow onto the rear wings. A blown engine wrecked Emerson's hopes of maintaining his Championship lead, while Denny and Mike salvaged 6-7. Ferrari drivers Lauda and Regazzoni demoted the Brazilian to third place in the points table.

The British GP was run at Brands Hatch where Emerson was armed with a brand-new M23/8, featuring low-offset front suspension with revised steering geometry, and parallel lower link rear suspension replacing the old reversed wishbone system. Emerson liked the reduced steering effort achieved by the new front suspension and would race the car. He drove a steady, typically intelligent race to inherit second place at the finish behind Scheckter's Tyrrell, Denny was a distant sixth and Mike spun and stalled to lose fourth place. His engine had been running hot and he was using one gear higher than usual in his efforts to conserve it. With insufficient torque available to kick the car straight when it suddenly slid out of line he spun helplessly onto the grass and then found his hot engine impossible to restart. The Yardley M23 was absolutely unmarked.

Two weeks later, the German GP was held at Nürburgring. Now the Marlboro-Team Texaco spare car M23/5 had been completed with parallel-link rear suspension and low-offset front end, while Denny's and Mike's two Yardley cars all retained the earlier set-up. During practice Mike had a frightening experience in M23/1 when it slammed sharp right out of the corner before the pits and damaged itself severely against the Armco. Hailwood leapt out shaken and bewildered, convinced something had broken, though continuing in M23/7.

Emerson was quick in practice but not quick enough for the front row and on the warm-up lap around the pits loop found his engine wouldn't rev cleanly. Consternation reigned. He seemed set to take the team spare sitting on the pit lane, but after some frantic work took his place on the grid in his allotted car. As the flag fell the horrified Brazilian's heart leaped as he found he couldn't pick-up first gear. Stranded near the head of the grid he flung his hand high and cowered down in his cockpit. Cars swerved past on both sides, inevitably someone wouldn't miss the stranded McLaren, and ironically it was Denny whose right-rear wheel thumped Emerson's left-rear to send 'The Bear' slithering into retirement twenty yards further on with his car's suspension shattered. Emerson got away but his damaged left-rear tyre was deflating and he limped into the pits to change it. Denny wasn't there. He had jumped smartly into the team spare and set off into the race, surviving two laps before officialdom disqualified him. Emerson's gearbox failed after three laps, but Mike's Yardley car was running fifth on lap 12 when it landed askew after a yump on the back of the circuit and then speared head-on into the Armco. The front of the car was demolished, and Mike trapped in it with a broken ankle, shin and complicated knee fracture. Initially it was thought he would be out of racing for three months. In fact it was the end of the popular English ace's motor racing career. It was a dark day for McLaren . . .

Phil Kerr's Yardley division of the team had both chassis severely damaged, and for the Austrian race two weeks later they had taken over Marlboro-Team Texaco's spare M23/4 which Denny had last raced at Jarama, and resprayed it in their livery for David Hobbs to drive. Emerson's latest-spec M23/8 was on hand for him, while Denny's older M23/6 retained the reversed wishbone rear suspension. Spare car M23/5 was to the latest spec. Emerson drove hard to head the field and compensate for his mid-season set-backs but his engine blew while running third. Denny made the most of a steady drive to inherit second place behind Reutemann, and Hobbs drove as competently as ever into seventh place.

The same cars appeared at Monza where Lotus team-mates of the preceding year, Emerson Fittipaldi and Ronnie Peterson, tigered for the lead, McLaren M23 versus Lotus 72. Lauda's Ferrari led and retired. Regazzoni's Ferrari followed suit. The Lotus and McLaren emerged, locked in combat for the lead . . .

Just before Regazzoni's red car smoked into the pit lane Emerson rushed deep inside Peterson's black Lotus under braking for the first chicane approaching the *Curva Grande*. The McLaren scrabbled-in on such a tight line that both cars were forced almost to a walking pace to stay on the road without colliding, Ronnie was better-placed on the exit and he retook the lead away through the high-speed curve beyond. They had battled this way, as Lotus team-mates, the previous year, but now there was no thought of either giving precedence. Twelve laps to go, Emerson trying the inside again into that first chicane. Ronnie held him out and drew slightly away. They were closing on Denny's M23, ready to lap it. Could 'The Bear' do anything to assist his team-mate? Ronnie had no doubts, slamming round outside the New Zealander in the first of the twin corners at Lesmo. Emerson found himself boxed-in for a few hundred yards, but through the left-hander at

ROMAN BRIO. MEN'S TOILETRIES

Champions! The Texaco-Marlboro McLaren crew erupt onto the trackside to greet Emerson's World Championship-clinching fourth place finish in the '74 US GP at Watkins Glen.

Vialone Denny stepped aside and Emerson blasted through. He could hold the Lotus through the turns but Ronnie drew away on the straights with his narrow-track car, and round the final lap it was Peterson and Lotus all the way, though the winning margin was only 0.8 second.

McLaren displaced Ferrari at the head of the Constructors' Championship. Regazzoni led the Drivers' title-chase with 46 points to Scheckter's 45 and Emerson third now with 43.

Only two Championship rounds remained; the Canadian GP at Mosport Park and the United States GP at Watkins Glen, where the title would be decided.

Jochen Mass, who had walked out of the Surtees team earlier in the year, was to take Hobbs' place in the Yardley M23 for these North American races, inheriting M23/4 while Fittipaldi and Hulme were to drive their regular cars. Emerson was holding nothing back and made his bid for the Championship in practice with a spectacular drive showing all his old skill and commitment to qualify on pole. Niki Lauda's Ferrari led for much of the race, with Emerson second, until 11 laps from the end he went off the road on debris flung onto the road by John Watson's wayward Brabham. Emerson inherited the lead and won comfortably from Regazzoni's second-string Ferrari. Denny finished sixth, while Mass had a torrid

debit in the Yardley car, beset with handling problems but finishing 16th.

McLaren now led the Constructors' Championship by 70 points to Ferrari's 64, while into the last round at Watkins Glen, Emerson and Regazzoni were tied for the Drivers' title on 52 points each, and Scheckter still had a mathematical chance of pipping them both for the Championship, third with 45 points; and nine available for a win . . .

It was the closest finale to the World Championship since 1964, when Jim Clark, Graham Hill and John Surtees could all win into the final lap of the final race . . .

Tactics could decide the Championship, so for Watkins Glen Teddy Mayer had his USAC team's two-way radios fitted in the Marlboro-Team Texaco M23s, which were as at Mosport. Pulling brakes caused Emerson fright in first practice, the spare car's set being fitted and curing the problem. Of the Championship contenders, Scheckter qualified best, on row three, with Emerson behind him and Ferrari – in acute handling problems – with Regazzoni on row five and already feeling he had no chance. Denny survived four race laps before his engine blew. He strode to a waiting helicopter in the paddock and flew away, out of Watkins Glen, and out of motor racing. "I'm a retired racing driver right now" he tittered to a questioning pressman. The 1967 World Champion, former double CanAm Champion for McLaren, had hung up his helmet . . . It was the low-key end to a fine career . . .

Out on circuit, Emerson settled down to keep Scheckter's dark-blue Tyrrell in his sights. With Regazzoni out of contention, his Ferrari handling diabolically badly, all the Brazilian had to do was finish on the Tyrrell's tail and he would be World Champion. It happened on lap 44. The Tyrrell fell victim to a mysterious fuel pick-up ailment which interrupted flow to the engine, and Jody was slowing and pulling in against the barrier to park it. Emerson dodged by and knew then he had his second World Championship sewn-up. If he failed to finish, Regazzoni was too far behind to score points, except by a miracle. He could afford to sit back and he cruised happily home fourth, securing the coveted Drivers' title for himself, and the Constructors' Championship at long last for Team McLaren – ten years after Bruce and Teddy had founded their team and company . . .

1975

Through 1975, Niki Lauda and Ferrari achieved dominance as Gordon's M23-series cars raced through their third season, substantially unaltered from original form. Early in the new season various suspension revisions were tried to improve front-end adhesion and 'turn-in' performance. Four cars were used in the course of the season, two being written-off by Emerson's now regular number two Jochen Mass at Nürburgring. Ferrari had the most powerful and reliable cars of the year, but their 75 per cent finishing record only marginally shaded Alastair Caldwell-managed McLaren reliability of 74 percent; 20 finishes from 27 starts. Lauda deposed Emerson as title holder and the Brazilian's final tally of two GP victories in the season showed how he drove extremely rapidly and competitively in those races before settling back merely to accumulate place points rather than tiger for outright victory in the rest. Towards the end of the summer, people close to him were talking of his having decided to retire from racing. But by the time of the Italian GP at Monza he'd changed his mind. And it showed, as he drove in magnificent style there and at Watkins Glen. Mass meanwhile matured into a happy number two driver, stable, content with his lot and normally very reliable.

In Argentina in January, Emerson had a bright shiny new car, M23/9, for his own use, carrying Brabham-like front suspension in which the original slender tubular links and rocker arms had been replaced by a substantial swept-back fabricated top rocker arm with pull-rods mounted under their outboard extremities, pulling-up a shaped actuating arm at the foot of gently inclined semi-inboard coil-spring/damper units. Mass's car M23/8 retained the old fully-inboard front suspension, while Emerson's new machine also ran appreciably narrower rear track and both cars wore shorter nose cones.

During the opening stages of the race Emerson was content to sit back in fifth place, pacing himself and his car in the hot Buenos Aires sun and awaiting developments. As the front runners hit trouble he began to force the pace, really racing in the final 30 laps and pressuring Hunt's leading Hesketh into the spin which cost it the race. James recovered quickly to fight back but Emerson sprinted to the line 5.9 secs clear for the 12th victory of his Grand Prix career.

In Brazil the cars were unchanged, and they finished 2-3 with Emerson beaten on his home ground by compatriot Carlos Pace's Brabham; Jochen Mass third.

The Brabham-crib front suspension on M23/9 employed swept-back arms in these South American races, and was modified in time for the South African GP in March with right-angle arms, in effect lengthening the wheelbase and moving the centre of gravity forward slightly. Jochen's car M23/8 had been converted to the new front suspension in South American form with the swept-back arms and shorter wheelbase. Old M23/6 was present as spare. Emerson had his engine blow in practice, gushing hot oil which sent Niki Lauda's pursuing Ferrari clattering into the catch-fencing. His spare car was prepared with the latest-style suspension but Emerson started from mid-grid. His engine began misfiring in the race and he had to stop three times for attention before a cracked and shorting-out plug lead was discovered and replaced. He lost virtually ten laps and was out of the running. Jochen, meanwhile, finished sixth.

At the Race of Champions, the spare M23/4 appeared with a third variant front suspension, with the coil/dampers mounted totally inboard again, but vertically. Emerson drove a lack-lustre race and Jochen was side-lined in an early collision. The season's second non-Championship race at Silverstone in April saw Emerson complaining of twitchy handling in practice and being beaten into second place by Lauda's Ferrari in the race. Non-rising rate fully-inboard front suspension had now been adopted, and the two regular race cars at Barcelona for the Spanish GP both carried it, while the spare M23/5 last used at Kyalami retained the South American-type rising-rate layout. But Emerson was deeply unhappy with circuit safety arrangements during practice and opted-out from driving in the race. Jochen took the start and when a terrible accident saw the red flag brought out after only 29 laps he was leading, and he and McLaren were awarded a cheerless race victory.

The regular cars reappeared at Monaco where they were presented in 1974 medium-wheelbase form in search of agility, and Emerson's featured a new cockpit-adjustable front anti-roll bar, enabling him to soften roll-stiffness as the fuel load burned off during the race. He finished second behind Lauda's Ferrari, Jochen losing fifth place to Depailler's Tyrrell on the last lap.

The long-wheelbase form returned for Zolder where a rapid practice change saw Emerson's M23/9 fitted with narrow track front suspension and going faster. But the Ferraris and Brabhams were quicker still. Emerson's brakes faded late in the race, dropping him out of the points while Jochen spun in the middle of the pack on the opening lap and became first retirement.

Gordon developed further suspension tweaks for M23/9 in time for Sweden, but Emerson was unimpressed and again missed the points with indifferent handling and fading rear brakes. Jochen clouted a water pipe by bounding over a kerb and cooked his Cosworth, and his chances . . .

Gordon smiling claimed "the Mark 197 arrangement" when M23/9 was unloaded at Zandvoort with further modified rear suspension, and rear-extension shrouds on the radiator side pods in an attempt to smooth the car's profile and ease airflow onto the rear wing. Emerson's engine failed while Jochen was afflicted by massive understeer and a metering unit on full rich which gave him "all or nothing" in terms of throttle response, and his M23/8 eventually got away from him and crashed quite heavily. Its front end was savaged, and for the following French GP Jochen was to race M23/6, while Emerson persevered with M23/9 in "Mark 197" form as in Holland. Jochen was to drive the best race of his career there at Ricard, finishing third close behind Hunt's second-placed Hesketh and the winning Lauda Ferrari. And World Champion Fittipaldi? He struggled against ill-handling to salvage fourth, a long way behind.

For the British GP at Silverstone, Emerson's regular car sported a new swallow-tailed rear wing, but the race was dominated by Brabham and Ferrari early on until after 15 laps it began to shower with rain out at Stowe Corner. Regazzoni spun out of the lead, and it began to rain steadily. Cloud cover was patchy, drivers had to wrestle with the decision whether to stay out on slick tyres or rush into the pits to change to wets, knowing they might have to stop again if the circuit dried out. Emerson stayed out, second as others stopped – pacing round after Hunt's leading Hesketh. But then James' engine lost its edge, Emerson closed and took the lead on lap 43. Ten laps later the heavens opened in a torrential downpour engulfing the back of the circuit. Cars slowed to near walking pace, pluming round in gentle bursts of throttle and slithering through the corners. Most of the field completed their 55th lap, but Emerson was the only one to complete a 56th. Rivers of rain-water were gushing across the track between Stowe and Club Corners. Swishing soggily into the catch-fencing at Stowe went three cars, including Jochen's McLaren. At Club Corner six more cars careered into the safety fences, and when Emerson arrived in the pit lane calling for wet tyres he was told the stewards had abandoned the race; it was all over, and he and McLaren had won the British Grand Prix . . .

Emerson had driven the whole way with a touch of the flair which had given him his 1972 World Championship with Lotus – as Alan Henry commented in *Motoring News*. "It really was a flash of the old Fittipaldi . . ." Less impressed, some others remarked "Look at McLaren, always winning the funny races, the Spanish GP cut short by Stommelen's accident, now the British in the rain . . ." but Emerson had kept his head and control while all around were losing their's . . . It was a mark of his class . . .

Jochen's Zandvoort-damaged M23/8 was rebuilt in time for Nürburgring and the German GP, only outward differences on the Marlboro cars there being contoured trailing flairs to the radiator side-pod cowlings and the addition of perspex vestigial skirts round the bottom periphery of the cars. Gordon had tried this idea at Dijon the previous year, uncertain whether they gave any aerodynamic advantage but willing to give them another try over the humps and bumps of Nürburgring. Emerson's M23/9 had lost its cockpit-adjustable front anti-roll bar.

Trying hard on his home ground, Jochen slid wide onto a streak of dust near *Brünnchen* and spun violently into the barrier, his just rebuilt car being comprehensively re-arranged again and obviously of no further use that weekend. Jochen emerged blaming nobody but himself for trying too hard. Still he had qualified faster than his team leader, and then on the first lap of the race in his spare car, old M23/4, he had a front tyre collapse at the bottom of the fearsomely-fast *Fuchsröhre* – "Fox's Throat" – dip. The car bottomed and thundered into the rightside barrier before richocheting back across the roadway, narrowly-missing the rest of the pack and destroying itself finally on the left-side Armco. The young German again emerged shaken but unhurt; smiling later "I wasn't sure whether I would get away with that one or not . . . I just kept my head down and hung on!"

Soon after losing their second-string car like this, the team's number one was overdue and was reported to be touring in slowly with a punctured left-rear tyre. After a replacement had been fitted Emerson found his car vibrating severely, and stopped for another. There was no improvement, clearly something had been damaged at the rear so after three disconsolate laps the World Champion retired and the McLaren crew cleared-away their gear long before the race had ended, in a win for Reutemann's Brabham. Nürburgring was not their favourite circuit.

Home at Colnbrook, work began to resurrect a full complement of M23s, while Gordon's brand-new M26 was under design. No spare car was available for the trip to Österreichring and the Austrian GP, in which Emerson retained his regular

M23/9 and Jochen took over the ex-Hulme M23/6. In race-morning warm-up Mark Donohue, out of retirement this season to race Roger Penske's new F1 car, crashed heavily and subsequently succumbed to his injuries. Another McLaren star had gone.

In the race, heavy rain again caused a premature halt, Jochen was classified fourth and Emerson a distant ninth, not caring at all for this kind of racing . . .

There was a mid-season Marlboro-supported non-Championship 'Swiss GP' at Dijon in mid-August, and McLaren naturally appeared, with Emerson in a brand-new M23/10, his old regular car becoming team spare while Jochen retained M23/6 as in Austria. But the Brazilian cooked his clutch at the start and retired after six laps, while Jochen drove well to finish third, having started fourth-fastest.Ferrari won the 'Swiss', and simply dominated the Italian GP which followed at Monza, but it was there that Emerson really began to perform anew.

He had his new car, serialled M23/8-2, but really M23-10 replacing Jochen's milder Nürburgring write-off, and despite practice problems with engine failures and bending suspension by bounding too enthusiastically over the chicane kerbs, Emerson qualified on row two behind the Lauda and Regazzoni Ferraris, and Jochen was right behind him. The German's luck was out again as he became involved in a tangle at one of the slow chicanes on the opening lap, and while the Ferraris looked set to dominate, Emerson set about them, and eventually finished second as the meat in a Ferrari sandwich. Niki Lauda was World Champion.

The season ended at Watkins Glen in upstate New York, where Emerson again showed real fire and was only narrowly bumped off pole position by Lauda, lining-up on the front row beside the scarlet Ferrari. They ran in that order for the first 20 laps, Emerson challenging hard for the lead until they came upon Regazzoni in the delayed second Ferrari and prepared to lap him. Lauda slipped by, but Emerson was so badly baulked that he lost 13 seconds in five laps . . . The organisers black-flagged the Swiss Ferrari driver for a lecture so Emerson got by at last while Ferrari's team director scuffled with the large Clerk of the Course . . . But Emerson's chance of seriously challenging Lauda for the lead had gone, and he came home an honourable second, and Jochen completed a fine McLaren outing with third place. In 1975 it was no disgrace to be second and third behind Lauda in a Ferrari 312T . . .

So 1975's World Championship season ended, with Emerson runner-up for the Drivers' title and McLaren third behind Ferrari and Brabham in the Constructors' Championship . . .

1976

Towards the end of 1975, Emerson Fittipaldi's third-year McLaren contract option should have been exercised, but he delayed signing. Testing at Ricard in November '75 he crashed and broke a finger after setting fastest time amongst the teams running there. The following week Lord Hesketh announced that unless a major sponsor came forward within a week to back his Formula 1 team it would cease operations forthwith – leaving star driver James Hunt without a drive.

James had already taken insurance against such a closure, talking with both Brabham and Lotus. At Colnbrook Teddy Mayer had been trying to finalise Emerson's signature for another season, with a deadline of November 25. Then at 8pm on Saturday November 22 the 'phone rang in his home in Esher. It was the Brazilian double-World Champion, calling from a coin-box at Zurich Airport. "I've called to tell you I'm not going to sign. I have signed with my brother Wilson for our own team next year . . ."

Now Teddy and Marlboro moved and within thirty-six hours had James Hunt. "He was very good. Very businesslike. He said what he wanted and signed-on . . ." Hunt and John Hogan of Marlboro concluded their sponsorship deal; John later observing that Hunt must have been the cheapest World Champion in recent racing history.

New driver, new star, new problem – James Hunt on his winning way in the 1976 Spanish GP, showing off the M23's new low-level airbox to comply with revised regulations like the new forward roll-over bar just visible ahead of the steering wheel, a line from its peak to that of the rear roll-over bar having

to pass above the driver's helmet with him "normally seated". In post-race scrutineering the rear track would offend, and the race winner would be disqualified. It set the tone for a controversial but exciting and dramatic year.

He drove his first McLaren laps at a mist-shrouded Silverstone in December, using the ex-Fittipaldi M23/8-2, its pedal layout suitably moved forward to accommodate the Englishman's lanky frame instead of the stocky Brazilian's.

At Colnbrook, Gordon's new M26 was on the stocks, while the M23s would use a new Alastair Caldwell-developed six-speed version of the Hewland FGA transaxle in the new year. He had developed a pet theory into reality through the '75 season, working in cooperation with Hewland Engineering nearby in Maidenhead, who supplied parts to his specification. The six-speed box would allow Hunt and Jochen Mass – retained as team number two driver – to make best use of the John Nicholson-developed and rebuilt Cosworth DFVs' torque curve.

The '76 Argentine GP had been cancelled, the season commencing instead at São Paulo with the Brazilian GP on January 25. Around 30lbs weight had been trimmed off the M23s, in part by the use of lighter body panels, and other changes included a reversion to lower wishbone rear suspension in place of the parallel-link system. The race also introduced Marlboro's dayglo-red livery, prompted by John Hogan who wanted to improve the cars' TV identity over the original gloss-red and white scheme. "It was very effective, but expensive, because the day-glo paint tended to dull and had to be re-applied regularly . . ."

Although the M23s proved not ideal for the sinuous Interlagos circuit the six-speed gearbox certainly plugged some gaps and Hunt proved his class by qualifying on pole ahead of Lauda's Ferrari. But the Austrian and Regazzoni's second Ferrari beat the M23 off the mark. Clay suffered a puncture and fell back, Lauda led Hunt for two-thirds distance until James suffered a freak failure.

One of the DFV engine's fuel injection trumpets came adrift, taking the screwed-in injector nozzle with it. Running on only seven cylinders James dropped back, his ambitions now restricted to a third maybe fourth-place finish. But then the rattling trumpet jammed down behind the throttle slides, jamming them open and poking the M23 into a spin into the catch-fencing. He tried to continue but the rear-wing and oil coolers were damaged; and his race was over.

Jochen meanwhile in M23/6 drove an exemplary number two race, to finish sixth and accumulate his first Championship point of the season.

In March at Kyalami another Alastair Caldwell development appeared on the cars which would later be taken up by other teams. In place of the normal heavy electrical starter motor the M23s now used compressed-air starters with an onboard reservoir chargeable from any airline and activated by a small solenoid. This obviated the need for a heavy onboard battery and saved another valuable few pounds weight, and unnecessary complication. Both cars practised at Kyalami with plastic aerodynamic underskirts attached, but they had to be removed following protests before the race during a dispute about wing heights.

Once again James qualified on pole, 0.1 second faster than Lauda, but he was always wary of abusing his clutch off the line and lay fourth into the race's first corner. He drove tremendously hard and just failed to catch Lauda's Ferrari – handicapped by a punctured tyre – losing out by only 1.3secs at the finish. Jochen was equally competitive in his regular M23/6 and finished third behind his team-mate after a trying drive handicapped by unpredictable handling.

It was obvious that in James Hunt and the latest version M23 Marlboro-McLaren had a winning combination, and that first victory came the following weekend at Brands Hatch in the non-Championship Race of Champions.

James had a choice of the regular race cars, M23/8 and M23/6; had a troubled practice period and started from row three but the race was a sensation as Australian Alan Jones led until half-distance in a new Surtees until James found a way by and ran away to win comfortably, while Lauda's Ferrari retired. It was a hugely popular home win with the enthusiastic Brands Hatch crowd.

The team travelled to Long Beach, California, for the inaugural United States GP West, taking the regular cars for James and Jochen, both using CanAm brakes with 35 per cent greater pad area than normal in deference to the demands of the tight street circuit. James qualified on row two but there was nothing really between the front runners, Lauda alongside him, Regazzoni ahead on pole and Patrick Depailler's Tyrrell second quickest. James started well and raced away second to Regazzoni with Depailler on his tail, but on lap 2 his engine died at the hairpin, Depailler accelerated past, then the M23's engine cleared its throat and roared again – a vapour lock had cleared itself. On lap 3 Depailler ran wide, his Tyrrell bucking under braking and James was alongside into the first hairpin only for the blue Tyrrell to move across and slam the M23 hard into the retaining wall. The highly-strung Englishman erupted from the cockpit of his broken McLaren enraged and ready to fight anybody, especially Depailler. For several laps he stood in the circuit waiting for the Frenchman to come round, furiously shaking his fist as the Tyrrell went by, working off his anger and frustration. It was all part of the Hunt psyche. Before a race in which he felt he had some chance he would often be tense to the point of vomiting. In the car he drove with controlled aggression. If established in a comfortable lead the relaxation would spark another nervous reaction. He would retch. Race over, his nervous release would leave him edgy, snappy, occasionally even violent until cool calm drifted in . . . Not perhaps the most mature set of characteristics, but none of us can say how we want to be born and James Hunt's channelled tensions during the season of '76 made him one hell of a racing driver; and the team ran with him . . .

And Jochen finished fifth . . .

Back to Silverstone for the non-Championship International Trophy race, James was in a class of his own, the only driver in the 1:17 bracket during practice, starting on pole, leading all the way and setting fastest lap.

The serious business of World Championship racing returned with the Spanish at Jarama, where new Formula 1 regulations took effect, restricting the size of the engine induction airboxes – effectively banning the old tall scoops behind the driver's head – along with new dimensional requirements for the wings and cockpit roll-hoops. James drove his M23/8 as usual, but Jochen took over M23/9 – formerly the team's regular spare car – discarding M23/6. He simply felt the older car was deficient in some inexplicable manner, and what thoughts must have been going through 'Hermann's mind as he had to sit on the pit counter and watch James take it out and equal a time he'd just set in M23/8 . . .?

Essentially James was a winner, a regular front-runner, and tacitly he had been taken on to replace Fittipaldi as number one. But no such formal distinction was made, and as the new-boy in a team to which Jochen had belonged for more than a year, the German former saloon car star was out to prove his own claim. Beginning practice at Jarama Jochen lay fourth in the World Drivers' Championship with seven points, and James was behind him, fifth in the standings with six. Pole positions and front-running didn't accumulate points, while Mass's steady finishing record did just that. He had something to prove . . .

Practice ended with James on pole again, 0.3 sec faster than Lauda, driving with injured ribs in his Ferrari, alongside. Behind James was Depailler in the latest six-wheeled Tyrrell and beside him was Jochen Mass.

Another gentle start left James shadowing Lauda whose rib-cage gave him increasing pain as the strenuous tight-circuit race dragged on. Just before half distance James moved ahead, Mass following him through, close on his tail. Teddy put out a pit signal instructing him to hold position, but he ran James close until his engine blew near the end. James won comfortably, 30.97 secs clear of Lauda, his first *Grande Epreuve* victory for Marlboro-McLaren.

But then post-race scrutineering took it away. The new regulation had been framed around the widest car in the business, the McLaren M23 and the winning car was now found to be too wide across the rear wheels, by 1.8 centimetres, around ⅝-inch. The technical commissioners decided to exercise their muscle, and promptly disqualified the car. James was bemused, Teddy enraged, the team stunned.

Teddy's legal background bubbled to the surface. "It's like being hanged for a parking offence" he declared, and promptly appealed against the CSI's decision. He admitted the car had been too wide – even if only because the team had been running new wheels and it hadn't occurred to anybody to measure their rim ledge overhang just to make sure. There was no dicker there, but since that minute oversight could have given James no advantage he should at least be able to keep his points. A fine would be more just. No performance advantage to him, and the team's infraction, not his . . .

In the short-term Marlboro-McLaren had to accept the fact, *pro tem*, that they had no points from Jarama, and it was not until the French GP weekend in June that hey presto the Spanish win was restored along with its prize money, though they were fined $3,000 for their indiscretion.

Meantime, the team's fortunes slumped. For Zolder and the Belgian GP the rear track was pulled within the 214cm limit by machining the inside wheel hub faces and adjusting the wishbone mounting points to suit. Oil coolers had returned to the side pods, but Jochen's M23/9 lost oil pressure early in practice and the coolers migrated back onto the tail of the car next day to reduce lubricant temperatures. The Ferraris monopolised the front row, James third quickest on row two, but in the spare car after crashing his regular mount. Jochen was way off the pace. James led the Ferraris off the line but was soon engulfed, his car's handling was "positively evil" and then it began to smoke, more and more heavily, and finally retired with dry transmission. Lauda and Regazzoni made it a dominant Ferrari 1-2. Jochen salvaged a further Championship point – sixth.

The oil cooler move in the Zolder paddock returned them to virtually their original South American mounting, but not quite. That "not quite" proved vital, for the M23s proved virtually impossible to balance in the same old way, and the problem cost a month's competitiveness before it was pinpointed.

At Monaco, Jochen's car ran experimentally with an additional low-level rear wing in practice, while James had endless problems with a jamming gear selector rod. They started down the grid, Jochen faster. In race morning warm-up they tried running without the airbox. It improved airflow over the rear wing and the handling. Starting so far back was an impossible handicap for someone with the Hunt mentality at Monaco where it is so difficult to pass a slower car starting ahead of you. He spun, dropped to the tail of the field and thankfully retired with engine failure after 24 laps. Jochen kept going, profited by retirements amongst the leaders, and salvaged fifth place – and two more points.

Anderstorp hosted the Swedish GP again where lack of rear-end adhesion sent James into two lurid high-speed spins during first practice and four more on the Saturday. He managed to climb to fifth place at the finish ... It was a points-scoring result at last ...

Then back at Colnbrook in near-panic, brainstorming their lost form, the team opted to return the cars effectively to Spanish GP trim. The oil coolers were resited. Testing began at Ricard, prior to the French GP and like magic the old manoeuvrability, the old balance had been restored. At that point in the season, with half the series to run, James was a monstrous 47 points behind his main rival – Championship leader Niki Lauda.

The French GP weekend saw the team's Spanish win restored, while at Ricard the revamped M23s confirmed their true form. James promptly qualified on pole and started on a part-worn set of soft-compound Goodyear tyres which experience had shown gave consistent characteristics and were quicker. Lauda led until lap 8 when his Ferrari engine failed, and 11 laps later Regazzoni's sister engine went the same way – crankshaft broken, in his case spinning him into the catch-fencing. James inherited the lead from Depailler's Tyrrell and was able to maintain it as the blue car fell back despite retching, dry, into his Nomex face mask. The finish was sweet relief – his second win of the season as the Spanish appeal was accepted in Paris next morning. Nine more points for James and the marque, three docked from Lauda and Ferrari as they were demoted from their Spanish first place back to second. James' 26-point total now trailed Niki's 52; exactly half as many, with half the season to run.

At Brands Hatch the confrontation between Hunt and Lauda, McLaren and Ferrari, was promoted for all it was worth, a fever-pitch showdown between the blue-eyed home team and the Continentals who had stood to benefit by the Spanish disqualification. But Niki took pole, with James alongside him, Regazzoni and Mario Andretti's Lotus behind.

James made his usual hesitant start, Lauda a good one, Regazzoni a fabulous one from the second row, spearing through like a scarlet cross-bow bolt, hurtling inside Lauda over the crest of Paddock Hill into the first right-hander. Niki turned in and the two Ferraris met, James a spectator, then braking savagely, far too close – he was going to be involved in this too!

Regazzoni's car spun to the outside, James punted from behind diving for the diminishing gap between the Ferrari's tail and the outside bank. He almost made it, but the M23's right rear wheel crashed over the tail-first Ferrari's right-rear and the McLaren planed crazily into the air, briefly two wheels high before crashing

James on the charge – British GP '76; the M23 showing-off its under-chassis draught excluders and hurtling round after the sensational first-corner multiple collision which caused the race to be stopped and restarted. Amidst great confusion it was first announced

down to earth, right side up. Engine still running, appalled that the race he was set to win was probably ended so soon, James found a gear and limped away up to Druids Hairpin and the rest of the lap. The car wasn't steering properly, its suspension obviously deranged, but suddenly there were crossed yellow and oil-flags all round the course, the Clerk of the Course had stopped the race.

James Hunt: "I thought all my birthdays had come at once . . . I wanted the team to switch my race wheels and tyres on to the spare car. I didn't know we weren't allowed to use the spare car, but the team did a very professional thing. They decided to repair the race car as well as getting the spare car ready as they didn't know exactly which car we would be able to run at the restart. In fact we took the spare car to the grid and put it in position while all the arguments went on about whether we could do it or not, and by the time all the arguments had finished, the race car had been repaired and the lads brought it up . . ."

In retrospect in fact it seemed that the race had been stopped too hastily. There

that the McLaren star would not be allowed to take the restart and a near riot in the crowd contributed to changing the organisers' minds . . . James won on the road but was subsequently disqualified, and this time it stuck . . .

Another restart – James leading imperiously after the German GP '76 had been stopped by Niki Lauda's fiery near-fatal Ferrari accident and then flagged away a second time. He led from start to finish, the works M23 absolutely uncatchable. Here his pursuers are led by Clay Regazzoni (Ferrari), the Tyrrell six-wheelers of Patrick Depailler (4) and Jody Scheckter, Carlos Pace's Brabham-Alfa Romeo and Jochen Mass in the sister M23.

was a clear path through the debris at Paddock Hill and Niki Lauda had cleared the incident and led comfortably away round that opening lap. Only the number one McLaren, Regazzoni's Ferrari and Laffite's Ligier had been badly damaged in the collision, and they had their spare cars on the grid as it was reformed. Then came the announcement that only those drivers who had completed that first lap would be allowed to restart, and James had turned-in to the service road behind the pits, so would not qualify.

Eoin Young described the scene: "It sparked an uproar from the crowd such as had never been heard from a British crowd at any motor race. From the football crowds on the terraces at Wembley, yes. From the enthusiasts at Brands Hatch, no. The heat of the crowd added to Hunt's determination. He would start the British Grand Prix, no matter what. He counted the crowd as his, and he would perform for them . . ."

The argument raged on the grid between drivers, team principals and officialdom. Hunt couldn't start in his spare car. He wasn't going to, he was going to restart in his original race car. Ferrari chipped in. If Hunt started, so would Regazzoni in his spare car. A new steering arm and front suspension link had the race M23 mobile again. The race would run now, potential protests would be made later. The crowd, at fever-pitch, settled expectantly. The rolling lap, the second start, and Lauda leading from James and Regazzoni. The M23 handled better on right-handers than left until its fuel load diminished and James found he could toss it oversteering into the lefts and avoid the understeer which had slowed him. Half-distance, still Lauda leading but Hunt closing. The Ferrari delayed by backmarkers, James on its tail, feinting and stabbing to go by. Lap 45, a gap inside the Ferrari into the right-hand hairpin at Druids, James was there, Lauda had to back off and give way, the McLaren and its home-town driver taking the lead they held to the finish, to the delirious glee of a most un-British vocal crowd. Curiously James felt little such elation.

After he had been passed Niki Lauda did not fight back, he settled for second – James: "I was a bit annoyed with everybody else at Brands, because where were they? I needed Niki to get a whole lot less than six points for second place and in the normal way there would have been five cars in the 50sec lead I had built up over him . . ."

But in the race control office the protests were already being lodged while James accepted the laurels, trophies and Champagne. The protests claimed that James had not been running when the first race was stopped. He had been running, though very slowly – limping along in fact – and the Stewards made an offer to the teams who protested; Tyrrell, Copersucar (the Fittipaldi brothers' team which stood to gain a finish in the points rather than Emerson's seventh place on the road) and Ferrari. The Stewards suggested they should withdraw their protests to save face and their protest fees. Tyrrell and Copersucar agreed, accepting the evidence presented against their case, but Ferrari's *Direttore Sportivo* Daniele Audetto could not withdraw, explaining he had no permission to do so from Mr Ferrari in Italy. So the Ferrari protest stood, and it would prove a bone of sore contention in the weeks to come . . .

Nürburgring, the German GP, unchanged McLarens and James qualifying on pole alongside Lauda who was vocally ill-at-ease with the circuit after nasty accidents there in previous years. Rain threatened on raceday, most runners opted to start on wet-weather tyres while Jochen would make the most of his specialist circuit knowledge on dries. His gamble paid off, he took the lead on the second lap while most of the field, James included, blasted into the pits to change onto dry tyres – the damp patches on the course were drying fast. Jochen led with James second, Teddy and Alastair Caldwell agonising in the pits if the order should remain this way – how could they tell their German driver to pass-up the chance of victory in his home GP in favour of Hunt, the team and the World Championship chase? Then Lauda's misfortune solved the problem for them. After changing his tyres he lost control of his Ferrari out on the back of the circuit and suffered a ghastly accident which stopped the race as four brave drivers and a marshal struggled to pull the Austrian from his burning car. He was taken to hospital, suffering critically from flame and toxic fume inhalation and burns, some serious. The drivers who stopped at the scene, including James after completing most of another 14-mile lap before reaching it, believed his injuries were fairly mild considering the severity of the incident and were not too downcast.

James was in quite good spirits as he faced the second World Championship GP restart in two weeks. Doubts about the weather had been set aside and dry tyres were universal. Ending lap 1 he had ten seconds in hand, and he had the race totally under control from that point forward, winning by nearly half-a-minute from Jody Scheckter's Tyrrell and Jochen third – first and third, joy for the team which had always suffered so badly at Nürburgring. Perhaps their luck was changing; and James' third consecutive victory . . . His main Championship rival sidelined . . . where would they go from here?

At that point Lauda still led the World Drivers' Championship with 58 points to James' 44, while Ferrari's lead in the Constructors' Championship was by 61 points to McLaren's 49.

While Niki Lauda clung to life and virtually willed himself better by harnessing his competitive nature, Ferrari made the tactical error which would eventually cost him his World Championship. Instead of possibly robbing Hunt of points in Austria, they withdrew from the race – claiming ostensibly it was a gesture against the governing body which could restore a GP victory to an illegal car – in Spain – and allow a national club – the British RAC – to reject their protest about Hunt's allegedly illegal restart at Brands Hatch. James remarked at the time "I can't understand Old Man Ferrari. With Niki away they ought to be entering two, maybe three cars to try and keep me out of the points. This way they're giving Niki no help at all . . ." Perhaps what should have been more to the point, given Ferrari's interest in cars rather than drivers, he was cutting-off his own nose to spite his face in the Constructors' Championship, in which at that time his legendary marque stood to score their second consecutive annual title.

Gordon's prototype M26 had been completed at Colnbrook and was taken to Österreichring for the Ferrari-less Austrian GP that August, along with the regular M23s. The car's low-profile aluminium and Nomex-honeycomb monocoque chassis featured in-built deformable structure with the foil cell structure sandwiched between the double skins of its aerospace sheet panelling, while its suspension was virtually pure M23 in latest '76 form. During testing James lapped in 1:35.4 with the new car but its fuel system proved reluctant to pick-up the last few gallons and with more potential to come it was clearly a long-term prospect, best set aside while the M23s remained so well understood, and so competitive. Just how competitive James proved in M23/8, which he qualified on pole position from John Watson's Penske, on 1:35.02. His M26 testing time would have put the new car on third spot on the starting grid . . . McLaren had an embarrassment of riches at this time, though Jochen had his problems in mid-grid.

The GP itself was a terrific race with James leading initially, only to be swallowed-up by Watson, then Ronnie Peterson's March, Scheckter's six-wheeled Tyrrell and Gunnar Nilsson's Lotus. James had been unhappy with his car's balance, suffering an understeer problem on full tanks. In race morning warm-up he felt the balance had been restored, but the car's handling deteriorated in the race. On lap 14 Scheckter survived an enormous accident and James tore by, through the scattered mud and debris lying on the track but by that time was already in trouble and doubted that this incident caused his problem. He finished a tardy fourth, and when his crew examined the car afterwards they found the left-front nose wing had been thumped from underneath and its angle of attack flattened slightly. Something had punctured the wing's under-surface – the working part of the aerofoil – and the hole was stuffed with mud suggesting it had been there when James hit the detritus from Scheckter's crash. He had no recollection of any earlier incident which could have caused such damage, but at least they had isolated the cause of the handling problem. John Watson won for Penske, where one year before Penske's star driver and friend Mark Donohue had been fatally injured in that team's March. Jochen was seventh, out of the points, but fourth for James meant only three more points, and he was still trailing the hospital-bound Niki Lauda by eleven . . .

James stuck with his M23 for the Dutch GP where Ferrari returned to the fray with a lone car for Clay Regazzoni to protect the now fast-recovering Lauda's chances in the Championship. McLaren brought the M26 out for its race debut after promising tests at Silverstone, Jochen was to drive it, but he had a miserable time in practice with persistent understeer and eventually crashed mildly when the right-side half-shaft broke leaving him with braking on only three wheels at the end of the fast pit straight. The car was repaired for him to race, while up on the front of the grid James was narrowly pipped for pole position by Ronnie Peterson's March.

For 30 race laps James fought a scorching battle with John Watson showing real class at last in the Penske, after both had disposed of Peterson. It was James' birthday, August 29, he was brim-full of confidence and drove around yet another understeer problem, a flapping brake cooling duct interrupting airflow over one of those sensitive front wings. The battle ended on lap 47 when the Penske suffered a transmission failure and with 30 laps to run the McLaren crew began flashing signals to their race leader that Regazzoni was staging a late charge in the lone Ferrari, and closing fast. The finish was nerve-tingling, with the gangling, athletic Englishman just holding-off the moustachioed swarthy Ticinese by less than a second at the flag. It was his fifth GP win of the season, and a full nine points tally brought him within two points of Lauda's Championship lead. Behind the venetian blinds in his office at Maranello, Mr Ferrari pondered Regazzoni's future – he had sparked the Brands Hatch collision, he believed, and now at Zandvoort he had started his charge for the lead far too late . . .

Jochen Mass meanwhile, had a miserable debut race with the M26, spinning it, being lapped and finishing a distant ninth . . .

Between Zandvoort and the Italian GP a growing campaign of vilification against Marlboro-McLaren reached its height in the Italian press. It was all good cheerful stirring stuff, guaranteeing a monster crowd for the Italian GP showdown at Monza, where it was learned Lauda would be returning in a third Ferrari, although 'the Old Man' had taken insurance against the effect of his star driver's Nürburgring injuries and had signed-on a willing Carlos Reutemann, who bought himself out of a Brabham-Alfa Romeo contract to make the move. There would be three Ferraris defending the faith on home soil, and McLaren were under fire . . .

How could their old cars be so quick? How could they deny the best flat-12 Ferraris? How had they recovered so miraculously from their bad patch after Jarama, where their cars had been proved illegal? The Italian press had the answer. They were illegally lacing their fuel with methanol. They had experience of the eye-watering fuel brew at Indianapolis. It all fitted. They probably had a supply hidden in their onboard extinguisher bottles, cockpit-tapped into the system whenever the driver wanted extra boost. Hadn't "reliable" drivers following Hunt's M23 testified to smelling methanol in its exhaust?

Teddy and the Colnbrook team had fair warning that their cars would be microscopically scrutineered at Monza, and fuel tests were virtually certain after such "revelations" in the press. Texaco knew it too, and hit trouble immediately on crossing the Italian frontier. Customs officials held them for no apparent reason. Then during practice at the Milanese autodrome a fuel check was made, samples being drawn off for laboratory analysis. The Formula 1 fuel regulation seemed clear to Texaco and to McLaren. They could use the top grade of fuel commercially available within the team's country of origin, within a one-octane tolerance. Since 101-octane fuel was available on service station pumps in the UK,

McLaren could run legally up to 102-octane. The nub of the argument which followed was that only 100-octane is the best available in most countries of Continental Europe, which for teams like Ferrari and Ligier would mean no more than 101-octane. The technical commission of the *Automobile Club d'Italia* had decided to secure their stance, and checked with the CSI governing body in Paris for clarification of the rules. They replied with a Telex *wrongly* stating that the maximum octane rating allowed was 101. This was true for a Formula 1 car made in France where they were based; not for a team from Britain . . . It was a peculiar anomaly, but true under the fuel requirements as then laid down. The CSI later corrected their Telex, but by then it was too late.

Overnight the fuel sample from the McLaren tanks was analysed and registered 101.6 octane. Texaco checked in their own laboratory and recorded 101.2. Irrespective, under the CSI's misleading "clarification" Telex the ACI stewards of the meeting were right in cancelling McLaren's Saturday practice times. The local press was overjoyed, right again!

Friday practice had been run in heavy rain and James had a mildly damaging spin during it in M23/8, while the dry Saturday times were obviously quicker and it was then that the fuel checks had been made. Teddy: "I think Ferrari began to believe that if James could beat them, we must be cheating, and they began to try and find excuses. In a way it was beneficial to us because they spent less time on development than perhaps they should have . . ."

Interestingly the AGIP fuel company seemed well-prepared for the spot-check on fuel quality; Ferrari's checking-out at 98.6, against McLaren's 101.6 and the Penske team's hapless 105.7 – impossibly way over the top . . .

With Texaco's muscle behind him, Teddy successfully appealed against the findings of the fuel check, but his cars' dry circuit Saturday times were still disqualified and their wet-weather Friday times only allowed to stand because "there is no proof what fuel you were using in those sessions". So James and Jochen had to start near the back of the grid.

Meanwhile, Lauda was back, and he qualified fifth fastest for Ferrari; uncomfortably for Maranello behind Laffite's Ligier-Matra on its first pole position, the two six-wheeled Tyrrells and Carlos Pace's Alfa Romeo-engined Brabham, which must have stung.

The seething crowd's jeers, cat-calls and index-and-little-finger evil-eye gestures at Hunt's McLaren as it was wheeled to the tail of the grid set the seal. Steam was coming from his ears as the cars set off on their rolling lap and he found himself cut out by traffic into the first chicane as the race began, dead-last. Ahead of him Jochen's M26 was bound for the pits on lap 2 with ignition problems, to thunderous applause from the packed grandstand, while James charged. He rushed up to 12th place after ten laps but couldn't get by Tom Pryce's new Shadow, which had extremely powerful brakes, as well as being very quick on the straights. Then a tiny gap opened and James was through, catching Jacky Ickx's Ensign, but he was even harder to pass and Pryce closed-up again. Out of the first chicane James grabbed the next gear and missed it, grabbing again while Pryce accelerated up alongside. Into the next chicane the Welshman relied on his car's superb braking and sat James out: "It was my fault" the McLaren number one would later admit, but only at the end of the season: "I'd had a hell of a job passing him already, so I decided to go for it. When we did get to the corner he was inside me, I couldn't get in and I went off the road of my own accord . . ."

The McLaren shuddered to a stop in the sand drag and nothing James could do would retrieve it. His race was over there and then. Two points at Zandvoort would be the closest he'd ever get to the World Championship, Lauda would see to that; finishing fourth, sore, near-exhausted, but back in the fray . . . "Niki's race really spoke for itself. To virtually step out of the grave and six weeks later to come fourth in a Grand Prix is a truly amazing achievement especially as there wasn't much practice time. He just got in the car and had a go. It was bloody good . . ."

Three Championship rounds left; Lauda 61 points, James Hunt 56 . . . five points adrift.

The come-back after Jarama seemed to be going bad. One week after Monza, James was in Atlanta, Georgia, for the opening of the International Race of Champions TV series in which star-name drivers raced one another on a variety of courses in ostensibly identical Chevrolet Camaros. He became involved in a 160mph spin on the stock car circuit's bankings, and hit the barriers, hard. He was unhurt, but a week after that the CSI Court of Appeal in Paris upheld Ferrari's British GP protest and disqualified James and McLaren from their Brands Hatch victory, elevating Lauda and Ferrari in his place. The CSI ignored a Ferrari request to reopen the Spanish case. The net effect of their decision was damaging enough to British hopes for the Championship, for James' points score now fell back to 47, Niki's swelling to 64 – a 17-point gulf with three GPs to run . . .

Ferrari's case pivoted on their contention that the McLaren had been stationary at the moment the red flag went out to stop the Brands Hatch race. The relevant regulation stated that those whose cars were running "at the time" the race was stopped could restart, and those whose cars were not running could not restart. Numerous witnesses declared that at the moment the race was stopped James' car was still mobile, but the Appeal Court chose to disbelieve them.

The McLaren view was the the governing body had found in their favour over the Spanish infringement, and were now evening the score for the sake of keeping Ferrari reasonably happy.

Teddy Mayer: "What happened in Spain was, in my opinion, simply a mistake. A natural one, obviously – or it should be obvious – with no intent to cheat, and the sentence of disqualification was very very heavy. Too heavy in our view, and our appeal was upheld. I can understand Ferrari's reaction to that, possibly feeling they should have had the race, but I don't understand the self-righteousness that was then shown by Ferrari in going around and saying that they never broke rules. It's all right to say those things, but to say them and believe them – that's something else. We all live in glass houses. No-one adheres to the rules absolutely, any more than anyone adheres to the whole of the law which is the law of the land absolutely because that's almost impossible. So to display the sort of self-righteousness that Ferrari did seems to me childish.

"The saddest of all was the appeal over the British GP because James won the race fair and square; there was no question about that, there was no question of his car being illegal. They were trying to use the rules to get out of competing with him and to me that's sad . . . the sad thing about the Brands Hatch accident was that it was Ferrari's fault – one of their drivers hit the other – and they were trying to take advantage of their own mistakes . . ."

Until this time James and Niki had always been on quite good terms. With the CSI Appeal Court's decision Niki was understandably delighted and said as much to inquiring TV news teams and journalists. His attitude incensed James, and for the first time there was genuine needle between them as the teams flew to Canada for the next Championship round, at Mosport Park on October 3, although there was nothing like the explosive situation which the popular press depicted.

Still James was intent upon closing that gap and he was uncatchable in practice, despite reservations about safety features at the frost-damaged track. James consciously tried to give his Austrian rival the impression that he was so fired-up he would not be averse to pushing the Ferrari off the track if necessary, but despite his German accident the Austrian, a genuine tough-nut, was largely unimpressed.

McLaren had set aside the M26 to concentrate upon wringing the best out of their M23s, and despite a blown engine James qualified resoundingly on pole position, alongside Peterson's March. Ronnie made the best start to lead initially, but the Englishman was soon ahead and after a challenge from Depailler's Tyrrell the McLaren team leader won handsomely. Lauda suffered a rear suspension problem which dropped him out of the points. Jochen was fifth in the second M23. Niki still led the World Championship, but the gap was closing. After the race both Championship contenders denied many of the more bitter quotes attributed to them in the popular press; the hatchet had been burried.

At Watkins Glen for the US GP East, James was again driving as though all the season's pent-up frustrations were being released in his handling of the car. He took his eighth pole position of the season, this time from Scheckter's Tyrrell, but it was the South African ex-McLaren driver who made the best start to lead away. They began a terrific running battle, which James only won with 13 laps to go.

In his final sprint to the flag he broke the lap record, and another nine points were his for the win. Lauda was troubled by increasing understeer in the Ferrari and fought hard to hold off Jochen's M23, finishing third from the German in fourth place; four more points to him, and now his Championship lead over James was just three points, 68 to 65, with one race remaining.

The newly-inaugurated Japanese GP at Mt Fuji could not have had a more propitious debut, but the weather spoiled it. Heavy rain swept the circuit, low cloud shrouded the hills. Immediately after the Watkins Glen race an M23 had been taken to Japan for James to test on the Fuji course. Ferrari's by this time beleaguered management were paranoid about almost anything the McLaren team did, and issued some unconsciously hilarious press statements condemning such pre-race testing as "unsporting and unfair".

As it happened Mario Andretti qualified on pole ahead of James with Lauda third fastest on row two. Race morning dawned to those leaden skies and persistent rain, puddles deep across the circuit. Discussion began. Should the race be run or not? James and Niki exchanged their personal views. The McLaren driver agreed they should ideally race another day, but if the organisers decided otherwise he would race today, but he would drive for the title, only as hard as necessary – only as hard as Niki made him go. The Austrian Ferrari star, conscious of his own mortality after the German fire had his doubts. The race Stewards eventually decided the start would be delayed but the race be run.

The start saw James spearing away into an immediate lead, leaving the rest of the field to grope their way through his spray while he alone had a clear view of the road ahead. Behind him Niki drifted back in the pack, cars pluming past on both sides. And after two laps the blood-red Ferrari came barking down the pit lane, stopped by its crew and the Austrian switched-off. His fire-ravaged eyelids, his difficulty in blinking, were a handicap in the rain and spray. He had difficulty focussing, but he didn't make those excuses. He told team manager Audetto he simply found conditions impossible, and was not going to risk his life or anyone else's by going on. He had abdicated responsibility for this World Championship – its outcome now lay in the lap of the Gods, in James Hunt's hands, and in those of the Colnbrook crew who had prepared the McLaren . . .

But then the rain eased, and stopped. The circuit was drying rapidly in the breeze off the mountains. The heavily-treaded Goodyear wet-weather tyres would overheat and blister without cooling water to run in. After 15 laps James eased back to save his tyres, but Andretti following him wondered why he seemed to stay on the normal line, now driving rapidly through the turns, instead of finding the puddles and damp patches to conserve the tyres. Two-thirds distance, the Championship seemed assured, James leading confidently, the McLaren's V8 exhaust note crisp and strong.

But then James was slowing. His left-rear tyre was rapidly deflating. If he finished lower than fourth, scoring less than those three vital Championship points to clinch the title from Lauda on his greater number of race wins, the title would be lost. Teddy in the pits: "We figured he should know best how long he could run on that tyre – we weren't about to over-rule his own opinion and signal him in for a change . . . It was down to him . . ."

Depailler took the lead, but briefly as he punctured a tyre. Andretti moved ahead, and James was limping, still second but with his car visibly slumped at one side, bottoming in showers of sparks on the broad pit straight's bumps and undulations. And the pace of leading on a dry road had now tortured the left-front tyre enough. On lap 68 in the final corner onto the pit straight the tyre

burst and he had no alternative but to flounder into the pits. It was fortunate the failure had happened where it did, rather than in the first corner *after* the pits which would have meant a long, long crawl home for help.

As it was the McLaren crew flung themselves on the car, the rear wheels were off and fresh refitted almost instantly, but the jack wouldn't fit under the sagging front-left corner. For an agonising moment it looked as if James was out of the contest for good, then his mechanic Howard Moore grabbed the punctured wheel and lifted the front of the car bodily to allow the jack to slide beneath. Wheel changed and James hurtled out of the pit-lane, fifth, almost in tears, choked with frustration and fury; cursing his luck, his tyres, the weather, the circuit, Teddy and his team. Why hadn't they brought him in before *this* happened?

Driving in real anger James Hunt slammed into those final laps. Lap 70 – three to go – Andretti led Depailler, Regazzoni, Alan Jones, Surtees and Hunt, fifth. Jones and Regazzoni were duelling for third place on near-bald tyres, their pace could not compare with James' on fresh rubber and he was past them both virtually without noticing it. Lap 71 – Andretti, Depailler, Hunt third. Lap 72 – he was closing on the leading duo. Last lap, chequered flag unfurled at the finish line and three cars hurtling towards it from the last turn. They slammed across the line virtually as one, Andretti winning and lapping Depailler just before the flag, James third – four points, World Champion at last . . .

And he didn't realise it.

Boiling with fury he completed a rapid final lap and rapped into the pit lane, blipping the throttle. Bursting out of his seat belts he towered in the cockpit bawling at Teddy's smiling face: "But I couldn't hear what he was saying because of his helmet, though I realised he thought he'd blown it from the expression on his face. Then he dragged his helmet off and paused for breath and I just said 'You've won. You've won. You were third. You've done it. You're the Champion . . .' and he calmed down . . ."

James couldn't believe it, and didn't believe it until he had checked other lap charts and had it officially confirmed by the time keepers, without protests from any of the other teams.

The Marlboro-McLaren driver had clinched the Drivers' Championship in this dramatic manner after a season in which he had unofficially broken Jimmy Clark's record of seven Championship GP victories in a season, though officially only equalling it, and after the most fraught and controversial Grand Prix season ever. But McLaren could not match his title with the Constructors' Championship, for Ferrari salvaged that from the season. And Jochen Mass had driven hard, intent on impressing, and he had been second and closing rapidly on James much to Teddy's mounting alarm until lap 46 when he hit a puddle, the M23 snapped right and demolished its right-front corner against the inside barrier on the long corner opening onto the pit straight. Still he would be confirmed as Hunt's number two for the coming season of '77, and the defence of the Englishman's World title.

The drama of James' Japanese GP pit-stop at Mt Fuji with wheels hastily changed to replace a blown left-front tyre, and the scene after the finish as Teddy indicates 'You finished third, you've won, you've won'; James, in a towering rage after his tyre failure, convinced he has lost the Championship, still has to be convinced . . .

1977

Barely two and a half months after settling the '76 Championship in Japan, the 1977 season got under way at Buenos Aires with the Argentine GP. The brief closed season had seen intensive development testing of the M26, but for the South American races the team played safe by relying upon their familiar trio of M23s with six-speed transaxles, James as usual in his faithful M23/8, Jochen in M23/9 and M23/6 as spare. The World Champion was on sparkling form, qualified comfortably on pole and led the race until a bolt broke in his car's right-rear suspension putting him off through the catch-fencing and lightly into the barriers. Jochen had run as high as third before settling down to nurse a seriously overheating and misfiring engine, which eventually spun him off.

The suspension fitting which had failed on James' car was reinforced in time for the Brazilian race, where James and Jochen qualified on pole and fourth fastest

Things didn't go so well in 1977 until the new M26 was sorted-out; here at Long Beach in the crowded first corner James' M23 goes for the high hurdle over John Watson's Brabham-Alfa Romeo (7) while a startled Mario Andretti (5) glimpses the goings-on in his rearview mirror. After a hasty pit stop to check damage James hustled back through the field to finish seventh, just out of the points . . .

respectively, emphasising the fact that the Marlboro-McLaren M23 was still very much the car to beat. But the race saw James dogged by excessive understeer in the scorching heat which forced him into the pits after 24 of the 40 laps to fit fresh tyres. He finished second behind Reutemann's Ferrari. Jochen lay third early on until lap 12 when under pressure from Mario Andretti's new ground-effects Lotus 78 he slid fractionally too wide on the disintegrating surface of a double left-hander. His M23/9 crashed heavily and was severely damaged.

Prior to the South African GP in early-March, the M26 was tested extensively at Kyalami but the programme was disrupted when a bolt on one of the double front brake calipers worked loose and cut through the wheel-rim, deflating the tyre and pitching James into a major accident at Leeukop Corner, virtually writing-off the new car. In his old faithful M23 he was sixth quickest in testing, and the team then began official practice for the GP with their trio of M23s, exactly four years after Denny Hulme had placed the prototype on pole there.

After Jochen's Brazilian crash, Depailler's Tyrrell had inflicted further damage on M23/9 as it lay by the trackside. The team had not suffered a major frontal impact on the M23 since Hailwood's 1974 German GP accident, and examination of Jochen's wreck prompted detail monocoque reinforcement in preparation for the South African trip. James had a new car M23/11, Jochen old M23/6, and M23/8 had been hastily shipped to replace the severely-distorted M26 as spare.

James qualified on pole yet again, but lost the lead to Niki Lauda on lap 7 as the Austrian tore away to his first win since the Nürburgring fire. The two McLarens finished 4-5 in team order.

Back home for the Race of Champions, James' M23/8 was fitted with a cockpit-operated adjustable rear anti-roll bar for the first time and after practice problems with both cars he qualified third fastest. Andretti's ground-effects Lotus 78 led from the start and had Hunt well in control in second place until with only six laps to go Andretti was sidelined by sudden electrical failure. James inherited victory by over 20 seconds from Scheckter's new Wolf.

A new M23/12 was completed in time for Jochen to use it at Long Beach, James in his new regular mount M23/11 maintaining his normal margin over his team-mate, but unable to qualify higher than eighth. Emerson Fittipaldi was faster in his Copersucar . . . Suddenly the M23 looked its age . . . James was involved in a spectacular first-corner collision with Watson's Brabham but continued, to finish seventh while Jochen retired with an awful transmission vibration. Andretti's trend-setting ground-effects Lotus won its first Championship-qualifying round . . . This was the way ahead . . .

The European season opened at Jarama with the Spanish GP in May. M26/2 was completed for James' use but its erratic handling and imbalance gave him a fraught time during practice, leaving him eighth fastest again. Spaniard Emilio de Villota had purchased M23/6 and made the tail of the grid. James retired from the race with misfiring after a miserable run, but Jochen was right on form and finished fourth, narrowly losing a frenzied scrap for third place to Scheckter's Wolf. Villota finished 13th.

The team relied upon its M23s for Monaco, the street circuit not being the place to wrestle with the M26's development problems. They tried five-speed 'boxes in early practice, reverting to six-speeds for the race, but again they qualified poorly. James used a new Cosworth 'development' DFV – one of a small, radically-tuned batch being made available to leading teams at that time to combat Ferrari's dominant flat-12 power unit – and it failed in the race, while Jochen drove well for fourth place, on the same lap as Scheckter's victorious Wolf.

At Zolder the M26 was back, with revised wings and oil cooler residing in a nose duct. It proved more progressive, better balanced but still not quick. Jochen qualified faster in his M23/12. Villota's private M23/6 made the back of the grid with Brett Lunger's newly-acquired Chesterfield-sponsored M23/14, sold as a new customer car and prepared by B S Fabrications in England to replace the American ex-CanAm driver's March. Raceday proved rainswept and Hunt

gambled on the track soon drying out; the only starter on slicks. Lunger's private McLaren developed an oil system problem at the last moment, and could not start. But James was lapped by lap 7, and at one stage as the circuit did begin to dry and tyre changes were being made it was Jochen who led, but only for two laps before he came in for dry tyres. After the stops Lauda led for Ferrari with Jochen second until lap 39 when he spun off on a wet patch and crashed into the barriers beyond the pits. James' non-stop run lost too much time early on to stand a chance of success, and he finished seventh, just out of the points. It was a bad tyre choice.

The M26 was better-suited to the tricky constant-radius corners of Anderstorp for the Swedish GP where James qualified third, ran second early on but then had to stop for fresh tyres after hurling the car round at all kinds of extraordinary angles to hold the pace. He finished twelfth, but Jochen inherited a valuable second place at the finish. Brett Lunger's private M23 was eleventh.

Now the M26 was improving with every race, and at Dijon for the French GP, James had M26/2 even more wound-up and took second place on the front row of the grid, beside Andretti's Lotus 78. He made an uncharacteristically good getaway and led until lap 4 when John Watson's Brabham appeared in the lead. Andretti burst past James on lap 17 and he could hold neither of them, finishing third. Jochen punted Reutemann's Ferrari in the opening mêlée and called at the pits ending lap 1 to have a bent steering arm and damaged wheel replaced. After resuming at the tail of the field he finished ninth. Lunger failed to qualify.

At last the M26 was showing true competitiveness, and M26/1 had been reconstructed since its Kyalami incident for Jochen to drive at Silverstone in support of James' regular M26/2. Teddy was also giving a debut Formula 1 drive to the young French-Canadian driver Gilles Villeneuve who had made his name in North American Formula Atlantic. The field was so large the RAC had to run a pre-qualifying session for privateers and newcomers, to decide who could begin official practice in the attempt to qualify for a race start. Gilles dominated it in M23/8, driving within an inch of the car's physical limit all the time, and learning how far he could push it only when control was gone and the car spun. Gordon Coppuck estimated he spun eight times in the six days he spent driving the car . . .

Marlboro-McLaren team-mates – James Hunt and Jochen Mass – eventually had a falling out at Mosport Park in the '77 Canadian GP when one fell over the other. Jochen was a good number two until he began to show a growing unwillingness to listen and learn from the faster man. He was unable to establish himself as team leader although he'd been driving with McLaren for more than a year before Hunt joined. Perhaps understandably, it rankled.

Meanwhile James was on top form and the M26 carried him to pole position, just like old times, Villeneuve was ninth on the grid for his impressive debut and Jochen slower in his M26 – which had been dogged by brake problems – eleventh-quickest, starting on his new team-mate's tail. Brett Lunger also ran.

Beside James on the front row was John Watson's Brabham-Alfa Romeo and it was the Ulsterman who dominated the first 50 laps, initially holding off Lauda's Ferrari, then James' charging M26. But on lap 51 of the 68 the Brabham stuttered into the pits with a fuel system problem and James was away to win handsomely on home ground to a rapturous reception from the partisan British crowd. And Jochen was fourth. He had been headed by Villeneuve early on, but only until lap 9 when the stocky little newcomer came into the pits thinking he had terminal overheating problems. In fact the water temperature gauge had failed and its needle was jammed against the end stop. He had been over a kerb and thought he had damaged the piping down below the tub. He was promptly shoo'd away back into the race, to finish eleventh. Lunger was two places behind him, after a lurid spin on spilled oil. But the race pointed the way ahead, for Renault made their modern GP debut with a 1.5-litre turbocharged Formula 1 car . . .

The German GP was at Hockenheim and James ran third there in his Silverstone-winning mount until an exhaust pipe broke, his development DFV engine sounding flat and losing its edge. Its performance fell away more with a faulty mechanical fuel pump, and Jochen charged hard before his home crowd until M26/1's gearbox failed. A similar problem sidelined Lunger.

Four McLarens started the Austrian GP, both Lunger and Villota qualifying down the grid, while James was on the front row, fractions slower than Lauda. James led most of the way until his engine blew in a smother of smoke and steam after 43 of the 54 laps. Jochen salvaged sixth for the team.

James had won two consecutive Dutch GPs at Zandvoort, but Andretti's Lotus and Laffite's Ligier qualified faster. Jochen was out in his new M26/3 but crashed after the first corner in the race following a tangle with Alan Jones's Austrian GP-winning Shadow. James stole the lead meanwhile after a terrific catapulting start, but he could not deny Andretti once the black Lotus had displaced Laffite. On lap 5 Mario was alongside as they hurtled down the 180mph straight into the right-handed Tarzan Loop beyond the pits. James held on, Andretti sitting him out round the outside of the right-hander and at the exit the cars touched, the M26 pitching-up into the air over the Lotus 78's right-front wheel, crashing down on its sump and smashing the water pump casting. Mario continued, but James was out, bitterly denouncing the rugged Italian-American's driving tactics in a manner and at such a length which earned him little sympathy. Brett Lunger had two M23s to choose between, his original M23/14 and now the ex-works M23/11 which B S Fabrications had just acquired. He finished eighth.

Back at Monza, the scene of such drama the previous year, the team ran their three M26s, plus M23/8 for Bruno Giacomelli the Italian comingman who had made his name in Formula 2 March cars. James had injured a ligament in his leg playing a celebrity football match, and was walking with difficulty, but driving with all the old controlled fury, and this time thoroughly 'in' with the capricious Monza crowd. He qualified on pole from Andretti, but it was the Lotus driver's day on his native soil while James tigered along third in the opening stages only to spin off and eventually retire, after a pit stop, with brake problems. Jochen was fourth, Lunger's engine failed on lap 5 and Giacomelli ran well before his engine matched Lunger's and spun him off on its own oil.

James set stupendous times in practice for the US GP East at Watkins Glen in October. His M26/2 was the only car in the 1:40 lap time bracket, and he beamed as he reported "The car feels really good, and I like this place a lot . . ." He still had a wickedly fast spin into the Armco on Friday practice, putting a mild rumple in the monocoque skinning, but the crew had it repaired for the Saturday.

It was a wet race, and Hans Stuck led the first 14 laps from Hunt in his Brabham-Alfa Romeo before it jumped out of gear and spun into the

Jeddy
with All Best Wishes And Thanks From Your New Driver

catch-fences. This left James a comfortable lead over Andretti, a lead which he maintained until his engine began to overheat and he sensed a tyre deflating towards the end. By that time all those still running were nursing their wet-weather tyres on a drying road surface, and James was able to run out victor for the second consecutive year, by barely two seconds. It was a mature, finely-judged race – the M26s' second *Grande Epreuve* success. Brett Lunger finished tenth, his team suffering lack of a proper engineer to keep the M23s competitive, while Jochen's engine cut out.

The Canadian GP at Mosport Park was a fraught event which Marlboro-McLaren men prefer to forget. Jochen had something break on his M26 which spun it gently into the Armco during practice, but despite the gentle impact the barrier virtually collapsed which impressed nobody. Ian Ashley hurt himself in a monstrous accident with his Hesketh and safety facilities had indeed proved extremely poor. James mused "This is a nice circuit to drive on, but it's not so nice to drive *off* . . ." There was tension in the air.

Andretti took pole narrowly quicker than James, while Jochen was on row three. It was another wet race and Andretti led the two M26s. He and James drew away and began remorselessly lapping the field as Jochen fell far back though still third. On lap 59 the two leaders came round to lap 'Hermann the German', who had Scheckter not far behind him.

Lap 60 – the trio blasted past the pits, Mass narrowly leading Andretti and Hunt on the road. Mario got out of shape at the hairpin trying to lap the German's M26

During the winter Jackie Stewart track-tested a number of contemporary F1 cars at Ricard-Castellet, briefly interrupting their annual test and development sessions there. The triple World Champion, winner of more Championship-qualifying GPs than any other driver, was impressed with the M26.

and James was past to lead the race, right on his team-mate's tail. Ending that lap and round into the right-handed Turn Four Jochen moved left and raised his hand to signal James through on the right. He felt a sudden bump and his car was spinning!

James had moved to the left to pass and Jochen had simply side-stepped into him. That was how James saw it, and his leading McLaren scythed through the catch-fences and smashed head-on into a wall. The impact was the heaviest even 'Hunt the Shunt' had ever experienced, and he was trapped by his feet, twisting sideways and wriggling out of his shoes to extricate himself from the cockpit. He stamped back along the verge and made to cross the the track. A marshal ran up to attempt to restrain him and the volatile Briton rounded and felled him with a punch. As he stalked back to the pits James waved angrily at Jochen every time he came by, having recovered from his own spin unscathed. "Here I am" James raged, "second and a half a lap faster than him, coming up to lap him and he pushed me right off the bloody road . . ."

It was another fairly mindless release of tension on his part, and for a Superstar to punch a volunteer marshal was unforgiveable. Marlboro certainly didn't appreciate the publicity and the organisers fined Hunt $2,000 for the assault plus $750 for walking along the track in a dangerous place. McLaren's chance of another GP win, indeed a fine 1-2 had been thrown away by one of those split-second misunderstandings which will happen in motor racing. Jochen eventually finished third after his spin, Andretti's leading Lotus having blown up when a lap clear of the field with only three to run . . .

The '77 season ended at Mt Fuji, Japan, where James began practice in M26/1, his own M26/2 having been severely re-arranged by its impact with the wall in Canada. The older car understeered badly under power, and James took over Jochen's car, M26/3. It was Jochen's final McLaren drive, after three years duty.

Andretti's standard-setting Lotus 78 took pole, but James was alongside him and Jochen on row four. And it was the deposed World Champion's McLaren which rocketed into an immediate lead and Andretti – trying to compensate for a very poor start, – pushed too hard on the opening lap, collided with Laffite's Ligier and crashed heavily into the Armco. James' main opposition had thus been removed, and Jochen moved into a strong second place on his team-leader's tail. The M26s really were operating well by this stage of the season, despite their lengthy and often problematic development period, and a Marlboro-McLaren 1-2 seemed very likely until lap 28 when the German's engine failed, and his career with the team was over, as Hunt thundered home to an easy victory. It would be his last in Formula 1, and McLaren's last for four long, parched, unhappy years . . .

Chapter 4
The Low Years 1978-79

"We were in agony, thrashing around trying to find where we had lost our grip . . ."

Teddy Mayer, 1983

To begin the 1978 World Championship season McLaren took three M26s to Buenos Aires for James Hunt and new driver Patrick Tambay, including M26/4 brand-new. The monocoque sides ahead of the rear wheels now carried flares, but the more radical 'M26½' tested at Ricard during the off-season with different wing side plates and repositioned radiators was not present. James drove the latest car, Tambay M26/3. Old M26/1 was available as spare. They finished 4-6.

The Brazilian GP was run at Rio de Janeiro's new Jacarepagua Autodrome and there James qualified on the front row beside Ronnie Peterson's ground-effect Lotus 78 on pole, and ran third early in the long, hot race until his pace destroyed his front tyres and he stopped to change them. Attempting to regain ground rapidly he dived for a narrowing gap left by Patrese's new Arrows, and spun into retirement. Tambay spun out of fifth place, suffering from the heat, and spun again two corners later, simply exhausted. He wisely gave up. Brett Lunger's M23/14 qualified very well in mid-grid but succumbed to overheating.

A brand-new M26/5 was available for Patrick to drive at Kyalami, where McLaren had such a good record. He qualified on row two alongside his team-leader, proving his potential, but James' engine failed after only four race laps and Patrick was in clutch trouble off the line, but sliced his way back through the field in great style thereafter. Then he hit an oil slick and spiralled into the catchfences, out of the race with damaged radiators and rear wing, although he managed to limp the car back to the pits. Lunger finished eleventh.

Silverstone hosted the one remaining non-Championship race in the calendar in March, and it proved catastrophic for the leading teams. Marlboro-McLaren entered James with a brace of M26s to choose between, while Lunger was awaiting delivery of a new M26 for his private operation, and had sold M23/14 for Tony Trimmer to campaign in the British Club Formula 1 series, relying on M23/11 in the meantime. Emilio de Villota appeared with his M23/6. Torrential rain flooded the circuit on raceday and James spun off at high speed through the fast fifth-gear Abbey Curve on the opening lap, along with several others. Trimmer and Lunger finished 3-4, Villota's electrics drowned-out.

Long Beach was another poor outing, James went out early on after clipping corner markers too hard, and Patrick was disputing fifth place with Laffite's Ligier when with six laps to go they collided and the M26's right-front tyre was deflated. He had earlier bent a steering arm in another collision with Scheckter's Wolf, and his exciting day finally saw him classified 12th and last . . .

Lunger's private M26/6 was out and running at Monaco where the works cars appeared unchanged, but the American's car failed to pre-qualify. Patrick finished a distant seventh and James retired when his rear anti-roll bar snapped, leaving his car with insuperable understeer.

Three works cars entered the Belgian GP at Zolder, James in M26/4, Patrick M26/5 and Bruno Giacomelli reappearing in the team after his Formula 1 debut at Monza the previous year, in a new M26/7; Patrick's entry being withdrawn due to a badly infected burn on his leg. Lunger's M26/6 just scraped onto the back of the grid. A multiple pile-up at the start ended Hunt's hopes, and Lunger and Giacomelli finished 7-8.

In practice for the Spanish GP at Jarama, James' M26/4 was badly damaged in a practice collision with Villota's M23/6. He had to race the spare M26/3, and led the race from a second-row start, but could not match the opposition's pace and finished sixth, Patrick spinning off in the early stages.

Brabham wheeled out their answer to the Lotus 78/79 ground-effect cars for the Swedish GP at Anderstorp, their sucker-system 'fan car' – drawing on Chaparral 2J CanAm innovation – dominating the meeting. After the Spanish practice accident, James had to rely on M26/3 but it had neither traction nor grip. Patrick crashed his M26/5 mildly, tail-first into the barrier, and was gentleman enough to apologise to his mechanics for it as he crabbed back into the pits. But Patrick finished fourth in the race, James eighth, without ambition . . .

At Ricard the Leo Wybrott-run Marlboro-McLaren 'B-team' reappeared with Italian Formula 2 star Bruno Giacomelli driving M26/7, and all were thrashing around trying to rediscover lost pace. Minor rear suspension geometry changes were tested on James' M26/3 in practice, but it reverted to the same spec as Patrick's M26/5 and the spare M26/1 on the second day. The spare car also featured apertures cut into the monocoque top just behind each rocker arm to relieve air pressure beneath the car. Testing proved inconclusive . . . James qualified promisingly, fourth on the second row behind the two Lotuses of Andretti and Peterson, and he finished there, third overall – best McLaren result of the season. Patrick was ninth, Bruno's engine failed, as did Lunger's.

For the British GP the Brands Hatch pit lane was crammed with McLarens; six variegated M26s and two old M23s. James' intended race car was M26/3, Patrick's M26/5 and Bruno's M26/7, with the rebuilt prototype chassis as spare. But interest centred upon a modified car based upon M26/4 after its Jarama practice collision. The monocoque had been reconstructed with rectangular side sponsons attached like the dominant Lotus ground-effect designs though curiously without underwing floors inside them, but with sliding skirts beneath the sponson side-panels, and the whole rear end of the car boxed-in beneath a smooth-contoured rear deck. The rear wing was still pylon-mounted, and the rear suspension incorporated inboard coil-spring/damper units to clear underwing airflow once wing sections could be fitted. Teddy: "It's thirty per cent of the way to being a Lotus, but it's only twenty per cent the way towards our new car . . ."

Brett Lunger's M26/6 was accompanied by his spare M23/11 and Tony Trimmer was also attempting to qualify with Melchester Racing's ex-Lunger M23/14. He didn't make it.

Neither regular works driver came to grips with practice or the race, James spinning off after only eight laps, and Patrick leading home Giacomelli and Lunger in a 6-7-8 result, speeding-up towards the finish. Bruno's great claim to prominence in this race was that he had put Lauda's leading Brabham off-line near the finish, allowing Reutemann's Ferrari to nip through and win! Ferrari just loved McLaren . . .

Hockenheim saw the M26E left at home, the regular cars again off the pace and none finishing. Patrick's car was thumped on the startline, later had a tyre deflate and crashed heavily into the *Ostkurve* fencing. James drove determinedly to hold fourth place until a front tyre deflated, he took a short-cut round the back of the pits to have it changed and was disqualified for his ingenuity; but only after completing another 14 race laps on a fresh tyre . . .

Austria was little better, Lunger qualifying and placing eighth in his private car while the works M26s went out, James colliding with Derek Daly's Ensign and bouncing off into the Armco early on and Patrick inheriting fifth place later, only to spin off. They had swopped cars, James taking chassis '5', Patrick chassis '3', for this race, and they kept them for the Dutch GP which followed, and Nelson Piquet was entered in Lunger's spare M23/11 as in Austria, where he crashed.

James Hunt was no longer driving with the old hunger and sustained nervous energy of 1976-77, and showed little sign of materially helping McLaren pull themselves up from midfield. He ran ninth just ahead of Patrick until a tyre began to deflate, and within twenty yards of the finish Patrick reversed their positions. The three other McLarens each retired.

In fact the former World Champion was on his way out of the team. Teddy Mayer: "He no longer seemed too interested in driving – I mean *really* driving. His contract was expiring anyway at the end of '78 and I had to say 'James, we're not going to renew this'. He wanted to continue, but it wasn't going to work, and John Hogan of Marlboro and myself told him so."

James had always been fiercely independent, laudably so in many ways, but there were right times and wrong times to insist on wearing jeans and tee-shirt and open-toed sandals, and certain functions for which one's paymasters were spending top dollar were the wrong time. After his final victory in the '77 Japanese GP one reporter was moved to observe: "Unfortunately there was to be no official prize giving on the rostrum, no champagne throwing by the winner, and no cheers for him from the crowd. Everybody stood around like idiots while James quickly changed out of his overalls and left the track for the airport in a tearing hurry. All the Japanese dignitaries were left on their podium with no winner to congratulate and a very bitter taste was left in everybody's mouth as a result.

"We know that James has his unconventional ways, we accept that he defies convention, but on this occasion he went too far. He will argue very strenuously that he had got a good reason for going so quickly, but the fact of the matter is that he was wrong. He soured a brilliant victory with a thoughtless display once the race was over. It was an unprofessional act from somebody who prides himself over his professional approach to his business . . ."

Such a reasoned broadside in a community as tight-knit as Formula 1 said it all. The assault on the Canadian marshal, the Zandvoort kerfuffle with Andretti did little for the image of the sport, its '76 World Champion or Marlboro-McLaren, and lack of success through '78 widened the rift. James undoubtedly felt his cars were no longer as competitive as they should be – and with some reason – but the men working to put him on the grid felt he was no longer driving with all his heart, like the old days: "he's stroking it", they would say, and he was out . . .

Teddy talked with Ronnie Peterson and his enthusiastic patron, the Italian Count 'Googie' Zanon. Ronnie had been teamed with Andretti in the standard-setting Lotuses and had enjoyed a brilliant season, but it was only a stop-gap commitment and now with Marlboro support Ronnie was signed to take Hunt's vacated seat at McLaren's. The atmosphere at Colnbrook brightened immensely. Ronnie was coming, the fastest driver of his day, now things would improve . . .

The news was released the week before the Italian GP on September 10. The M26s ran there all with revised front suspension geometry, and both Lunger and Piquet made the grid in their B S Fabrications cars. The start was fudged, and running on the right of the broad start-straight James was alarmed to see Patrese's normally aggressive Arrows storming up the pit-lane area to his right. Ahead the track funnelled down into the first chicane and James jinked left, possibly made contact and spun, sparking a huge multiple accident in which Peterson's Lotus 78 speared head-on into a barrier and erupted into flame, its front end demolished. James bravely plunged into the fire to heave-out the Swede, severely injured with both legs broken. Ronnie was taken to Niguarda Hospital in Milan; prognosis seemed hopeful, but he would be out for some months.

The race was eventually restarted, with James in his spare M26/1 but he could not compete and went out with engine failure. Patrick salvaged fifth place, Giacomelli was 14th, Piquet ninth. Lunger's car was damaged in the first-start accident. That night a lengthy operation to set Ronnie's legs went wrong, bone marrow escaped into his bloodstream and clots formed, obstructing flow to brain, lungs and kidneys, and he died . . .

Teddy: "In many ways Ronnie's death so soon after the euphoria of signing him for '79 was an even bigger blow than Bruce's. We were really looking forward to great things with him driving for us, but in an instant it had all gone. And he was bringing a lot of sponsorship money with him which would have meant a lot. It had all looked terrific, and now it couldn't happen. We were in agony that season and this had been the new dawn, and then Monza . . ."

James Hunt meanwhile had signed-on with Walter Wolf's team. Teddy and Marlboro talked with him to see if the new contract was binding, and decided it was. Few other leading drivers were free – Teddy: "I spoke to Bernie Ecclestone of Brabham and told him we were in a bad way. John Watson was his number two driver, teamed with Niki Lauda, and Bernie wasn't too happy with him, and since John was keen to become a true number one he was happy to make the move and Bernie released him and he joined us with Patrick . . ."

Meanwhile the US GP East and Canadian GPs ended the season. For these two races the hitherto familiar dayglo-red and white M26s were repainted in two-tone blue livery advertising Löwenbräu beer, a company owned by Philip Morris subsidiary Miller Beer, whose promotions people had effectively 'borrowed' the Formula 1 team for these North American events.

James ran his usual M26/5 while Patrick took over the Giacomelli M26/7, M26/3 being relegated to spare. James qualified better than of late, on row three, and ran fifth before burning out his front tyres again and stopping to replace them. Tambay had run fifth but finished sixth, stuttering, low on fuel, just ahead of James' seventh place. The Canadian race was run on the Île Notre Dame circuit at Montreal for the first time. Neither works driver liked M26/7 and Patrick reverted to his original car, aviating it over Hector Rebaque's private Lotus 78 in the hairpin during practice. The new circuit proved very hard on brakes and both works M26s suffered, James spinning off to end his McLaren career after 51 of the 70 laps, while Patrick survived to finish eighth . . . When James climbed into his car before the start he found a note on its steering wheel: "This is the last one, good luck buddy – it's been a great three years . . ."

Back home Gordon's brand-new ground-effects M28 prototype had just been completed, and Patrick tested it at Silverstone on October 17.

1979

The new M28 was one of several cars built new for the 1979 season based on Lotus 79 ground-effects technology with skirted underwing sections either side of a narrow centre monocoque. Gordon was happy to admit that Lotus had provided the inspiration, but his Nomex honeycomb M26-type monocoque formed the basis of a large plan-area car seeking to improve upon Lotus downforce figures by using larger area underwings. The result was one of the largest of modern Formula 1 cars, with inboard suspensions front and rear to clear airflow through the sidepods, a wheelbase of no less than 113-inches, front track 70-inches and rear track 64-inches. The car was taken to the Lockheed wind tunnel facility at Atlanta, Georgia, for full-size testing before further circuit tests commenced through the winter at Ricard in the South of France, preparatory to the South American races commencing the 1979 Championship series. Later tests at Rio and Buenos Aires seemed to show real potential, for John Watson set the pace . . .

From that point forward, it was virtually all downhill . . .

The prototype car suffered structural problems. The bonding between cast magnesium beams and honeycomb monocoque proved suspect and the car had to be reworked. It was available to join a new M28/2 for the Argentine GP, where the two new cars were driven respectively by Tambay and Watson, with M26/5 as spare. John was held responsible for triggering a multiple accident soon after the start and was subsequently fined by the governing body in controversial manner.

Immediately after the accident Tambay's M28 was cannibalised to repair John's and he rewarded the team with a third place finish. In Brazil the M28s' problems surfaced. They generated insufficient grip, were too bulky, slow on the straight, heavy to accelerate and brake. Patrick had a fraught practice period in which he severely damged his car, racing the spare M26 instead and colliding with Regazzoni's Williams. A new M28/3 was completed in time for the South African trip, where the cars displayed a general lack of grip despite revised side pods. The cars tested poorly at Jarama before the flight to Long Beach, where the cars wore blue Lowenbrau livery. M28/1 was left home at Colnbrook being redesigned. A Race of Champions report mentioned "the wretched McLaren M28" with which poor Wattie was still struggling, unable to make any sense of it, while Gordon and the rest of the McLaren crew worked feverishly to complete their reconstruction of M28/1 in an attempt to retrieve something worthwhile from the season.

At Jarama M28/1B reappeared, 5-inches shorter and some 50lbs lighter, with new rear spring location behind the axle line instead of ahead of it, revised front suspension geometry and generally more compact dimensions. Patrick took M28/3, and M28/2 became team spare. In testing at Zolder prior to the Belgian GP, Wattie crashed heavily, M20/2B being completed to latest spec for him with further revised suspension geometry. Tambay's M28/3 was left at Colnbrook being reworked to B-spec at the time of the race, so he ran old M26/7 ex-Giacomelli instead, and failed to qualify. John finished sixth, his best result since Buenos Aires.

At Monaco an M28C emerged, actually M28/3 reconstructed with completely inboard front suspension, revised bodywork and reprofiled side pods, Patrick driving M28/2B and failing to qualify again . . . John inherited a fourth place finish through reliability and his care in keeping clear of the barriers which developed such a magnetic attraction for so many others.

Dijon saw two M28Cs for John and Patrick, and they finished 10-11, but meanwhile on May 1 serious detail design had begun upon a more conventional, compact replacement car, the M29. Teddy Mayer: "With the M28 we didn't do a good job for John Watson at all. What we had tried to do was create a competitively light monocoque tub carrying the maximum possible ground-effect area. I think that was the right approach but the execution was just appalling. When we were doing it there wasn't any great time constraint, and we had a pretty free rein with the budget, but the M28 honeycomb tub subsequently proved to have about 10 percent the stiffness it should have had . . .

"We were misled by initial testing because Goodyear had a very good tyre for us. It was fairly quick in the South American tests and at Buenos Aires, quicker than the Lotuses which after all were still the standard-setters, we thought. In fact we didn't appreciate just how much the tyres were contributing, nor how much Lotus had fallen back . . ."

The new M29/1 made its debut in the British GP meeting at Silverstone, where John drove it, and in unofficial testing had already got down to lapping just under 1:15 whereas the M28's best was only 1:16.8. John qualified the new car on row four and finished fourth on merit, while Patrick brought M28/2C home seventh.

It was an improvement but it could not be sustained. Two M29s were ready for the German GP at Hockenheim and a third was available after the Austrian GP, in time for the Dutch. Monza saw revised suspension geometry but results, as can be seen in the Appendix on page 266, did not come.

Teddy: "The M29 wasn't that bad. It was really Gordon's copy of a Lotus monocoque and the tub was nice, with a lot of help from John Thompson" – the monocoque fabrication specialist – "Who made the first tub in his place at Northampton . . ." Gordon disputes the "Lotus copy" suggestion: "There's better reason to describe it as a Williams – definitely not a Lotus".

At the time Teddy was asked how damaging production of a lemon like the M28 could be to a specialist company like his? "Well it's bad from several points of view. It costs a lot of money to rectify because you've spent a lot of money in the first

place. You have to do it all over again. You lose points and prize money. It's not very good for the morale of the team. And of course the sponsors are not desperately happy. But we have Marlboro through to the end of 1980 and they've been very good; in no way discouraging or damaging at all. They feel like members of the team and are just as disappointed about it as we are . . .

"To get the first M29 on the road will cost us £100,000, and the cost of development from that point on is anybody's guess. The M28 was built with three fuel cells, one in the tub and one in each sidepod, which made it very tricky and complicated to modify, and a honeycomb structure is inherently difficult to modify in any case.

"So we said we wouldn't build the new chassis out of honeycomb – there is some in it, but the very minimum – and we've also designed it with a single seat fuel cell. The basic philosophy is to keep it light, simple and easy to change . . ."

John Watson rounded-off this traumatic season with sixth place in both the Canadian and US GPs, somewhat bewildered at what had befallen him, while Patrick Tambay had been with McLaren through their worst two seasons ever, his confidence had taken a knock with his mid-season non-qualifications and he was not to be retained. It looked like the end of his Formula 1 career as he fell back on CanAm racing in the 'States, but he would bounce back . . .

In November testing at Ricard, the team ran an interim M29 using a new rear suspension set-up with outboard rear brakes developed by Coppuck and with new underwings. John's best time in a standard sister car was 1:9.0, the new car slammed round in 1:6.3. Prospective new team drivers were also given a go. American Kevin Cogan showed little aptitude in Teddy's opinion, but when French F3 star Alain Prost took over, his opening laps were quicker than John Watson's and Teddy: "Watched him for ten laps then ran to my car to get out a contract . . ." Paddy McNally of Marlboro had introduced the stocky, serious-minded little Frenchman to Teddy at Watkins Glen, and here he was showing all kinds of potential. He was duly signed-on for 1980.

By common consent, a great gormless device – the tragic ground-effects M28 of 1979 very nearly killed McLaren as a credible force in Formula 1. The broad sidepods housed the largest-area underwings possible within the regulation overall width and length, and although the outer skin looked smooth and sleek the car was too big, slow on the straights, unwieldy and initially at least its monocoque suffered a notable lack of rigidity.

Chapter 5
New Beginning – Into the 'Eighties

The World Champion way, Long Beach 1982: "When I was leading near the finish I slowed down. There was nothing wrong with my car, I just slowed down. So long as you win what difference does the gap to the next car make? It doesn't make sense to keep going quickly . . ."

Niki Lauda

On his debut for the team at Buenos Aires, Alain Prost qualified his M29C faster than John Watson with his and that set the pattern for most of the year, Alain faster, in practice the number one, with Teddy and the team regarding him that way while poor Wattie seemed utterly at odds with his car, incapable of fingering its problems and of driving himself out of despondency. It looked for much of the year as though his days as a competitive Formula 1 driver were over, and the same for the team as a whole . . .

Alain's sixth place in Argentina was followed by fifth in Brazil, then came a test session at Ricard with the M29C variant featuring a longer bell-housing between engine and transaxle, but swept-back front suspension elements to maintain the standard wheelbase, merely altering the weight-distribution. The car also carried revised side pods and suspension geometry but Prost crashed it apparently when something broke, in practice at Kyalami. He took over M29/1B to resume, but a suspension link failed, the right-rear wheel turned-in and he crashed again, this time damaging a bone in his wrist and being unable to race.

Stephen South, the English F2 driver, had tested quite promisingly for the team and was tipped to take Prost's place at Long Beach, but Teddy announced his preference for Hans Stuck, the experienced German. BMW contractual clashes scotched that idea, so South took the second car in California and failed to qualify. John thankfully inherited fourth place for his first 1980 Championship points.

An experimental 'low-drag' M29 was tested at Brands Hatch but the standard cars raced in Belgium where Alain again out-qualified his senior team-mate, and at Monaco John's performance was lamentable and he did not qualify, while Alain went out in a first-corner collision. It was McLaren's nadir . . .

In Spain the spare M29C appeared with a totally revised front end, but it failed in practice, pitching Alain into the barrier. For the French GP at Ricard the M29s were further developed, Alain qualifying seventh and John 14th, better than of late, but the Frenchman's transmission apparently failed and John was seventh. At Brands Hatch for the British GP improved rear suspension helped Alain to finish sixth and in the points again, John was eighth, but tall new Goodyears saw the M29Cs all at sea again at Hockenheim before Alain narrowly missed another points score, seventh, in Austria. Gordon's new 50 per cent stiffer M30 with all-inboard suspension, all-outboard brakes, made its debut in Alain's hands at Zandvoort and thereafter he was slower than Wattie, though finishing sixth there, and seventh in the Italian GP at Imola while the Ulsterman retired both times. In Italy the M29Cs ran M30 front uprights and brakes, but by that time major change had come about, and Bruce McLaren's old team had effectively ceased to exist . . .

Looking back on that year, Teddy recalls: "In 1980 John wasn't able to contribute much technically. When he'd tell me 'It's understeering' it took me a long time to deduce it wasn't necessarily doing that at all. I figured he's the guy in the cockpit so he must know what's happening, but that wasn't altogether true. He'd think about it a lot and tell us what he thought was happening, and in fact he didn't always know. He might have been complaining of understeer when his instincts were making him drive the car that way, because really it always wanted to stick its tail out and oversteer. It took me a long time to appreciate that . . .

"Prost was more adaptable, and he quickly got his car to the point where he was quite happy with it. He claimed he was embarrassed at continually qualifying faster than John, but he was happy as hell . . . wouldn't you be? People talk about number one drivers and number two drivers, and occasionally sign on two stars and call them equal number ones, but really there's always a *de facto* number one . . . and Prost was ours ."

"But the M29 was in trouble. In June/July I took one myself to MIRA for major aerodynamic tests in their wind tunnel and we got some real improvement, which the M30 followed up . . .

"By that time we were in deep trouble, we'd fallen off the tight-rope where you're competitive, and once a team has done that it's just so hard to climb back on. Marlboro told us something had to be done. It came down to that. When John Barnard came back to England in the Autumn of '79 I'd offered him a job as head of research and development. But after his experience with Jim Hall taking most of the credit for the Chaparral USAC car he'd designed, he was ambitious for public recognition, and didn't want his work to be diluted by Gordon's input. They wanted me to get rid of Gordon, and I wasn't willing to do that. So John Barnard went to Ron Dennis who had been running F3s and F2s and ProCar-series BMW M1s with Marlboro sponsorship. Ron had Formula 1 ambitions and John was going to build him a car . . .

"At that time Ron and Marlboro came to me and suggested a merger between Team McLaren and Ron's Project Four team and we weren't interested.

"About a year later, in the late-summer of 1980 they came back again and this time Marlboro told us we'd better do it, because we weren't doing any good alone. Now it's bloody difficult to find an alternative sponsor as good as Marlboro when you're in the situation we were in at that time, and I realised it would be the sensible thing to do. What hurt was that we'd been trying to build-up a reasonable design staff in depth for years to take some of the load off Gordon and we'd never quite managed it. Anyone we had who showed real promise had moved on, like John Barnard. Now part of the merger deal was that Gordon had to go. He wasn't included in it. He wasn't surprised when I told him, nor even very unhappy, though he wasn't by any means over-joyed. He was tired. He'd had all this pressure for all those years and now we'd been pressing him to do all kinds of things he didn't necessarily believe in, because I knew we had to get better results just to survive." So the merger went through, and Gordon went off to join March, then set-up his own Spirit team with March's former F2 team manager, John Wickham. He'd be back in Formula 1 . . .

The merger, forming a new company titled McLaren International, was announced in early-September 1980, just before the Italian GP. Both Team McLaren and Project Four contributed assets, the new concern residing in the Colnbrook works while looking for more spacious premises elsewhere. "We thought we'd find somewhere in a month – it took us nearer six . . ." Teddy took care of administration, accounting and ran one of the cars in the field, as he had since the CanAm days; drawing more on his long experience of what *not* to do in effectively compensating for his lack of formal engineering. Ron Dennis ran the sponsorship side, looking towards the future and development of new Chief Engineer John Barnard's carbon-fibre monocoque car. Tyler Alexander ran the test team, and engineered the other car at race meetings. Ron and Teddy were officially joint Managing Directors, Teddy becoming Chairman and Tyler and John Barnard taking Directorships. Teddy had owned 85 per cent of Team McLaren and now took the largest single shareholding in McLaren International, 45 per cent.

One press announcement of the new company announced "McLaren International is to continue development of the existing McLaren M30 and will

Watson on the charge; John in the much-modified M29/2C during his reputation-saving drive in the 1980 Canadian GP, Montreal, when he held a strong second place only to spin, coming home fourth. At one stage before Prost went off in the M30, Team McLaren were running 3-4; on their way out of despair.

Alain Prost achieved the leap from Formula 3 to Formula 1 in great style during 1980. Here he is in the last of the Colnbrook-designed and built McLarens, the one-off M30, on the way to seventh place in the year's Italian GP at Imola. For McLaren by that time this was a 'good result'.

unveil Project Four's John Barnard designed Formula 1 car in December, The Barnard design features a carbon-fibre tub, and if successful will presumably supercede the M30 . . . Ron Dennis has confirmed that Project Four's Formula 2, 3 and Procar teams will be wound up at the end of the year and that McLaren International will concentrate solely on Formula 1 . . ."

At that time it was made known that Alain Prost would continue driving for the team in 1981, but there was no mention of John Watson's future and F2 drivers Stefan Johansson, Roberto Guerrero and Eliseo Salazar would test drive.

But John Barnard tackled the M30 in preparation for the Canadian GP where it appeared with new underbody, engine cover, spring rates and anti-roll bars, and John Watson's further-improved M29C was at last being driven with his old application and fire. He proved he was not yet over the hill by setting fourth fastest time in Friday practice, and only misfortune delayed him to qualify seventh in the Saturday sessions. Prost was slower, twelfth in the revised M30 and while he spun off in the race John drove hard and finished fourth, for three more World Championship points. At Watkins Glen Alain had something fail on the M30 in practice and crashed heavily, writing-off the last of the line of Colnbrook McLarens, and he was not fit enough to start the race. John was quicker in the M29C, bolstered by his Canadian result, and ran seventh in the GP before his car's handling began to deteriorate as the left-rear damper failed. A lengthy pit stop traced the problem but a replacement had to be fetched from the garage. This cost nine long laps and dropped him too far behind to be classified as a finisher under the 'ninety per cent of the distance' rule.

There was a feeling that John might, just, "have saved his bacon". His two seasons with McLaren had not been very productive. While the universally popular, thoughtful Ulsterman was the first to admit his performances hadn't been outstanding, he felt Teddy was often unsympathetic for his problems with the cars. Teddy stated he hadn't "been very impressed with John's determination this year" but he valued experience in the team – "Prost has told me just how much he has learned from having John around . . ."

In November '80 it looked as though McLaren International's driver pairing for '81 would be Prost and young Italian hope Andrea De Cesaris, but the little Frenchman was being courted by Renault, and driving for his national turbo team was an attraction he could not resist.

After much controversy he made the move, pleading that his contract had been with Team McLaren and that organisation no longer existed. Teddy made things very hot for both Prost and Renault, but the French as usual in motor racing got their way . . . By Christmas it was clear John Watson's McLaren place was safe, with young De Cesaris as his number two. To add to all this controversy there was a deep rift in Formula 1 between the mainly British-based Cosworth-engined teams with skirted ground-effect aerodynamic technology maintaining their competitive position and the *Grande Costruttore* major manufacturer Continental teams like Renault, Ferrari and Alfa Romeo building dominance on turbo power and lobbying FISA – the sport's governing body – to ban sliding-skirt ground-effect aerodynamic devices. This dispute rumbled on through the winter of 1980-81 and at one point it looked very much as though two separate Formula 1 series would be organised, one by the Formula 1 Constructors' Association and another by FISA for the 'Grandees'. The South African GP – ostensibly a Championship round – was run at Kyalami in February with no participation from Renault, Ferrari, Alfa Romeo, Talbot (Ligier) or Osella. The FOCA teams ran sliding skirts, FISA withheld Championship status, but agreement was reached on banning such aerodynamic aids thereafter and a degree of stability was assured.

1981

In practice at Kyalami, John was out-qualified by Andrea de Cesaris, whose M29/5C had its left front suspension damaged by a wild spin; John's M29/4C suffering a seized fuel metering unit which left them sharing the spare car for the rest of the session. The race was started in heavy rain, which rapidly dried, it became another tyre changing saga, and on laps 28 and 29 the dayglo-red and white Marlboro-McLaren with John Watson driving actually led across the timing line. It was the Ulsterman's first GP lead since Monaco '78 and although John subsequently had to stop to change onto slick tyres and eventually finished fifth he was most encouraged, as were the team, setting aside any thoughts of where he might have finished in a full entry . . . Young Andrea slid off at Leeukop corner, mildly damaging his car on his GP debut for the team, now on Michelin tyres.

On March 6 the new John Barnard-designed Marlboro MP4 Formula 1 car was shown to the press at a rain-swept Silverstone, ready to be flown out to Long Beach for its public debut. The new car marked the realisation of Ron Dennis' ambition to run his own F1 programme, as first discussed with John two years before. One release notice read: "The futuristic new aerospace-technology monocoque in carbon-fibre was formed in conjunction with Hercules Incorporated of Salt Lake City, Utah, a chemicals company specialising in work on missile rocket motors. Hercules are deeply involved in carbon-fibre technology and make the monocoque sections specially for McLaren International. The sections are flown to Britain where they are bolted and glued together to form a light and extremely rigid monocoque.

"This approach cuts the component parts of the monocoque to about one-tenth of those used in conventional aluminium construction. Barnard estimates that as many as 50 sections of aluminium are required to build a conventional monocoque, but this carbon-fibre design uses only five pieces, plus the outer shell.

"The underbody . . . and side panels of the Marlboro MP4 are made from carbon-fibre honeycomb and the radiators are mounted on either side abreast the dash panel in carbon-fibre boxes which double as ductings and mountings, replacing the conventional framework and fibreglass. 'Apart from the suspension, there isn't a great deal of metal in the chassis', explains Barnard.

"As far as general chassis configuration is concerned, the Marlboro MP4 is pretty conventional by current standards, employing inboard-mounted coil-spring/dampers activated by rocker arms, and wishbones all round.

"Aerodynamic testing has been carried out in the Maritime Institute wind tunnel at Feltham, using models . . ."

The MP4 (named simply to reflect 'Marlboro-Project Four' although popularly the cars were very much 'McLarens') broke new ground in its use of carbon-fibre mouldings to form its chassis monocoque, but coincidentally Lotus had made a considerable fuss of their introduction of Kevlar and other composite fibre mouldings in their latest monocoques. John Barnard had independently matched Colin Chapman's team step for step, and matching the maestro to that extent was a promising launch-pad for McLaren International's first product. Many critics of carbon-fibre's structural use came forward, however, warning of its poor impact resistance relative to conventional metal monocoque materials, and predicting dire effects should an MP4 suffer a heavy accident. All credit is due to John Watson and Andrea de Cesaris, for ignoring such prophets of doom, and driving the cars as hard as they did. Andrea's lengthy crash-testing programme proved them wrong.

The MP4 was too new to race effectively at Long Beach, but the team management was keen to run the car there in deference to Hercules' interest. The sleek newcomer made the ageing M29s look positively vintage in comparison, and it won the Californian organisers' *concours d'elegance*, to some surprise. It was not race-worthy and Andrea and John qualified their M29s right on the back of the grid. The impetuous Italian went out in a first-lap collision, taking both Rebaque's Brabham and ironically Alain Prost's Renault with him – two races, two accidents. John's engine misfired until he quit after 15 laps. It was not an impressive World Championship beginning . . .

Two weeks elapsed before the Brazilian GP at Rio, before which a lengthy test programme had been set-up at Donington Park only to be washed-out by rain. But Wattie was bubbling with newfound confidence: "In eight laps, without any adjustments, I was easily quicker than I'd ever been with a skirtless M29 . . ." Driving the older cars at Rio neither McLaren driver could find adequate balance, and Andrea spun repeatedly. His engine cut out early in the race but John splashed through the rain into fifth place and held it comfortably until lap 35 when he slid the tail out of line as usual but this time it kept on sliding and he spun. "It was nobody's fault but my own" he cursed, dropping back to eighth for the finish.

Back home the MP4 again tested well, and was flown to Buenos Aires for the following Argentine GP and John promptly lapped fourth fastest during pre-race testing. Understeer – as of old – dogged him in early practice, the team not tracing it to a dud damper until too late. Andrea spun and spun again. Ron Dennis had a quiet chat with him, "Don't try to run before you can walk. Don't try to get more out of the old car than there is in it . . .".

John ran eighth but competitively until severe rear end vibration ended his race, and Andrea placed eleventh. It was progress.

Having been robbed of their sliding skirts to contain ground-effect aerodynamic depression beneath the cars, the ingenuity of British chassis designers had surfaced in a different and controversial manner. The revised regulations specified a given ground clearance to prevent devices bridging the gap between car underside and road surface. Gordon Murray and David North of Brabham appreciated that under such regulations they could use a lowering device which would allow their cars to sit at verifiable clearance when stationary, but settle down on circuit to bring fixed skirts within viable range of the road surface. The new skirts would then prevent ambient-pressure air rushing in beneath their underwing side-pod sections to 'fill-in' the low-pressure area created by airflow beneath the working under-surfaces of these wings which in turn created the immense downforces which smeared modern F1 cars down onto the road through corners and contributed to their ever-increasing lap speeds. In effect it would side-step the sliding-skirt ban, and retain near equality with the turbo cars.

The European F1 season commenced at Imola in Italy for the so-called San Marino GP, and there McLaren International fielded two MP4s, the latest one fitted with a progressive double spring system, though John found it bottoming badly before going well later on. Ron decided against giving Andrea an MP4 as it would put him under "unacceptable pressure" there on home soil. He drove M29/5F very well until spinning late in practice and knocking-off a rear corner. John qualified seventh, while in race morning warm-up Andrea crumpled his M29F's nose. At the end of the opening lap John was harrying Rene Arnoux's Renault for fifth place but while attempting to pass the French car he misjudged things slightly and knocked-off the MP4's full-width nose wing. Again he made no excuses. "It was a foolish mistake" he admitted after having a new nose fitted in the pits and chasing back through the field into 11th place, and setting second fastest race lap on the way. Andrea did his job well, trailing Villeneuve's sixth-placed Ferrari until the last lap, when the French-Canadian's slipping clutch allowed the youngster by to score his first World Championship point. It was promising.

There was still no MP4 for Andrea at Zolder, where John cumpled the latest car's rear wing and side pod in practice on his way to qualifying fifth on the grid. Andrea's M29F ended practice 23rd; his Italian sighs and wistful looks at Wattie's spare MP4/1 saying it all . . .

John was charging along fourth in the race until his car began jumping out of gear and he fell away to finish seventh. It was a disappointment. Just twelve months previously it would have been a triumph! Andrea's race ended early, with gearbox failure.

Hydro-pneumatic lowering suspension appeared on the MP4s at Monaco, but John abandoned it on his car, complaining it felt too stiff and twitchy "just like a go-kart". Andrea was allowed MP4/1 for the first time, but the streets of Monte Carlo were not the best place and he clipped the chicane and bent a rocker arm. Nobody minded, John and the Italian qualified 10-11 – a good effort in such a competitive situation. Unfortunately on the opening lap Andrea got his wheels interlocked with those of Prost's Renault and attempted to accelerate his way out of trouble. The MP4 bounded high over the Renault's wheels and crashed down on top of Andretti's Marlboro-Alfa Romeo nose, taking both out of the race. John had a good run and looked bound to finish fourth, when his engine quit.

Jarama, Spanish GP; John qualified fourth fastest on row two, as one report described: "It was heart-warming to see the popular Ulsterman pull off such an impressive practice performance and everybody in the McLaren International camp had their fingers well and truly crossed in preparation for the race . . ." John's time was set on the second of only 11 laps he managed in the all-important final hour after earlier troubles. Andrea meanwhile spun with a broken steering arm on his MP4 but made the middle of the grid. The race became a classic victory

Wonderful Wattie – after being brought virtually to a standstill by an early multiple collision in his path, John Watson recovered to challenge for the lead of the British GP, Silverstone '81, and inherited victory when the leading Renault failed. To finish first, you must first finish, and to a deliriously partisan reception 'Wattie' brought McLaren International their first-ever Grande Epreuve victory, and the McLaren marque's first since Hunt's Japanese win in the M26, 1977. It was the maiden victory for the John Barnard-designed carbon-fibre-chassised MP4.

for Gilles Villeneuve, blocking a train of four other cars to produce some sensational TV coverage, with just 1.24 seconds covering all five across the line . . . and amongst them John's MP4 was third, 0.58 second behind the Ferrari. Early on, Andrea had become involved in a battle for 15th place with Hector Rebaque's Brabham which the Mexican won, though not before the Italian had banged wheels furiously with him into the first corner beyond the pits. Andrea dropped the MP4 and slid gently into retirement amongst the catch-fencing halfway round lap 10.

The MP4 looked terrific at Dijon, fast and stable on the tight French GP venue's climbs, dips and swerves. John set fastest time on Friday practice, and in a battle royal for pole position in the final Saturday session he was almost immediately down to 1:6.3 while his rivals were still in the 1:7s. But then came Arnoux's final spurt for Renault, and Wattie was demoted to line-up alongside him on the front row, second fastest. Andrea performed very well, qualifying fifth and being well briefed to keep out of trouble on the charge into the first corner.

Unfortunately the race was stopped after 58 laps due to torrential rain and the cars were fitted with soft qualifying tyres for a 22-lap resumption, final results being decided on aggregate of these two 'heats'. John was third when the first part was flagged down, and finished second in part two for second overall. He had driven aggressively throughout the meeting and the MP4 was the fastest of the Cosworth brigade. Andrea seemed set to finish in the top six only to stop for wet tyres just before the 'first heat' was flagged down falling from eighth to 14th, and finally being classified eleventh overall.

Third in Spain, second in France, could Wattie win at Silverstone? After dominating the 1977 race until his Brabham faltered, he seemed owed victory in the British GP but fairy-tales don't come true.

He and Andrea qualified 5-6, their dayglo-red and white cars packing row three of the starting grid behind the two Renaults on row one and a Brabham and Ferrari on row two. Andrea drove coolly and smoothly for his good time, but spoiled it in race morning warm-up, crumpling his MP4's wings in the catch-fencing at Stowe. The damage was rapidly repaired but on the fourth lap of the race Gilles Villeneuve whacked his Ferrari over the kerbing at the Woodcote chicane and the turbocharged car bounced into a lurid high-speed spin, tyre smoke blinding the queue of cars hot on his heels which included both MP4s. John came almost to a halt on the verge before selecting first and tearing away after the field, but Andrea had no such luck, locked-up everything and hurtled into the catch-fencing at high speed, erupting from the cockpit furious in his frustration.

John resumed ninth, and flying . . . He made up places and profited from retirements amongst the leaders. When Piquet crashed his Brabham on lap 11 John took fifth, two laps later outbraking Reutemann's Williams at the chicane for fourth. Squeezing ahead of Pironi's Ferrari the Italian turbo car promptly blew-up, John third and clear. Only the Renaults of Prost and Arnoux were ahead of him, until lap 17 when the former McLaren's driver's retired. John ran second more than half a minute behind Arnoux's leading Renault and for 30 laps the race was processional. But the Renault's exhaust note ran ragged, and by lap 51 Arnoux was clearly in trouble.

John gained four seconds in one lap, three seconds on the next. The crowds packed all round the circuit were waving him on, he could see the flurry of movement, the fluttering programmes. By lap 57 the gap was down to 4.5 seconds, lap 58 only 2.5.

Still closing, lap 60 John on the Renault's tail, lap 61 the MP4 lunging for the inside at Copse Corner, clinging to the tight inside line round the right-hander and wheel-to-wheel with the Renault away, round the left-hand kink at Maggotts, leaving John on the favoured inside line for the tighter right-hander at Becketts. Arnoux fell away, the enthusiastic crowd thundered its approval, and John Watson and the McLaren MP4 were leading the British GP. Seven laps to go, would it last?

It did, and Wattie scored a marvellous emotional victory on home soil, the first for McLaren International and John Barnard's carbon-fibre MP4, McLaren's first since James Hunt, the M26 and the Japanese GP of 1977. It had been a long dry three-and-a-half years for the team, and over four years since John's only previous *Grande Epreuve* victory – for the Penske team in Austria '76.

The Ulsterman again was objective as ever: "I just can't get used to the idea it's me they're cheering for . . . Sure it's a justification and reward for all the bad years. But I'm not totally satisfied. It wasn't a win from the front. I was slightly lucky, even though I had to work pretty hard to make up the ground I'd lost. There is a difference between winning and coming first . . .

"The car was better in the race than it had been in the warm-up during the morning. It *was* good by comparison with everything but Piquet's Brabham and the Renaults. But I still couldn't pitch it into the corners and nail the throttle like I wanted to. The back end was pretty skittish. Sure I'm over the moon, but we've still got to improve if we want to win again . . ."

It was down to earth with a bump at Hockenheim where the MP4s 'porpoised' badly over the undulations of the super-fast *Autodrom*. Angle of incidence between the underwing floors and the road surface could be critical in ground-effect cars, and fore-and-aft pitching would alter the wings' angle of attack and in certain cases their downforce. This effect could become self-exciting, with the wings making and breaking downforce and making the car progressively oscillate until the driver either backed off to regain control or flew off the road. Andrea was a gnat's whisker off John's best time when he spun off on the last lap of qualifying, rumpling his car's underside over the chicane kerbing. They lined-up on row five, John spun further back down the field in the early stages and Andrea spun under braking on lap 5, slightly bent a steering arm and in any case was stranded on the grass, unable to restart his hot engine. Wattie was having a dreadful time: ". . . without doubt the worst-handling car I've ever driven in my life. I couldn't believe how badly it was porpoising. My feet were being thrown up off the pedals and smashed against the steering rack. The front wheels almost seemed to be coming off the ground at one point on the circuit . . ."

But he tucked his chin down and persevered, and was rewarded with sixth place and another Championship point. At this stage of the season he was sixth in the Drivers' competition, as were McLaren in the Constructors'.

In Austria the McLaren enclave was still an unhappy place, John complaining they must get their downforce under control, and the understeer. And Andrea surpassed himself. He set off for the second timed session and on his first lap crashed heavily, the MP4's carbon-fibre monocoque again surviving well as the suspension, wings and pods absorbed the impact. But John struggled home sixth for another point in the race and a muted Andrea survived for eighth.

At Zandvoort the MP4s wore new underwing panels in an effort to eradicate the porpoising problem, and Andrea walked back to the pits close to tears after trying to brake late into the Tarzan Loop, locking-up the wheels and slithering straight-on very rapidly into the rubber tyre barrier there. His reception was frosty and the management were to decide he would not stay on. John inherited a distant fourth place in the race before his electrical system cut-out on lap 51, while Andrea was denied a start.

Ron Dennis, Teddy Mayer and John Barnard had each had a word with the impetuous Italian, he would nod and agree he must temper his enthusiasm.

He did manage to keep everything in one piece during practice at Monza, where John qualified seventh and Andrea 17th on his home ground. The Ulsterman was running sixth on lap 20 during the race when he ran wide out of the second 150mph fourth-gear right-hander at Lesmo. The MP4 put both left-side wheels up the polished kerb and began to spin. It spiralled back across the track and slammed violently tail-first into the right-side Armco. The steel rails forced apart and literally 'bit off' the left-rear wheel and suspension, while the right-hand corner complete with gearbox were yanked off the back of the engine and bounded back across the circuit. John, strapped in the monocoque with just a shattered engine bolted behind it, went scuttering along the right-hand verge, a brief flash of flame from the disrupted fuel-system's dry-break couplings caused no fire, and the British GP winner, miraculously unhurt, was able to unstrap himself and walk away unaided. Andrea was running consistently and would have taken sixth place only to slide off on oil from Piquet's blown Brabham on the last lap. He was classified seventh instead.

A new MP4 was available for John in Canada and at last the team seemed to have taken a grip on the 'bouncing' problem. It was a horribly wet race but John groped his way up to second place behind Jacques Laffite's Talbot-Matra in the murk, proving the value of Michelin's wet-weather tyres as the Goodyear runners all struggled. Andrea made a late stab to pass Piquet for fifth place, just as Laffite was poised to pass them both. The Italian banged wheels with the Brabham giving Piquet a horrible moment while the McLaren MP4 spun to a halt on the soggy verge, unable to restart and out of the race.

The final World Championship round was at Las Vegas on a sinuous course laid-out around the carpark of Caesars Palace Hotel. There in practice John was suffering from sinus trouble and took sixth place on the grid despite feeling himself a danger on-circuit. Andrea qualified 14th in what would be his last McLaren ride and this time kept his car intact. Mid-way round the second race lap, however, he dived inside Patrick Tambay's Talbot into one of the tight right-hand corners, made contact and spun the Frenchman round. Andrea stopped to complain of bad handling and resumed with four new wheels and tyres. A later stop replaced a bent steering arm, shortly before John came in to complain of dreadful oversteer and resumed with fresh Michelin tyres. He finished seventh, Andrea twelfth.

Meanwhile as early as August, Marlboro had been rumoured to be making 'big money' offers for a star driver to join John Watson in a McLaren International 'Superteam' for the forthcoming season. Rumours of "more than half a million dollars" being offered to attract Nelson Piquet from Brabham or Carlos Reutemann from Williams were being bandied about.

In September it became known that Niki Lauda, who had abruptly retired from race-driving during practice for the Canadian GP in 1979, was showing interest in a come-back. His former sponsor Parmalat, the Italian dairy company which still backed Brabham, was said to be interested in massaging him into a renewed place with the team. In mid-September the Austrian double-World Champion returned to the wheel of a Formula 1 car, test-driving a Marlboro MP4 at Donington Park.

He drove Watson's MP4/2 for more than 50 laps, and showed he'd lost little of his old skill with a best time only 0.6 second slower than Wattie's best that day. Niki's mind was made up to return immediately after his testing performance. It seemed a choice between McLaren and Williams. John Watson joked "We'll leave the number two seat open!" in response to questions from friendly journalists worried on his behalf that he'd be pushed aside. In fact he and Niki had been team-mates at Brabham and got on very well together.

In that silly season during October '81 there was also talk of both James Hunt and Jackie Stewart being lured back into racing by big-money sponsorship. It was Las Vegas madness, but Marlboro ensured the Lauda deal went through and it was formally announced in a November function at the team's new Woking factory – which they had moved into from Colnbrook that July.

"We've got The Rat in the trap at last" announced Teddy Mayer, and a couple of days later Niki and Wattie began energetic testing at Ricard. The TAG-Porsche turbo engine project was also detailed; Ron Dennis' far-sighted investment in the future . . .

Emerson Fittipaldi nudges-on opposite lock at Silverstone's Copse Corner during his drive to victory in the 1975 British Grand Prix, his Texaco-Marlboro McLaren wearing number '1' in honour of their reigning position as Champions of the World.

Magical moment – James Hunt during his sensational World Championship-winning drive in the Marlboro-McLaren M23; Japanese Grand Prix, Mount Fuji, 1976.

Overleaf: 'Super Rat's' return – Niki Lauda very rapidly proved that he had lost none of his old double-World Championship winning skill when he came out of retirement to drive the McLaren International MP4s in 1982-83. Here he rides the rails at Rio's Jacarepaguà Autodrome, Brazilian GP 1983.

—————————— **1982** ——————————

That winter of '81-82 saw John Barnard's engineering team sort out their wind tunnel programme reasonably well, fitting their own moving-ground gear in the National Maritime Institute's wind tunnel at Feltham in order to simulate a realistic aerodynamic interface between car and road surface. Full-size testing at Ricard and at Michelin's Ladoux test centre near Clermont-Ferrand in France helped find better grip through aerodynamic means. The Michelin track has built-in weight balances to record load as a vehicle passes over them. Watson and Lauda would start the new season with mildly-revised MP4B cars based on existing carbon-fibre tubs which were proving extremely durable, having been thoroughly crash-tested by poor Andrea de Cesaris, and by John occasionally – as at Monza – during the preceding season. Through 1982 Barnard would admit to ". . . paring off some weight, changing the suspension a little bit and trying to improve stiffness everywhere." While other teams improved rigidity by replacing their old conventional fabricated top rocker arm inboard suspensions with Brabham-like pull-rod systems, John retained the rocker arms.

Early in the year he was troubled by the manner in which Michelin's radial tyres squidged down under load at high speed, so taking-up precious skirt movement before even hitting a bump. Cross-ply Goodyear tyres as used by much of the main opposition would grow at speed under centrifugal force, in effect compensating for aerodynamic downthrust increasing with speed to force the car down against the road surface. The conflict of growing tyres and lowering car compensated one for another to maintain a pre-set ride-height, while the Michelin radial runners had to set-up their cars very finely in the pit lane to compensate for 'squidge' on-circuit. John reflected: "We spent a lot of time setting-up to the nearest sixteenth of an inch with spacers and bump rubbers. If you had to ride severe bumps at high speed you'd find too much of the skirt travel had already been taken up. We had generally to tune to finer limits than the Goodyear runners . . ."

But McLaren International added to their stature with early-season success, and Michelin responded with great help later on. They made special 15-inch diameter front tyres which reacted better than the 13s and in-between metric-size TRXs run formerly. Michelin traction was very good and on many circuits McLaren could run narrow rears for a useful drag reduction – tyres which the turbo Renaults for example with their much greater power could not make survive race distance. This was also a function of car balance. During the year John also varied both track and wheelbase of his MP4Bs ". . . most times running the front track as wide as possible, adding 3½-4 inches wheelbase at one point, then pulling back to a couple of inches longer than original . . ."

The team also experimented with carbon brake discs in Brazil and at Long Beach to achieve an immense weight-saving *a la* Brabham, but John decided further experience was necessary before they could be adopted as standard. The team usually had four cars assembled at any one time, normally taking only three to meetings in rotation to even-up mileage.

Kyalami marked the return of Niki Lauda for the South African GP on January 23. He had emerged from a considerable testing accident at Ricard with his nerve thoroughly tested, and not found wanting. This was emphasised as in practice at Kyalami he bent a bottom wishbone brushing the wall at Crowthorne Corner, then continued to set a time before threatened rain began to fall. Wattie set the faster time in the T-car before spinning off the damp track later on. John's race car was brand-new carrying the reinforced footwell area soon to become mandatory. During the race Niki played himself in gently to take a distant fourth place and John finished sixth – both MP4Bs in the points immediately.

In Brazil, Niki was fastest Michelin qualifier after shrewdly completing only twelve timed laps throughout the two days of qualifying. His fifth fastest time contrasted with John's twelfth-best in the second MP4B. Unfortunately Carlos Reutemann saw fit to bang wheels with the Lauda car early in the race, putting the Austrian out for the day with bent rear suspension. The team were crestfallen, for

Niki's chances in the race were highly-rated. John proved as resilient as ever in tropical heat and humidity, and finished fourth. This was immensely valuable as both Piquet's Brabham which won on the road and Keke Rosberg's Williams which was second were subsequently disqualified and fourth place and three Championship points abruptly became second place, and six . . .

Lauda proved he had lost little of his old skill and wilyness at Long Beach where after wiping off the nose in a first-session spin he set fastest time in the final period after a sustained seven-lap burst of smooth, controlled artistry behind the wheel. Pole position seemed assured until the closing moments of the session, when discarded McLaren driver Andrea de Cesaris suddenly slammed-in a stunningly fast lap in his works Alfa Romeo and stole it from under his former employers' noses. John Watson, meanwhile was again in agony. A broken fuel pump drive ended his first session after half a lap, and by the time his spare car was ready only 20 minutes remained – he was 26th fastest. On the Saturday his MP4B was jumping out of gear but in the final hour the Ulsterman took eleventh spot.

Many were worried about De Cesaris starting on pole. Would he forget himself again and do something silly ahead of the pack? He did not, and was leading smoothly on lap 8 with Lauda pressing Arnoux's Renault hard on the Alfa's heels. As the pursuing cars headed into the hairpin leading out onto the straight Arnoux was slow, having missed a gear accelerating from the previous turn. Niki was about to challenge when he spotted Giacomelli's Alfa about to strike on his left. The crafty Austrian simply dodged right, leaving room for the Italian to charge by, misjudge his braking for the hairpin and ram Arnoux hard in the tail. Two down, Niki was second . . .

John was charging hard, fifth, his car much improved in race morning warm-up and already have stormed up through the pack. Up front De Cesaris was nervously watching his pit signals as Niki closed. On lap 15 the Alfa came up to lap Raul Boesel's March in the tight chicane on the back straight. Andrea chose the wrong side of the March, was held up and Lauda nipped by to lead. The McLaren pulled away, smoothly, relentlessly, to establish and hold a 9-second cushion over the Italian's Alfa Romeo, but then De Cesaris glanced in his mirrors too long and looked up to find himself heading into the wall, *Bang*; out of the race. John's good run ended when he had to stop for fresh tyres on lap 29, but he salvaged sixth place, while Niki Lauda won.

Niki Lauda's shapely Marlboro-McLaren MP4/1B dominated the US GP (West) at Long Beach, California, 1982. The carbon-fibre car achieved the best balance of traction and handling in the field and gave the double-World Champion Austrian ace his 18th World Championship-qualifying victory in only his 3rd race since coming out of retirement to join McLaren International.

He strode into the post-race press conference, the Parmalat cap, the waspish grin, buck-teeth gnawing an apple. Not waiting to be formally introduced he ambled up to the waiting battery of microphones and barked "Any kvestions?" SuperRat was back – after three races with Marlboro-McLaren. He and McLaren were second in the World Championships, to Alain Prost, and Renault. Wattie was third-equal.

In common with other leading FOCA teams McLaren boycotted the San Marino GP at Imola, leaving it to Ferrari and Renault. They returned at Zolder in Belgium, a meeting overshadowed by Gilles Villeneuve's death in a dreadful practice accident to his Ferrari. Niki qualified fourth, John tenth, and the race developed with Rosberg dominant for Williams and Niki his closest challenger. But tyre trouble for both meant that Wattie running the perfect tyre combination for the day came steaming through the field to take the lead sensationally on the penultimate lap, and win again! Niki was third on the road but at post-race scrutineering his car was found to be 1.8Kg below the minimum weight limit, and he was therefore disqualified. The team had miscalculated weight loss through tyre and brake wear and were hugely relieved as John's car just passed the weight-check – by 1Kg... He was now second to Prost in the Drivers' Championship with 17 points to the Frenchman's 18, McLaren headed the Constructors' table by 29 points to Renault's 22 ...

Now they were really back in business with a vengeance. The tribulations of '78-80 when Marlboro-McLaren had been mere also-rans, were laid to rest ...

It was a happy team which approached Monaco but there neither MP4B performed well over the bumps. They lacked traction which was baffling after the Long Beach performance, Wattie blew his engine on Thursday morning and had to resort to his spare chassis, and Niki blew-up in the afternoon. He was spending most of his time adjusting skirts and ride height, and in the McLaren pits Teddy Mayer was becoming increasingly irritated. Looking back on that weekend he recalls: "That was the low point for me. Until then I'd been very happy to go along with everything John Barnard did, and without trying to enhance my reputation for interfering I just thought the cars' set-up was far too stiff for such a slow circuit. He was worried about the cars bottoming and wearing-out their skirts on the bump after the tunnel and refused to soften them at all. I reckoned skirts hardly mattered on such a slow circuit, it was just ridiculous, but I didn't really want to create waves so I just altered the set-up on John Watson's car and let John Barnard and Niki get on with it. I believed Niki was learning all over again and he was unknowingly misleading John Barnard. Watson was being forced to follow where Niki led, and that wasn't always right ..."

More times John was right, or the tyres worked well, which was to prove the ultimate arbiter of success or failure.

The upshot was that Wattie qualified ahead of Lauda, and the Austrian fell back in the early stages of the race as John forged ahead. But a leaking oil cooler shorted-out the Ulsterman's battery and Niki's engine lost oil pressure. Both McLarens were out after running only eighth at best.

The inaugural Detroit GP followed in the USA, another street circuit which should suit the MP4Bs on Long Beach form. But neither driver was particularly happy, Niki qualifying tenth despite being quickest in one wet session, and John a lowly 17th after a collision with Chico Serra's Fittipaldi.

The race was stopped after seven laps due to the organisers over-reacting to a minor incident. This was crucial; good news for McLaren. John had found his car understeering too much, and in the interval before the restart harder-compound Michelins were fitted.

He was 13th at the restart, Niki seventh, rapidly striding forward to join a battle for third. John rapidly hacked his way past four cars; the leading Renault broke. John found he had a huge braking advantage at three points round the circuit and made the most of it to climb into sixth place. While Rosberg's Williams led, he was pursued by a second-place battle involving Didier Pironi's Ferrari, Eddie

Cheever's Talbot, Niki and Giacomelli, and as they bobbed and weaved, feinting for position and advantage, so they slowed each and John closed up.

He promptly hacked past Giacomelli's Alfa but ran wide in the next turn, the Italian fighting back, drawing level. Wattie wasn't about to be denied and took the corner, the cars touched and the Alfa smeared along the barrier, out of the race. John's car accelerated away, unscathed, Pironi, Cheever and Lauda in his sights.

He was into a rhythm he'd rather not break. He knew if he became locked into the duel ahead he would be slowed to their pace. That he could do without, so he tried the alternative, and it came off. He passed them. Just like that. In one lap they fell, and ending lap 33 mild, enigmatic old Wattie was second and carving seconds off Rosberg's lead. The Williams was in trouble with tyres and transmission, the Finn could not defend his lead and by lap 37 the Marlboro-McLaren was leading. Niki seemed inspired by his team-mate's passing and established himself in third, closed on Rosberg and then made an error in trying to pass in an impossible manoeuvre, spinning himself into retirement.

There was no chance of the McLaren 1-2 which at one time had seemed possible, but John Watson rushed on to comfortable victory, after a sensational drive through most of the field. He now headed the Drivers' Championship, with 26 points to Pironi's 20. McLaren now held a twelve point Constructors' Championship lead over Ferrari and Williams, second-equal; 38 points to 26 . . .

One week later on Montreal's Île Notre Dame circuit, John was fastest Cosworth-engined qualifier, sixth on the grid with Niki eleventh. The Brabhams dominated, Piquet winning in his new BMW turbo car from team-mate Riccardo Patrese's Cosworth version, and John placed third, Niki going out with clutch failure. John stretched his Championship lead to 10 points, McLaren twelve clear now of Brabham.

At Zandvoort Niki took over the mantle of quickest Cosworth runner as the turbos came on song, improved aerodynamics giving the MP4B better straight-line speed. John couldn't find a clear lap when it mattered in qualifying and was 1 second per lap slower. Niki finished fourth while John's tyres were bad, he stopped for a new set and classified ninth, out of the points. Pironi won for Ferrari, closing within one point of John at the top of the Drivers' table, McLaren now led Brabham in the Constructors' Cup by 45 points to 36.

The British GP at Brands Hatch saw Niki start fifth on the grid, John twelfth. Rosberg's Williams failed to start from pole, and the other half of the front row went out as Patrese stalled his Brabham and was rammed from behind by Arnoux. Piquet led away with Niki immediately second, the race moments old and events already going his way. The leading Brabham was out after only nine laps, Niki left in the lead with a comfortable time cushion over the rest of the delayed field. He maintained it comfortably to the finish, to bring McLaren International their second British GP victory in their two seasons' existence. John spun-off early on avoiding someone else's moment, and he lost his Championship lead to Pironi, with Niki now third, 35 points to 30 and 24 respectively. McLaren still headed the Constructors' Cup, 54 points to Ferrari's 45.

The French GP was at Ricard, where the turbos had a great advantage. The McLarens were out of luck, John retiring early, with of all things a broken battery lead, and Niki finishing eighth, out of the points, after a stop for tyres. Pironi now had a nine point lead over John, McLaren survived at the top of the Constructors' table, but just two points clear of Ferrari.

Then in practice at Hockenheim poor Pironi suffered massive leg injuries in another ghastly Ferrari accident and clearly would play no further part in the Championship. John was *de facto* Championship leader, but practice also saw Niki spin off. He had been on the grass at the previous corner, avoiding Rupert Keegan's March, and thought dirt on his tyres might have contributed to his uncharacteristic spin. But after practice ended he felt pain in one wrist, and it signalled ligament damage. He kicked himself for not having let go of the wheel at the moment of impact, and missed the race to save himself for the Austrian GP, one week later, on his home soil. John therefore was sole McLaren runner in the

Wattie in Motown – John Watson slaughtered all opposition at Detroit '82. The MP4/1B was one of the neatest and most integrated F1 designs of its period, tribute to John Barnard's lengthy and unfettered design gestation period with his first Formula 1 car.

German GP and he was set to take an excellent third in the race with only nine laps to go when the front suspension broke, probable legacy of a morning warm-up incident in which he locked-up under braking for a chicane and bounded over the kerb. The suspension elements had not been changed pre-race because Wattie swore he had hit nothing.

Austria was another poor race for the team, the MP4Bs could not be trimmed properly during practice leaving Niki tenth quickest, still troubled by his tender wrist and John 18th. John went out with a ruptured cooling system after running seventh, Niki finished fifth. Now Rosberg with 33 points had moved ahead of John's 30 point total in the Championship chase, and Ferrari's 64 points displaced McLaren's 56 for the Constructors' title lead.

The so-called Swiss GP was a new Championship round run at Dijon. Niki lay third fastest for a long time in qualifying only to be bumped down to fourth at the end of the period. John was all at sea, eleventh. Niki finished third in the race while John's hopes took a jolt as he ran over a tall kerb early on while passing Patrese and damaged a skirt. He stopped for a replacement to be fitted, and a hard recovery drive was ill-rewarded with only 13th place. Now he had tumbled to fourth-equal in the Drivers' competition, or third discounting Pironi's points. Rosberg led with 42, from Prost's 31 and John and Niki together on thirty.

Ferrari led McLaren, 64 points to 60.

Monza, Italian GP; no grip for the McLarens out of the slow chicanes. Niki and John qualifying 10-12, but John driving aggressively into fourth place to score his first points in three months and so keep his Championship hopes just alive, with only Las Vegas remaining to decide the title. It was between Rosberg, leading with 42 points, Wattie on 33 and Prost with 31. Niki retired with handling and braking problems.

An appeal had been registered against Niki's Belgian disqualification and that could bring him into contention for the Championship in Arizona. If the Court found in his favour then he might take his third World crown if he won on Saturday, September 25, with Rosberg placing lower than fifth. This gave him a better chance than Wattie's for he had to win with Rosberg scoring no points whatsoever. John relaxed by staying in Los Angeles before the race, visiting Hercules Incorporated at Salt Lake City on the Monday, before arriving in Las Vegas the Wednesday prior to the race. He spun several times in practice and was not happy. As usual he qualified well down the grid, on row five, and Niki was on row seven after dialling-in his car nicely on race rubber, adjusting it painstakingly onto qualifiers and then having the engine tighten just as he was about to attempt a serious time.

The race saw John drive brilliantly to overcome his lowly grid position, slicing through the field to finish second behind Michele Alboreto, winning his maiden GP for Tyrrell. But it was not good enough to give John Watson the World Championship; Keke Rosberg took it coolly, driving a reliable race to finish fifth, two points; taking the title by 44 points to John's 39, ironically equalling the injured Pironi's total. Niki was fifth in the Championship, with 30 points. McLaren International were runners-up in the Constructors' Cup, 69 points, to Ferrari's 74 . . .

For Teddy Mayer the pivotal race of the year had been the Swiss GP at Dijon: "During qualifying John ran not too well, while Niki was just brilliant. But on race morning Niki's car was rubbish, I altered John's and suddenly he was going like gang-busters. He flew early in the race but got just a little too impetuous going around the outside of Patrese and that damaged a skirt which we had to change and that lost him a lap. He was a second-and-a-half quicker than Niki after that, and although Niki finished third he couldn't really compete during the race . . ."

Whatever Teddy had done he kept secret, making no entry in the vehicle records . . .

Towards the end of the year it became clear that the gifted and ambitious former Project Four principals didn't really need Mayer and Alexander, the surviving original Directors from Team McLaren. Both Ron Dennis and former employee John Barnard were ambitious men. Ambition achieved meant ambition extended. John in particular would like public credit for his work. A thoroughly likeable man and forthcoming engineer, to outsiders he made no bones about that. As long as Mayer and Alexander were there his contribution might seem diluted; right or wrong that's the way they saw it. Teddy: "In fact we got along better than I thought we would, but Ron eventually made me an offer to buy out my share in the company which I accepted . . ."

They discussed terms that winter, from October to December, and just before Christmas 1982 Dennis and Barnard bought out Teddy's 45 per cent plus Tyler's small personal shareholding, and they left the racing team they had helped found with Bruce himself nearly twenty action-packed years before. Teddy: "We ran the show with Bruce like friends with a shared enthusiasm for the first six years, then Bruce was killed in 1970, and from then until the merger well into 1980 it was all down to me, I made the decisions, and good or bad that made it more interesting. After the merger, with three or four people all trying to make the big decisions it wasn't so rewarding and it was right for me to get out when I did.

"Where would I be relatively if I'd followed a normal US tax law career? I guess I'd probably be better off, but I wouldn't have had anything like the same job-satisfaction. Hell, we had our bad times, and the effort demanded was immense – but we achieved a lot, it was a lot of fun along the way . . ."

Chapter 6
TAG-Turbos and Beyond

"TAG's support for the engine project shows a lot of careful
thought and real vision on Mansour Ojjeh's part. It's a
massive investment in the future . . ."

Ron Dennis, 1983

During the winter of 1982-83 the long-running Formula 1 regulations dispute finally stabilised with a new flat-bottom chassis being demanded to ban ground-effects tunnel sections once and for all. Some small measure of under-chassis airflow management was still permitted ahead of the front axle line and behind the rear axle but winter testing proved the advantages to be obtained were indeed minimal. Now at last the turbocharged teams could use their power advantage over the Cosworths to pull bigger, higher-drag wings through the air. The Cosworth brigade's one-time aerodynamic advantage was lost, and although the Ford-backed F1 engine company responded with a redesigned DFY version of their legendary V8 racing engine, their fifteen years of virtual Formula 1 domination were clearly at an end.

In response to the altered regulations many constructors radically altered the shape of their cars. Gordon Murray of Brabham produced a slender harpoon-like design in the turbo BMW-powered BT52 – Ligier, Tyrrell and others following suit – while the Ferraris and Renaults slimmed down to a lesser extent. John Barnard's lengthy experience of the large plan-area MP4/1 configuration persuaded him to develop further what the McLaren International team knew and understood, while development of the Ron Dennis-inspired TAG Turbo V6 engine being designed and made for the team (initially on an exclusive basis) by Porsche was being progressed in Germany.

John Barnard was one of the more upset of F1 engineers at the winter's abrupt rule-change, but like all others he then considered: "Well, at least we're all starting equal again. Let's get at 'em . . ." and away they went. Studying the new problem prompted basic thoughts like "It's going to be difficult to achieve downforce from the underside any more, and the front wing already works well, so let's concentrate on the rear. There's a problem finding downforce at all, and another putting its centre of pressure where we want it. We've got the TAG-Porsche turbo engine coming along, so it might be counter-productive to go all the way with a new Cosworth car for what might be less than a season . . ."

The upshot of such thought-process was that the Marlboro-MP4/1C for '83 was visually little altered from its 1982 predecessor apart from its regulation flat bottom, missing skirts, and waisted platform abaft the side radiator mountings, with low-level flat aerodynamic trays just ahead of the rear wheels.

"We used the same rear end – Cosworth engine/suspension/gearbox – as in 1981-82, while thinking of the turbo engine with its inter-coolers and extra plumbing, persuaded us not to go too far up the slimline route. We have great experience of the large plan-area car and with our still large plan-area flat bottom I still think we have one of the best lift/drag ratios amongst current cars. People say how sensitive it must be to ride height and suspension rate changes and both are significant in setting it up, but recently that hasn't been much of a problem . . ."

With attached nose and tail wings absolutely critical in supplying 80 per cent of the flat-bottom F1 car's downforce much research and experimentation had been devoted to them; "But without a turbo engine the trade-off is simple – horsepower versus aerodynamics . . ."

Running their Michelin tyres, like the established turbo teams of Renault, there was little doubt that McLaren suffered from an extraordinary 3-litre versus turbo car turn-around in car characteristics with the new flat-bottom chassis. During 1982 the MP4/1Bs' ground-effect sections in cars which were right down to the Formula 1 minimum weight limit, matched McLaren tyre loadings very closely to those of the less aerodynamically-effective turbo Renaults. Into 1983 the 3-litre weight limit had been trimmed and the MP4/1Cs were lighter still, as well as being robbed of their ground-effect underwing loadings. Renault harnessed their extra turbo horsepower to haul enormous barn-door wings through the air and probably had more downforce than the Marlboro MP4s , so the relative change in tyre loading proved much less for them than was the case for McLaren International. The Woking team's cars struggled to heat-up '82-style tyres with only one-third of that season's aerodynamic downloads, so John and Ron had to lean on Michelin to make them lighter tyres better tailored to the new MP4/1Cs' demands. The prototype tyres finally arrived in second practice at Monaco, proving around 1.0 secs per lap quicker than the original boots, but as rain fell the agonised team had to rely on their first-day times and both John Watson and Niki Lauda failed to qualify . . . That was the team's nadir . . .

It proved a freak, and as the season progressed so the team bounced back to establish its cars as the best of the Cosworth-engined brigade in hopeless pursuit of the turbos until the Dutch GP in late-August, and the debut of the new TAG Turbo TTE-PO1 V6 turbo engine.

The season had begun in Brazil in March where Niki finished strongly third, and then at Long Beach for round two the team was again in agony; a bad bump on the revised circuit causing ride-heights to be jacked-up during first practice, then civil engineering removing the problem overnight and allowing spring platforms to be wound down again, whereupon the cars seemed just as bad. Ron Dennis: "We had a huge problem at Long Beach in practice but after John and Niki qualified twenty-second and twenty-third conditions were transformed for the race . . ."

It proved a storybook Grand Prix, with the two dayglo-red and white Marlboro MP4s scything through the entire field. Their Michelin tyres survived the entire distance untroubled, unlike the Goodyears and Pirellis of the opposition, and at one-third distance a collision between Tambay's leading Ferrari and Rosberg's Williams fired a chain of events which retired both cars. Laffite's Williams inherited the lead from Patrese's Brabham-BMW, but the Frenchman was in tyre trouble and then Patrese went hustling down an escape road in his efforts to get by. Meanwhile John and Niki had progreessed surgically through the field, passing all who did not eliminate themselves, and with thirty laps to go Wattie was into the lead he held to the finish, with team-mate Lauda on his wheel-tracks for a superb team 1-2, Niki setting fastest lap and breaking his existing record into the bargain.

It was a remarkable performance, but the realistic Ron Dennis dismisses suggestions of the team weaving some mysterious technical magic for race-day: "Conditions change, it's as simple as that. Once they changed our tyres began to generate grip, and when you generate grip the tyres start to heat up, and the hotter they become the more grip you get. So within certain limits it just gets better and better . . . But we suffered again at Imola and especially at Monaco, where neither luck nor magic came to help us . . ."

Both cars failed in the early-season French GP at Ricard-Castellet, and at Imola for the San Marino GP Wattie could only salvage fifth place. Both cars failed to qualify in the Monaco debacle, both cars failed again at Spa-Francorchamps, but at Detroit John finished third on the scene of his 1982 triumph. In Canada he was sixth, second Cosworth runner home behind the turbos. At Silverstone the turbo-circuits half of the season was really into its stride and Cosworth runners could have little hope. Niki was first Cosworth-runner home, sixth, with John ninth. At Hockenheim Niki and John placed 5-6 on the road only for the Austrian to be disqualified for reversing in the pit lane after overshooting his refuelling-stop marks, elevating those who finished behind him.

Still Niki and John had dominated the Cosworth race-within-a-race, and the Austrian did it again at Österreichring to finish sixth behind the turbos – again first Cosworth runner home, while John had a nose-wing knocked off in the first corner, made a pit stop to replace it but could only finish ninth after a charge back through the field.

Meanwhile the very first carbon-fibre MP4 tub had been rigged as the MP4/1D test hack for the new TAG Turbo engine, and in initial testing at Silverstone soon after the British GP it showed instant promise, lapping in 1:12.8 – a time which would have elevated the team three places on the British GP grid the previous weekend.

The team worked its heart out to complete the prototype MP4/1E turbo car in time for the Dutch GP on August 28 at Zandvoort where it was entrusted to Niki Lauda. The car impressed immensely with its integrated design and careful packaging for the compact new V6 engine and its associated turbochargers and intercoolers. John Barnard had worked closely with Porsche chief engineer Hans Mezger in arranging the car's layout and engine installation as an integrated "no compromise" package and the result was a tribute to all involved in its design, construction and assembly although an all-new turbo car with long-life development potential was even then taking shape in John Barnard's mind.

The team's investment in the turbo engine extended to a very expensive tailor-made Bosch Motronic MS3 electrical management system using two micro-processors to monitor every aspect of engine/turbo performance on each bank of three cylinders, the two units interlinked to effect near-instantaneous performance management corrections bank to bank. While BMW, for example, used electronic control governing an old-style mechanical fuel injection metering unit, McLaren's new system was all electronic, with solenoids opening and shutting the nozzles.

Ron declared after practice that the hastily completed car had performed "with fewer problems than we anticipated", and was one of the fastest of all on the long pit straight, reaching 285km/h – 177 mph – to prove itself easily competitive with Ferrari and Renault in a straight line. Niki commented: "It's pretty good for a brand new car, but we've still got a lot of things to try. There's work to be done on suspension adjustments, we can try bigger wings and of course there's a touch of turbo lag when you go back on the throttle. It feels powerful enough . . ." He went out of the race with a brake problem after a promising mid-field debut while John was in the groove again – perhaps miffed by not having a turbo of his own? – and finished third behind the victorious turbo Ferraris, the Marlboro team easily winning the Cosworth race yet again in their last outing with the classical V8 engine.

For Monza and the Italian GP in September both McLaren International drivers had TAG Turbo V6 engines and both retired, but race development is invaluable to reach true race-worthiness as rapidly as possible.

Further development of the interim TAG-Porsche powered cars saw them wearing Ferrari-like 'barn-door' rear wings at Brands Hatch where the European GP had been hastily organised to replace a cancelled inaugural World Championship round in New York City. Wattie's rear wing progressively collapsed, finally ripping off completely on the long back straight into Hawthorn's corner where, robbed of its downforce, he found the car spearing off into the catchfences. Niki's sister car went out when valves met pistons on the over-run; symptomatic of underdevelopment with a progressive rev-limiter and radical cam timing.

The final Championship round of the year was at Kyalami on October 15th. A third MP4/1E was on hand for the first time as spare. Pre-practice testing was

The TAG-Turbo Porsche V6 engine made its race debut here in Niki Lauda's interim McLaren, hastily completed by a massive team effort just in time for the Dutch Grand Prix, Zandvoort, 1983.

fraught with problems but the team engineers Steve Nichols and Alan Jenkins got the chassis well sorted for qualifying and the race. Niki drove with terrific aggression in pursuit of ultimately victorious Brabham-BMWs and despite a slow refuelling stop rushed into second place behind Riccardo Patrese in the last ten laps and looked set to challenge seriously for the lead. But a regulator failed due to heat and vibration and the V6 Marlboro-McLaren spluttered to a halt half-way round lap 72 of the 77.

An even more bitter fate befell John Watson in what would prove to be his last drive for the team. Engine problems dictated he race the spare car, it refused to start on the grid ready for the rolling lap and he set off after the rest had left. In

such a case the delayed driver has to start from the back of the grid. With over 150 GPs behind him, Wattie should have known better, but in the heat of the moment once he caught up with the pack he weaved through to his original position; inevitably he was disqualified, after 18 laps when lying 11th overall. . . .

So the season ended, with John sixth equal in the Drivers' Championship alongside Renault's Eddie Cheever on 22 points; Niki tenth with 12. Marlboro-McLaren finished fifth in the Constructors' table, with 34 points, against Ferrari's victorious total of 89; four points behind Williams in fourth place, but 16 ahead of Alfa Romeo in sixth.

Despite the often-bitter rearguard action being fought by predominantly British Formula 1 team interests to maintain normally-aspirated 3-litre engine parity with the 1.5-litre turbos, it had been clear from the time of McLaren International's foundation that turbocharged engines would eventually win the day.

Ron Dennis and John Barnard had been determined to find such an engine for their new team, and despite the doubts of some of Ron's co-directors he approached the people he considered the most experienced and best-equipped to develop it; Porsche. For years they had stayed clear of Formula 1, preferring long-distance racing to prove their wares and enhance their image. They had stated publicly that Formula 1 was of little interest to them, and it was largely the Dennis attitude of "If you don't ask, you don't get" which won them over. Sure that Porsche would not be interested, nobody had approached them before Ron made his overtures, delightedly to find the enthusiastic German concern only too happy to do the work. But he would have to find the money to under-write the job which they would undertake purely on a customer project basis.

"We signed a six-month design contract on my assurance that I would find the backing to build the engine. That effectively bought us six months during which time I approached three or four potential backers. Just before the end of that period we entered into partnership with TAG to build and promote the engine initially for our exclusive use in Formula 1, and subsequently for other purposes and customer sale. . . . Phase 1 had been signed in mid-'81 and we signed the construction contract with Porsche in December '82. . . ."

The TAG logo had become familiar in recent years on the highly-successful Williams team cars, standing for *Techniques d'Avant Garde*, a Saudi-connected corporation established in 1977 by Akram Ojjeh to consolidate his family's commercial activities between Europe and the nations of the Middle East.

The man behind TAG's involvement with Williams and Formula 1 was Akram Ojjeh's enthusiastic son Mansour, and he also provided much of the impetus behind TAG Turbo Engines, the new company formed with Ron and McLaren International to handle the new 1.5 litre turbo V6 engine being developed for them by Porsche.

Now for the new season of 1984 John Barnard was developing a new MP4/2 car using a new-generation carbon-fibre monocoque based on the original design but with revised fuel cell and side shaping, a new aerodynamic form demanding new rear suspension, revised turbo mountings and a new McLaren-made brake package. Further transmission developments and a third-generation chassis design – the MP4/3 – were also in the pipeline for later in the 1984 season.

Meanwhile, in the week following the South African race the driver situation was settled for 1984, when Alain Prost suddenly became available having been sacked by Renault despite coming within an ace of winning the World title. Prost promptly returned to Marlboro-McLaren in Watson's place, bringing with him both his mature skills and all that youthful long-term potential.

Kyalami '83 had marked the emergence of the McLaren TAG-Porsche turbo as a properly competitive threat. With Lauda and Prost signed for 1984, and John Barnard's definitive turbocar designs on the way, the McLaren marque entered its 19th season of racing.

243

Appendices

Appendix 1 – McLaren Type Numbers 1964-1983

M1A	Original Group 7 sports car, productionised as McLaren-Elva-Oldsmobile Mark 1, versions also with Ford V8 and Chevvy V8 engines.
M1B	1965-66 rebodied development of M1A sports car, sold in US as McLaren-Elva Mark 2.
M1C	1967 Trojan-built spaceframe customer CanAm sports cars, sold in US as Mark 3s.
M2A	Robin Herd's 1965 Firestone tyre test car; Mallite monocoque chassis, Traco-Olds and Ford V8 engines.
M2B	The 1966 works team F1 Mallite monocoques intended for Ford Indy V8 power, also used Serenissima V8.
M3	The spaceframe 'whoosh-bonk' *Formule Libre*/hillclimb/MGM camera car single-seaters.
M4A	Robin Herd 1967 F2/F3 bath-tub monocoque car, one developed with 2.1 BRM V8 engine as works team interim F1 car. This took M4B title, also used by Trojan production versions for US Formula B racing.
M5A	Robin's 1967 one-off works team F1 monocoque with 3.0 BRM V12 engine sold on to Jo Bonnier.
M6A	1967 CanAm Champion monocoque-chassised sports-racing cars with Chevrolet V8 power.
M6B	1968 Trojan production version of the Championship-winning M6A design.
M6GT	1969 Coupe based on the CanAm/production sports-racing tub. Prototype sold to David Prophet who raced it, later converting it to open form. Claimed total of four built on various tubs.
M7A	Robin Herd's final McLaren design for 1968 F1 Cosworth-DFV engine.
M7B	Integral sponson fuel-tanked experimental F1 for Bruce's use 1969, sold to Antique Automobiles F1 team, written-off.
M7C	Formula 5000-based full monocoque version of M7-series for Bruce's use 1969, sold to John Surtees 1970, then Bonnier.
M7D	1970 Alfa Romeo V8-engined version of M7-series.
M8A	1968 works CanAm Champion sports cars, semi-stressed engine mounting.
M8B	1969 CanAm Champion winged cars unbeaten in the series . . .
M8C	1970 Trojan production version of the M8A with non-stressed engine mounting to allow customers to fit alternative units.
M8D	1970 works CanAm Champion sports cars, 'Batmobile' finned bodies; Bruce McLaren killed testing in one, June 1, Goodwood.
M8E	1971 Trojan production CanAm cars based on M8D.
M8F	1971 CanAm Champion works sports cars.
M8FP	1972 Trojan production CanAm cars.
M9A	Jo Marquart's experimental four-wheel drive 1969 F1 car.

M10A	Gordon Coppuck's 1969 Formula A/5000 production customer car.
M10B	1970 Formula 5000 car, like M10A in production at Trojan's.
M11	Designation not used due to likely confusion with 'Mark II'.
M12	1969 Trojan production CanAm sports car, M8-type body clothing M6-series monocoque tub.
M13	Designation not used for superstitious reasons.
M14A	1970 works Formula 1 cars.
M14D	Alfa Romeo V8-powered version used in 1970 Formula 1 with M7D.
M15A	Gordon Coppuck's 1970 Indianapolis/USAC track cars using Offenhauser 4-cylinder turbocharged engines.
M16A	Epochal wedge-shaped 1971 Indianapolis/USAC track cars using turbo-Offy power again, works and Penske team.
M16B	1972 Indianapolis/USAC cars, as with whole series, all built at Colnbrook for either works or Penske teams, only passed on into private hands from those sources.
M16C	1973 Indianapolis/USAC cars.
M16C/D	1974 Indianapolis/USAC cars.
M16E	John Barnard re-worked 1975/76 Indianapolis/USAC cars.
M17	Designation allocated to 3-litre prototype sports-racing car but project abandoned.
M18	1971 Trojan production Formula 5000 car for customer sale.
M19A	Ralph Bellamy's 1971 works Formula 1 car with DFV power and initially rising-rate suspension systems. Continued use through 1972, into '73.
M20	1972 CanAm Championship defender with 'coke-bottle' planform low polar moment chassis, beaten by the turbo Porsches.
M21	1972 Bellamy-designed works F2 car planned for production by Trojan, formed basis of 1973 Trojan-designed and built (non-McLaren) F5000 customer car.
M22	1972 Trojan production Formula 5000 car for customer sale.
M23	1973 deformable structure works Formula 1 car won 1974 and 1976 World Championships. One of the classic Grand Prix cars of all time.
M24	1977 Indianapolis/USAC track car using Cosworth DFX turbocharged V8 engine, developed into M24B in 1978; type based on M23 experience.
M25	John Barnard's still-born 1975 Formula 5000 car based on M23 experience.
M26	Gordon Coppuck's M23 replacement, used 1976-78 in Formula 1.
M27	Shelved M26 replacement, non ground-effects design.
M28	1979 ground-effects Formula 1 car; a disastrous failure.
M29	1979 hasty "Williams-copy" ground-effects Formula 1 car, replacing M28.
M30	1980 advanced ground-effects Formula 1 car intended to retrieve McLaren competitiveness, failed and lone M30 written-off US GP East, 1980.
MP4/1	John Barnard's innovative carbon-fibre monocoque 'Marlboro-Project 4' Formula 1 car produced by McLaren International in time for the 1981 season.
MP4/1B	Updated MP4 for 1982.
MP4/1C	Updated MP4B for 1983.
MP4/1D	TAG-Porsche turbo test car 1983.
MP4/1E	Interim TAG-Porsche turbo race cars for late 1983.

Appendix 2 – The Formula 5000 cars

During 1967 Britain's motor racing promoters were casting around for a crowd-drawing single-seater Formula to provide racing which they could afford which would attract viable gate receipts. Regulations were drafted for Formula Britain, catering for single-seaters with British-made 3-litre engines, but no industry support was forthcoming and the idea died. Coincidentally in the USA, the Sports Car Club of America decided to promote single-seater road racing on something better than club level, and modified their F1-like Formula A to admit 5-litre production-based or 'stock-block' engines alongside the 3-litre cars. This gave their European-style road racing a more American accent, and won wide acclaim. Lola Cars began building chassis for Formula A, and at Colnbrook McLaren Cars were interested, with the prospect of Trojan in Croydon laying-down a production batch of McLaren-designed and developed single-seaters alongside the CanAm sports-racing cars. So British Formula 5000 was born, maximum capacity 5000cc, engines based on a minimum production run of 5000 units. For British and what would become European F5000, 3-litre racing engines were banned, as were FIA graded drivers who had qualified for their grading with Formula 1 results – as opposed to long-distance endurance Championship performances.

McLaren's tiny design team based their F5000 on the M7A Formula 1 design, Gordon Coppuck adding rear horns to the basic tub to accept a race-tuned Chevvy V8 stock-block, unstressed unlike the F1 DFV unit. The M10A was a more sophisticated car than its main market rival, the Lola T140 which was a simple spaceframe compared to the monocoque McLaren. Trojan earmarked most of their M10A production for the North American market. They were still smarting from the awful reputation established by the Chequered Flag team M4A F2/F3 cars in 1968, and wanted to do it properly this time . . . Only one car was to run in Britain, a quasi-works entry for Peter Gethin, maintained and entered by Church Farm Racing, run by Derek Bell's step-father, Col. Bernard Hender. M10A price in the UK was £7,055, over £1,500 more than the Lola, but it was to be the car to beat. Bruce did much of the original testing on the prototype car which became Gethin's CFRT entry, and with an A1 Bartz-prepared Chevvy V8 installed Peter won the first two British races easily, but lost the lead on the final lap at Jarama when the engine failed. He won again at Brands Hatch and Mallory Park, where David Hobbs' new Surtees offered real opposition for the first time. A brief tour in North America yielded one win and two retirements, before the team returned to home shores and eventually clinched the Guards F5000 Championship from Trevor Taylor's Surtees in the last round, when both were put off the road by an errant back-marker . . . It was that kind of Formula . . .

Meanwhile in North America Tony Adamowicz won the 1969 Formula A title with an Eagle, facing strong opposition from Sam Posey's McLaren M10A and a number of Lola and Surtees cars, plus Gethin's visiting M10A. John Cannon of CanAm fame replaced his Eagle with a new M10B for 1970, the car running at Sebring as early as December 28, 1969, and he won at Riverside, Kent and Elkhart Lake to clinch the SCCA Continental Championship.

For 1970 the successful M10A design was modestly updated as the M10B with revised steering geometry using low-offset wheels and an altered engine bay lowering the engine fully 2-inches. The rear suspension top beam was deleted and a Hewland DG300 gearbox replaced the original LG600 to save considerable weight. Lambretta-Trojan had produced 17 M10As and now followed-up with 21 M10Bs.

Irishman Sid Taylor ran the works car for Peter Gethin who won eight races and took three second places from 13 starts before being given a works McLaren F1 drive. Reine Wisell took over the F5000 ride, winning three times and taking a second place in his six starts to find himself a place in Team Lotus at the US GP . . .

Mike Walker won twice in Alan McKechnie's McLaren, and former team mechanic Howden Ganley, crew-chief on *'Big Ed'* the Ford GTX of 1965, found his way into a Barry Newman-owned M10B on Bruce's recommendation for 1970 F5000 in Europe, and his 18 starts secured one win, five seconds and six third places. Graham McRae came from New Zealand to Europe and was a regular front runner in his McLaren, but had a torrid time with numerous spins and accidents before cooling-down sufficiently to win the UK finale at Brands Hatch in September.

After two consecutive Champion years in European F5000, McLaren introduced the stressed-engine M18 to replace the well-sorted and extremely popular M10-series cars. The first M18 was delivered to Sid Taylor as a semi-works car, to be driven by Brian Redman. It immediately proved a difficult child. It was difficult to sort in initial testing, and proved unpredictable when loaded through corners. Its debut race at Snetterton saw it blown-off with depressing ease by Hailwood's Surtees, and at the end of the season Brian had won only two of its 16 races, though others tried their hand on occasion. Graham McRae was to have run an M18 for Trojan but the deal fell through and he was probably relieved to concentrate on his old M10B which with progressive modification proved good enough to win three times.

There were two other M18s on the British and European scene, Barry Newman's driven by Howden Ganley, Tim Schenken and Jean-Pierre Jaussaud, and the Swedish privateer Ulf Norinder's. Howden modified his car progressively with M10B features, while Norinder raced for fun and found the M18 so enjoyable he retired in mid-season and the car remained garaged.

Frank Gardner won the Championship laurels in his works Lola. McRae and Pink Stamps team driver Ray Allen both performed well in old M10Bs, as did Belgian Teddy Pilette in Count van der Straaten's Team VDS entry, and David Prophet on spasmodic occasions in his private car. Tony Dean appeared in a beautifully-converted ex-F1 M7A – chassis M7A/2 – but crashed it at the first corner of the first race at Mallory Park and subsequently aquaplaned into a marshal's post at Castle Combe, breaking its creator's neck. Happily, he recovered. Keith Holland dropped his M10B into the Mallory Park lake and in general McLaren's star was on the wane as the Formula now held little interest for the Colnbrook works, deep into Formula 1, CanAm and now USAC racing . . .

The McLaren F5000s had enjoyed great success in the revamped Tasman

Championship in New Zealand and Australia, to which they had been admitted from the Antipodean summer of 1969-70.

For the 1971 L & M Continental Championship in America, English driver David Hobbs took over trucking executive Carl Hogan's older M10B – in which Cannon had won the 1970 title – and it was proved thoroughly competitive again as David won five rounds and added a second place in the eight-race series to bring yet another US Championship to the McLaren marque.

In 1972 David Hobbs was then hired to race an updated version of the unfortunate M18, known as the M22, down-under, and it was another disappointment, although he finally succeeded in sorting it out to the point where he could win the final round at Adelaide, and by that time the car had been redesignated as an 'M18B' the real M22 being prepared for the European season.

In fact Trojan's F5000 production line trickled to a halt in '72, VDS ordering an M22 for Teddy Pilette but it was not delivered until May. They raced the ex-Redman/Hobbs M18B instead but neither car proved very competitive. Ray Allen raced the ex-Norinder M18 while the circuit promoters' other entry, for Ray Calcutt and Tony Lanfranchi on occasion, was the ex-Ganley M18. Redman drove an ex-Broadspeed M10B for Sid Taylor until a new Chevron became available and the old warhorse won twice. Keith Holland's M10B was remarkably competitive before being sold to Clive Baker for the end of the season, and Holland also assembled another car from his Mallory Park submarine version of '71 fame, and this one was sold to a newcomer named Chris Oates. A number of variously aged and unkept M10-family cars also-ran, while Tony Dean converted an ex-works F1 M14A – M14A/2 – to Formula 5000 trim but appeared infrequently. In the US L&M Championship series, Al Lader and Lothar Motschenbacher performed notably – surprisingly so to European eyes – with production M18s.

No McLaren chassis won an F5000 race in 1973. Trojan who had built McLaren's customer cars since 1964 were to have laid down a batch of replica F1 M19s for the class, but dropped the idea and produced their own Trojan T101 instead. In essence this combined the front end of the 1972 McLaren M21 Formula 2 car – as raced successfully by Jody Scheckter – with the M22 F5000 after-part. Design was by Trojan's Paul Rawlinson, and former Brabham designer Ron Tauranac was subsequently brought-in on a consultancy basis to develop it. Certainly it was an improvement over the 1971 M18 and the M22 which followed it. Some felt that Trojan should have continued development of the M10 theme through those two poor seasons, as did Graham McRae, Frank Matich in Australia and the US, Keith Holland, Tony Kitchiner etc whose M10Bs all proved far quicker than the later models.

During 1973 Colnbrook sold its three M19s for F5000 use, the first going to Tony Dean who before its conversion was completed sold it to Brian Robinson. McLaren did the conversion at Colnbrook and after Dean tested Robinson's finished car he wanted very much to buy it back. It was "at least as good as my Chevron", he said. Robinson would not sell, and before Dean could complete a deal on the remaining pair they had gone to Tony Kitchiner's team, for 1974. But none of these hybrids would prove as effective in competition as they seemed in testing.

In North America the CanAm sports car series had collapsed, the Porsche turbos pricing the competition out of existence, and the SCCA replaced it with Formula A/5000. With an eye on a works team return to the CanAm forum an all-new M23 F1-based 5-litre prototype known as the M25 was completed at Colnbrook, and tested by Howden Ganley early in 1975. But it was never raced, Formula 1 taking priority, and the tub lay unloved for long months on the roof of a Colnbrook outhouse. It was the end of McLaren's interest in production single-seater racing cars.

Appendix 3 – Formula one McLaren racing record
KEY TO ABBREVIATIONS:

PP	Pole position
FR	Front row of grid qualification
FL	Fastest lap
DNQ	Did not qualify
DNS	Did not start after qualifying
DNA	Did not appear at meeting
WDN	Entry withdrawn
DISQ	Disqualified
UNC	Completed too little distance to be classified, though placed 'Nth' on road

1966
22-5-66 MONACO GRAND PRIX, Monte Carlo

1 Chris Amon	M2B-Ford		DNA
2 Bruce McLaren	M2B-Ford	M2B/2	Rtd oil

13-6-66 BELGIAN GRAND PRIX, Spa-Francorchamps

24 Bruce McLaren	M2B-Serenissima	M2B/2	DNS bearings
25 Chris Amon	M2B-Ford		DNA

3-7-66 FRENCH GRAND PRIX, Reims-Gueux

28 Bruce McLaren	M2B-Serenissima	—	DNA

16-7-66 BRITISH GRAND PRIX, Brands Hatch

14 Bruce McLaren	M2B-Serenissima	M2B/2	6th
15 Chris Amon	M2B-Ford	—	DNA

24-7-66 DUTCH GRAND PRIX, Zandvoort

20 Bruce McLaren	M2B-Serenissima	M2B/2	DNS eng.
22 Chris Amon	M2B-Ford	—	DNA

7-8-66 GERMAN GRAND PRIX, Nürburgring

16 Bruce McLaren	M2B-Ford	—	WDN*

Entry taken over by David Bridges' Brabham BT11 for John Taylor

4-9-66 ITALIAN GRAND PRIX, Monza

32 Bruce McLaren	M2B-Ford	—	WDN*
34 Chris Amon	M2B-Ford	—	WDN*

Entries taken over by Amon Brabham-BRM BT11 and Phil Hill Eagle-Climax.

2-10-66 UNITED STATES GRAND PRIX, Watkins Glen

17 Bruce McLaren	M2B-Ford	M2B/1	5th

23-10-66 MEXICAN GRAND PRIX, Mexico City

17 Bruce McLaren	M2B-Ford	M2B/1	Rtd eng.

1967
12-3-67 Race of Champions, Brands Hatch
Two heats and Final:

Heat 1:	11 Bruce McLaren	M4B-BRM V8	M4B/1	4th
Heat 2:	McLaren			6th
Final:	McLaren			Rtd cams't

15-4-67 Spring Trophy, Oulton Park

14 Bruce McLaren	M4B-BRM V8	M4B/1	5th
Heat 2: McLaren			5th
Final: McLaren			5th

29-4-67 International Trophy, Silverstone

8 Bruce McLaren	M4B-BRM V8	M4B/1	5th

7-5-67 MONACO GRAND PRIX, Monte Carlo

16 Bruce McLaren	M4B-BRM V8	M4B/1	4th

4-6-67 DUTCH GRAND PRIX, Zandvoort
17 Bruce McLaren   M4B-BRM V8   M4B/1   Crashed*
Car subsequently burned out, Bruce took second Eagle works entry for mid-season.
1-7-67 FRENCH GRAND PRIX, Le Circuit Bugatti, Le Mans
8 Bruce McLaren   Eagle-Weslake V12 102   Rtd
15-6-67 BRITISH GRAND PRIX, Silverstone
10 Bruce McLaren   Eagle-Weslake V12 102   Rtd
6-8-67 GERMAN GRAND PRIX, Nürburgring
10 Bruce McLaren   Eagle-Weslake V12 102   Rtd
27-8-67 CANADIAN GRAND PRIX, Mosport Park
19 Bruce McLaren   M5A-BRM V12*   M5A/1   7th
New 3.0 V12 monocoque works McLaren.
10-9-67 ITALIAN GRAND PRIX, Monza
4 Bruce McLaren   M5A-BRM V12   M5A/1   FR Rtd
16-9-67 Gold Cup, Oulton Park
23 Alan Rollinson   M4A-Cosworth
FVA F2   20011/E   9th o/a
1 10 67 UNITED STATES GRAND PRIX, Watkins Glen
14 Bruce McLaren   M5A-BRM V12   M5A/1   Rtd hose
22-10-67 MEXICAN GRAND PRIX, Mexico City
14 Bruce McLaren   M5A-BRM V12   M5A/1   Rtd oil p.
12-11-67 Madrid GP, Jarama, Spain
11 Alan Rollinson   M4A-Cosworth
FVA F2   20011/E   Rtd, pedal

1968
1-1-68 SOUTH AFRICAN GRAND PRIX, Kyalami
1 Denis Hulme   M5A-BRM V12   M5A/1   5th
17-3-68 Race of Champions, Brands Hatch
1 Denis Hulme   M7A-DFV*   M7A/2   3rd
2 Bruce McLaren   M7A-DFV*   M7A/1   PP FL FIRST
* *New 3.0 Cosworth-Ford V8 works cars.*
25-4-68 International Trophy, Silverstone
1 Denis Hulme   M7A-DFV   M7A/2   PP FIRST
2 Bruce McLaren   M7A-DFV   M7A/1   2nd
12-5-68 SPANISH GRAND PRIX, Jarama
1 Denis Hulme   M7A-DFV   M7A/2   FR 2nd
2 Bruce McLaren   M7A-DFV   M7A/1   Rtd oil
26-5-68 MONACO GRAND PRIX, Monte Carlo
12 Denis Hulme   M7A-DFV   M7A/2   5th
14 Bruce McLaren   M7A-DFV   M7A/1   Crashed
9-6-68 BELGIAN GRAND PRIX, Spa-Francorchamps
5 Bruce McLaren   M7A-DFV   M7A/3   FIRST
6 Denis Hulme   M7A-DFV   M7A/2   Rtd UJ
23-6-68 DUTCH GRAND PRIX, Zandvoort
1 Denis Hulme   M7A-DFV   M7A/2   Rtd ign.
2 Bruce McLaren   M7A-DFV   M7A/3   Crashed
7-7-68 FRENCH GRAND PRIX, Rouen-les-Essarts
8 Denis Hulme   M7A-DFV   M7A/2   5th
10 Bruce McLaren   M7A-DFV   M7A/3   8th
20-7-68 BRITISH GRAND PRIX, Brands Hatch
1 Denis Hulme   M7A-DFV   M7A/2   4th
2 Bruce McLaren   M7A-DFV   M7A/3   7th
4-8-68 GERMAN GRAND PRIX, Nürburgring
1 Denis Hulme   M7A-DFV   M7A/2   7th
2 Bruce McLaren   M7A-DFV   M7A/1   13th
17-8-68 Gold Cup, Oulton Park
1 Bruce McLaren   M7A-DFV   —   DNA

8-9-68 ITALIAN GRAND PRIX, Monza

1 Denis Hulme	M7A-DFV	M7A/2	FIRST
2 Bruce McLaren	M7A-DFV	M7A/1	FR Rtd eng.
3 Jo Bonnier	M5A-BRM V12	M5A/1	6th

22-9-68 CANADIAN GRAND PRIX, Mont Tremblant-St Jovite

1 Denis Hulme	M7A-DFV	M7A/2	FIRST
2 Bruce McLaren	M7A-DFV	M7A/1	2nd
11 Dan Gurney	M7A-DFV	M7A/3	Rtd o'heat

6-10-68 UNITED STATES GRAND PRIX, Watkins Glen

1 Denis Hulme	M7A-DFV	M7A/2	½-shaft/Crash
2 Bruce McLaren	M7A-DFV	M7A/1	6th
14 Dan Gurney	M7A-DFV	M7A/3	4th
17 Jo Bonnier	M5A-BRM V12	M5A/1	'14th' UNC

3-11-68 MEXICAN GRAND PRIX, Mexico City

1 Denis Hulme	M7A-DFV	M7A/2	Susp/Crash
2 Bruce McLaren	M7A-DFV	M7A/1	2nd
14 Dan Gurney	M7A-DFV	M7A/3	Rtd susp.
17 Jo Bonnier	M5A-BRM V12	M5A/1	T-car

1969

1-3-69 SOUTH AFRICAN GRAND PRIX, Kyalami

5 Denis Hulme	M7A-DFV	M7A/2	FR 3rd
6 Bruce McLaren	M7A-DFV	M7A/3	5th
18 Basil van Rooyen	M7A-DFV	M7A/1	Rtd brakes

16-3-69 Race of Champions, Brands Hatch

3 Denis Hulme	M7A-DFV	M7A/2	3rd
4 Bruce McLaren	M7A-DFV	M7A/3	Rtd ign.

30-3-69 International Trophy, Silverstone

3 Denis Hulme	M7A-DFV	M7A/2	Rtd eng.
4 Bruce McLaren	M7C-DFV	M7A/4	6th
15 Jo Bonnier	M5A-BRM V12	—	DNA

4-5-69 SPANISH GRAND PRIX, Barcelona

5 Denis Hulme	M7A-DFV	M7A/2	4th
6 Bruce McLaren	M7C-DFV	M7A/4	2nd

18-5-69 MONACO GRAND PRIX, Monte Carlo

3 Denis Hulme	M7A-DFV	M7A/2	6th
4 Bruce McLaren	M7C-DFV	M7A/4	5th

21-6-69 DUTCH GRAND PRIX, Zandvoort

6 Bruce McLaren	M7C-DFV	M7A/4	Rtd susp.
7 Denis Hulme	M7A-DFV	M7A/2	4th
18 Vic Elford	M7A-DFV	M7A/3	10th

6-7-69 FRENCH GRAND PRIX, Clermont Ferrand

4 Denis Hulme	M7A-DFV	M7A/2	FR 8th
5 Bruce McLaren	M7C-DFV	M7A/4	4th
10 Vic Elford	M7A-DFV	M7A/3	5th

19-7-69 BRITISH GRAND PRIX, Silverstone

5 Denis Hulme	M7A-DFV	M7A/2	FR Rtd eng.
6 Bruce McLaren	M7C-DFV	M7A/4	3rd
19 Vic Elford	M7A-DFV	M7A/3	6th
20 Derek Bell	M9A-DFV 4WD	M9A/1	Rtd susp.

3-8-83 GERMAN GRAND PRIX, Nürburgring

9 Denis Hulme	M7A-DFV	M7A/2	Rtd trans
10 Bruce McLaren	M7C-DFV	M7A/4	3rd
12 Vic Elford	M7A-DFV	M7A/3	Crashed
42 Un-nominated	M9A-DFV 4WD	—	DNA

7-9-69 ITALIAN GRAND PRIX, Monza

16 Denis Hulme	M7A-DFV	M7A/2	FR 7th
18 Bruce McLaren	M7C-DFV	M7A/4	4th*

*Only 0.19 second behind the winner!

20-9-69 CANADIAN GRAND PRIX, Mosport Park

4 Bruce McLaren	M7C-DFV	M7A/4	5th
5 Denis Hulme	M7A-DFV	M7A/2	Rtd dist.
35 Vic Elford	M7A-DFV	—	DNA

5-10-69 UNITED STATES GRAND PRIX, Watkins Glen

5 Denis Hulme	M7A-DFV	M7A/2	FR Rtd tran
6 Bruce McLaren	M7C-DFV	M7A/4	DNS eng.

19-10-69 MEXICAN GRAND PRIX, Mexico City

5 Denis Hulme	M7A-DFV	M7A/2	FIRST
6 Bruce McLaren	M7A-DFV	M7A/4	Rtd fuel sys.

1970

7-3-70 SOUTH AFRICAN GRAND PRIX, Kyalami

5 Bruce McLaren	M14A DFV	M14A/1	Rtd eng.
6 Denis Hulme	M14A-DFV	M14A/2	2nd
7 John Surtees	M7C-DFV	M7A/4	Rtd eng.

22-3-70 Race of Champions, Brands Hatch

4 Bruce McLaren	M14A-DFV	M14A/1	Crashed
5 Denis Hulme	M14A-DFV	M14A/2	3rd
6 Peter Gethin	M7A-DFV	M7A/2	6th
7 John Surtees	M7C-DFV	M7A/4	Rtd throt

19-4-70 SPANISH GRAND PRIX, Jarama

5 Denis Hulme	M14A-DFV	M14A/2	FR Rtd ign.
8 John Surtees	M7C-DFV	M7A/4	Rtd g'box
11 Bruce McLaren	M14A-DFV	M14A/1	2nd
20 Andrea de Adamich	M7D-Alfa Romeo V8	M7D/1	DNQ

26-4-70 International Trophy, Silverstone

Aggregate result of two heats:

Heat 1:	4 Bruce McLaren	M14A-DFV	M14A/1	4th
	5 Denis Hulme	M14A-DFV	M14A/2	FR 6th
	6 Reine Wisell	M7A-DFV	M7A/2	9th
	7 John Surtees	M7C-DFV	M7A/4	DNA
	16 Andrea de Adamich	M7D-Alfa V8	M7D/1	DNA
	*21 David Prophet	M10B-Chev V8	400-04	Rtd eng.
	*42 Howden Ganley	M10B-Chev V8	400-05	Rtd fuel
	*52 Graham McRae	M10B-Chev V8	400-11	Rtd eng.
	*54 Mike Walker	M10B-Chev V8	400-03	12th
	*61 Peter Gethin	M10B-Chev V8	400-06	7th o/a: FIRST

*Formula 5000 entries in combined race.

Heat 2:	McLaren	5th
	Wisell	6th
	Walker	9th o/a
	Hulme	'10th' fuel
	McRae	Crashed
	Gethin	Rtd eng.

Aggregate: McLaren 4th, Wisell 5th, Hulme 6th, Walker 10th.

10-5-70 MONACO GRAND PRIX, Monte Carlo

10 Andrea de Adamich	M7D-Alfa V8	M7D/1	DNQ
11 Denis Hulme	M14A-DFV	M14A/2	4th
12 Bruce McLaren	M14A-DFV	M14A/1	Crashed
14 John Surtees	M7C-DFV	M7A/4	Rtd oilp

7-6-70 BELGIAN GRAND PRIX, Spa-Francorchamps

4 Bruce McLaren	M14A-DFV	—	WDN
5 Denis Hulme	M14A-DFV	—	WDN
6 Andrea de Adamich	M7D-Alfa V8	—	WDN
17 John Surtees	M7C-DFV	—	WDN

21-6-70 DUTCH GRAND PRIX, Zandvoort

20 Peter Gethin	M14A-DFV	M14A/2	Crashed
21 Andrea de Adamich	M14D-Alfa V8	M14D/1	DNQ
32 Dan Gurney	M14A-DFV	M14A/1	Rtd eng.

5-7-70 FRENCH GRAND PRIX, Clermont Ferrand

16 Andrea de Adamich	M7D-Alfa V8	M7D/1	15th
17 Dan Gurney	M14A-DFV	M14A/1	5th
19 Denis Hulme	M14A-DFV	M14D/1	4th
15 John Surtees	M7C-DFV	—	DNA

19-7-70 BRITISH GRAND PRIX, Brands Hatch

9 Denis Hulme	M14A-DFV	M14D/1	3rd
10 Dan Gurney	M7A-DFV	M7A/1	Rtd eng.
11 Andrea de Adamich	M7D-Alfa V8	M7D/1	DNS f.leak
12 Peter Gethin	M7A-DFV	—	DNA
21 Trevor Taylor	M7C-DFV	—	DNA
30 Jo Bonnier	M7C-DFV	—	DNA

2-8-70 GERMAN GRAND PRIX, Hockenheimring

4 Denis Hulme	M14A-DFV	M14A/2	3rd
20 Andrea de Adamich	M14D-Alfa V8	M14D/1	DNQ
24 Peter Gethin	M14A-DFV	M14A/1	Rtd camst

16-8-70 AUSTRIAN GRAND PRIX, Österreichring

21 Denis Hulme	M14A-DFV	M14A/2	Rtd eng.
22 Andrea de Adamich	M14D-Alfa V8	M14D/1	12th
23 Peter Gethin	M14A-DFV	M14A/1	10th

22-8-70 Gold Cup, Oulton Park

Aggregate result of two heats:

Heat 1:	6 Andrea de Adamich	M14D-Alfa V8	—	DNA
	*12 Howden Ganley	M10B-Chev V8	400-05	2nd
	*21 David Prophet	M10B-Chev V8	400-04	4th
	*41 Reine Wisell	M10B-Chev V8	400-06	Rtd g'box
	*42 Graham McRae	M10B-Chev V8	400-11S	DNS
	*44 Mike Walker	M10B-Chev V8	—	DNA
	*48 Robin Darlington	M10A-Chev V8	—	DNA
Heat 2:	Ganley			5th
	Prophet			13th
	Wisell			Rtd g'box

6-9-70 ITALIAN GRAND PRIX, Monza

30 Denis Hulme	M14A-DFV	M14A/2	4th
32 Peter Gethin	M14A-DFV	M14A/1	'9th' UNC
34 Andrea de Adamich	M14D-Alfa V8	M14D/1	8th
36 'Nanni' Galli	M7D-DFV	M7D/1	DNQ

20-9-70 CANADIAN GRAND PRIX, Mont Tremblant-Ste Jovite

5 Denis Hulme	M14A-DFV	M14A/2	Rtd eng.
6 Peter Gethin	M14A-DFV	M14A/1	6th
8 Andrea de Adamich	M14D-Alfa V8	M14D/1	Rtd eng.

4-10-70 UNITED STATES GRAND PRIX, Watkins Glen

8 Denis Hulme	M14A-DFV	M14A/2	7th
9 Peter Gethin	M14A-DFV	M14A/1	14th
10 Andrea de Adamich	M14D-Alfa V8	M14D/1	DNQ
27 Jo Bonnier	M7C-DFV	M7A/4	Rtd pipe

25-10-70 MEXICAN GRAND PRIX, Mexico City

8 Denis Hulme	M14A-DFV	M14A/2	3rd

9 Peter Gethin	M14A-DFV	M14A/1	Rtd eng.
27 Jo Bonnier	M7C-DFV	—	DNA

1971

24-1-71 Argentina GP, Buenos Aires
Aggregate result of two heats:

Heat 1:	16 Carlos Reutemann	M7C-DFV	M7A/4	6th
	22 David Prophet	M10B-Chev V8	400-04	8th
	24 Gordon Spice	M10B-Chev V8	400-05	'12th' UNC
Heat 2:	Reutemann			3rd
	Prophet			4th
	Spice			5th

Aggregate result: Reutemann 3rd, Prophet 4th, Spice '8th' UNC.

6-3-71 SOUTH AFRICAN GRAND PRIX, Kyalami

11 Denis Hulme	M19A-DFV	M19A/1	6th
12 Peter Gethin	M14A-DFV	M14A/1	Rtd fuel sys.
23 Jo Bonnier	M7C-DFV	M7A/4	Rtd susp.

21-3-71 Race of Champions, Brands Hatch

9 Denis Hulme	M19A-DFV	M19A/1	FR Rtd eng.
10 Peter Gethin	M14A-DFV	M14A/1	Rtd o'heat
11 Jo Bonnier	M7C-DFV	—	DNA

28-3-71 Questor GP, Ontario Motor Speedway, California, USA
Aggregate result of two heats:

Heat 1:	6 Denis Hulme	M19A-DFV	M19A/1	4th
	7 Peter Gethin	M14A-DFV	M14A/1	9th
Heat 2:	Hulme			5th
	Gethin			7th

Aggregate result: Hulme 3rd, Gethin 6th

9-4-71 Spring Cup, Oulton Park

6 Peter Gethin	M14A-DFV	M14A/1 = FL FR 2nd	
7 Denis Hulme	M19A-DFV	—	DNA

18-4-71 SPANISH GRAND PRIX, Barcelona

9 Denis Hulme	M19A-DFV	M19A/1	5th
10 Peter Gethin	M14A-DFV	M14A/2	8th
23 Jo Bonnier	M7C-DFV	M7A/4	DNA

8-5-71 International Trophy, Silverstone
Aggregate of two heats:

Heat 1:	6 Peter Gethin	M14A-DFV	M14A/2	6th
	25 Keith Holland	M10B-Chev V8	—	DNA
	33 Teddy Pilette	M10B-Chev V8	—	DNA
	44 Gordon Spice	M10B-Chev V8	400-05	19th
	51 Brian Redman	M18-Chev V8	500-01	10th
	52 Tony Dean	M7A-Chev V8	M7A/2	11th
	54 John Myerscough	M10B-Chev V8	400-18S	Rtd oil
	56 Graham McRae	M18-Chev V8	—	DNA
	57 Ulf Norinder	M18-Chev V8	500-05	20th
	58 Ray Allen	M10B-Chev V8	400-21	Crashed
	62 J-P Jaussaud	M18-Chev V8	500-04	16th
	71 David Prophet	M10B-Chev V8	400-04	Rtd o'heat
Heat 2;	Gethin			4th
	Dean			9th
	Jaussaud			10th
	Norinder			13th
	Spice			16th
	Redman			Rtd elec.

Aggregate result: Gethin 2nd, Dean 7th, Jaussaud 8th, Norinder UNC, Spice UNC, Redman UNC.

23-5-71 MONACO GRAND PRIX, Monte Carlo

9 Denis Hulme	M19A-DFV	M19A/1	4th
10 Peter Gethin	M14A-DFV	M14A/2	Crashed

13-6-71 Jochen Rindt Memorial, Hockenheim, West Germany

21 Peter Gethin	M14A-DFV	M14A/2	Rtd throt

20-6-71 DUTCH GRAND PRIX, Zandvoort

26 Denis Hulme	M19A-DFV	M19A/2	12th
28 Peter Gethin	M19A-DFV	M19A/1	'15th' UNC

4-7-71 FRENCH GRAND PRIX, Ricard-Castellet

9 Denis Hulme	M19A-DFV	M19A/2	Rtd elect
10 Peter Gethin	M19A-DFV	M19A/1	9th

17-7-71 BRITISH GRAND PRIX, Silverstone

9 Denis Hulme	M19A-DFV	M19A/2	Rtd eng.
10 Peter Gethin	M19A-DFV	M19A/1	Rtd eng.
11 Jack Oliver	M14A-DFV	M14A/2	Crashed

1-8-71 GERMAN GRAND PRIX, Nürburgring

18 Denis Hulme	M19A-DFV	M19A/2	Rtd fuel
19 Jack Oliver	M14A-DFV	—	DNA
20 Peter Gethin	M19A-DFV	M19A/1	Crashed

15-8-71 AUSTRIAN GRAND PRIX, Österreichring

9 Denis Hulme	M19A-DFV	M19A/2	Rtd eng.
10 Jack Oliver	M19A-DFV	M19A/1	9th
28 Jo Bonnier	M7C-DFV	M7A/4	DNS fuel

22-8-71 Gold Cup, Oulton Park
Aggregate result of two heats:

Heat 1:	1 Brian Redman	M18-Chev V8	500-01	Rtd o'heat
	4 John Myerscough	M10B-Chev V8	400-18S	DNS crash
	8 Ray Allen	M10B-Chev V8	400-19	Rtd oilp.
	12 J-P Jaussaud	M18-Chev V8	—	DNA
	21 David Prophet	M10B-Chev V8	400-04	9th
	22 Graham McRae	M10B-Chev V8	400-11S	Rtd fire
	25 Keith Holland	M10-Chev V8	—	DNA
	43 Teddy Pilette	M10B-Chev V8	—	DNA
	44 Gordon Spice	M10B-Chev V8	400-05	Crashed
Heat 2:	McRae			6th
	Spice			8th
	Prophet			9th

Aggregate result: Prophet 7th, McRae '9th' UNC, Spice '15th' UNC.

5-9-71 ITALIAN GRAND PRIX, Monza

14 Jack Oliver	M14A-DFV	M14A/2	7th
28 Jo Bonnier	M7C-DFV	M7A/4	10th

19-9-71 CANADIAN GRAND PRIX, Mosport Park

9 Denis Hulme	M19A-DFV	M19A/2	FL 4th
10 Mark Donohue	M19A-DFV	M19A/1	3rd

3-10-71 UNITED STATES GRAND PRIX, Watkins Glen

7 Denis Hulme	M19A-DFV	M19A/2	FR Crashed
20 Jo Bonnier	M7C-DFV	M7A/3	16th
31 David Hobbs	M19A-DFV	M19A/1	10th

24-10-71 World Championship Victory Race, Brands Hatch

10 Jack Oliver	M19A-DFV	M19A/2	Rtd brakes

1972

23-1-72 ARGENTINE GRAND PRIX, Buenos Aires

17 Denis Hulme	M19A-DFV	M19A/2	2nd

18 Peter Revson	M19A-DFV	M19A/1	Rtd eng.

4-3-72 SOUTH AFRICAN GRAND PRIX, Kyalami

12 Denis Hulme	M19A-DFV	M19A/2	FIRST
14 Peter Revson	M19A-DFV	M19A/1	3rd

19-3-72 Race of Champions, Brands Hatch

3 Brian Redman	M10B-Chev V8	400-15	Rtd spun
4 Guy Edwards	M10B-Chev V8	400-18S	DNS oil l.
7 Gordon Spice	M10B-Chev V8	400-05	DNS
9 Ray Allen	M18-Chev V8	500-05	14th
10 Ray Calcutt	M18-Chev V8	500-04	DNQ
21 David Prophet	M10B-Chev V8	400-04	DNQ
25 Keith Holland	M10B-Chev V8	400-06	DNQ
33 Teddy Pilette	M18-Chev V8	500-01	11th
55 Denis Hulme	M19A-DFV	M19A/2	3rd
56 Peter Revson	M19A-DFV	M19A/1	8th

23-4-72 International Trophy, Silverstone

3 Denis Hulme	M19C-DFV	M19C/1	4th
4 Peter Revson	M19A-DFV	M19A/2	5th
18 Clive Santo	M10B-Chev V8	400-19	13th
21 David Prophet	M10B-Chev V8	400-04	'14th' UNC
25 Keith Holland	M10B-Chev V8	—	DNS eng.
33 Teddy Pilette	M18-Chev V8	500-01	11th
42 Tony Dean	M14A-Chev V8	—	DNA
43 Brian Redman	M10B-Chev V8	400-15	DNS
44 Guy Edwards	M10B-Chev V8	—	DNA
47 Gordon Spice	M10B-Chev V8	400-05	Rtd eng.
48 Ray Allen	M18-Chev V8	500-05	Crashed
50 Ray Calcutt	M18-Chev V8	—	DNA

1-5-72 SPANISH GRAND PRIX, Jarama

11 Denis Hulme	M19A-DFV	M19A/1	FR Rtd trans
20 Peter Revson	M19A-DFV	M19A/2	5th

14-5-72 MONACO GRAND PRIX, Monte Carlo

14 Denis Hulme	M19C-DFV	M19C/1	15th
15 Brian Redman	M19A-DFV	M19A/2	5th

19-5-72 Gold Cup, Oulton Park

2 Tony Dean	M14A-Chev V8	M14A/2	DNS clutch
3 Gordon Spice	M10B-Chev V8	400-15	DNS
4 Guy Edwards	M10B-Chev V8	400-18S	7th
7 John Kendall	M10B-Chev V8	400-05	DNS
8 Ray Allen	M18-Chev V8	500-05	6th
10 Ray Calcutt	M18-Chev V8	500-04	'10th' UNC
18 Clive Santo	M10B-Chev V8	400-19	DNS
21 David Prophet	M10B-Chev V8	400-04	'11th' UNC
23 Pierre Soukry	M10B-Chev V8	400-20	DNS
25 Keith Holland	M10B-Chev V8	400-06	Rtd chass.
33 Teddy Pilette	M22-Chev V8	1/72	9th
46 Denis Hulme	M19A-DFV	M19A/1	FR FIRST

4-6-72 BELGIAN GRAND PRIX, Nivelles

9 Denis Hulme	M19C-DFV	M19C/1	FR 3rd
10 Peter Revson	M19A-DFV	M19A/2	7th

2-7-72 FRENCH GRAND PRIX, Clermont Ferrand

2 Denis Hulme	M19C-DFV	M19C/1	FR 7th
11 Brian Redman	M19A-DFV	M19A/1	9th

15-7-72 BRITISH GRAND PRIX, Brands Hatch

18 Denis Hulme	M19C-DFV	M19C/1	5th
19 Peter Revson	M19A-DFV	M19A/1	3rd
20 Brian Redman	M19A-DFV	—	DNA

30-7-72 GERMAN GRAND PRIX, Nürburgring

3 Denis Hulme	M19C-DFV	M19C/1	Rtd eng.

5 Brian Redman	M19A-DFV	M19A/1	5th

13-8-72 AUSTRIAN GRAND PRIX, Österreichring

12 Denis Hulme	M19C-DFV	M19C/1	FL 2nd
14 Peter Revson	M19C-DFV	M19C/2	3rd

10-9-72 ITALIAN GRAND PRIX, Monza

14 Denis Hulme	M19C-DFV	M19C/1	3rd
15 Peter Revson	M19C-DFV	M19C/2	4th

24-9-72 CANADIAN GRAND PRIX, Mosport Park

18 Denis Hulme	M19C-DFV	M19C/1	FR 3rd
19 Peter Revson	M19C-DFV	M19C/2	2nd

8-10-72 UNITED STATES GRAND PRIX, Watkins Glen

19 Denis Hulme	M19C-DFV	M19C/1	FR 3rd
20 Peter Revson	M19C-DFV	M19C/2	FR Rtd elec.
21 Jody Scheckter	M19A-DFV	M19A/1	9th

22-10-72 World Championship Victory Race, Brands Hatch

7 Jody Scheckter	M19A-DFV	M19A/1	'18th' UNC
8 Brian Redman	M19C-DFV	M19C/1	7th
31 Chris Oates	M10B-Chev V8	—	DNA
32 Tony Dean	M14A-Chev V8	M14A/2	DNQ
34 Guy Edwards	M10B-Chev V8	400-18S	DNS
37 Roger Williamson	M10B-Chev V8	400-05	Rtd tyres
38 Ray Allen	M18-Chev V8	500-05	Rtd
40 Tony Lanfranchi	M18-Chev V8	500-04	DNS
48 Clive Santo	M10B-Chev V8	400-19	DNS
51 David Prophet	M10B-Chev V8	400-04	DNS
53 Pierre Soukry	M10B-Chev V8	400-20	DNQ
57 Clive Baker	M10B-Chev V8	400-06	Rtd
63 Teddy Pilette	M22-Chev V8	1/72	Rtd o'heat

1973

28-1-73 ARGENTINE GRAND PRIX, Buenos Aires

14 Denis Hulme	M19C-DFV	M19C/1	5th
16 Peter Revson	M19C-DFV	M19C/2	8th

11-2-73 BRAZILIAN GRAND PRIX, Interlagos

7 Denis Hulme	M19C-DFV	M19C/1	3rd
8 Peter Revson	M19C-DFV	M19C/2	Rtd g'box

3-3-73 SOUTH AFRICAN GRAND PRIX, Kyalami

5 Denis Hulme	M23-DFV	M23/1	PP 5th
6 Peter Revson	M19C-DFV	M19C/2	2nd
7 Jody Scheckter	M19C-DFV	M19C/1	9th

17-3-73 Race of Champions, Brands Hatch

28 John Bowtell	M10A-Rover V8	300-16	DNQ
31 Chris Oates	M10B-Chev V8	—	DNA
33 Teddy Pilette	M18-Chev V8	500-01	Crashed
57 Denis Hulme	M23-DFV	M23/1	2nd
57 Clive Baker	M10B-Chev V8	400-06	DNS
58 Jody Scheckter	M19C-DFV	M19C/1	Crashed
78 Willie Wood	M14A-DFV	M14A/2	DNQ

8-4-73 International Trophy, Silverstone

9 Denis Hulme	M23-DFV	M23/1	Rtd eng.
10 Peter Revson	M23-DFV	M23/2	4th
28 John Bowtell	M10A-Rover V8	300-16	DNQ

29-4-73 SPANISH GRAND PRIX, Barcelona
5 Denis Hulme	M23-DFV	M23/1	FR 6th
6 Peter Revson	M23-DFV	M23/2	4th

20-5-73 BELGIAN GRAND PRIX, Zolder
7 Denis Hulme	M23-DFV	M23/1	FR 7th
8 Peter Revson	M23-DFV	M23/2	Crashed

3-6-73 MONACO GRAND PRIX, Monte Carlo
7 Denis Hulme	M23-DFV	M23/1	6th
8 Peter Revson	M23-DFV	M23/2	5th

17-6-73 SWEDISH GRAND PRIX, Anderstorp
7 Denis Hulme	M23-DFV	M23/1	FL FIRST
8 Peter Revson	M23-DFV	M23/2	7th

1-7-73 FRENCH GRAND PRIX, Ricard-Castellet
7 Denis Hulme	M23-DFV	M23/1	8th
8 Jody Scheckter	M23-DFV	M23/3	FR Crashed

14-7-73 BRITISH GRAND PRIX, Silverstone
First start:
7 Denis Hulme	M23 DFV	M23/1	FR 4th
8 Peter Revson	M23-DFV	M23/2	FR 6th
30 Jody Scheckter	M23-DFV	M23/3	Crashed*

His accident on lap 2 sparked multiple collision, race stopped and retstarted using original grid and running total distance. Results:
Revson	FIRST
Hulme	3rd

29-7-73 DUTCH GRAND PRIX, Zandvoort
7 Denis Hulme	M23-DFV	M23/1	Rtd eng.
8 Peter Revson	M23-DFV	M23/2	4th

5-8-73 GERMAN GRAND PRIX, Nürburgring
7 Denis Hulme	M23-DFV	M23/1	12th
8 Peter Revson	M23-DFV	M23/2	9th
30 Jacky Ickx	M23-DFV	M23/4	3rd

19-8-73 AUSTRIAN GRAND PRIX, Österreichring
7 Denis Hulme	M23-DFV	M23/1	8th
8 Peter Revson	M23-DFV	M23/2	Rtd clutch

9-9-73 ITALIAN GRAND PRIX, Monza
7 Denis Hulme	M23-DFV	M23/1	15th
8 Peter Revson	M23-DFV	M23/4	FR 3rd

23-9-73 CANADIAN GRAND PRIX, Mosport Park
0 Jody Scheckter	M23-DFV	M23/2	Crashed
7 Denis Hulme	M23-DFV	M23/1	13th
8 Peter Revson	M23-DFV	M23/4	FR FIRST

7-10-73 UNITED STATES GRAND PRIX, Watkins Glen
0 Jody Scheckter	M23-DFV	M23/2	Rtd susp.
7 Denis Hulme	M23-DFV	M23/1	4th
8 Peter Revson	M23-DFV	M23/4	5th

1974

13-1-74 ARGENTINE GRAND PRIX, Buenos Aires
5 Emerson Fittipaldi	M23-DFV	M23/5	10th
6 Denis Hulme	M23-DFV	M23/6	FIRST
33 Mike Hailwood	M23-DFV	M23/1	4th

27-1-74 BRAZILIAN GRAND PRIX, Interlagos
5 Emerson Fittipaldi	M23-DFV	M23/ 5	PP FIRST
6 Denis Hulme	M23-DFV	M23/6	12th
33 Mike Hailwood	M23-DFV	M23/1	5th

3-2-74 President Medici GP, Brasilia, Brazil
5 Emerson Fittipaldi	M23-DFV	M23/5	FL FR FIRST

17-3-74 Race of Champions, Brands Hatch
5 Emerson Fittipaldi	M23-DFV	M23/4	3rd
6 Denis Hulme	M23-DFV	M23/6	'13th' UNC
33 Mike Hailwood	M23-DFV	M23/1	4th
54 Alan Kaye	M14A-Chev V8	M14A/2	DNQ
59 Brian Robinson	M19A-Chev V8	M19A/2	DNQ

30-3-74 SOUTH AFRICAN GRAND PRIX, Kyalami
5 Emerson Fittipaldi	M23-DFV	M23/5	7th
6 Denis Hulme	M23-DFV	M23/6	9th
23 Dave Charlton	M23-DFV	M23/2	19th
33 Mike Hailwood	M23-DFV	M23/1	3rd

7-4-74 International Trophy, Silverstone
4 Mile Hailwood	M23-DFV	M23/7	Rtd clutch
5 Emerson Fittipaldi	M23-DFV	—	DNA
6 Denis Hulme	M23-DFV	M23/4	Rtd Clutch
54 Alan Kaye	M14A-Chev V8	—	DNA
58 Brian Robinson	M19A-Chev V8	M19A/2	Rtd eng.

28-4-74 SPANISH GRAND PRIX, Jarama
5 Emerson Fittipaldi	M23-DFV	M23/5	3rd
6 Denis Hulme	M23-DFV	M23/4*	6th
33 Mike Hailwood	M23-DFV	M23/7	9th

* M23/6 practice car

12-5-74 BELGIAN GRAND PRIX, Nivelles
5 Emerson Fittipaldi	M23-DFV	M23/5	FIRST
6 Denis Hulme	M23-DFV	M23/6	FL 6th
33 Mike Hailwood	M23-DFV	M23/7	7th

26-5-74 MONACO GRAND PRIX, Monte Carlo
5 Emerson Fittipaldi	M23-DFV	M23/5	5th
6 Denis Hulme	M23-DFV	M23/6	Crashed
33 Mike Hailwood	M23-DFV	M23/1	Crashed

9-6-74 SWEDISH GRAND PRIX, Anderstorp
5 Emerson Fittipaldi	M23-DFV	M23/4	4th
6 Denis Hulme	M23-DFV	M23/6	Rtd susp.
33 Mike Hailwood	M23-DFV	M23/7	Rtd fuel

23-6-74 DUTCH GRAND PRIX, Zandvoort
5 Emerson Fittipaldi	M23-DFV	M23/5	3rd
6 Denis Hulme	M23-DFV	M23/6	Rtd ign.
33 Mike Hailwood	M23-DFV	M23/7	4th

7-7-74 FRENCH GRAND PRIX, Dijon-Prenois
5 Emerson Fittipaldi	M23-DFV	M23/5	Rtd eng.
6 Denis Hulme	M23-DFV	M23/6	6th
33 Mike Hailwood	M23-DFV	M23/1	7th

20-7-74 BRITISH GRAND PRIX, Brands Hatch
5 Emerson Fittipaldi	M23-DFV	M23/8	2nd
6 Denis Hulme	M23-DFV	M23/6	7th
33 Mike Hailwood	M23-DFV	M23/1	Rtd spun

4-8-74 GERMAN GRAND PRIX, Nürburgring
5 Emerson Fittipaldi	M23-DFV	M23/8	Crashed
6 Denis Hulme	M23-DFV	M23/6	Crashed
33 Mike Hailwood	M23-DFV	M23/7	Crashed

18-8-74 AUSTRIAN GRAND PRIX, Österreichring
5 Emerson Fittipaldi	M23-DFV	M23/8	'18th' UNC
6 Denis Hulme	M23-DFV	M23/6	2nd
33 David Hobbs	M23-DFV	M23/4	7th

8-9-74 ITALIAN GRAND PRIX, Monza
5 Emerson Fittipaldi	M23-DFV	M23/8	2nd
6 Denis Hulme	M23-DFV	M23/6	6th

33 David Hobbs	M23-DFV	M23/4	9th

22-9-74 CANADIAN GRAND PRIX, Mosport Park

5 Emerson Fittipaldi	M23-DFV	M23/8	PP FIRST
6 Denis Hulme	M23-DFV	M23/6	6th
33 Jochen Mass	M23-DFV	M23/4	16th

6-10-74 UNITED STATES GRAND PRIX, Watkins Glen

5 Emerson Fittipaldi	M23-DFV	M23/8	4th
6 Denis Hulme	M23-DFV	M23/6	Rtd eng.
33 Jochen Mass	M23-DFV	M23/4	7th

FITTIPALDI AND McLAREN — FORMULA 1 WORLD CHAMPIONS

1975

12-1-75 ARGENTINE GRAND PRIX, Buenos Aires

1 Emerson Fittipaldi	M23-DFV	M23/9	FIRST
2 Jochen Mass	M23-DFV	M23/8	14th

26-1-75 BRAZILIAN GRAND PRIX, Interlagos

1 Emerson Fittipaldi	M23-DFV	M23/0	FR 2nd
2 Jochen Mass	M23-DFV	M23/8	3rd

1-3-75 SOUTH AFRICAN GRAND PRIX, Kyalami

1 Emerson Fittipaldi	M23-DFV	M23/9	'19th' UNC
2 Jochen Mass	M23-DFV	M23/8	6th
31 Dave Charlton	M23-DFV	M23/2	14th

16-3-75 Race of Champions, Brands Hatch

1 Emerson Fittipaldi	M23-DFV	M23/9	5th
2 Jochen Mass	M23-DFV	M23/8	Crashed

13-4-75 International Trophy, Silverstone

1 Emerson Fittipaldi	M23-DFV	M23/4	= FL 2nd

27-4-75 SPANISH GRAND PRIX, Barcelona

1 Emerson Fittipaldi	M23-DFV	M23/9	DNS*
2 Jochen Mass	M23-DFV	M23/8	FIRST*

Refused to race in protest at track safety state, Mass won when race red-flagged after accident involving bystander fatalities.

11-5-75 MONACO GRAND PRIX, Monte Carlo

1 Emerson Fittipaldi	M23-DFV	M23/9	2nd
2 Jochen Mass	M23-DFV	M23/8	6th

25-5-75 BELGIAN GRAND PRIX, Zolder

1 Emerson Fittipaldi	M23-DFV	M23/9	7th
2 Jochen Mass	M23-DFV	M23/8	Crashed

8-6-75 SWEDISH GRAND PRIX, Anderstorp

1 Emerson Fittipaldi	M23-DFV	M23/9	8th
2 Jochen Mass	M23-DFV	M23/8	Rtd eng.

22-6-75 DUTCH GRAND PRIX, Zandvoort

1 Emerson Fittipaldi	M23-DFV	M23/9	Rtd eng.
2 Jochen Mass	M23-DFV	M23/8	Crashed

6-7-75 FRENCH GRAND PRIX, Ricard-Castellet

1 Emerson Fittipaldi	M23-DFV	M23/9	4th
2 Jochen Mass	M23-DFV	M23/6	3rd

19-7-75 BRITISH GRAND PRIX, Silverstone

1 Emerson Fittipaldi	M23-DFV	M23/9	FIRST*
2 Jochen Mass	M23-DFV	M23/6	'7th'

Declared winner after race stopped due to torrential rain with 11 laps still to run. Fittipaldi was still running; Mass had crashed.

3-8-75 GERMAN GRAND PRIX, Nürburgring

1 Emerson Fittipaldi	M23-DFV	M23/9	Rtd susp.
2 Jochen Mass	M23-DFV	M23/4	Crashed

17-8-75 AUSTRIAN GRAND PRIX, Österreichring

| 1 Emerson Fittipaldi | M23-DFV | M23/9 | 9th |
| 2 Jochen Mass | M23-DFV | M23/6 | 4th |

24-8-75 Swiss GP, Dijon-Prenois

| 1 Emerson Fittipaldi | M23-DFV | M23/10 | FR Rtd clutch |
| 2 Jochen Mass | M23-DFV | M23/6 | 3rd |

7-9-75 ITALIAN GRAND PRIX, Monza

| 1 Emerson Fittipaldi | M23-DFV | M23/10 | 2nd |
| 2 Jochen Mass | M23-DFV | M23/6 | Crashed |

5-10-75 UNITED STATES GRAND PRIX, Watkins Glen

| 1 Emerson Fittipaldi | M23-DFV | M23/10 | FL FR 2nd |
| 2 Jochen Mass | M23-DFV | M23/6 | 3rd |

1976

25-1-76 BRAZILIAN GRAND PRIX, Interlagos

| 11 James Hunt | M23-DFV | M23/8 | PP Crashed |
| 12 Jochen Mass | M23-DFV | M23/6 | 6th |

6-3-76 SOUTH AFRICAN GRAND PRIX, Kyalami

| 11 James Hunt | M23-DFV | M23/8 | PP 2nd |
| 12 Jochen Mass | M23-DFV | M23/6 | 3rd |

14-3-76 Race of Champions, Brands Hatch

| 11 James Hunt | M23-DFV | M23/8 | FL FIRST |

28-3-76 UNITED STATES GRAND PRIX (WEST), Long Beach

| 11 James Hunt | M23-DFV | M23/8 | Crashed |
| 12 Jochen Mass | M23-DFV | M23/6 | 5th |

11-4-76 International Trophy, Silverstone

| 11 James Hunt | M23-DFV | M23/9 | PP FL FIRST |

2-5-76 SPANISH GRAND PRIX, Jarama

| 11 James Hunt | M23-DFV | M23/8 | PP FIRST* |
| 12 Jochen Mass | M23-DFV | M23/9 | FL Rtd eng. |

16-5-76 BELGIAN GRAND PRIX, Zolder

| 11 James Hunt | M23-DFV | M23/6 | Rtd trans. |
| 12 Jochen Mass | M23-DFV | M23/9 | 6th |

23-5-76 MONACO GRAND PRIX, Monte Carlo

| 11 James Hunt | M23-DFV | M23/8 | Rtd eng. |
| 12 Jochen Mass | M23-DFV | M23/9 | 5th |

13-6-76 SWEDISH GRAND PRIX, Anderstorp

| 11 James Hunt | M23-DFV | M23/8 | 5th |
| 12 Jochen Mass | M23-DFV | M23/9 | 11th |

4-7-76 FRENCH GRAND PRIX, Ricard-Castellet

| 11 James Hunt | M23-DFV | M23/8 | PP FIRST |
| 12 Jochen Mass | M23-DFV | M23/9 | 15th |

18-7-76 BRITISH GRAND PRIX, Brands Hatch

| 11 James Hunt | M23-DFV | M23/8 | FR FL DISQ |
| 12 Jochen Mass | M23-DFV | M23/9 | Rtd clutch |

1-8-76 GERMAN GRAND PRIX, Nürburgring

| 11 James Hunt | M23-DFV | M23/8 | PP FIRST |
| 12 Jochen Mass | M23-DFV | M23/9 | 3rd |

15-8-76 AUSTRIAN GRAND PRIX, Österreichring

| 11 James Hunt | M23-DFV | M23/8* | PP FL 4th |
| 12 Jochen Mass | M23-DFV | M23/9 | 7th |

Set pole time in M23/8

29-8-76 DUTCH GRAND PRIX, Zandvoort

| 11 James Hunt | M23-DFV | M23/8 | FR FIRST |
| 12 Jochen Rindt | M26-DFV | M26/1 | 9th |

12-9-76 ITALIAN GRAND PRIX, Monza

11 James Hunt	M23-DFV	M23/8	Crashed
12 Jochen Mass	M26-DFV	M26/1	Rtd ign.

3-10-76 CANADIAN GRAND PRIX, Mosport Park

11 James Hunt	M23-DFV	M23/8	PP FIRST
12 Jochen Mass	M23-DFV	M23/9	5th

10-10-76 UNITED STATES GRAND PRIX, Watkins Glen

11 James Hunt	M23-DFV	M23/8	PP FL FIRST
12 Jochen Mass	M23-DFV	M23/9	4th

17-10-76 JAPANESE GRAND PRIX, Mr Fuji

11 James Hunt	M23-DFV	M23/8	FR 3rd
12 Jochen Mass	M23-DFV	M23/9	Crashed

JAMES HUNT WORLD CHAMPION DRIVER FOR McLAREN

1977

9-1-77 ARGENTINE GRAND PRIX, Buenos Aires

1 James Hunt	M23-DFV	M23/10*	PP FL Rtd
2 Jochen Mass	M23-DFV	M23/9	Rtd eng.

*'M23/8-2'

23-1-77 BRAZILIAN GRAND PRIX, Interlagos

1 James Hunt	M23-DFV	M23/10	PP FL 2nd
2 Jochen Mass	M23-DFV	M23/9	Crashed

5-3-77 SOUTH AFRICAN GRAND PRIX, Kyalami

1 James Hunt	M23-DFV	M23/11	PP 4th
2 Jochen Mass	M23-DFV	M23/6	5th

20-3-77 Race of Champions, Brands Hatch

1 James Hunt	M23-DFV	M23/10	FL FIRST

3-4-77 UNITED STATES GRAND PRIX (WEST), Long Beach

1 James Hunt	M23-DFV	M23/11	7th
2 Jochen Mass	M23-DFV	M23/12	Rtd trans.

8-5-77 SPANISH GRAND PRIX, Jarama

1 James Hunt	M26-DFV	M26/2	Rtd misf.
2 Jochen Mass	M23-DFV	M23/12	4th
36 Emilio de Villota	M23-DFV	M23/6	13th

22-5-77 MONACO GRAND PRIX, Monte Carlo

1 James Hunt	M26-DFV	M26/2	7th
2 Jochen Mass	M23-DFV	M23/12	Crashed
30 Brett Lunger	M23-DFV	M23/14	DNS fuel
36 Emilio de Villota	M23-DFV	M23/6	DNQ

5-6-77 BELGIAN GRAND PRIX, Zolder

1 James Hunt	M26-DFV	M26/2	7th
2 Jochen Mass	M23-DFV	M23/12	Rtd spun

19-6-77 SWEDISH GRAND PRIX, Anderstorp

1 James Hunt	M26-DFV	M26/2	12th
2 Jochen Mass	M23-DFV	M23/12	2nd
30 Brett Lunger	M23-DFV	M23/14	11th
36 Emilio de Vilotta	M23-DFV	M23/6	DNQ

3-7-77 FRENCH GRAND PRIX, Dijon-Prenois

1 James Hunt	M26-DFV	M26/2	FR 3rd
2 Jochen Mass	M23-DFV	M23/12	9th
30 Brett Lunger	M23-DFV	M23/14	DNQ
36 Emilio de Villota	M23-DFV	—	DNA

16-7-77 BRITISH GRAND PRIX, Silverstone

1 James Hunt	M26-DFV	M26/2	PP FL FIRST
2 Jochen Mass	M26-DFV	M26/1	4th
30 Brett Lunger	M23/DFV	M23/14	13th
36 Emilio de Villota	M23-DFV	M23/6	DNQ

40 Gilles Villeneuve	M23-DFV	M23/8	11th

31-7-77 GERMAN GRAND PRIX, Hockenheimring

1 James Hunt	M26-DFV	M26/2	Rtd fuelp.
2 Jochen Mass	M26-DFV	M26/1	Rtd g'box
30 Brett Lunger	M23-DFV	M23/14	Crashed
36 Emilio de Villota	M23-DFV	M23/6	DNQ

14-8-77 AUSTRIAN GRAND PRIX, Österreichring

1 James Hunt	M26-DFV	M26/2	FR Rtd eng.
2 Jochen Mass	M26-DFV	M26/1	6th
30 Brett Lunger	M23-DFV	M23/14	10th
36 Emilio de Villota	M23-DFV	M23/6	Crashed

28-8-77 DUTCH GRAND PRIX, Zandvoort

1 James Hunt	M26-DFV	M26/2	Crashed
2 Jochen Mass	M26-DFV	M26/3	Crashed
30 Brett Lunger	M23-DFV	M23/14	9th
36 Emilio de Villota	M23-DFV	M23/6	DNQ

11-9-77 ITALIAN GRAND PRIX, Monza

1 James Hunt	M26-DFV	M26/2	PP Spun off
2 Jochen Mass	M26-DFV	M26/3	4th
14 Bruno Giacomelli	M23-DFV	M23/8	Rtd eng.
30 Brett Lunger	M23-DFV	M23/14	Rtd eng.
36 Emilio de Villota	M23-DFV	M23/6	DNQ

2-10-77 UNITED STATES GRAND PRIX, Watkins Glen

1 James Hunt	M26-DFV	M26/2	FR FIRST
2 Jochen Mass	M26-DFV	M26/3	Rtd fuel p.
30 Brett Lunger	M23-DFV	M23/11	10th

9-10-77 CANADIAN GRAND PRIX, Mosport Park

1 James Hunt	M26-DFV	M26/2	FR Crashed
2 Jochen Mass	M26-DFV	M26/3	3rd
30 Brett Lunger	M23-DFV	M23/14	11th

23-10-77 JAPANESE GRAND PRIX, Mt Fuji

1 James Hunt	M26-DFV	M26/3	FR FIRST
2 Jochen Mass	M26-DFV	M26/1	Rtd eng.

1978

15-1-78 ARGENTINE GRAND PRIX, Buenos Aires

7 James Hunt	M26-DFV	M26/4	4th
8 Patrick Tambay	M26-DFV	M26/3	6th
30 Brett Lunger	M23/DFV	M23/14	13th

29-1-78 BRAZILIAN GRAND PRIX, Rio de Janeiro

7 James Hunt	M26-DFV	M26/4	FR Crashed
8 Patrick Tambay	M26-DFV	M26/3	Crashed
30 Brett Lunger	M23-DFV	M23/14	Rtd o'heat.

4-3-78 SOUTH AFRICAN GRAND PRIX, Kyalami

7 James Hunt	M26-DFV	M26/4	Rtd eng.
8 Patrick Tambay	M26-DFV	M26/5	Crashed
30 Brett Lunger	M23-DFV	M23/14	11th

19-3-78 International Trophy, Silverstone

7 James Hunt	M26-DFV	M26/4	Crashed
28 Emilio de Villota	M23-DFV	M23/6	Rtd elec.
30 Brett Lunger	M23-DFV	M23/11	4th
40 Tony Trimmer	M23-DFV	M23/14	3rd

24-3-78 Gold Cup, Oulton Park

1 Tony Trimmer	M23-DFV	M23/14	PP FL FIRST
5 Emilio de Villota	M25-DFV	M25/1	2nd

27-3-78 Evening News Trophy, Brands Hatch

1 Tony Trimmer	M23-DFV	M23/14	FR FIRST

5 Emilio de Villota	M25-DFV	M25/1	3rd

2-4-78 UNITED STATES GRAND PRIX (WEST), Long Beach

7 James Hunt	M26-DFV	M26/4	Crashed
8 Patrick Tambay	M26-DFV	M26/5	12th
30 Brett Lunger	M23-DFV	M23/11	DNQ

16-4-78 Anglia TV Trophy, Snetterton

1 Tony Trimmer	M23-DFV	M23/14	PP FL FIRST
5 Emilio de Villota	M25-DFV	M25/1	2nd

1-5-78 Sun Trophy, Mallory Park

1 Tony Trimmer	M23-DFV	M23/14	PP 2nd
5 Emilio de Villota	M25-DFV	M25/1	FL 4th

7-5-78 MONACO GRAND PRIX, Monte Carlo

7 James Hunt	M26-DFV	M26/4	Rtd susp.
8 Patrick Tambay	M26-DFV	M26/5	7th
30 Brett Lunger	M26-DFV	M26/6	DNQ

15-5-78 Whitsuntide, Zandvoort

1 Tony Trimmer	M23-DFV	M23/14	DNS eng.
5 Emilio de Villota	M25-DFV	M25/1	Rtd fuelp.
30 Brett Lunger	M26-DFV	M26/6	PP FL 6th

21-5-78 BELGIAN GRAND PRIX, Zolder

7 James Hunt	M26-DFV	M26/4	Crashed
8 Patrick Tambay	M26-DFV	—	DNA
30 Brett Lunger	M26-DFV	M26/6	7th
33 Bruno Giacomelli	M26-DFV	M26/7	8th

21-5-78 Donington F1 Trophy, Donington Park

1 Tony Trimmer	M23-DFV	—	DNA
5 Emilio de Villota	M25-DFV	M25/1	FR 5th

29-5-78 Radio 210 European Trophy, Thruxton

1 Tony Trimmer	M23-DFV	M23/14	FIRST

4-6-78 SPANISH GRAND PRIX, Jarama

7 James Hunt	M26-DFV	M26/3	6th
8 Patrick Tambay	M26-DFV	M26/5	Rtd clutch
28 Emilio de Villota	M23-DFV	M23/6	DNQ
30 Brett Lunger	M26-DFV	M26/6	DNQ

17-6-78 SWEDISH GRAND PRIX, Anderstorp

7 James Hunt	M26-DFV	M26/3	8th
8 Patrick Tambay	M26-DFV	M26/5	4th
30 Brett Lunger	M26-DFV	M26/6	DNQ

24-6-78 F1 Trophy Oulton Park

5 Emilio de Villota	M23-DFV	M23/6	PP Rtd elct

1-7-78 FRENCH GRAND PRIX, Ricard-Castellet

7 James Hunt	M26-DFV	M26/3	3rd
8 Patrick Tambay	M26-DFV	M26/5	9th
30 Brett Lunger	M26-DFV	M26/6	Rtd eng.
33 Bruno Giacomelli	M26-DFV	M26/7	Rtd eng.

16-7-78 BRITISH GRAND PRIX, Brands Hatch

7 James Hunt	M26-DFV	M26/3	Crashed
8 Patrick Tambay	M26-DFV	M26/5	6th
30 Brett Lunger	M26-DFV	M26/6	8th
33 Bruno Giacomelli	M26-DFV	M26/7	7th
40 Tony Trimmer	M23-DFV	M23/14	DNQ

30-7-78 GERMAN GRAND PRIX, Hockenheimring

7 James Hunt	M26-DFV	M26/3	DISQ*
8 Patrick Tambay	M26-DFV	M26/5	Crashed

Short-cut to pits – Tambay crashed after a puncture

30-7-78 Travis Trophy, Mallory Park

1 Tony Trimmer	M23-DFV	M23/14	PP 2nd

5 Emilio de Villota	M23-DFV	M23/6	FR FL 4th

13-8-78 AUSTRIAN GRAND PRIX, Österreichring

7 James Hunt	M26-DFV	M26/5	7th
8 Patrick Tambay	M26-DFV	M26/3	16th
29 Nelson Piquet	M23-DFV	M23/11	Crashed
30 Brett Lunger	M26-DFV	M26/6	19th

Race re-started after stop due to torrential rain:
Lunger, 8th, Hunt crashed, Tambay crashed.
Result overall, aggregate of two parts: Lunger 8th

27-8-78 DUTCH GRAND PRIX, Zandvoort

7 James Hunt	M26-DFV	M26/5	10th
8 Patrick Tambay	M26-DFV	M26/3	9th
29 Nelson Piquet	M23-DFV	M23/11	Rtd trans.
30 Brett Lunger	M26-DFV	M26/6	Rtd eng.
33 Bruno Giacomelli	M26-DFV	M26/7	Spun

28-8-78 Fuji Tapes Trophy, Brands Hatch

1 Tony Trimmer	M23-DFV	M23/14	FIRST
5 Emilio de Villota	M23-DFV	M23/6	Rtd oil l.

10-9-78 ITALIAN GRAND PRIX, Monza

7 James Hunt	M26-DFV	M26/1	Rtd ign.
8 Patrick Tambay	M26-DFV	M26/3	5th
29 Nelson Piquet	M23-DFV	M23/11	9th
30 Brett Lunger	M26-DFV	M26/6	Crashed

10-9-78 Radio Victory Trophy, Thruxton

1 Divina Galica	M23-DFV	M23/14	7th
5 Emilio de Villota	M25-DFV	M25/1	PP 8th

24-9-78 Budweiser Trophy, Snetterton

1 Tony Trimmer	M23-DFV	M23/14	2nd
5 Emilio de Villota	M23-DFV	M23/6	PP 8th

1-10-78 UNITED STATES GRAND PRIX, Watkins Glen

7 James Hunt	M26-DFV	M26/5	7th
8 Patrick Tambay	M26-DFV	M26/7	6th

8-10-78 CANADIAN GRAND PRIX, Montreal

7 James Hunt	M26-DFV	M26/5	Spun
8 Patrick Tambay	M26-DFV	M26/3	8th

1979

21-1-79 ARGENTINE GRAND PRIX, Buenos Aires

7 John Watson	M28-DFV	M28/2	3rd
8 Patrick Tambay	M28-DFV	M28/1	Crashed

3-3-79 SOUTH AFRICAN GRAND PRIX, Kyalami

7 John Watson	M28-DFV	M28/2	Rtd ign.
8 Patrick Tambay	M28-DFV	M28/1	10th

8-4-79 UNITED STATES GRAND PRIX (WEST), Long Beach

7 John Watson	M28-DFV	M28/2	Rtd fuel.
8 Patrick Tambay	M28-DFV	M28/3	Crashed

15-4-78 Race of Champions, Brands Hatch

7 John Watson	M28-DFV	M28/2	Rtd g'box

29-4-79 SPANISH GRAND PRIX, Jarama

7 John Watson	M28-DFV	M28/1	Rtd eng.
8 Patrick Tambay	M28-DFV	M28/3	13th

29-4-79 Sun Trophy, Mallory Park

88 Iain McLaren	M26-DFV	M26/6	DNQ

13-5-79 BELGIAN GRAND PRIX, Zolder

7 John Watson	M28-DFV	M28/2	6th
8 Patrick Tambay	M26-DFV	M26/7	DNQ

20-5-79 Anglia TV Trophy, Snetterton

2 Gordon Smiley	M23-DFV	M23/14	7th

27-5-79 MONACO GRAND PRIX, Monte Carlo

7 John Watson	M28-DFV	M28/3	4th
8 Patrick Tambay	M28-DFV	M28/2	DNQ

28-5-79 Rivet Supply Trophy, Thruxton

2 Gordon Smiley	M23-DFV	M23/14	4th
17 Riccardo Zunino	M23-DFV	M23/11	5th

4-6-79 Whitsuntide, Zandvoort

2 Gordon Smiley	M23-DFV	M23/14	5th

30-6-79 F1 Trophy, Oulton Park

88 Iain McLaren	M26-DFV	—	DNA

1-7-79 FRENCH GRAND PRIX, Dijon-Prenois

7 John Watson	M28-DFV	M28/3	11th
8 Patrick Tambay	M28-DFV	M28/2	10th

14-7-79 BRITISH GRAND PRIX, Silverstone

7 John Watson	M29-DFV	M29/1	4th
8 Patrick Tambay	M28-DFV	M28/2	7th

29-7-79 GERMAN GRAND PRIX, Hockenheimring

7 John Watson	M29-DFV	M29/1	5th
8 Patrick Tambay	M29-DFV	M29/2	Rtd susp.

12-8-79 AUSTRIAN GRAND PRIX, Österreichring

7 John Watson	M29-DFV	M29/1	9th
8 Patrick Tambay	M29-DFV	M29/2	10th

26-8-79 DUTCH GRAND PRIX, Zandvoort

7 John Watson	M29-DFV	M29/3	Rtd eng.
8 Patrick Tambay	M29-DFV	M29/2	Rtd eng.

9-9-79 ITALIAN GRAND PRIX, Monza

7 John Watson	M29-DFV	M29/3	Crashed
8 Patrick Tambay	M29-DFV	M29/2	Rtd eng.

9-9-79 Radio Victory Trophy, Thruxton

24 Dennis Leech	M23-DFV	M23/11	9th

16-9-79 Dino Ferrari GP, Imola, Italy

8 Patrick Tambay	M28-DFV	M28/3	8th

30-9-79 CANADIAN GRAND PRIX, Montreal

7 John Watson	M29-DFV	M29/3	6th
8 Patrick Tambay	M29-DFV	M29/2	Rtd eng.

7-10-79 UNITED STATES GRAND PRIX, Watkins Glen

7 John Watson	M29-DFV	M29/3	6th
8 Patrick Tambay	M29-DFV	M29/2	Rtd eng.

1980

13-1-80 ARGENTINE GRAND PRIX, Buenos Aires

7 John Watson	M29-DFV	M29/2	Crashed
8 Alain Prost	M29-DFV	M29/1	6th

27-1-80 BRAZILIAN GRAND PRIX, Interlagos

7 John Watson	M29-DFV	M29/2	11th
8 Alain Prost	M29-DFV	M29/1	5th

1-3-80 SOUTH AFRICAN GRAND PRIX, Kyalami

7 John Watson	M29-DFV	M29/1	11th
8 Alain Prost	M29-DFV	M29/3	DNS Crash

30-3-80 UNITED STATES GRAND PRIX (WEST), Long Beach

7 John Watson	M29-DFV	M29/2	4th
8 Stephen South	M29-DFV	M29/4	DNQ

4-5-80 BELGIAN GRAND PRIX, Zolder

7 John Watson	M29-DFV	M29/2	'13th' UNC
8 Alain Prost	M29-DFV	M29/4	Rtd brake

18-5-80 MONACO GRAND PRIX, Monte Carlo

7 John Watson	M29-DFV	M29/2	DNQ
8 Alain Prost	M29-DFV	M29/4	Crashed

1-6-80 SPANISH GRAND PRIX, Jarama

7 John Watson	M29-DFV	M29/2	Crashed
8 Alain Prost	M29-DFV	M29/4	Rtd eng.

29-6-80 FRENCH GRAND PRIX, Ricard-Castellet

7 John Watson	M29-DFV	M29/2	7th
8 Alain Prost	M29-DFV	M29/4	Rtd trans.

13-7-80 BRITISH GRAND PRIX, Brands Hatch

7 John Watson	M29-DFV	M29/2	8th
8 Alain Prost	M29-DFV	M29/4	6th

10-8-80 GERMAN GRAND PRIX, Hockenheimring

7 John Watson	M29-DFV	M29/2	Rtd eng.
8 Alain Prost	M29-DFV	M29/5	11th

17-8-80 AUSTRIAN GRAND PRIX, Österreichring

7 John Watson	M29-DFV	M29/3	Rtd eng.
8 Alain Prost	M29-DFV	M29/5	7th

31-8-80 DUTCH GRAND PRIX, Zandvoort

7 John Watson	M29-DFV	M29/2	Rtd eng.
8 Alain Prost	M30-DFV	M30/1	6th

14-9-80 ITALIAN GRAND PRIX, Monza

7 John Watson	M29-DFV	M29/2	Rtd susp.
8 Alain Prost	M30-DFV	M30/1	7th

29-9-80 CANADIAN GRAND PRIX, Montreal

7 John Watson	M29-DFV	M29/2	4th
8 Alain Prost	M30-DFV	M30/1	Crashed

5-10-80 Pentax Trophy, Silverstone

34 Dennis Leech	M23-DFV	M23/11	11th

5-10-80 UNITED STATES GRAND PRIX, Watkins Glen

7 John Watson	M29-DFV	M29/2	'12th' UNC
8 Alain Prost	M30-DFV	M30/1	DNS T-crash

1981

7-2-81 SOUTH AFRICAN GRAND PRIX, Kyalami

7 John Watson	M29-DFV	M29/4	5th
8 Andrea de Cesaris	M29-DFV	M29/5	Crashed

15-3-80 UNITED STATES GRAND PRIX (WEST), Long Beach

7 John Watson	M29-DFV	M29/4	Rtd eng.
8 Andrea de Cesaris	M29-DFV	M29/5	Crashed

29-3-81 BRAZILIAN GRAND PRIX, Rio de Janeiro

7 John Watson	M29-DFV	M29/4	8th
8 Andrea de Cesaris	M29-DFV	M29/5	Rtd fuelp.

12-4-81 ARGENTINE GRAND PRIX, Buenos Aires

7 John Watson	MP4-DFV	MP4/1	Rtd vibes
8 Andrea de Cesaris	M29-DFV	M29/5	11th

3-5-81 SAN MARINO GRAND PRIX, Imola-Italy

7 John Watson	MP4-DFV	MP4/2	10th
8 Andrea de Cesaris	M29-DFV	M29/4	6th

17-5-81 BELGIAN GRAND PRIX, Zolder

7 John Watson	MP4-DFV	MP4/1	7th
8 Andrea de Cesaris	M29-DFV	M29/4	Rtd g'box

31-5-81 MONACO GRAND PRIX, Monte Carlo

7 John Watson	MP4-DFV	MP4/2	Rtd eng.
8 Andrea de Cesaris	MP4-DFV	MP4/1	Crashed

21-6-81 SPANISH GRAND PRIX, Jarama

7 John Watson	MP4-DFV	MP4/2	3rd
8 Andrea de Cesaris	MP4-DFV	MP4/1	Crashed

5-7-81 FRENCH GRAND PRIX, Dijon-Prenois
7 John Watson	MP4-DFV	MP4/2	FR 3rd
8 Andrea de Cesaris	MP4-DFV	MP4/1	14th

18-7-81 BRITISH GRAND PRIX, Silverstone
7 John Watson	MP4-DFV	MP4/2	FIRST
8 Andrea de Cesaris	MP4-DFV	MP4/1	Crashed

2-2-81 GERMAN GRAND PRIX,
7 John Watson	MP4-DFV	MP4/2	6th
8 Andrea de Cesaris	MP4-DFV	MP4/1	Crashed

16-8-81 AUSTRIAN GRAND PRIX, Österreichring
7 John Watson	MP4-DFV	MP4/3	6th
8 Andrea de Cesaris	MP4-DFV	MP4/1	8th

30-8-81 DUTCH GRAND PRIX, Zandvoort
7 John Watson	MP4-DFV	MP4/3	Rtd elect.
8 Andrea de Cesaris	MP4-DFV	MP4/1	DNS Crashed

13-9-81 ITALIAN GRAND PRIX, Monza
7 John Watson	MP4-DFV	MP4/3	Crashed
8 Andrea de Cesaris	MP4-DFV	MP4/1	7th

27-9-81 CANADIAN GRAND PRIX, Montreal
7 John Watson	MP4-DFV	MP4/4	FL 2nd
8 Andrea de Cesaris	MP4-DFV	MP4/1	Crashed

17-10-81 UNITED STATES GRAND PRIX, Las Vegas
7 John Watson	MP4-DFV	MP4/4	7th
8 Andrea de Cesaris	MP4-DFV	MP4/1	12th

1982

23-1-82 SOUTH AFRICAN GRAND PRIX, Kyalami
7 John Watson	MP4-DFV	MP4/5	6th
8 Niki Lauda	MP4-DFV	MP4/4	4th

21-3-82 BRAZILIAN GRAND PRIX, Rio de Janeiro
7 John Watson	MP4-DFV	MP4/5	2nd
8 Niki Lauda	MP4-DFV	MP4/4	Rtd susp.

4-4-82 UNITED STATES GRAND PRIX (WEST), Long Beach
7 John Watson	MP4-DFV	MP4/2	6th
8 Niki Lauda	MP4-DFV	MP4/4	FR FL FIRST

9-4-82 Gold Cup, Oulton Park
6 Arnold Glass	M29-DFV	M29/4	'4th' UNC

12-4-82 Caribbean Airways Trophy, Brands Hatch
6 Arnold Glass	M29-DFV	M29/4	6th

25-4-82 SAN MARINO GRAND PRIX, Imola, Italy
Team entries withdrawn

9-5-82 BELGIAN GRAND PRIX, Zolder
7 John Watson	MP4-DFV	MP4/2	FL FIRST
8 Niki Lauda	MP4-DFV	MP4/6	DISQ*

Car judged underweight

23-5-82 MONACO GRAND PRIX, Monte Carlo
7 John Watson	MP4-DFV	MP4/2	Rtd ign.
8 Niki Lauda	MP4-DFV	MP4/6	Rtd eng.

31-5-82 Rivet Supply Trophy, Thruxton
6 Arnold Glass	M29-DFV	M29/4	4th

6-6-82 DETROIT GRAND PRIX, USA
7 John Watson	MP4-DFV	MP4/5	FIRST
8 Niki Lauda	MP4-DFV	MP4/6	Crashed

13-6-82 CANADIAN GRAND PRIX, Montreal
7 John Watson	MP4-DFV	MP4/5	3rd
8 Niki Lauda	MP4-DFV	MP4/6	Rtd clutch

3-7-82 DUTCH GRAND PRIX, Zandvoort

7 John Watson	MP4-DFV	MP4/5	9th
8 Niki Lauda	MP4-DFV	MP4/6	4th

18-7-82 BRITISH GRAND PRIX, Brands Hatch

7 John Watson	MP4-DFV	MP4/5	Spun
8 Niki Lauda	MP4-DFV	MP4/6	FIRST

25-7-82 FRENCH GRAND PRIX, Ricard-Castellet

7 John Watson	MP4-DFV	MP4/7	Rtd
8 Niki Lauda	MP4-DFV	MP4/6	8th

8-8-82 GERMAN GRAND PRIX, Hockenheimring

7 John Watson	MP4-DFV	MP4/7	Rtd susp.
8 Niki Lauda	MP4-DFV	MP4/6	DNS

15-8-82 AUSTRIAN GRAND PRIX, Österreichring

7 John Watson	MP4-DFV	MP4/5	Rtd eng.
8 Niki Lauda	MP4-DFV	MP4/6	5th

15-8-82 Donington Summer International, Donington Park

6 Arnold Glass	M29-DFV	M29/4	'6th' UNC
18 John Foulston	M19A-DFV	—	DNA

29-8-82 SWISS GRAND PRIX, Dijon-Prenois, France

7 John Watson	MP4-DFV	MP4/5	13th
8 Niki Lauda	MP4-DFV	MP4/7	3rd

30-8-82 Caribbean Airways Trophy, Brands Hatch

6 Arnold Glass	M29-DFV	—	DNA
16 John Foulston	M19A-DFV	—	DNA

12-9-82 ITALIAN GRAND PRIX, Monza

7 John Watson	MP4-DFV	MP4/5	4th
8 Niki Lauda	MP4-DFV	MP4/2	Rtd susp.

25-9-82 UNITED STATES GRAND PRIX, Las Vegas

7 John Watson	MP4-DFV	MP4/5	2nd
8 Niki Lauda	MP4-DFV	MP4/7	Rtd eng.

ADD 1-8-82 Historic SCC Trophy, Donington Park

2 John Foulston	M19A-DFV	M19A/1	FR Rtd eng.
7 Mike Littlewood	M19A-DFV	M19A/2	PP 3rd

1983

13-3-83 BRAZILIAN GRAND PRIX, Jacarepagua

7 John Watson	MP4-DFV	MP4/1C-6	Rtd eng.
8 Niki Lauda	MP4-DFV	MP4/1C-7	3rd

27-3-83 UNITED STATES GRAND PRIX (WEST), Long Beach

7 John Watson	MP4-DFV	MP4/1C-6	FIRST
8 Niki Lauda	MP4-DFV	MP4/1C-7	FL 2nd

10-4-83 Race of Champions, Brands Hatch

7 John Watson	MP4-DFV	MP4/1C-2	Rtd vibration

17-4-83 FRENCH GRAND PRIX, Ricard-Castellet

7 John Watson	MP4-DFY	MP4/1C-6	Rtd eng.
8 Niki Lauda	MP4-DFT	MP4/1C-7	Rtd wheel bearing

30-4-83 SAN MARINO GRAND PRIX, Imola

7 John Watson	MP4-DFY	MP4/1C-6	5th
8 Niki Lauda	MP4-DFY	MP4/1C-7	Crashed

15-5-83 MONACO GRAND PRIX, Monte Carlo

7 John Watson	MP4-DFY	MP41/C-8	DNQ
8 Niki Lauda	MP4-DFY	MP4/1C-7	DNQ

22-5-83 BELGIAN GRAND PRIX, Spa-Francorchamps

7 John Watson	MP4-DFY	MP4/1C-8	Rtd collision
8 Niki Lauda	MP4-DFY	MP4/1C-7	Rtd eng.

5-6-83 DETROIT GRAND PRIX, USA
7 John Watson   MP4-DFY   MP4/1C-8 FL 3rd
8 Niki Lauda   MP4-DFY   MP4/1C-7 Rtd damper

12-6-83 CANADIAN GRAND PRIX, Montreal
7 John Watson   MP4-DFY   MP4/1C-8 6th
8 Niki Lauda   MP4-DFY   MP4/1C-7 Rtd spun out

16-7-83 BRITISH GRAND PRIX, Silverstone
7 John Watson   MP4-DFY   MP4/1C-8 9th
8 Niki Lauda   MP4-DFY   MP4/1C-7 6th

7-8-83 GERMAN GRAND PRIX, Hockenheimring
7 John Watson   MP4-DFY   MP4/1C-2 6th*
8 Niki Lauda   MP4-DFY   MP4/1C-7 5th*
*Niki disqualified for reversing in pit-lane, John classified 5th

14-8-83 AUSTRIAN GRAND PRIX, Osterreichring
7 John Watson   MP4-DFY   MP4/1C-2 9th
8 Niki Lauda   MP4-DFY   MP4/1C-7 6th

2-8-83 DUTCH GRAND PRIX, Zandvoort
7 John Watson   MP4-DFY   MP4/1C-2 3rd
8 Niki Lauda   MP4-TAG   MP4/1E-6 Rtd brakes

11-9-83 ITALIAN GRAND PRIX, Monza
7 John Watson   MP4-TAG   MP4/1E-5 Rtd elect.
8 Niki Lauda   MP4-TAG   MP4/1E-6 Rtd eng.

25-9-83 EUROPEAN GRAND PRIX, Brands Hatch
7 John Watson   MP4-TAG   MP4/1E-5 Crashed
8 Niki Lauda   MP4-TAG   MP4/1E-6 Rtd eng.

15-10-83 SOUTH AFRICAN GRAND PRIX, Kyalami
7 John Watson   MP4-TAG   MP4/1E-7 DISQ
8 Niki Lauda   MP4-TAG   MP4/1E-6 '11th' elect.